Disability and Employment

A contemporary disability human rights approach applied to Danish, Swedish and EU law and policy

School of Human Rights Research Series, Volume 43.

The titles published in this series are listed at the end of this volume.

Disability and Employment
A contemporary disability human rights approach applied to Danish, Swedish and EU law and policy

Maria Ventegodt Liisberg

intersentia
Cambridge – Antwerp – Portland

Intersentia Ltd
Trinity House | Cambridge Business Park | Cowley Road
Cambridge | CB4 0WZ | United Kingdom
mail@intersentia.co.uk

Maria Ventegodt Liisberg
Disability and Employment
A contemporary disability human rights approach applied to Danish, Swedish and EU Law and Policy

Cover image: © Antonprado – Dreamstime.com

ISBN 978-1-78068-028-6
NUR 828

British Library Cataloguing in Publication Data. A catalogue record for this book is available from the British Library.

Acknowledgements

This book is the result of my research as an external PhD student at Maastricht University. First and foremost, I am deeply grateful for the unwavering support of my main supervisor Lisa Waddington who has commented on all the drafts of my thesis as well as helping me with the practicalities associated with being an external PhD student. Lisa has continuously inspired me to seek to improve my analytical skills and my clarity of writing. I am also indebted to my co-supervisor Ruth Nielsen of Copenhagen Business School for highly useful feed-back and guidance. Special thanks also to my friend Brigit Toebes who has provided me with academic and moral support during the last years of this long-lasting process.

I would also like to acknowledge the support of the Danish Institute for Human Rights where I have had the pleasure of working both before, during and after the writing of my thesis. I thank the former Director of the Institute, Morten Kjærum, and the former Head of the National Department, Birgitte Kofod Olsen, for giving me working tasks related to disability human rights law and for supporting my wish to write this thesis. I have also appreciated the stimulating and supportive atmosphere of the Research Department under the leadership of Hans-Otto Sano, Eva Maria Lassen and Peter Scharff Smith.

Moreover, I am grateful to Stig Langvad, Chairman of the Disabled Peoples' Organisation Denmark, and Holger Kallehauge, former High Court Judge and Chairman of the Danish Society of Polio and Accident Victims, who both so excellently promote the human rights of persons with disabilities in Denmark and globally, for encouraging me to do research on disability human rights.

In addition, thanks are due to Jan Høgelund of the Danish National Centre for Social Research for providing me with special calculations on the employment of persons with disabilities in Denmark. Many thanks also to Louise Rayar for translating the English summary of the thesis into Dutch.

I am also grateful to the members of the Reading Committee who provided helpful comments: Hildegard Schneider, Ann Numhauser-Henning (Lund University) and Anne Pieter van der Mei.

Finally, I would like to acknowledge the substantial financial support of the Danish Research Council.

I dedicate this book to my husband, Jonas, with love and gratitude.

Contents

Chapter V
Employers' Obligations

List of Abbreviations

CAT	Convention Against Torture and Other Forms of Cruel, Inhuman and Degrading Treatment or Punishment
CEDAW	Convention on the Elimination of All Forms of Discrimination Against Women
CERD	Convention on the Elimination of All Forms of Racial Discrimination
CRC	Convention on the Rights of the Child
CRMW	Convention on the Protection of the Rights of All Migrant Workers and Members of Their Families
CRPD	Convention on the Rights of Persons with Disabilities
ECHR	European Convention of Human Rights
ECJ	Court of Justice of the European Communities
ECtHR	European Court of Human Rights
ESC	European Social Charter
CJEU	Court of Justice of the European Union
ICCPR	International Covenant on Civil and Political Rights
ICESCR	International Covenant on Economic, Social and Cultural Rights
ICF	International Classification of Functioning, Disability and Health (WHO)
ICIDH	World Health Organization International Classification of Impairments, Disabilities and Handicaps (WHO)
UDHR	Universal Declaration of Human Rights
UN	United Nations
WHO	World Health Organisation

Part I

Introduction

Chapter I
Introduction

This thesis defines a contemporary disability human rights approach in the field of employment based on an analysis of human rights law and policy and applies the approach to Danish, Swedish and European Union (EU) law and policy. The research in this thesis has been triggered by three factors. Firstly, disability human rights law over the past two decades has developed tremendously and there is a need to reflect this transformation in domestic law and policy. The second factor is that Denmark, in comparison with Sweden has a surprisingly low employment rate of persons with disabilities. Thirdly, this research was prompted by the development of EU disability policy and law, which is exerting an increasingly strong influence on the disability policies and laws of the EU Member States.[1] The research questions that arise from the above developments are explored below.

Human rights law concerned with disability has been transformed since the 1990s due to a change in the underlying perception of disability. Whereas limitations in participation in social life were formerly seen as inevitable consequences of impairment, they are now perceived as resulting from the interaction between man-made barriers and impairment. Previously disability-related human rights were limited to rights to rehabilitation and social security, whereas today, it is recognised that persons with disabilities may encounter discrimination in the enjoyment of all human rights. Gradually human rights bodies are embracing this new perception of the human rights of persons with disabilities. For example, in 2009 the European Court of Human Rights held for the first time that a violation of the European Convention of Human Rights had occurred on the grounds of disability discrimination.[2] By far the strongest evidence of this new approach to disability under human rights law is the United Nations Convention on the Rights of Persons with Disabilities (CRPD) adopted in 2006. A few years after it was opened for signatures and ratifications, the CRPD has already been signed by nearly 150 and ratified by almost 100 countries. In this thesis, I intend to define how a contemporary approach to human rights of persons with disabilities would impact on employment and how Danish, Swedish and EU employment law and policy may be improved from a human rights perspective.

---

1 According to Article 1(2) of the Lisbon Treaty amending the Treaty on European Union and the Treaty establishing the European Community of 13 December 2007, the European Union shall replace and succeed the European Community. I will therefore refer only to the European Union in this thesis.

2 European Court of Human Rights, *Glor v. Switzerland,* Application no. 13444/04, judgment of 30 April 2009.

A considerable proportion of the Danish and Swedish populations have a disability: In both countries, approximately one fifth of the population between the ages of 15 and 64 years have a disability and approximately one tenth of the population between the ages of 15 and 64 years have a disability *and* a reduced working capacity. However, the rates of employment of persons with disabilities are strikingly different in these two Scandinavian countries. Whereas only approximately one quarter of persons with disabilities and reduced working capacity are employed in Denmark, more than half are employed in Sweden. In other words, persons with disabilities and reduced working capacity are twice as likely to be in employment in Sweden than in Denmark. Further, Denmark has the highest overall rate of employment in the EU, closely followed by Sweden. Therefore the low rate of employment of persons with disabilities in Denmark cannot be explained with reference to an overall rate of employment.[3] The low participation of persons with disabilities is all the more interesting due to the fact that the *flexicurity* model, on which the Danish labour market is founded, has been hailed as an ideal labour market model in the EU.[4] The Danish *flexicurity* model consists of a combination of low job protection, active labour market policies and a generous social security system. The low rate of employment of persons with disabilities in Denmark raises the question whether the Danish *flexicurity* model leads to the exclusion of persons with disabilities from the labour market. In this thesis, a comparison is made of the employment policies and laws in Denmark and Sweden in order to pinpoint the main reasons for this striking difference in employment participation of persons with disabilities. Proposals will be made for an improvement in Danish employment policy and law in relation to persons with disabilities and the possible implications for the Danish *flexicurity* model are discussed.

EU law and policy in the field of employment has also developed quite significantly since the 1990s and exert an increasingly strong influence on the policies and laws of the Member States. Although the EU has adopted harmonising legislation only to some extent in the field of employment, the EU does seek to influence employment policy and law through the open method of co-ordination and the European Employment Strategy. As mentioned above, the EU promotes the implementation of the so-called flexicurity-model on the labour market and the possible consequences of implementation of the flexicurity-model for employment of persons with disabilities and reduced working capacity will be examined. In relation to disability-specific EU law and policy, the EU's disability law and policy has also strengthened during this period. A directive on equal treatment in employment was adopted in

---

3 In 2008, three top-scorers were Denmark (78.1%), The Netherlands (77.2%) and Sweden (74.3%) in 2008. Source: Eurostat.

4 European Council Decision (EC) 2008/618 of 15 July 2008 on guidelines for the employment policies of the Member States, OJ [2008] L198/47, Annex, third paragraph; European Commission Communication COM (2007) 359 final of 26 June 2007, Towards Common Principles of Flexicurity: More and better jobs through flexibility and security, p. 20.

the year 2000[5] and in 2010, the CRPD became the first international human rights treaty formally concluded by the European Union.[6] In the present thesis, I assess EU law and policy from a human rights perspective and examine how EU law and policy influences Danish and Swedish law.

1. Research Questions and Purposes

As illustrated by *Diagram 1* below, this thesis examines the relevant human rights law and policy, EU law and policy, and Danish and Swedish law in their own right and comparatively.

Diagram 1. Overview of Research Framework

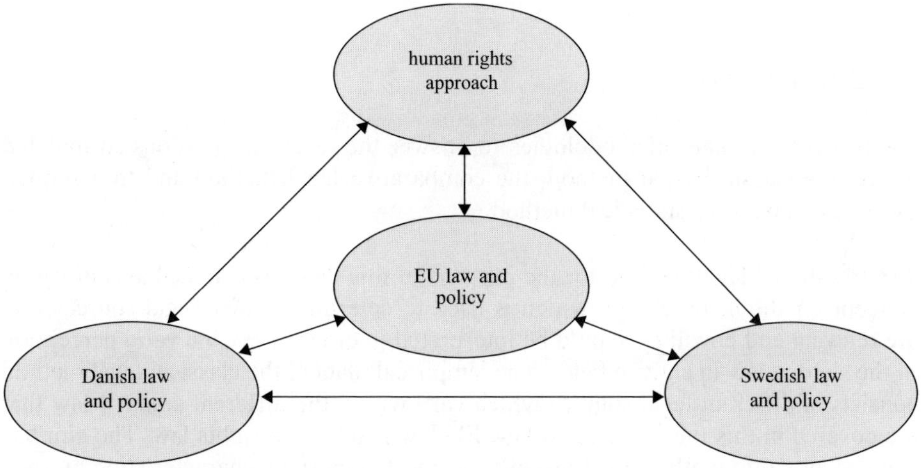

The above diagram translates into the following four research questions:

What is the 'contemporary disability human rights approach' and what are the practical implications of this approach for employment law and policy? (Chapter II)

What is the content of EU employment law and policy with regard to persons with disabilities and how could EU law and policy be adjusted to better comply with the 'contemporary disability human rights approach'? (Chapter III)

5 Council Directive (2000) 78 of 27 November 2000 'establishing a general framework for equal treatment in employment and occupation', OJ [2000] L303/16.

6 The European Union "formally confirmed" its consent to be bound by the CRPD on the 23 of December 2010, cf. Article 43 of the CRPD.

What are the main differences between Danish and Swedish employment law and policy in relation to persons with disabilities and how should Danish law and policy be amended to achieve the same high level of labour market participation for persons with disabilities as Sweden? (Chapter IV-VII)

To what extent is Danish and Swedish employment law and policy based on the 'contemporary disability human rights approach' and how should they be reformed to comply with the 'contemporary disability human rights approach'? (Chapter IV-VII)

To what extent does Danish and Swedish employment law and policy in relation to persons with disabilities comply with EU employment law and policy and in what direction is EU law and policy influencing Danish and Swedish law and policy? (Chapter IV-VII)

2. Methodology

I will use three main methodologies to answer the research questions formulated above: the classical legal method, the comparative legal method and to a limited extent a comparative statistical method.

The traditional legal method for the purpose of this thesis is clarified as a unifying concept for the methodology which is used to determine which legal sources that are relevant and how they should be interpreted in order to reach a valid perception of the state of law in a given field.[7] The 'empirical' data of the classical legal method consists of different legal sources which vary within the different areas of law that are covered in this thesis: national law, EU law and human rights law. The aim has been to use this method to draw out the most important characteristics of each sphere of law within each of the different areas of law and policy that are covered. While it would be impossible to cover all legal sources within each area, this research aims to locate the most important ones in order to extract from them essential and relevant learning about law and policy in a given field.

The comparative legal method consists of a comparison of rules in different legal systems in different countries or international legal systems, such as EU and human rights law. It is a well-established legal method and theories on possibilities, and risks associated with this legal method are abundant.[8] One discussion within the field of the comparative legal method concerns the importance of the social and political context of the rules, which are compared. Concern about the importance of this has led some writers to suggest that rule-comparison can only take place

7 Nielsen 1999, p. 19.

8 Bogdan 2004; Gordley 1998; Hoecke and Warrington 1998; Kahn-Freund 1974.

between legal systems sharing the same social and political context.[9] Denmark and Sweden are both Scandinavian countries with similar languages and similar cultural, social and political contexts which make it relatively unproblematic to compare the rules of these two countries.[10] Naturally, one should not be lulled into thinking that the two countries are identical by the presence of many commonalities. However, the many common traits make it more interesting that the rules and values underlying disability law and policy in the field of employment differ. The value of performing a comparison between Denmark and Sweden is that it provides two different models which can be held up against each other. The different rules and policies in the two countries can serve as sources of inspiration or warning depending on their content.[11] Again, I will not be able to perform a full comparison of all sources of laws and policies, but I hope to identify the most important ones.

Finally, the analysis and comparison of laws and policies in Denmark and Sweden will be qualified with statistical material on labour market participation of persons with disabilities. Fortunately, both the Danish and Swedish national statistical agencies (*Statistics Denmark* and *Statistics Sweden)* conduct surveys of labour market participation based on the methodology of the European Labour Force Surveys which ensures that the statistics are comparable.[12] In addition to the already-publicised statistics, the *Danish National Centre for Social Research* has provided special statistical extract on labour market participation of persons with disabilities for the purposes of this thesis. More details on comparability of statistics will be provided in Section 5 below where I provide an overview of the rates of employment of persons with disabilities in Denmark and Sweden. I will use statistics on labour market participation to give an overview of the differences in employment rates of persons with disabilities. In addition, I will also use statistics where I can qualify my analysis of law and policy in different areas. For example, I will use statistics on the use of state promotional measures and social security benefits in order to compare their practical use and if possible, their effect on employment rates of persons with disabilities.

3. Scope and Structure

This thesis is divided into four parts. Part I contains the introduction. In Part II, I will analyse human rights law and provide the analytical framework for the

9 Bogdan 2004, p. 1237.

10 Scheinin 2008, p. 135, who mentions 'Scandinavian realism', which has been a common and predominant school of thought in Nordic legal thinking and 'social democracy' as a broadly shared political ideology in the Nordic countries and Halvorsen and Hvindén 2009b, p. 178 who describe the Nordic model of disability protection.

11 Bogdan 2004, p. 1235.

12 Council Regulation (1998) 577 of 9 March 1998 on the organization of a labour force sample survey in the Community, OJ [1998] L77/3.

subsequent analysis of EU and domestic law which is contained in Part III. Part IV contains the conclusion.

Part II of the thesis – International law and Analytical Framework

The aim of Part II of the PhD is to provide an overall description and analysis of the relevant international law. In this part of the thesis, I seek to define the principles and concepts which characterise the 'contemporary disability human rights approach' with regard to employment. As mentioned above, the 'contemporary disability human rights approach' is a distillation of the main human rights principles relevant to persons with disability in employment. The 'contemporary disability human rights approach' provides the overall framework for an ideal approach to disability law and policy from a disability human rights' perspective. In Part II, I analyse the legal status of the 'contemporary disability human rights approach' as well as the methodology for defining its contents. In addition, I seek to determine to what extent Denmark and Sweden are legally obliged, as States Parties to different human rights treaties, to ensure that their disability policies and laws comply with the 'contemporary disability human rights approach'.

Part III of the thesis – EU and domestic law and policy

In the third part of the thesis, I compare EU, Danish and Swedish law and policy. In addition, I assess the compliance of Danish and Swedish law and policy with the 'contemporary disability human rights approach' which was defined in Chapter II of the thesis. I also examine to what extent Swedish and Danish laws are compliant with EU law and policy. In Chapter III of the thesis, I give an overview of policy and legal developments in the specific fields of law and policy that are covered by this thesis and I seek to determine to what extent EU law complies with the 'contemporary disability human rights approach'. The analysis of domestic law and policy in relation to the contemporary disability human rights approach is done in Chapter IV to VI, each chapter covering different aspects of disability employment law and policy:

Equality law and policy – Chapter IV of the thesis

Legislation which prohibits discrimination on the grounds of disability and imposes a duty to provide reasonable accommodation for persons with disabilities is covered in this section. In addition, it will be examined to what extent equality laws permit or oblige employers to undertake positive action to realise substantive equality for persons with disabilities. Policies to support the effective implementation of equality laws, for example, through the establishment of State Equality bodies will also be examined. Equality laws and policies in Denmark and Sweden will be compared to each other and to EU and human rights law respectively.

Employers' Obligations – Chapter V of the thesis
Employers' obligations of special relevance to this thesis include duties to adapt working conditions to the needs of employees with disabilities under health and safety laws and policies. Employers have a duty to provide reasonable accommodation to employees with disabilities under equality laws, but it is of central importance to the effective realisation of this obligation that it is mainstreamed into the general health and safety law. The extent of employers' obligations towards employees with disabilities comes to its ultimate test when an employer seeks to dismiss an employee due to his or her reduced working capacity. Therefore, the laws and policies governing dismissals on grounds relating to the employee will also be examined. Finally, laws and policies regarding the dismissal of employees with disabilities due to restructuring or other grounds relating to the undertaking will be analysed. Employers' obligations in Denmark and Sweden will be compared to each other and to EU and human rights law and policy respectively.

Employment Promotion – Chapter VI of the thesis
Employment promotional measures are measures undertaken by employment services to promote the employment of persons with disabilities who are unemployed. Examples hereof are training, wage subvention and job placement with individual undertakings. The organisation and degree of privatisation of the employment services will also be examined since this may influence the level of priority accorded to assisting persons with disabilities to obtain employment. In addition, I will examine the laws and policies governing the employment of persons with disabilities in sheltered employment workshops under this heading even though this may be classified under domestic legislation as a social measure rather than an employment promotional measure. State promotional measures in Denmark and Sweden will be compared to each other and to EU and human rights law respectively.

Income-Replacement Benefits – Chapter VII of the thesis
Social security benefits aimed at compensating persons with disabilities for lack of income from employment will be examined on the grounds that access to such benefits may influence the motivation of persons with disabilities to obtain employment and to stay employed negatively. Also, one could argue that the eligibility criteria for social security benefits provide a definition of when it is socially acceptable for the labour market to decline to find employment for a person. In addition to benefits for long-term reduced working capacity (disability pensions), benefits for short-term reduced working capacity (sickness benefit and rehabilitation benefit) will be examined. In addition, I have chosen to examine the eligibility criteria for compensation of persons who have incurred a reduced working capacity due to a work injury since this is also a quantitatively important benefit which serves to compensate for a lack of income from the labour market due to loss of working capacity.

This thesis focuses specifically on the field of *employment* rather than analysing access to all types of occupation, including self-employment. However, the statistics on persons with disabilities on the labour market cover both persons who are employed by undertakings which they do not own themselves, and self-employed persons.

Clearly, many other areas of policy and law influence the labour market participation of persons with disabilities. For example important areas of education and general accessibility to transportation and the physical environment also influence the inclusion of persons with disabilities in the labour market, but fall outside the scope of this study.

4. Some Definitions

I will return to the definition of *disability, impairment* and *reduced working capacity* several times throughout the thesis including in Chapter II where I examine the development of the concept of disability under human rights law. However, as I will use them throughout the thesis, I will give a brief introductory definition of these three central concepts in the present section.

Whereas *impairments* are a characteristic, a feature or an attribute of an individual, such as a mental illness, a missing limb or blindness,[13] *disability* is the limitation that results from the interaction between impairments and social barriers, and hinders participation of persons with impairment in social life. Thus, there is no deterministic relationship between all impairments and disability. A person with an impairment could in principle lead a life without suffering limitations in social life and thus not become disabled. Limitations in the possibilities for participation in social life may occur as a result of the impairments themselves in the form of tiredness or pain for example, which limits a person's ability to take part in social life. Limitations may also occur as a result of negative attitudes or barriers in the environment or social structures such as the built environment or the internet.

As described by for example *Shakespeare* and *Kayess and French*, the perception that an impairment may in itself lead to limitations and thus to disability is controversial 'within the broader disability movement', which appears to have moved 'towards a radical social constructionist view of disability'.[14] According to the radical social constructionist view of disability, impairment has no underlying reality and all limitations are the result of social constructions.[15] For example, it would be a social construct that a blind person is disabled due to his or her

13 Kayess and French 2008, p. 21.

14 Kayess and French 2008, p. 7.

15 Ibid.

impairment. According to the social constructionist view, in an ideal society, a blind person would never find himself or herself in a situation where being blind would place him or her at a disadvantage compared to people who are not blind.[16] According to *Kayess and French* this radical social constructionist view is not predominant in academic literature on disability. In the present thesis, it is assumed that impairment may be disabling just as negative attitudes and the social environment may exclude persons with an impairment from taking part in social life, and therefore can be disabling.

In this thesis, the concept of 'persons with disabilities' will be used as a broad term which covers both persons with impairments who are *not* disabled, persons with impairments who *are* disabled as well as persons who do not presently have an impairment, but who may nonetheless be subjected to differential treatment due to future, past or perceived impairment.

In line with the UN Convention on Human Rights of Persons with Disabilities (CRPD), the impairment in question must be a longer-lasting impairment in order to distinguish it from impairments resulting from a temporary sickness. The concept of 'persons with disabilities' will be used because it is the preferred terminology in both literature and human rights documents. Thus, I use the term 'persons with disabilities' in spite of the fact that using the term 'persons with impairments' would underline that disability is not a necessary consequence of impairment.

Lastly, a *reduced working capacity* implies that the ability to perform work is limited. A person's working capacity may be reduced in relation to some work, but not in relation to other work. For example, a person's reduced capacity to perform physically demanding work does not necessarily mean that the person's capacity to perform sedentary work is also reduced. Reduced working capacity may have many different causes, such as drug-abuse or personal problems due to a divorce, and is not necessarily associated with an impairment. In the present thesis, when I am referring to reduced working capacity then I am only considering persons whose reduced working capacity is related to a longer-lasting impairment.

5. Disability Employment in Denmark and Sweden in Figures

In the present Section, I will give a brief overview of the differences in labour market participation of persons with disabilities in Denmark and Sweden, which constitute one of the reasons for choosing to compare these two countries in the present thesis.

---

16 See for a critique of radical social constructivism of the social model and the 'ignorance of the problematic reality of biological impairment' for example Shakespeare 2006, p. 40.

In order to compare the labour market participation of persons with disabilities in Sweden and Denmark, one first needs to verify whether the definitions of disability used in the different national surveys are comparable. Both the Danish and Swedish surveys on participation of persons with disabilities in the labour market are performed as supplements to the National Labour Market Surveys which ensures the general comparability of the data.[17]

In the Danish Survey, the interviewees were asked whether they had *"a disability or a longer lasting health problem"*. The inclusion of persons who have a 'longer-lasting health problem' ensures that not only persons who have a traditional physical disability, but also persons with less serious impairments, mental illness and other longer-lasting illnesses are included. According to this survey, 19% of the population between the ages of 16 and 64 had a disability or longer-lasting health problem in 2008 in Denmark.[18] The persons who replied that they did have a disability or a longer-lasting health problem were also asked how they assessed their working capacity on a scale from 1 to 10, with 1 being no working capacity and 10 being full working capacity. Of the interviewees with disabilities or a longer-lasting health problem, 52% placed themselves between 1 and 6 and were considered to have a reduced working capacity.[19] Accordingly, approximately 10% of the Danish labour force was disabled with a reduced working capacity in Denmark in 2008.

In Sweden, the interviewees were told that the survey was about the labour market situation for persons with disabilities and it was explained that *"disability means that one has reduced eyesight or hearing, speaking or voice problem, movement impairment, allergy or any form of mental disability. One may also have diabetes, heart or lung problems, illness of the digestive system, psoriasis, epilepsy, dyslexia or the like"*.[20] The persons who said that they had a disability were asked if they found that their *"disability leads to a reduction in working capacity"*. According to this survey, almost 16% of the population between the age of 14 and 64 years has a disability and approximately 10% of the population between the ages of 14 and 64 years has a reduction in working capacity in Sweden.

In sum, in Denmark and Sweden, similar definitions of disability, which included not only traditional impairments, but also longer-lasting and serious illnesses, were used in the surveys in both countries. Moreover, the proportions of the population

---

17 Denmark: Larsen and Høgelund 2009, 28. The special extracts by the Danish Social Research Institute, which were made for this thesis have been made on the basis of the same data that was used in Larsen and Høgelund 2009. Sweden: Statistics Sweden 2009. On comparability see Statistics Denmark, Arbejdskraftundersøgelsen 2006, Statistiske Efterretninger, 2007:5, p. 3.

18 Larsen and Høgelund 2009, p. 23.

19 Extract by Social Research Institute 2009 for this thesis, kol 2.

20 Statistics Sweden 2007, addendum 4, introductory question and question 2 on reduction in working capacity.

which have a disability and which have both a disability and reduced working capacity are relatively similar: 19 and 16 percent of the populations in Denmark and Sweden respectively have a disability and 10 percent of the population in both Denmark and Sweden have a disability and reduced working capacity. National surveys of disability in Sweden and Denmark in previous years show that the proportions of persons with disabilities and especially persons with disabilities and reduced working capacity are also relatively similar over time, as may be seen in *Table 1* below.

Table 1. Proportions of persons with disabilities and of persons with disabilities and reduced working capacity of the population between the age of 14 and 64 years[21]

	Denmark		Sweden	
2008	19	10	16	9
2005 for Denmark and 2006 for Sweden	20	9	16	10
2002	20	10	20	10

The fact that the two countries have relatively similar general health situations also supports the assumption that the two countries do in fact have comparable rates of disability.[22] In conclusion, it is my assessment that the figures on labour market participation of persons with disabilities in Denmark and Sweden are comparable, especially as regards the figures on persons with disabilities and reduced working capacity which have hovered around 10% in both countries in national surveys since 2002.

In *Table 2* below, I compare the level of employment of persons with disabilities with and without reduced working capacity. These figures show that the overall rate of employment is a little higher in Denmark, but that the rate of employment of persons with disabilities is lower in Denmark than in Sweden. While 83% of persons without disabilities are in employment in Denmark, only 77% of persons without disabilities are in employment in Sweden. However, in spite of higher rate of employment for persons without disabilities in Denmark, persons with disabilities are less likely to be on the labour market in Denmark than in Sweden. While 56% of persons with disabilities in Denmark are in employment, 62% of persons with disabilities are in employment in Sweden. It is however quite interesting to note that

21 Extract by Social Research Institute 2009 for this thesis kol 1 and 2, Larsen and Høgelund 2009, p. 32, Statistics Sweden 2009. The rate of persons with disabilities and reduced working capacity for 2002 is an estimation based on the fact that the rate of persons with reduced working capacity was practically unchanged from 2002 to 2005, cf. Larsen and Høgelund 2009, p. 56. Statistics Sweden 2009, p. 18.

22 Eurostat, Healthy Life Years at Birth for both Denmark and Sweden was 67 years while EU average was 62 years in 2007.

persons with disabilities *without* reduced working capacity do not have lower employment rates than persons without disabilities. Persons with disabilities *without* reduced working capacity have employment rates of 83% and approximately 78% in Denmark and Sweden respectively. Thus, the difference in employment rates of persons with disabilities is explained by the striking difference in the employment rates of persons with disabilities *and* reduced working capacity. While only one quarter of persons with disabilities *and* reduced working capacity are in employment in Denmark, twice as many are in employment in Sweden.

Table 2. Labour market participation of persons with disabilities in 2008[23]

	Denmark	Sweden
Persons with disabilities, % of population between 15 and 64 years of age	19	16
Persons with reduced working capacity, % of population between 15 and 64 years of age	10	9
General employment rate, % of population between 15 and 64 years of age	78	74
Persons without disabilities in employment, % of total persons without disabilities	83	77
Persons with disabilities in employment, % of persons with disabilities	56	62
Persons with disabilities, but without reduced working capacity, in employment, % of total persons with disabilities, but without reduced working capacity	83	78
Persons with disabilities and reduced working capacity in employment, % of total persons with disabilities and reduced working capacity	26	50

6. This Thesis in the Context of Existing Research

The components of the contemporary disability human rights approach have been developed by other authors, but it is to my knowledge, the first time that the four components have not been merged as a unified proposal for a contemporary disability human rights approach for the field of employment which takes into account the UN Convention of Human Rights.[24] Several legal studies have been made of EU disability employment law and policy, but since *Waddington's* thesis from 1996, no in-depth analysis from a disability human rights perspective has been

23 General employment rates: Eurostat. Denmark: Special Extract by Social Research Institute 2009 for this thesis, kol 3, 4 and 6. Sweden: Statistics Sweden 2009.

24 See for example Annardottir 2009 on the development of the concept of equality, Fredman 2005b on the participation of disability organisations in the conduct of State functions, Bickenbach 1999 who links the disability concepts with the different concept of equality and Stein 2007 who defines a disability rights paradigm based on the social model of disability, the right to development and a capabilities approach.

made in relation to both anti-discrimination, employment protection, employment promotion and income-replacement laws and policies.[25] No in-depth comparison of Danish and Swedish law and policy, which covers all the above-mentioned areas has ever been made.[26] Danish studies of disability employment law are relatively scarce. Writings have been made, which cover either the protection against discrimination on the grounds of disability, income-replacement benefits for persons with disabilities or the efficiency of disability-specific employment promotional measures, but no single work provides an in-depth analysis of Danish disability employment law and policy.[27] Swedish disability employment studies are relatively more developed. Most importantly, *Inghammar* published a thesis in 2006, which contains an in-depth analysis of Swedish disability employment law as compared to German and British (but not Danish) law and policy. *Inghammar's* thesis analyses the disability employment laws in relation to a goal of inclusion of persons with disabilities and an assessment of whether the laws in question create individual rights. However, *Inghammar* does not relate the analysis to specific obligations under human rights law and also he does not perform an assessment of the actual effects of different laws in policies through analysis of statistical data on employment of persons with disabilities. Other authors on Swedish law have written on the individual areas of disability employment law and policy, but have not performed an overall analysis of these laws and policies.[28]

7. Conclusion

A tremendous development has taken place in human rights law since the 1990s, which has resulted in the recognition of the human right of persons with disabilities to be included in the labour market. This thesis seeks to explore what the contemporary disability human rights approach entails for national disability employment law and policy. Denmark and Sweden will be studied and compared in order to determine whether the significant disparity in employment rates of persons with disabilities and reduced working capacity could be a result of lack of compliance with the contemporary disability human rights approach in Denmark. In addition, EU law and policy will be examined since EU law and policy exerts an increasingly strong influence on the disability policies of the Member States in the area of employment.

---

25 Waddington 1995. See for example Schiek, Waddington and Bell 2007a and Gijzen 2006 on anti-discrimination law and Barnard 2006 on employment law.

26 For example Johansson and Hvindén 2007 compare employment promotion and income-replacement policies.

27 Nielsen and Roseberry 2008 on labour law, Justesen 2008 on disability anti-discrimination law, Andersen, Nielsen and Precht 2008 on anti-discrimination law, Ketscher 2008 on income-replacement benefits.

28 Lunning and Toijer 2006 and Calleman 2000 on employment law, Iseskog 2003 on anti-discrimination, Norström 2010.

Part II

Analytical Framework

Chapter II
Human Rights

In the present Chapter, I will seek to define a 'contemporary disability human rights approach' with regard to employment based on an analysis of present-day protection of persons with disabilities under human rights law. The 'contemporary disability human rights approach' is the paradigm for designing laws and policies to ensure compliance with the international human rights of persons with disabilities today.

In Section 1 below, I develop a description of the 'contemporary disability human rights approach'. I begin with a discussion of the methodology for describing the 'contemporary disability human rights approach' before continuing with the discussion of the substantive contents of the 'contemporary disability human rights approach'. Section 2 is very different from the first Section as it analyses the legal status of human rights law in Denmark and Sweden.

Although the definition of the contemporary disability human rights approach is initiated in the present Chapter, I will flesh out its meaning in later Chapters that deal with the substantive areas of the law: *Chapter IV Equality Law and Policy, Chapter V Employers' Obligations, Chapter VI State Promotion* and *Chapter VII Income-Replacement Benefits*. In these later Chapters, I will perform more detailed analyses of what the contemporary disability human rights approach entails in relation to the specific topics and I will examine Danish and Swedish laws and policies in relation to the contemporary disability human rights approach. The analysis of EU disability employment law and policy in relation to the contemporary disability human rights approach takes place in *Chapter III EU law and policy.*

1. The Contemporary Disability Human Rights Approach

The aim of this section is to provide an understanding of the 'contemporary disability human rights approach'. In the first Sub-Section, I will describe why and how I establish the contents of the contemporary disability human rights approach. In the subsequent three Sub-Sections, I will examine the principle of equality and the model of disability during the following three periods of time: from the end of World War II until the end of the 1960s, from the 1970s to the 1990s and finally, their contemporary meanings. In the fifth Sub-Section, I explore the role of the State and different private parties under the human rights approach. The sixth Sub-Section contains a conclusion.

1.1. Methodology for Determining the "Contemporary Disability Human Rights Approach"

The aim of defining a contemporary disability human rights approach is to provide a general framework for assessing employment laws and policies from the perspective of human rights law. By defining a contemporary disability human rights approach in this thesis, I identify the key principles that should inform the development of ideal policies and laws in the field of employment in relation to persons with disabilities. The reliance on principles of human rights law such as substantive equality rather than just specific articles in human rights conventions allows for a more general discussion of the reasons why one national law or policy is better than another. Also, disability human rights law is still in its early stages and so specific provisions on for example the obligations of States in relation to the realisation of the right to work are relatively few. A description founded on human rights principles allows for more in-depth understanding of the human rights obligations in question.

Principles of human rights law are not in themselves legally binding on States Parties, but they are important in the sense that they provide the conceptual framework for understanding a given human rights treaty. It follows from Article 31 of the Vienna Convention on the Law of Treaties of 1969 that a treaty shall be interpreted "*in light of its object and purpose*".[29] Thus, the legally binding obligations contained in the provisions of a human rights convention shall be interpreted in the light of the principles underlying the Treaty. In the UN Convention on the Rights of Persons with Disabilities of 2006 (CRPD).[30] the founding principles of the Convention are defined in Article 3. In addition, the Vienna Convention on the Law of Treaties provides that founding principles may be extracted from for example the Preamble or from the context of the Treaty in question.[31]

Although human rights principles are not in themselves legally binding, reference is made to the human rights principles in legally binding provisions of human rights treaties. For example, the CRPD provides, in almost all of the substantive articles, that persons with disabilities have a right to enjoy rights on an equal basis with others. For example, Article 27 of the CRPD on the right to Work and Employment provides that "*States Parties recognize the right of persons with disabilities to work, on an equal basis with others*". Moreover, the understanding of the principles

---

29 United Nations, Vienna Convention on the Laws of Treaties of 23 May 1969, Treaty Series, vol. 1155, p. 331.

30 United Nations Convention on the Rights of Persons with Disabilities, 13 December 2006, General Assembly Resolution, Doc.A,/61/611.

31 According to Article 31(2) of the Vienna Convention on the Law of Treaties of 1969, Vienna Convention on the Law of Treaties of 1969, the "context for the purpose of the interpretation of a treaty shall comprise [...] [inter alia the] preamble and annexes".

underlying the contemporary disability human rights approach are qualified by authoritative interpretations of relevant human rights obligations by for example treaty bodies or courts, including the European Court of Human Rights (ECtHR). Thus, it is my understanding that States Parties to for example the CRPD will be under a legal obligation to progressively realise the obligations under the contemporary disability human rights approach as it is described in the present thesis.[32] In addition, States Parties may be under an obligation to ensure immediate compliance with for example the prohibition of discrimination on the grounds of disability which also forms part of the contemporary disability human rights approach in the field of employment law and policy.[33]

The principle of equality is the most central principle informing the position of persons with disabilities under international human rights law. This is evidenced by Article 1 CRPD which states that the purpose of the CRPD is to *"promote, protect and ensure the full and equal enjoyment of all human rights and fundamental freedoms by all persons with disabilities, and to promote respect for their inherent dignity"* and the fact the term "*equal*" or "*same*" is repeated in practically all material provision of the CRPD.[34]

In addition to specifying the concept of equality, the concept of disability also needs to be described in the context of defining the contemporary disability human rights approach. The concept of disability has developed over time and in parallel with the concept of equality. The understanding of what disability is and how the negative effects of disability can be alleviated are decisive for the definition of human rights of persons with disabilities. If disability is seen as an inevitable consequence of impairment, the human rights of persons with disabilities will centre around habilitation and rehabilitation. If disability is seen as a consequence of barriers in social life, human rights of persons with disabilities will focus on the right to inclusion and equal treatment.

Moreover, one could have added the principles of dignity and individual autonomy to qualify further the contemporary disability human rights approach. This would be justified on the grounds *inter alia* that dignity is a fundamental human rights principle and that all the UN core conventions including the CRPD proclaim that

---

32 Article 4(2) of the CRPD, Article 2(1) of ICESCR, Part I of ESC of 1961 and of Revised ESC of 1996.

33 Article 4(2) of the CRPD, Articles 2(1) and 26 of ICCPR, Articles 1 and 14 of ECHR.

34 (My emphasis.) Out of the first 30 Articles of the Convention, 'equal' is not mentioned in Article 4 on general obligations, Article 8 on awareness-raising, Article 11 on situations of risk, Article 16 on freedom from exploitation, Article 20 on personal mobility and Article 26 on habilitation and rehabilitation.

human rights are derived *"from the inherent dignity of the human person"*.[35] The principle of individual autonomy has not been given such a prominent place in human rights instruments, but it is mentioned in Article 3 of the CRPD together with the principle of dignity. However, it is my assessment that the principle of equality coupled with the social model of disability covers the essence of the principles of dignity and individual autonomy. I have therefore chosen not to include them explicitly in the characterisation of the contemporary disability human rights approach.

Finally, the concept of equality has in legal literature been linked with specific perceptions of the duties of the State to be inclusive of civil society in decision-making processes.[36] I have therefore chosen to qualify the contemporary disability human rights approach with an analysis of the role of different actors on the labour market. The issue of the role of State and non-State actors in realising human rights is of special relevance when examining the labour markets in Denmark and Sweden where the social partners have a large degree of regulative power.

The analysis of the models of equality and disability and the role of different actors on the labour market is based on the classical legal method as well as more theoretical legal literature. Special weight is given to the CRPD because it is a recent and specialised core UN human rights convention. Also, the European Social Charter of 1961 (ESC) and the Revised European Social Charter of 1996 (Revised ESC) are considered to be important sources of human rights law in relation to Denmark and Sweden because of the existence of authoritative interpretations by the European Committee of Social Rights of Article 15(2) on the right of persons with disabilities to employment in the Committee's examinations of State Reports.[37] Finally, the European Convention of Human Rights of 1950[38] (ECHR) is essential when dealing with human rights in Europe and although the ECtHR has made only few judgments of direct relevance to the employment of persons with disabilities, I will also deal in some detail with the ECHR. Other human rights instruments such as ILO conventions which apply to Sweden and Denmark and concern the employment of persons with disabilities will also be mentioned, but will not be given the same weight.

In *Sub-Sections 1.2, 1.3.* and *1.4.*, I examine the evolution of human rights law with a special focus on equality and disability: from the end of World War II to the end

---

35 CAT preamble, The UN Bill of Rights: UN Human Rights Declaration of 1948, ICCPR and ICESCR; the UN core conventions: ICERD, CEDAW, CAT, CRC, CRMW and CRPD.

36 Fredman 2005b pp. 370–371.

37 European Council, European Social Charter of 1961, European Treaty System No. 35 and the Revised ESC of 1996, European Treaty System No. 163.

38 European Council, Convention for the Protection of Human Rights and Fundamental Freedoms, European Council Treaty System No. 5.

of the 1960s, from the 1960s to the 2000s and current trends. In *Section 1.5.*, I examine the role of State and non-State actors in improving human rights in the labour market and finally, in *Section 1.6.*, I sum up what the contemporary disability human rights approach entails.

1.2. From the End of World War II until the End of the 1960s – Formal Equality and the Medical Model of Disability

1.2.1. Models of Equality and Disability

The model of *formal equality* was the predominant theoretical equality model from the end of World War II until the end of the 1960's, i.e. during the years when the Universal Declaration of Human Rights and the first legally binding human rights conventions were drafted in the UN and in Europe. The formal equality model is based on an idea of 'sameness' or a 'symmetrical approach' because it is based on the assumption that all persons should be treated in the same way or are 'symmetrical' irrespective of the unequal consequences of this treatment. This approach is formal or procedural in character, in the sense that it does not require a substantive or normative test of the contents of the treatment as long as there is consistency in treatment.[39]

The advantage of the formal equality approach is that it is relatively simple and therefore potentially easy to implement. The weakness of the formal equality approach is that it does not address the structural disadvantage facing persons belonging to certain groups and therefore it does not provide a foundation for prohibiting indirect discrimination or allowing positive action. Also, since the formal equality approach does not recognise potentially unjust social structures, equality must be achieved by *disregarding* a certain characteristic.[40] However, disregard for potentially relevant group-characteristics may in fact perpetuate inequality instead of promoting equality.

The concept of disability was in the period after the Second World War (as well as earlier) based on the so-called 'medical model' according to which disadvantages faced by persons with disabilities are the consequence of the individual's condition or impairment.[41] It is the individual's aberration from the social norm which leads to disadvantage experienced by the disabled person. The medical model receives its name not only because it sees the medically diagnosable deviance as the cause of disadvantage, but also because medical treatment and rehabilitation are seen as the

39 Anardóttir 2003, p. 22.
40 Anardóttir 2003, p. 23, Barnard and Hepple 2000, p. 562.
41 Hendriks and Liisberg 2009, Waddington 1995, p. 38; Hendriks 2002, p. 200.

main solutions to this disadvantage.[42] Once the disability is cured then any disadvantage will have been removed. This model has also been labelled the 'functional limitation model', the 'biological inferiority model' and the 'individual model'.[43] The importance of the medical model in shaping disability policies around the world cannot be exaggerated. Based on the medical model of disability, disability policies have sought to reduce the disability through rehabilitation and to compensate through/by means of welfare subsidies and to provide separate structures for persons with disabilities who are seen as unable to take part in mainstream society.[44]

Common to the model of formal equality and the medical model of disability is the belief that the social structures are a constant, and should not be changed. Any difference in opportunities for participation in society which is associated with a certain personal characteristic must therefore be overcome by disassociating the individual with that personal characteristic or by accepting that there is a difference in opportunities. In relation to the labour market, the problems faced by persons with disabilities had to be overcome therefore not by adjusting the labour market to their needs, but primarily by rehabilitating persons with disability so that they were no longer disabled. In addition, a separate labour market was also created in many countries in order to provide persons with disabilities with employment opportunities without changing the general structures of society. The result was that persons with disabilities were kept outside the ordinary labour market.[45]

1.2.2. The United Nations

In the wake of the Second World War, the Universal Declaration of Human Rights was adopted in New York as a bulwark against a new World War and against the hideous crimes against humanity that had characterised the war. It marked the first time that individual rights and freedom were set out in detail. The principle of equality was central to the Universal Declaration which states in Article 1 that "All human beings are born free and equal in dignity and rights" and in Article 2 that *"Everyone is entitled to all the rights and freedoms set forth in this Declaration, without distinction of any kind, such as race, colour, sex, language, religion, political or other opinion, national or social origin, property, birth or other status."*

This Universal Declaration was ground-breaking, but it was also a product of its time. It states in Article 2 that no distinction must be made on the grounds of for

42 Gijzen 2006, p. 382. Traustadóttir 2009, p. 8.
43 Hendriks 2002, p. 200.
44 Waddington and Diller 2002, p. 245.
45 Ibid.

example race, gender or religion. This provision reflects the idea that equality is achieved by disregarding the fact that a person belongs to a certain group.

When one considers the fact that as many as one million persons with disabilities were victims of the German Euthanasia programme and many more disabled persons were victims of involuntary sterilisation and medical experimentation, it is striking that persons with disabilities were not identified as a group vulnerable to discrimination in the Universal Declaration or the ECHR.[46]

During the 1960s and after many years of negotiation, the important UN Covenants on Economic, Social and Cultural Rights (ICESCR)[47] and Civil and Political Rights (ICCPR)[48] were adopted. As was the case with the UN Universal Declaration of Human Rights (UDHR), the two UN Covenants did not contain specific provisions on persons with disabilities.[49] Article 5 of the ICCPR nonetheless provides that "no one shall be subjected without his free consent to medical or scientific experimentation". As such the ICCPR recognises the crimes that *inter alia* persons with disabilities were subject to in the Concentration Camps during the Second World War.[50]

Treaty-Monitoring Bodies have been established to monitor the implementation of each of the UN core conventions. They provide guidance on the interpretation of the conventions in their examination of State Reports and in General Comments on specific topics or articles of the conventions. The Committee on Economic, Social and Cultural Rights explained that

> *"The absence of an explicit, disability-related provision in the Covenant can be attributed to the lack of awareness of the importance of addressing this issue explicitly, rather than only by implication, at the time of the drafting of the Covenant over a quarter of a century ago."*[51]

While the two UN Covenants on Economic, Social and Cultural and Civil and Political Rights do not mention 'disability' explicitly, they do not exclude that

46 Hendriks and Liisberg 2009.

47 United Nations, International Covenant on Economic, Social and Cultural Rights, 16 December 1966, *Treaty Series*, vol. 993, p. 3.

48 United Nations, International Covenant on Civil and Political Rights, 16 December 1966, *Treaty Series*, vol. 999, p. 171.

49 United Nations, Universal Declaration of Human Rights of 10 December 1948, UN Doc A/810/71.

50 Hendriks and Liisberg 2009.

51 Committee on Economic, Social and Cultural Rights, General Comment No. 5, *Persons with Disabilities,* 9 December 1994, point 6. The Committee was established under ECOSOC Resolution 1985/17 of 28 May 1985 to carry out the monitoring functions assigned to the United Nations Economic and Social Council (ECOSOC) in Part IV of the Covenant.

'disability' may become a protected ground of discrimination. Common Article 2, which has almost the same wording in both Covenants, provides for an open-ended ban against discrimination:

> *"Each State Party to the present Covenant undertakes to respect and to ensure to all individuals within its territory and subject to its jurisdiction the rights recognized in the present Covenant, without distinction of any kind, such as race, colour, sex, language, religion, political or other opinion, national or social origin, property, birth or other status."*[52]

In line with the model of formal equality, the emphasis is on prohibiting distinctions on the grounds of personal characteristics rather than on removing obstacles in society to allow for the full participation of persons with certain characteristics. The fact that the prohibition of discrimination is tied to the material provisions of the Covenant also underlines the view that the concept of equality implies consistency in treatment and is not a free-standing substantive right with a normative content of its own. In addition, the fact that the list of grounds is open-ended may on the one hand be seen as positive since it means that a 'new' discrimination ground such as disability may be recognised after the drafting of the provision. On the other hand however, differential treatment on grounds that are not explicitly mentioned in the provision, such as disability for example, may not enjoy the same level of protection as grounds that are listed in the provisions, such as race and gender for example.[53] In comparison, for example the European Community Directive Establishing a General Framework for Equal Treatment in Employment and Occupation is not open-ended and it mentions disability as a protected ground. According to the Directive, differential treatment on the grounds of disability is in principle only justifiable where the disability constitutes an occupational requirement.[54]

Interestingly however, the ICCPR also includes an additional prohibition on discrimination in its Article 26, which has the following wording:

> *"All persons are equal before the law and are entitled without any discrimination to the equal protection of the law. In this respect, the law shall prohibit any discrimination and guarantee to all persons equal and effective protection against discrimination on any ground such as race, colour, sex, language, religion, political or other opinion, national or social origin, property, birth or other status."*

52 ICCPR Article 2(1). ICESCR Article 2(2) uses the word 'discrimination' rather than 'distinction'.

53 Arnardóttir 2009, p. 49.

54 Council Directive 2000/78 Establishing a General Framework for Equal Treatment in Employment and Occupation, OJ [2000] 303/16, Articles 3 and 4.

The fact that it was deemed necessary to include a non-discrimination provision in addition to Article 2 indicates that the ICCPR is not entirely limited to a formal equality model and that there was a development towards a more substantive model of equality. Although Article 26 ICCPR has later been given a substantive content of its own which goes beyond the model of formal equality, its content was originally disputed.[55]

1.2.3. The Council of Europe

During the 1950s and 1960s, the Council of Europe also adopted two fundamental instruments protecting civil and political rights and economic, social and cultural rights. In parallel to the ICCPR, the ECHR only mentions disability in relation to medical treatment. Thus, Article 5(e) on deprivation of liberty mentions "*persons of unsound mind*" together with "*persons who can spread infectious diseases, alcoholics, drug addicts and vagrants*". According to the ECtHR, the rationale for allowing deprivation of liberty is that *"there is a link between all those persons in that they may be deprived of their liberty either in order to be given medical treatment or because of considerations dictated by social policy, or both on medical and social grounds"*.[56] The fact that persons with disabilities were only mentioned in relation to medical treatment reflects the perception of disability during the 1950s and 60s.

The ECHR contains an open-ended prohibition of discrimination which, similarly to ICCPR and ICESCR Article 2, is tied to the scope of application of the convention and has an open-ended list of discrimination grounds indicating that the provision was formulated with model of formal equality in mind. ECHR Article 14 has the following wording:

> *"The enjoyment of the rights and freedoms set forth in this Convention shall be secured without discrimination on any ground such as sex, race, colour, language, religion, political or other opinion, national or social origin, association with a national minority, property, birth or other status."*

As opposed to the ICESCR, the European equivalent, namely the European Social Charter of 1961 (ESC), does contain a specific provision on persons with disabilities. In line however with the medical model of disability, the ESC of 1961, Article 15, emphasises rehabilitation and vocational training of the individual rather than seeking to remove social barriers to participation:

55 Nowak 2005, p.605.

56 European Court of Human Rights, 25 january 2005, *Enhorn v. Sweden*, Application No. 56529/00, § 43.

"The right of physically or mentally disabled persons to vocational training, rehabilitation and social resettlement
With a view to ensuring the effective exercise of the right of the physically or mentally disabled to vocational training, rehabilitation and resettlement, the Contracting Parties undertake:
to take adequate measures for the provision of training facilities, including, where necessary, specialised institutions, public or private;
to take adequate measures for the placing of disabled persons in employment, such as specialised placing services, facilities for sheltered employment and measures to encourage employers to admit disabled persons to employment."

In sum, during the 1940s, -50s and -60s groundbreaking moves were made with regard to the recognition of the individual's justiciable rights under international law. In terms of equality models and the position of persons with disabilities under human rights law, the adopted human rights instruments were based on the medical model of disability and did not take into account that persons with disabilities did not have the same opportunities in a society based on structures that favour persons without disabilities. During the following decades, this recognition changed the model of equality and the position of persons with disabilities under human rights law.

1.3. From the 1970s until 2000s – Substantive Difference Equality and the Minority Model of Disability

1.3.1. The Models of Equality and Disability

During the 1970s, '80s and '90s, the first steps were taken to redress the absence of specific human rights protection for persons with disabilities. The new perception of the position of persons with disabilities under human rights law reflected a change in the model of equality from formal equality to a substantive difference approach and a change from the medical model of disability to a social minority model of disability.

The *substantive* difference *equality model* differs from the formal equality model in that it is not merely procedural, but requires a normative assessment of the result of a treatment.[57] Thus, under the substantive difference model, it is recognised that some differences relating to personal characteristics cannot simply be ignored and must be acted upon in order to achieve equality. In other words, asymmetrical treatment may be necessary to comply with the standard of substantive equality. As opposed to the formal equality model, which only recognises direct discrimination, the substantive equality model with its asymmetrical approach recognises both

57 Arnardóttir 2003, p. 24; Arnardóttir 2009, p. 49; Gijzen 2006, p. 23; Fredman 2002, p. 8.

direct and indirect discrimination as well as discrimination due to lack of reasonable accommodation. It may also allow for positive action understood as active measures taken to address structural inequalities. However, according to the substantive difference equality model the starting point is that equal treatment is sufficient and only in exceptional situations can it be required to make adjustments of the treatment in question by imposing positive action. In other words, the individual's special characteristics, which are different from those of the norm, may be taken into account, but only as an exception to the rule.

The advantage with the substantive difference equality model, as opposed to the model of formal equality, is that this model of equality has a normative content and that it recognises that special treatment may be required to take account of special characteristics. Its strengths lie also in the implied recognition of individual rights, which may be enforced by courts of law.[58]

The weakness of the substantive difference equality model is however that the dominating groups of society are the standard of measure. It is unclear exactly when a personal characteristic warrants special treatment. In addition, special treatment will only be warranted as an exception to the rule which is to uphold the status-quo. General social structures will as a rule not be subjected to change in order to ensure equality for groups who are different from the prevailing groups.[59] Other weaknesses with this model are linked with its reliance on individual rights enforced by the courts as catalysts for change. As identified by *Sandra Fredman*, four central difficulties are associated with the reliance on individual complaints to bring about change: Firstly excessive strain is put on victims of discrimination both in terms of cost and personal energy. Secondly court intervention is random and ad-hoc depending on whether a suited case has been presented to the courts. Thirdly, the basis in individual fault makes this system relatively unsuited to deal with institutional and collective inequality, which is not the fault of one specific perpetrator. Fourthly, individual claims are adversarial which leads to equality becoming a site of conflict rather than a common goal.[60]

In parallel with the movement from the model of formal equality towards the model of substantive difference equality, the period of time from the 1970s to the 1990s marked a shift away from the medical model of disability to the social model of disability. These two models may be perceived as opposites where the first explains disadvantage by pointing to the individual's deviation from the norm and where the second explains disadvantage by pointing to barriers in the environment. According to the social model of disability, the limitations faced by persons with disabilities in

58 Arnardóttir 2009, p. 50; Fredman 2002, p. 9.

59 Arnardóttir 2003, p. 26; Kimber 1996, p. 272.

60 Fredman 2005b, p. 372–373.

obtaining employment, housing and education are not the product of their medical condition, but of social attitudes of neglect and stereotypical perceptions of disabled persons.[61] This model entails that the policy approach to the limitations experienced by persons with disabilities should not focus on the individual, but on the environment.[62]

During the 1970s and 1980s, the minority rights model of disabilities or the social minority model of disability, dominated in disability theory. According to this model of disability, which is a sub-model to the social model of disability, *"disabled persons are a social minority who have been systematically discriminated against in all areas of life."*[63] Inspired by especially the racial equality movement in the United States of America, the minority rights proponents sought to show that persons with disabilities were also an insular minority with a specific form of human difference (disability instead of black skin colour) which had historically led to marginalisation. This school of thought has sought to underline the characteristic differences between persons with disabilities on the one hand and persons without disabilities on the other hand in order to justify the necessity for adaptation for the needs of persons with disabilities. Since the social minority model of disability is a sub-model of the social model of disability, the policies based on this model target the environment and attitudes towards disability rather than the individual. In addition, the advocates of the minority group have favoured anti-discrimination legislation as the prime tool to achieve substantive equality.[64]

As will be seen below, the social minority model of disability has been a successful promulgator of change in human rights law. The social minority model, which explains the exclusion of persons with disabilities in similar manner to the exclusion of other groups such as women and blacks, succeeded in obtaining recognition for the need to protect persons with disabilities from discrimination and to make accommodation for their special needs.

The problem with the social minority model is that it relies on an assumption that there is a minority consisting of persons with disabilities. The problem with this assumption is that it is very difficult to say who has and who does not have a disability. In doing so, one may draw on the medical model of disability and to require that only persons with a certain type of disability, a certain degree of disability at a certain time may be defined as within the group of persons with disability. By doing so, one risks excluding groups of persons who are discriminated and experience exclusion on the grounds of their disability, but who do not fall within the group of persons with disabilities as defined for example under a law

61 Gijzen 2006, p. 384, Traustadóttir 2009, p. 9. Hendriks 2002, p. 201.

62 Waddington and Diller 2002, p. 246.

63 Bichenbach and others 1999b.

64 Bickenbach 1999, p. 101. Hahn 1993, p. 746. Hendriks 2002, p. 202.

prohibiting discrimination on the grounds of disability founded on the social minority model.[65]

Another point of criticism of this model has been its reliance on discrimination legislation as the motor for change. Although indirect discrimination caused by social structures may to some extent be recognised, discrimination legislation is by its nature focussed on an individual victim of discrimination as well as backwards-looking and negative in that it is used on a case-by-case basis to be decided by the courts and that it prohibits certain behaviour rather than pointing towards certain behaviour.[66] The social universality model of disability, which will be described below under *Section 1.4.1.*, addresses these problems with the social minority model of disability.

1.3.2. The United Nations

During the 1970s, the first small steps were taken to rectify the absence of persons with disabilities from mainstream human rights documents such as the Universal Declaration of Human Rights and the two UN human rights Covenants of 1966. In 1971 and in 1975, the UN Declaration of the Rights of Mentally Retarded Persons and UN Declaration of the Rights of Disabled Persons were adopted.[67] These documents mark a shift towards to the civil rights approach according to which human rights shall be used to promote equality rather than for example social legislation. The UN Declaration of the Rights of Mentally Retarded Persons and the UN Declaration of the Rights of Disabled Persons proclaim that "Disabled persons have the same civil and political rights as other human beings", and urge that *"Disabled persons shall be protected against all exploitation, all regulations and all treatment of a discriminatory, abusive or degrading nature"*.[68] Nevertheless, most of the policy recommendations concerned medical treatment and rehabilitation and social security.

In 1976, the UN World Health Organisation (WHO) adopted a taxonomy of impairments, disability and handicaps entitled *"The International Classification of Impairments, Disabilities and Handicaps"* (ICIDH).[69] This first attempt by the WHO to define disability encountered heavy criticism by disability NGOs because it was founded on the medical model of disability which sees a disability as an

65 Bickenbach 1999, p. 107.
66 Fredman 2005a, p. 206–7; Gijzen 2006, p. 387.
67 UN Declaration of the Rights of Mentally Retarded Persons, General Assembly Resolution 2856; UN Declaration of the Rights of Disabled Persons, General Assembly Resolution 3447 of 1975.
68 Ibid.
69 World Health Resolution No. 29.35 of May 1976.

inevitable consequence of impairment.[70] The reliance on the medical model of disability was clear from the sub-title of the ICIDH: *"A manual of classification relating to the consequences of disease"*. A revised *"International Classification of Functioning, Disability and Health"* (ICF) was endorsed by the World Health Assembly in 2001.[71] This new classification builds on a synthesis of the medical and social models of disability in that it takes account of the fact that both the impairment *and* the environment context influence the limitations experienced by persons with impairments. This classification by the WHO is considered controversial by some Disability NGOs, which is also the reason that the CRPD fails to make reference to the ICF.[72] As mentioned in *Chapter I, Section 5. Some Definitions*, some disability NGOs seem to have moved towards a radical social constructionist view which completely denies that impairments may in themselves entail limitations in activities or participation in social life.[73]

During the 1980s, the shift away from the medical approach to disability and toward the civil rights approach became cemented with the proclamation of the International Year of the Disabled in 1981, the International Decade of Disabled Persons launched in 1983 and the appointment of the first Special Rapporteur on human rights and disability by the UN Sub-Commission on Prevention of Discrimination and Protection of Minorities in 1984.[74] The World Programme of Action adopted in 1982 promoted equality and was founded on the social model of disability described above under *Section 1.3.1. The Models of Equality and Disability.* The Programme of Action not only included Chapters on "*Prevention*" and "*Rehabilitation*", but also a Chapter on "*Equalization of Opportunities*" in which it was stated that to achieve the goals of "*full participation and equality, rehabilitation measures aimed at the disabled individual are not sufficient. Experience shows that it is largely the environment which determines the effect of impairment or a disability on a person's daily life.*"[75]

Also during the 1980s, the first legally binding human rights instrument specifically on persons with disabilities was adopted. In 1983, the International Labour Organisation (ILO) under the UN adopted Convention No. 159 on Vocational

---

70 Hendriks and Liisberg 2009. See for example the criticism by UN Special Rapporteur Leandro Despouy appointed by Resolution 84/20 of 20 August 1984 by the Sub-Commission on Prevention f Discrimination and Protection of Minorities entitled "Human Rights and Disabled People", paras. 94 to 98.

71 World Health Resolution No. 54.21 of 22 May 2001.

72 Kayess and French 2008, p. 25.

73 Kayess and French 2008, p. 7.

74 U.N. resolutions on International Year of the Disabled and the UN Decade of Disabled Persons: General Assembly Resolutions 31/123 and 37/53; Resolution on Special Rapporteur: Commission on Human Rights Resolution 1984/31.

75 UN World Programme of Action adopted by the General Assembly on 3 December 1982, by its resolution 37/52.

Rehabilitation and Employment (Disabled Persons). In spite of the fact that Article 4 of this Convention states that "Equality of opportunity and treatment for disabled men and women shall be respected" and *"Special positive measures [...] shall not be regarded as discriminating against other workers"*, the duties set out in this convention mainly target the individual and not social barriers for participation. Thus, this Convention may be seen as bridging the old medical model of disability and the newer social model of disability as well as the models of formal and substantive difference equality. The Convention does not fully embrace the social model of disability which would require it to focus on environmental barriers to participation and the model of substantive difference equality which would entail a duty to provide reasonable accommodation.

It was only at the end of the 1980s that the UN General Assembly adopted a legally binding human rights instrument, which contained a specific provision on persons with disabilities. The UN Convention on the Rights of the Child (CRC) of 1989 was the first UN human rights convention to include disability in its open-ended list of discrimination grounds and the first to include a specific article on persons with disabilities.[76] CRC Article 23 concerns children with disabilities. According to Article 23(1) States Parties shall recognise that disabled children should enjoy *"a full and decent life, in conditions which ensure dignity, promote self-reliance and facilitate the child's active participation in the community"*. In line with the social minority model of disability, the provision stresses the right to special care. As opposed however to under the diversity model of disability discussed below, the provision of special care shall be conducive to full integration, but integration is not a right in itself for the disabled child. Article 23(2) provides that:

> *"assistance [...] shall be designed to ensure that the disabled child has effective access to and receives education, training, health care services, rehabilitation services, preparation for employment and recreation opportunities in a manner conducive to the child's achieving the fullest possible social integration and individual development, including his or her cultural and spiritual development."*

In the 1990s a number of States, Non-governmental Organisations (NGOs) and individuals advocated for a comprehensive and legally binding instrument on the rights of persons with disabilities.[77] However, this initiative did not achieve sufficient support among the Member States of the UN. Instead, as a matter of compromise, the UN Standard Rules on the Equalization of Opportunities for Persons with Disabilities (UN Standard Rules) were adopted in 1993. Although the Rules are non-binding, they proclaim to be an *"international instrument of a*

76 United Nations, Convention on the Rights of the Child, General Assembly Resolution 44/25 of 20 November 1989, Article 2.

77 Hendriks and Liisberg, 2009.

different kind", and atypically for non-binding instruments, the rules provide for a monitoring mechanism, which includes a Special Rapporteur on Disability.[78]

The UN Standard Rules are founded on the substantive model of equality and the social model of disability according to which obstacles to equality of opportunities are found in the environment rather than at the level of the individual. In line herewith, the Standard Rules recommend that States should recognise *"the overall importance of accessibility in the process of equalization of opportunities" and "provide for appropriate sanctions in case of violations of the principles of non-discrimination"*. However, the UN Standard Rules merely provide that States should *"encourage employers to make reasonable adjustments"* instead of defining denial of reasonable adjustments as a form of discrimination.[79] This weak level of priority given to the duty to provide reasonable accommodation shows that the UN Standard Rules are based on substantive difference equality.

After the adoption of the Standard Rules, one could have expected that the Treaty monitoring bodies under the ICCPR and the ICESCR would have become more conscious of persons with disabilities. However in a study commissioned by the UN High Commissioner for Human Rights, it was found that the potential of the Committees to ensure respect for the human rights of persons with disabilities was not fully explored.[80] For example, the Committees did not systematically examine State compliance with the Covenants with regard to persons with disabilities and did not systematically mainstream disability issues in their General Comments on the interpretation of the covenants. Only the Committee on Economic, Social and Cultural Rights has adopted a General Comment which specifies in some detail how the ICESCR should be interpreted to ensure the full enjoyment of persons with disabilities.[81]

The Human Rights Committee, which monitors compliance with the ICCPR, considers individual complaints against States that have ratified the Optional Protocol on individual complaints. Under this procedure, the Human Rights Committee has addressed a few cases which specifically concerned persons with disabilities. In the *Hamilton* case, the Human Rights Committee found that Jamaica had violated Article 10(1) on the right of persons deprived of their liberty to be

---

78 UN Standard Rules on the Equalization of Opportunities for Persons with Disabilities adopted by the General Assembly on 20 December 1993 by its resolution 48/96 (UN Standard Rules), Introduction and Section IV on Monitoring Mechanisms.

79 U.N. Standard Rules Rule No. 7 on Employment. CRPD Article 5(2).

80 Quinn and Degener 2002.

81 Committee on Economic, Social and Cultural Rights, General Comment No. 5 on Persons with Disabilities adopted in 1994. The Committee on the Elimination of Discrimination Against Women also adopted a disability-specific General Comment, but it merely acknowledges double discrimination of women with disabilities and calls on parties to provide information on disabled women, General Comment No. 18 of 1991. Hendriks and Liisberg 2009.

treated *"with respect for the inherent dignity of the human person"* because a prison inmate paralysed in both legs was left dependent on the help of other inmates to reach recreational areas outside his cell and to empty his slop bucket. The Committee stated that *"the author has made very precise allegations, relating to the difficulties he has encountered as a disabled person [...]. In the Committee's opinion, the conditions described in para 3.1, are such as to violate the author's right to be treated with humanity and with respect for the inherent dignity of the human person, and are therefore contrary to article 10, paragraph 1."*[82] In the case *C. v. Australia*, the Committee found a violation of Article 7, which prohibits torture, inhuman and degrading treatment, because Australia deported a foreigner, who had been granted refugee status in his country, to a country, where he could not expect to receive treatment for his mental illness. The Committee noted the following:

> *"In circumstances where the State party has recognized a protection obligation towards the author, the Committee considers that deportation of the author to a country where it is unlikely that he would receive the treatment necessary for the illness caused, in whole or in part, because of the State party's violation of the author's rights would amount to a violation of article 7 of the Covenant."*[83]

Finally, in the *Wackenheim*-case, the Human Rights Committee acknowledged that Article 26 applies to differentiation on the grounds of dwarfism and in the field of employment.[84] The case concerned a complaint from a man with dwarf-growth who earned his living by being thrown in dwarf-throwing contests in France. The Committee found however that a legislative ban against dwarf-tossing was based on objective and reasonable grounds and thus did not constitute a violation of Article 26. The Committee stated that *"Differentiation constitutes discrimination when it is not based on objective and reasonable grounds."* In the case in question, the Committee considered *"that the State party has demonstrated, in the present case, that the ban on dwarf-tossing as practised by the author did not constitute an abusive measure but was necessary in order to protect public order which brings into play considerations of human dignity that are compatible with the objectives of the Covenant."*[85]

These three cases show that the Human Rights Committee has required of States that they take into consideration that persons with disabilities may require or warrant different treatment due to their disability. This indicates that the Committee

82 International Human Rights Committee, *Hamilton v. Jamaica,* Communication No. 616/1995 of 28 July 1999, para. 8.2. See also *Francis v. Jamaica,* Communication No. 606/1994 of 3 August 1995 regarding the deterioration of mental health during prolonged incarceration on death row.

83 C. v. Australia, Communication No. 900/1999 of 13 November 2002, para. 8.5.

84 Wackenheim v. France, Views of the UN Human Rights Committee in Communication no. 854/1999 of 26 July 2002, CCPR/C/75/D/854/1999. Hendriks and Liisberg 2009.

85 Ibid.

interprets the ICCPR in accordance with the model of substantive difference equality and the social model of disability. One may discuss whether the finding in the *Wackenheim*-case was paternalistic and could unintentionally perpetuate condescending attitudes towards persons with disabilities as being in need of protection. In my view however, tossing of dwarves in itself reflects a condescending perception of dwarves as non-human objects. I therefore agree with the Human Rights Committee that a prohibition on dwarf-tossing does not amount to discrimination on the grounds of disability.

1.3.3. The Council of Europe

In the present Section, I examine the protection of persons with disabilities firstly under the European Convention on Human Rights and secondly under the European Social Charter. The development in the protection under each of these conventions is analysed and examined in relation to the substantive difference equality model and the social minority model of disability.

1.3.3.1. European Convention on Human Rights

Being the only international human rights instrument applicable to Denmark and Sweden monitored by an international court, which takes legally binding decisions, the ECHR has a singular position in relation to these two countries.

The ECtHR began in the 1980s to recognise exceptions to the formal equality model and to interpret the European Convention on Human Rights in accordance with the substantive equality model.[86] Since then, the ECtHR has further embraced the substantive model of equality and has been increasingly willing to perceive equal treatment as requiring asymmetrical treatment. Thus it has been willing to recognise the occurrence of indirect discrimination, the duty to provide reasonable accommodation (although it does not use this phrasing) and that positive treatment may be permitted in order to promote equality.[87] For example in the *Thlimmenos*-

---

86 Arnardóttir 2009, p. 53, an example of an early cases recognising substantive equality are the Rasmussen v. Denmark, judgment of 28 November 1984, Application No. 8777/79 where it was found to be in accordance with ECHR Article 14 that a man could only challenge his paternity within a certain time limits after he gained knowledge of the alleged paternity, which did not apply to women in relation to their maternity.

87 In the case D.H. and Others v. the Czech Republic, judgment of 13 November 2007, Application No. 57325/00 (Grand Chamber), the Court for the first time found indirect discrimination in violation of Article 14 in conjunction Article 2 of the First Protocol on the right to education. The Court found discrimination on the grounds of race because many Roma children were placed in schools for intellectually disabled children as a result of tests which did not take account of their needs "as members of a disadvantaged class", para. 207. As the Chamber noted in its admissibility decision in the instant case, the choice between a single school for everyone, highly specialised structures and unified structures with specialised sections is not an easy one.

case, the ECtHR found that the exclusion of all persons with a criminal record from being appointed as chartered accountants amounted to discrimination because persons who had a criminal record due to conscientious objection on the grounds of religion should be treated differently from others with criminal records. The ECtHR stated that:

> *"The right not to be discriminated against in the enjoyment of the rights guaranteed under the Convention is also violated when States without an objective and reasonable justification fail to treat differently persons whose situations are significantly different. [...] However, the Court also considers that, unlike other convictions for serious criminal offences, a conviction for refusing on religious or philosophical grounds to wear the military uniform cannot imply any dishonesty or moral turpitude likely to undermine the offender's ability to exercise this profession. [...]It follows that the applicant's exclusion from the profession of chartered accountants did not pursue a legitimate aim. As a result, the Court finds that there existed no objective and reasonable justification for not treating the applicant differently from other persons convicted of a serious crime."*[88]

In line with the judgment in the *Thlimmenos*-case, the ECtHR passed a historic judgment in relation to persons with disabilities on 30 April 2009 in the *Glor*-case. In this case it was the first time that the Court found discrimination on the grounds of disability although it did not state this explicitly. The ECtHR noted that the case concerned possible discrimination of a person with a physical disability even if it was considered as a minor disability by the national authorities.[89] Moreover, the Court underlined that the ECHR must be interpreted in light of present day conditions and that there is a European and universal consensus today that persons with disabilities must be protected from discrimination as shown by the UN CRPD. The case concerned a man who had diabetes and who was found unfit to perform his military service even though he had stated that he wanted to perform his military service. In addition, he was required to pay a penalty tax over several years for not performing his military service. The rules on penalty tax only provided exemptions

---

It entails a difficult balancing exercise between the competing interests. As to the setting and planning of the curriculum, this mainly involves questions of expediency on which it is not for the Court to rule. In Stec and Others v. the United Kingdom, judgment of 12 April 2006, Grand Chamber, Application No. 65731/01, (Grand Chamber), the Court found that positive differential treatment of women did not constitute discrimination of men because of the "disadvantaged situation of women", para. 66.

88 European Court of Human Rights, *Thlimmenos v. Greece*, Application no. 34369/97, Judgment of 6 April 2000, para. 44 and 47. The Court found a violation of ECHR Article 14 in conjunction with Article 9 on freedom of religion.

89 European Court of Human Rights, *Glor v. Switzerland,* Application no. 13444/04, judgment of 30 April 2009, para. 53. A request by the Swiss government to have the case tried before the Grand Chamber of the European Court of Human Rights was rejected by the Court, Press Release issued by the Registrar of the European Court of Human Rights, no.962 of 15 December 2009.

for persons who were unfit for military service due to severe disability. Persons who were found unfit due to other health-related grounds, such as diabetes, were not exempted from paying the penalty tax. The lack of exemptions for persons found unfit to perform their military service on other health grounds than severe disability constituted discrimination on the grounds of ECHR Article 14 in conjunction with Article 8.[90] The ECtHR stated the following:

> *"In light of the aims and effects of the penalty tax, the objective justification for the distinction applied by the internal authorities, especially as regards persons unfit for service who are exempted from the penalty tax and persons unfit for service who are nonetheless obliged to pay the tax, does not seem reasonable considering the prevalent principles of democratic societies."*[91]

Moreover, Member States were obliged to choose the least intrusive limitation in a right if it was to be considered proportionate and necessary in a democratic society. Thus the ECtHR found that Switzerland could have required of persons with minor disabilities such as the plaintiff that they either carry out their military services with adaptation for their needs or that they be permitted to carry out a civil service instead of sentencing them to a penalty tax.[92] The ECtHR stated the following:

> *"The Court nonetheless asks itself what would hinder the establishment of special forms of military services for persons in a similar situation to that of the applicant. One may think particularly of activities which, although taking place at the heart of the armed forces, require lesser physical efforts and which could therefore be carried out by persons in a situation similar to that of the applicant. [...] It is true that civil service instead of military service is in the majority of countries open only to conscientious objectors as is the case in Switzerland. [...] The Court is however convinced that specific forms of civil service adapted to the needs of persons in the situation of the application are perfectly possible."*[93]

Both the above-mentioned *Thlimmenos*-case and the *Glor*-case illustrate the adherence of the ECtHR to the substantive equality model as in both cases it acknowledged that same treatment is not always adequate and that differential treatment may be necessary.

In accordance with its adherence to the substantive equality model, the ECtHR has also acknowledged the social model of disability and the ensuing duty to accommodate the environment, in certain cases, to the needs of persons with

90 Ibid. para. 96–97.

91 Ibid. Para. 97 (My translation from French).

92 Ibid. para. 94–95.

93 Ibid. Paras. 94 and 95. (My translation from French.) The importance of this case in relation to scope of application of the European Equal Treatment Directive is discussed in *Chapter III EU Law and Policy, Section 4 European Equal Treatment Directive.*

disabilities. This was the case in the *Glor*-case where the Court stated that Switzerland could have provided for possibilities for performing military or civil services for persons with disabilities. Another example is the *Price*-case, which resembles the *Hamilton*-case of the Human Rights Committee mentioned above. In the *Price*-case, the ECtHR found a violation of ECHR Article 3 because the complainant had been detained under conditions which did not take due account of the complainant's disability. In this judgment, the Court stated that:

> *"However, the Court considers that to detain a severely disabled person in conditions where she is dangerously cold, risks developing sores because her bed is too hard or unreachable, and is unable to go to the toilet or keep clean without the greatest of difficulty, constitutes degrading treatment contrary to Article 3 of the Convention."*[94]

Also in the *Kutzner*-case, which concerned a married couple who both had intellectual disabilities and who had their children removed and placed with foster parents, the ECtHR found a violation of Article 8 on the right to family life and noted that:

> *"the Bersenbrück Guardianship Court withdrew the applicants' parental responsibility for their two daughters, Corinna and Nicola, who were born in 1991 and 1993 respectively, and ordered their placement with foster parents, notably on the ground that the applicants did not have the requisite intellectual capacity to bring up their children.[...]Accordingly, although the educational-support measures taken initially subsequently proved to be inadequate, it is questionable whether the domestic administrative and judicial authorities have given sufficient consideration to additional measures of support as an alternative to what is by far the most extreme measure, namely separating the children from their parents."*[95]

In sum, the *Glor*, *Price* and the *Kutzner* cases quoted above show that the ECtHR has recognised that disability is a difference which may require an exception to the rule of same treatment. In all cases, the States were required to make reasonable accommodations (although this term was not used) to the ordinary treatment of prisoners and parents respectively. In other words, it is the substantive difference equality model and the minority disability model which constitute the foundation of the findings of the ECtHR.[96]

---

94 European Court of Human Rights, *Price v. UK,* Application no. 33394/96, judgment of 10 July 2001, para. 30.

95 European Court of Human Rights, *Kutzner v. Germany*, Application no. 46544/99, judgment of 26 February 2002, para. 68 and 75.

96 Other examples of cases where the European Court of Human Rights has found violations due to lack of accommodation for disability (without using this term) include also X. v. the Netherlands,.

A number of cases also illustrate the limitations of the substantive difference model and the minority disability model. The ECtHR has now in several cases treated questions of lack of accessibility to public places as a question of whether the negative consequences of accessibility for an individual complainant had been so grave as to warrant the imposition of a positive duty on Member States to change the existing design or practices. The framing of the question of exclusion of persons with disabilities from full participation in social life in this way results in the weakening of the protection of persons with disabilities under the European Convention on Human Rights. Thus, several authors have shown how the ECtHR could well provide stronger protection to persons with disabilities without breaking the existing boundaries of the European Convention of Human Rights, for example by being more willing to try disability cases under ECHR Article 14 which prohibits discrimination.[97]

For example in the *Botta*-case of 1998, the ECtHR found that the lack of accessibility to a public beach for a man using a wheelchair did not fall within the ambit of Article 8 ECHR on the right to private life. The Court stated the following:

> *"In the instant case the applicant complained in substance not of action but of a lack of action by the State. [...]The Court has held that a State has obligations of this type where it has found a direct and immediate link between the measures sought by an applicant and the latter's private and/or family life. [...] In the instant case, however, the right asserted by Mr Botta, namely the right to gain access to the beach and the sea at a place distant from his normal place of residence during his holidays, concerns interpersonal relations of such broad and indeterminate scope that there can be no conceivable direct link between the measures the State was urged to take in order to make good the omissions of the private bathing establishments and the applicant's private life. Accordingly, Article 8 is not applicable."*[98]

In the *Zehnalovà and Zehnal*-case, one could have expected a different finding than in the *Botta*-case since the *Zehnalovà and Zehnal*-case concerned lack of access for a wheelchair-user to public buildings (rather than a public beach) in the applicant's home town (as opposed his or her place of vacation) to which the applicant needed

---

97 De Schutter 2005, pp. 45–53, where the author identifies five potential routes for overcoming the *Botta* line of cases. ECHR Article 14 is accessory, which means that in only applies to differential treatment which falls within the ambit of the Convention. For an analysis of the protection against discrimination on the grounds of disability in the field of employment under the ECHR, see De Schutter 2005 pp. 56–60. The Twelfth Protocol to the ECHR, which was adopted in 2000 and entered into force in 2005, contains a free-standing right to non-discrimination. Neither Denmark nor Sweden have ratified the Twelfth Protocol to the ECHR. O'Cinneide 2009, pp. 185–189 where he sets forth arguments for strengthened protection of persons with disabilities under the ECHR by referring to case law in other areas.

98 European Court of Human Rights, *Botta v. Italy,* judgment of 24 February 1998, Application No. 153/1996/772/773, para. 33–35. See also the *Mołka*-case where the Court surprisingly rejected that lack of access to v.

access in her daily life (as opposed to during his or her vacation). However, also in this case, the ECtHR did not find that there was a direct link between the measures that the State was asked to take and the applicant's private life.[99]

Moreover, the *Mołka*-case concerned a wheelchair-user who could not cast his vote at a local election. Contrary to the other two cases, the ECtHR acknowledged that there could be a direct link between a lack of accessibility on the one hand and the applicant's private life on the other.[100] The case was however rejected as manifestly ill-founded because the Court found that a duty to ensure accessibility to local voting facilities would amount to a disproportionate burden on the State. The Court stated the following:

> *"Having regard to the above considerations, the Court does not rule out the possibility that, in circumstances such as those in the present case, a sufficient link would exist to attract the protection of Article 8. However, the Court does not find it necessary finally to determine the applicability of the Article in the present case since, for the reasons which follow, the application is in any event inadmissible on other grounds. [...] In view of their awareness of the funds available to provide such access for disabled persons, the national authorities are in a better position to carry out this assessment than an international court. Moreover, the Court notes that the applicant has not shown, as was pointed out by the domestic courts, that he could not have been assisted in entering the polling station by other persons. [...] It is also of relevance for the assessment of the respondent Government's compliance with their positive obligations under Article 8 in the present case that the situation complained of concerned one isolated incident as opposed to a series of obstacles, architectural or otherwise, preventing physically disabled applicants from developing their relationships with other people and the outside world.[...] Bearing in mind the above considerations, the Court considers that the respondent State cannot be said, in the special circumstances of the present case, to have failed to ensure respect for the applicant's private life."*[101]

Finally, in the *D.H.*-case, the Grand Chamber of the ECtHR found that Roma-children had been discriminated indirectly because they were quasi-automatically

---

99 European Court of Human Rights, *Zehnalova and Zehnal v. the Check Republic,* Decision of 19 February 2002, Application No. 38621/97. See also the Sentges v. Netherlands.

100 European Court of Human rights, Mołka v. Poland, Decision of 11 April 2006, Application No. 56550/00.

101 Compare with the reasoning of the Court in the Hirst-case which concerned the disenfranchisement of convicted prisoners who were detained in the United Kingdom and where the Court found a violation of Article 3 of Protocol 1 on Parliamentary elections (not local elections as in the *Mołka* -case). The Court stated: 'As pointed out by the applicant, the right to vote is not a privilege. In the twenty-first century, the presumption in a democratic State must be in favour of inclusion". European Court of Human Rights, Hirst v. United Kingdom (No. 2), Judgment of 6 October 2005, Application No. 74025/01, para. 59.

placed in schools for children with intellectual disabilities.[102] From a disability rights-perspective, it is interesting to note that the ECtHR stated explicitly that it could not make decisions on the appropriateness of placing children with intellectual disabilities in specialised schools. This is surprising in view of growing international consensus that children with intellectual disabilities should be included in the general educational system.[103] The ECtHR recognised that an education in the special schools made integration in society more difficult for Roma children:

> *"As a result, they received an education which compounded their difficulties and compromised their subsequent personal development instead of tackling their real problems or helping them to integrate into the ordinary schools and develop the skills that would facilitate life among the majority population. Indeed, the Government have implicitly admitted that job opportunities are more limited for pupils from special schools [...]"*[104]

However, the Court could not interfere in how the educational system excluded children with disabilities from general structures:

> *"[...] the choice between a single school for everyone, highly specialised structures and unified structures with specialised sections is not an easy one. It entails a difficult balancing exercise between the competing interests. As to the setting and planning of the curriculum, this mainly involves questions of expediency on which it is not for the Court to rule [...].*[105]

Especially these last two cases regarding access to voting facilities and education show the limitations of the substantive difference model and the minority disability model as applied by the ECtHR. Although the ECtHR recognises that a lack of physical access and specialised schools for intellectually disabled children respectively hinder the individual with a disability from taking part in social life, the Court still finds it almost impossible to require of the State to change general social structures. In the *D.H.*-case, the ECtHR noted explicitly that it could not interfere with the organisation of the educational system. And in the *Mołka*-case, views the lack of access to voting facilities as 'one isolated incident' which was not so disruptive to the individual as to warrant the imposition of a duty to change general structures. By referring to the limited disruption of the individual's life, the

---

102 European Court of Human Rights, D.H. and Others v. the Czech Republic, judgment of 13 November 2007, Application No. 57325/00 (Grand Chamber).

103 CRPD Article 24 (Persons with disabilities receive the support required, within the general education system, to facilitate their effective education) and Revised ESC Article 15 (take the necessary measures to provide persons with disabilities with guidance, education and vocational training in the framework of general schemes wherever possible).

104 European Court of Human Rights, D.H. and Others v. the Czech Republic, judgment of 13 November 2007, Application No. 57325/00 (Grand Chamber), para. 207.

105 Ibid., para. 205.

ECtHR underplays the fact that the exclusion took place on the grounds of the personal characteristic of disability which means that all persons with this type of disability will be affected similarly and treats the exclusion as if it were just a question of the individual's bad luck.

The case law of the ECtHR shows that the Court is more likely to examine a case under ECHR Article 14 regarding non-discrimination and that the strictness of scrutiny depends on whether or not the Court considers the grounds on which differentiation has taken place to be 'suspect'.[106] Grounds such as race and gender are considered 'suspect' and the ECtHR will thus be more likely to try these cases under ECHR Article 14 and it will be very difficult to justify differential treatment based on these grounds. These grounds immediately raise a suspicion of unreasonableness and prejudice.[107] In contrast, the fact that the ECtHR has to this day only found discrimination on the grounds of disability in one case (*Glor*-case) and has been relatively unwilling to even consider cases under ECHR Article 14 (*Price*-case, *Botta*-case, *Mołka-case, D.H.-case)* shows that disability has not to date been considered to be a 'suspect' ground of discrimination.[108]

One may ask whether this relatively low level of protection of persons of persons with disabilities under the ECtHR is a result of inherent limitations in the European Convention of Human Rights or whether it the result of a lack of understanding of disability as a human rights issue which may develop in the years to come. As pointed out above, the ECtHR still seems to view the exclusion of persons with disabilities from social life as a problem which the individual himself or herself should bear the consequences of. However, especially the recent *Glor*-case gives reasons to expect that a stronger protection of persons with disabilities under the European Convention of Human Rights could be under way. The *Glor*-case shows that the ECtHR will most probably be influenced by the view on disability which underlies the UN Convention on Rights of Persons with Disabilities and which is described in more detail below.[109] Other sources of influence will obviously be the national law of the Member States of the Council of Europe and EU law which are increasingly providing protection against discrimination on the grounds of disability. In sum, the ECtHR will most likely in time come to recognise disability as a suspect ground of discrimination.

---

106 Anardottir 2002.

107 Schiek, Waddington and Bell 2007b, p. 36.

108 Anardottir 2002.

109 European Court of Human Rights, *Glor v. Switzerland,* Application no. 13444/04, judgment of 30 April 2009, para. 53 where the Court underlines that the ECHR must be interpreted in light of present day conditions and that there is a European and universal consensus today that persons with disabilities must be protected from discrimination as shown by the UN CRPD. See also Björgvinsson 2009, p. 161; Liisberg 2009, p. 349.

In addition, from a non-disability specific perspective, it has been pointed out that there are signs that the ECtHR is beginning to *"conceptualise the previously biologically constructed discrimination ground of sex in terms of socially constructed gender"* which could subsequently influence the Court's conception of disability another step from the medical and individual model of disability towards the social model of disability.[110] The more this social construction of difference is accepted by the ECtHR, the more likely it will be that the Court questions general structures which perpetuate exclusion of specific groups.

1.3.3.2. European Social Charter

As mentioned above, the ESC as adopted in 1961 was the first human rights treaty to include a specific provision on persons with disabilities. In 1996, a Revised ESC was adopted which marked a change in relation to the provision on disability. The ESC of 1961 remains in force for the States which have ratified it and the Revised ESC only applies to the States which have ratified it. Article 15 of the ESC of 1961 was entitled *"The right of physically or mentally disabled persons to vocational training, rehabilitation and social resettlement"* and was as such clearly based on the medical model of disability. In contrast, Article 15 of the Revised European Social Charter was based on the social model of disability. The new title of the provision is: *"The right of persons with disabilities to independence, social integration and participation in the life of the community"*. According to this provision, Member States shall undertake:

> *"to promote their access to employment through all measures tending to encourage employers to hire and keep in employment persons with disabilities in the ordinary working environment and to adjust the working conditions to the needs of the disabled or, where this is not possible by reason of the disability, by arranging for or creating sheltered employment according to the level of disability."*[111]

Article E of the Revised European Social Charter prohibits discrimination based on *"any ground such as race, colour, sex, language, religion, political or other opinion, national extraction or social origin, health, association with a national minority, birth or other status."*

The European Committee of Social Rights established under the European Social Charter monitors whether States Parties fulfil their obligations under the ESC by means of the examination of State reports and the examination of collective complaints against States Parties to an Additional Protocol to the ESC. The findings

---

110 Arnardóttir 2009, p. 57 where the author refers to the Goodwin-case in which the Court, in the context of transsexual rights, rejects that the words 'men and women' in Article 12 on the right to marry "must refer to a determination of gender by purely biological criteria".

111 European Social Charter, Article 15(2).

of the Committee in its examination of State reports and under the collective complaints procedure provide an authoritative interpretation of the European Social Charter, but they are not legally binding on the Member States. Based on an examination of its case law it is clear that the European Committee of Social Rights interprets Article 15 of the European Social Charter of 1961 in accordance with the social model of disability and requires that Member States adopt a prohibition of discrimination on the grounds of disability in the field of employment.[112]

For example, the European Committee of Social Rights interprets Article 1(2) which provides that States must *"protect effectively the right of the worker to earn his living in an occupation freely entered upon"* and Article 15(2) on the duty of States Parties to *"undertake measures for the placing of disabled persons in employment"* of the ESC of 1961 as requiring the adoption of a prohibition of discrimination on the grounds of disability in the field of employment:

> *"The Committee considers that under Article 1§2 legislation should prohibit discrimination in employment at least on grounds of race, ethnic origin, religion, disability, age, sexual orientation and political opinion. Where a state party has accepted Article 15§2 of the Charter the Committee will examine legislation prohibiting discrimination on grounds of disability under this provision."*[113]

Under the collective complaints procedure the Committee on Social Rights has dealt with two cases on the rights of persons with disabilities. In both cases the Committee found that there was a violation of the Revised ESC due to a lack of access to education for children with intellectual disabilities.[114] In its Decision of 2003, the Committee found that the lack of available education as well as care and support facilities for children and adults with autism in France constituted a violation of Articles 15(1) on persons with disabilities and 17(1) on education (either alone or read in combination with Article E on discrimination of the Revised Social Charter). In its Decision, the Committee stated the following:

> *"In other words, human difference in a democratic society should not only be viewed positively but should be responded to with discernment in order to ensure real and effective equality. [...] The Committee recalls [...] that the implementation of the Charter requires the State Parties to take not merely legal action but also practical action to give full effect to the rights recognised in the Charter.[...] Nevertheless, it considers, as the authorities themselves acknowledge, and whether a broad or narrow definition of autism is adopted, that the proportion of children with autism being educated in either general or specialist schools is much lower than in the case*

112 See e.g. Conclusions XVI-2, vol. 1, p. 99, Belgium and p. 171, Czech Republic, p. 360, Greece.

113 European Committee of Social Rights, Conclusions XVIII-1 – Austria, Article 1, p. 27.

114 European Committee of Social Rights, Complaint No. 13/2002 by Autism-France v. France of 4 November 2003 and Complaint No. 41/2007 by Mental Disability Advocacy Centre v. Bulgaria of 3 June 2008.

of other children, whether or not disabled. It is also established, and not contested by the authorities, that there is a chronic shortage of care and support facilities for autistic adults."[115]

In its Decision from 2007, which concerned access to education for children with disabilities in Bulgaria, the European Committee on Social Rights firmly underscored to a greater degree, the duty to ensure access to the general educational system than in the case of 2003. It stated:

"Firstly, as regards taking special account of children with disabilities, the Committee points out that, while it is acceptable for a distinction to be made between children with and without disabilities in the application of Article 17§2, the integration of children with disabilities into mainstream schools in which arrangements are made to cater for their special needs should be the norm and teaching in specialised schools must be the exception. [...] In the present case, the criteria of accessibility and adaptability are at stake, i.e. educational institutions and curricula have to be accessible to everyone, without discrimination and teaching has to be designed to respond to children with special needs."[116]

In sum, the European Committee on Social Rights has embraced both the substantive equality model and the social model of disability by underlining that States must ensure 'effective equality' and that States must undertake positive action to provide persons with disabilities with education. The decision is founded on the assumption that the problem of the lack of participation in the educational system lies not with persons with disabilities themselves, but with the fact that the educational system is not inclusive towards them. Furthermore, in this decision the European Committee on Social Rights shows signs that it is moving beyond the requirements under the difference equality model and the minority model of disability. The European Committee on Social Rights found that the systemic absence of persons with disabilities from the mainstream educational system in Bulgaria constituted a violation of the ESC.[117] The mainstream educational system in Bulgaria had to be restructured so as to be universally inclusive to all, including children with disabilities. The diversity equality model and the social universality model of disability, which this decision seems to be based on, are described in detail under *Section 1.4. Current Trends* below.

---

115 European Committee of Social Rights, Complaint No. 13/2002 by Autism-France v. France of 4 November 2003, para. 52 and 53.

116 European Committee on Social Rights, Complaint No. 41/2007 by Mental Disability Advocacy Centre of 3 June 2008, para. 35 and 37. See also Quinn 2005 p. 279 on protection against discrimination on the grounds of disability under the European Social Charter.

117 European Committee on Social Rights, Complaint No. 41/2007 by Mental Disability Advocacy Centre of 3 June 2008, para. 35 and 37.

Finally, as regards the imposition of legally binding strict quotas for the promotion of employment of persons with disabilities, the European Committee of Social Rights has underlined that Article 15§2 of the European Social Charter does not require the introduction of quotas but, when such a system is applied, the Committee examines the effectiveness of the quotas when assessing conformity with Article 15§2.[118] The fact that the European Committee of Social Rights permits the use of, but does not require the enactment of positive action measures, is in conformity with the substantive difference equality model which places less importance on proactive measures than the substantive diversity equality model. Please see *Chapter IV Equality Law and Policy, Section 2 Contemporary Disability Human Rights Approach* for a more detailed discussion of quotas.

1.4. Current trends – Substantive Diversity Equality and Social Universality Model of Disability

1.4.1. The Models of Equality and Disability

The current trends in perceptions of equality are characterised by an attempt to achieve substantive equality by remedying each of the deficiencies of the substantive difference model of equality. This last model of substantive equality has many names: "proactive model", "multidimensional disadvantage model", "equality of results" and "diversity equality model".[119] I will use this last term because it underlines the positive and inclusive perception of human difference on which this model of equality is founded. An additional advantage of the latter term is that the word diversity is used in the CRPD which lists *"Respect for difference and acceptance of persons with disabilities as part of human diversity and humanity"* as one of the general principles of the Convention.

Similarly to the substantive difference equality model, the 'ubstantive diversity equality model has an asymmetrical approach to achieving equality which recognises uneven distribution of power, privilege and disadvantage among different groups in society. However, according to the substantive diversity equality model, measures to even out disadvantage between different groups in society are not seen as an exception to the rule of identical treatment. This model of equality is forward-looking and aims at changing general structures in society so that they reflect the equal rights of different groups in society. Thus, according to the substantive diversity equality model, society is diverse and general structures must reflect this. As put by *Kayess and French*, *"if formal equality was about ignoring difference, a*

118 Council of Europe, European Committee of Social Rights, *Conclusions XVIII-2, vol. 1, Hungary, 2007, p. 237.*

119 Arnardóttir 2009, p. 54 (multi-dimensional disadvantage equality, 'aims at equality of results'); Fredman 2005b, p. 373 (proactive models).

universality approach is about expecting difference".[120] There is no single norm against which all others are compared to evaluate whether a characteristic is relevant and can warrant different treatment.[121] The fact that general structures must reflect that persons with disabilities have an equal right to participation underlines the need for mainstreaming the interests of persons with disabilities. Without mainstreaming the interest of persons with disability into all laws and policies, general structures cannot be changed to reflect diversity in society.

A practical difference between the two models is that the substantive diversity equality model does not rely *mainly* on individual claims to bring about change, but leaves the principal initiative with policy makers and implementers, providers of goods and services, employers and others. This means that the four weaknesses associated with the individual claims-led model are addressed: individual victims are relieved of the burden of complaining; change is systemic rather than being based on a case-by-case approach; fault committed by a specific perpetrator must not be proven and equality becomes a common goal rather than a site of conflict.[122] However, although the proactive approach is important under the substantive diversity equality model, individual rights are still a necessary part of the approach – albeit as fall-back rights to be used if general structures are not changed to ensure full inclusion. Thus, the substantive diversity equality model is still a rights-based model.

The weakness in the substantive diversity equality model lies in its reliance on action by policymakers to amend existing social structures. For this model to lead to change, the good will of policy makers and others who set out the general structures of society is required.[123] However, the courts of law may still be drawn upon to adjudicate cases where proactive measures are needed to redress disadvantage. Where the courts apply the substantive diversity equality model, they will be much more likely to find indirect discrimination than was the case under the substantive difference equality model since the courts will be more willing to examine general structures under the diversity equality model. Although courts will not lay out the manner in which indirect discrimination should be redressed, the courts may still play an important role as catalysts of change under the substantive diversity equality model. The courts will however have to walk a thin line between protecting disadvantaged groups from discrimination and respecting the standard-setting role of democratically elected law-makers and governments.

---

120 Kayess and French 2008, p. 11.

121 Arnardottír, 2009, p. 54–55.

122 Arnardottír 2009, p. 54; Fredman 2005b, p. 373.

123 Fredman 2005b, p. 374.

Social construction theories such as the social model of disability form the backbone of the substantive diversity equality model.[124] In this respect, the social universality model of disability corresponds with the substantive diversity equality model. According to the social universality model of disability, disability is not a fixed characteristic of a specific group in society as was the view under the minority disability model. According to *Bickenbach, "[...] a disability should not be viewed as a human attribute that demarcates one portion of humanity from another (as gender does, and race sometimes does), but rather as an infinitely various but universal feature of the human condition. [...] ability-disability is a continuum and the complete absence of disability, like the complete absence of ability, is a limiting case of theoretical interest only."*[125] Once disabilities are seen as general human condition, it becomes clear that the range of 'normality' must be broadened and general social structures must be amended to reflect this norm. Universal design, which may be applied not only to physical structures but to all sorts of structures, e.g. rules and standards governing working hours, aims at enabling the widest possible range of disabled and non-disabled persons may make use of the design.

Although the social universality model of disability seeks to diminish the focus on differences between persons with and without disabilities, it is recognised that it may in some instances be necessary to define some persons as disabled and some as not-disabled, but the definition is not a given. One should be conscious that the delimitations are a result of political and economic considerations which should be open to challenge, debate and revision.[126]

In relation to the definition of disability under non-discrimination legislation, a definition based on the substantial diversity equality model and the social universality model of disability will be more inclusive than a definition based on the substantial difference equality model and the social minority model of disability. Whereas the difference equality model would have a tendency to emphasise differences between the 'norm' and persons who request protection from discrimination, the social universality equality model would be more willing to question 'norms' and their possible discriminatory effects of norms on persons who request protection from discrimination. Thus, a definition of disability under the substantial difference equality model and social minority model will be more likely to focus on whether or not the alleged victim is sufficiently disabled to qualify for protection against discrimination. In contrast, a definition of 'disability' under the substantial diversity equality model and social universality model of disability is more likely to focus on whether or not the person who subjected someone to differential treatment did this on the grounds of disability or not. As opposed to under the substantive difference equality model, the individual's disability may be

124 Arnardottír 2009, p. 55.

125 Bickenbach 1999, p. 112; Gijzen 2006, p. 388.

126 Bickenbach 1999, p. 112.

relevant only in the sense that it sheds light on what the grounds were for the action taken by the alleged perpetrator of discrimination. The severity of a person's disability should not be decisive since discrimination may take place both on the grounds of minor and major disabilities and be equally deserving of protection. Moreover it should not be relevant whether or not a person has experienced limitations in his or her social life in the past, since this will to a large extent depend on whether or not that person has met with inclusive design and attitudes. Again, persons who have not, to date, experienced limitations on their social life due to their impairment may well have the same impairments as others who have had such experiences, and be equally prone to discrimination on the grounds of disability.

In addition, since the heart of the matter concerns the grounds for the differential treatment, it follows that a person who is mistakenly perceived as having a disability, who has previously had a disability or who is developing a disability may be subjected to discrimination on the grounds of disability. It follows also that a family member's disability may motivate discrimination. In sum, the definition of disability under legislation providing protection against discrimination will be used to qualify illegitimate grounds for a certain treatment and not the health status of the alleged victim if it is based on the substantive diversity model and the social universality model of disability.

In contrast to non-discrimination legislation, social legislation has an entirely different aim, which includes, for example, the provision of personal assistance for needs related to a person's impairment. In this context, it may be necessary to make relatively narrow definitions of the individuals who may benefit from the legislation irrespective of whether the legislation is based on the social universality or social minority models of disability. Only discrepancies might concern the willingness to recognise the negative effects of the environment and prevailing social norms. For example under both models, only persons who suffer from serious limitations in their daily lives as a consequence of their impairment alone and in interaction with the environment may qualify for personal assistance. However, there would be a tendency to be more willing to give weight to the negative impact of environmental barriers and negative social attitudes on a person's daily life according to the social universality model, rather than according to the substantial difference equality model.

In the following Sub-Sections, I will examine whether there are grounds for arguing that the substantive diversity equality model and the social universality model of disability have in fact informed the development towards the current protection of persons with disabilities under human rights law.

1.4.2. The United Nations

In Section 2 above, I found that the Council of Europe instruments – the ECHR and the ESC – and the UN Covenants on human rights – the ICCPR and the ICESCR are all based on the *substantive difference equality model.* However, especially the treaty bodies and Court interpreting the ESC and to some extent also the ECHR and the ICESCR have taken steps towards the recognition of substantive diversity equality. Thus, there seems to be a movement towards the *substantive diversity equality model* both under the UN human rights system and under the European Council. In this Section, I will examine the CRPD more closely.

In December 2006, the General Assembly adopted the CRPD after a process involving a great number of States in an unprecedented open process, which allowed for the participation of civil society.[127] The CRPD is not only the first comprehensive and legally binding international human rights convention dedicated to persons with disabilities, but also the first UN human rights convention to be adopted in the twenty-first century and the first addition in sixteen years to the short list of now nine treaties which make up the core human rights treaties of the United Nations.[128] The CRPD was opened for signature on 30 March 2007, and entered into force on 3 May 2008 after its ratification by the 20th State.[129] Already on the day that the CRPD was opened for signature and ratification, eighty-one states and the European Community signed the Convention which is the highest number of opening signatures recorded for any human rights treaty.[130]

As mentioned above, the main characteristic of the substantive diversity equality model is that the claims-led anti-discrimination approach is complemented with a proactive approach according to which general structures must be changed to become inclusive. The role of the State is to ensure equality and participation as opposed to merely refraining from interferences with the individual. According to the social universality disability model, which corresponds with the substantive diversity equality model, all persons are more or less disabled, and persons with disabilities do not constitute a separate minority.

There is no doubt that the CRPD is based on a model of substantive equality as opposed to formal equality. CRPD Article 3 explicitly states that the Convention is based on 'equality of opportunity,' which means that formal equality is not sufficient. It is the effect of the treatment, which is measured. In addition, the CRPD is based on diversity rather than a difference substantive equality model. Thus, the

127 Lawson 2007, p. 588.

128 The other eight treaties are the UNDHR, ICCPR, ICESCR, CERD, CEDAW, CAT, CRC and CRMW.

129 CRPD Article 45(1). In May 2009, the CRPD had 56 Member States and 139 signatories.

130 Kayess and French 2008, p. 2.

proactive approach aimed at altering general structures in society so that they become inclusive towards persons with disabilities runs as a thread through the articles of the Convention. In spite of the fact that the CRPD was seen as an *"implementation convention"*, which would merely explain how existing rights should be understood in relation to persons with disabilities, during its drafting process, the CRPD has introduced both new rights and new proactive duties under existing rights.[131] These rights and duties are new in the sense that they are now explicitly stated and not dependent on a disability-sensitive interpretation of general rights. The Convention recognises that equality for persons with disabilities will not be achieved without changing general structures in society. Thus, the CRPD introduces new rights regarding awareness-raising and accessibility which in a pro-active manner seek to change general attitudes and physical structures in society. According to CRPD Article 8:

> *"States Parties undertake to adopt immediate, effective and appropriate measures (a) to raise awareness throughout society, including at the family level, regarding persons with disabilities [...]."*

CRPD Article 9 provides the following:

> *"To enable persons with disabilities to live independently and participate fully in all aspects of life, States Parties shall take appropriate measures to ensure to persons with disabilities access, on an equal basis with others, to the physical environment, to transportation, to information and communication [...] and to other facilities and services open or provided to the public."*

In addition, the proactive approach runs as a thread through the other substantive provisions of the Convention. Starting with civil and political rights, they contain proactive elements to ensure effective enjoyment of persons with disabilities, which do not limit themselves to duties to provide reasonable accommodation, but are aimed at dismantling general social and attitudinal barriers to participation and inclusion of persons with disabilities. For example Article 13 on access to justice provides both for a duty to provide accommodation for persons with disabilities, as well as a duty to proactively provide awareness training for those working in the field of administration of justice. As to economic, social and cultural rights, which are also found in the ICESCR, they provide firstly for the creation of inclusive general structures, practices and attitudes and secondly for the provision of specialist services and measures in a manner that facilitates inclusion in the general community.[132] For example, the right to work in Article 27 provides firstly that general structures shall be inclusive:

---

131 Kayess and French 2008, p. 20.

132 Kayess and French 2008, p. 31.

"States recognize the right of persons with disabilities to work, on an equal basis with others; this includes the right to the opportunity to gain a living by work freely chosen or accepted in a labour market and work environment which is open, inclusive and accessible to persons with disabilities."

In relation to positive action measures such as for example quotas for employment of persons with disabilities, the CRPD does not go so far as to impose a duty on States to undertake specific measures. However, the CRPD goes so far as to establish a duty to promote employment and to recommend the use of positive action measures:

"[States Parties shall] Promote the employment of persons with disabilities in the private sector through appropriate policies and measures, which may include affirmative action programmes, incentives and other measures"[133]

Other UN human rights conventions, such as the CRC, also provide explicit duties on the States Parties to ensure that all persons may effectively enjoy human rights, but the CRPD goes further than these instruments in 'its detail, range and precision'.[134] It has been argued by several authors that the CRPD breaks down the traditional dichotomy between civil and political rights, which have traditionally been perceived as duties to refrain from interferences (negative rights) to be complied with at all times, and the economic, social and cultural rights which were perceived as programmatic rights to be realised progressively through action by the State (positive rights).[135]

Other UN conventions have also allowed for the use of positive action measures, but none have emphasised as clearly as the CPRD has, that positive action measures should not be seen as an exception, but may be necessary in order to achieve substantive equality. Although no other UN convention is as explicit as the CRPD in this regard in their wording, several Expert Committees have interpreted core UN conventions in a similar manner. Most notably, General Recommendation No. 25 on Temporary Special Measures adopted by the Committee on the Elimination of Discrimination Against Women of 2004 states that

"the Committee considers that States parties are obliged to adopt and implement temporary special measures in relation to any of these articles if such measures can be shown to be necessary and appropriate in order to accelerate the achievement of overall, or a specific goal of, women's de facto or substantive equality."[136]

---

133 CRPD Article 27(1)(h).

134 O'Cinneide 2009, p. 167.

135 Koch 2009, p. 77 (one of the strongest manifestations of the notion of human rights as indivisible); O'Cinneide 2009, p. 167.

136 Committee on the Elimination of Discrimination Against Women, General Recommendation No. 25 on Temporary Special Measures, 2004, Para. 24.

The UN Committee on Economic, Social and Cultural Rights also came to the conclusion that positive action would not only be permitted, but would be required in some cases. Thus, the Committee stated that,

> *"the obligation in the case of such a vulnerable and disadvantaged group is to take positive action to reduce structural disadvantages and to give appropriate preferential treatment to people with disabilities in order to achieve the objectives of full participation and equality within society for all persons with disabilities".*[137]

In sum, the CRPD embraces the substantive diversity equality model in that it imposes far-reaching positive obligations on States Parties to alter existing social structures which prevent persons with disabilities from participating equally in society with others. The question of the extent of the duties under human rights law to use positive action measures in order to promote equality of persons with disabilities is explored in *Chapter IV Equality Law and Policy, Section 2 Contemporary Disability Human Rights Approach.*

Finally, the CRPD is based on the social model of disability and the social universality model of disability. Thus, Article 1 on the Purpose of the Convention states that *"persons with disabilities include those who have long-term physical, mental, intellectual or sensory impairments which in interaction with various barriers may hinder their full and effective participation in society on an equal basis with others."* With this description of the concept of disability, the CRPD recognises that it is not the impairment itself, which leads to reduced participation, but rather that reduced participation is a consequence of interaction between the impairment and social barriers. In line with the fact that the CRPD is based on the substantive diversity equality model, the CRPD is also based on the social universality disability model rather than the social minority disability model. According to CRPD Article 3 on the General Principles of the Convention, there must be *"respect for difference and acceptance of persons with disabilities as part of human diversity and humanity."* Also, the CRPD refers to universal design in Article 4(f) according to which States undertake to promote the development and use of universal design. Finally, as mentioned above, the CRPD emphasises that all social structures must be inclusive – they must reflect that the citizens of the society are diverse and have disabilities.

In conclusion, the CRPD, which reflects the most contemporary perception of disability in human rights law, is based on the substantive diversity equality model and the social universality model of disability.

---

137 UN Committee on Economic, Social and Cultural Rights, General Comment No. 5: The Rights of Persons with Disabilities, 1994, para. 9.

1.4.3. The Council of Europe

The current protection under the ECHR and ESC was examined above under *Sub-Section 1.3. From the 1970s until the 2000s.* The conclusion was that the ECtHR continues to base its interpretation of the ECHR on the principle of substantive difference equality model and the corresponding minority rights disability model. However, it was stressed that the ECtHR may be expected to develop its equality principle over the years, also under the influence of the CRPD. In contrast, the ESC is already to a large extent, being interpreted on the basis of the principle of substantive diversity equality and the social universality model of disability.

In addition, on 6 April 2006, the Committee of Ministers of the Council of Europe, which is the governing body of the Council of Europe, adopted a Recommendation on the Council of *"Europe Action Plan to promote the rights and full participation of people with disabilities in society: improving the quality of life of people with disabilities in Europe 2006–2015"*.[138] The Action plan is not legally binding, but the Member States have with this Action Plan made a political commitment to adopt policies and laws based on the principle of substantive difference equality and the minority rights disability model. Thus, the Action Plan provides that it is based on the principles of non-discrimination, equal opportunities, full citizenship and participation, autonomy and human diversity. The Action plan contains 15 "*Action lines*" encompassing all key areas of life including employment in Action line no. 5. According to Action Line No. 5, the objective of disability policy in the field of employment should be to promote employment within the open labour market and to ensure that people with disabilities have equality of opportunities. These goals should be achieved through enforcement of the prohibition on non-discrimination and positive action measures as well as through the mainstreaming of issues relating to employment of persons with disabilities in general employment policies.[139]

In conclusion, the present-day interpretation of the ESC and the Committee of Ministers Action Plan indicate that the Council of Europe is also moving in the direction of the equality principle and disability model found under the CRPD. In the next Sub-Section, I examine the involvement of civil society and social partners in accordance with the disability contemporary human rights approach.

1.5. The Involvement of Civil Society and Social Partners

Above, I have analysed the models of equality and disability on which the contemporary disability human rights approach is based. In this Section, I examine

138 Rec(2006)5.

139 Ibid, Section 1.5 on Implementation and Follow-up and Section 3.5. on Employment, Vocational Guidance and Training.

which roles are assigned to State and non-State actors in the human rights approach. State actors include national and local public authorities and both the executive, legislative and judicial branches of the State. Non-state actors include social partners, employers, individual persons and civil society, also understood as "*the arena of uncoerced collective action around shared interests, purposes and values [...] distinct from those of the state, family and market*".[140] It is given that the most important civil society organisations in relation to the topic of this thesis are organisations of persons with disabilities. I will consider social partners to be distinct from civil society due to their close relation to the labour market. *Sub-Section 1.5.1. Involvement of Civil Society* examines how the State should involve civil society and *Sub-Section 1.5.2 Involvement of Social Partners* examines how the social partners should be involved in accordance with the contemporary disability human rights approach.

1.5.1. Involvement of Civil Society

As parties to human rights treaties, States are legally obliged to comply with these treaties. As such, all the branches of the State, including national and local public authorities, as well as the executive, legislative and judicial branches bear direct responsibility for compliance under human rights law. In the present Sub-Section, I would like to examine more closely the duty of the State to involve civil society in the carrying out of its functions. This question has been taken up inter alia by *Sandra Fredman* who described how the different equality models are founded on specific views on the role of the State in relation to the individual. According to the traditional complaints-led models of equality, which includes the formal equality model and to some extent the substantive difference equality, equality comprises a negative duty to refrain from discriminating against the individual. The role of the individual is to vote at periodic elections on an equal footing with others. Standards are set by the legislature and there may be a debate about the work of the legislature and the executive and judiciary, but the public has no direct or indirect role in standard-setting.[141]

The drawback with this system is that it fails to take account of the majoritarian process in the legislative process, particularly where the minority is under-represented in all areas of social life, including the educational system, the labour market, and the public and political debate. Formal equality and to some extent the substantive difference equality model seek to ensure that the individual's rights are ensured through individual, justiciable rights. However, as mentioned above, the

140 Definition from "What is Civil Society" by Centre for Civil Society of London School of Economics, www.lse.ac.uk/collections/CCS/introduction/what_is_civil_society.htm.

141 Fredman 2005b pp. 370–371.

litigation process favours those with the relevant resources and not minority groups which may be disadvantaged.[142]

In contrast, *Fredman* argues that the substantive diversity equality model implies a participatory role for civil society both in relation to the standard-setting and in relation to enforcement.[143] Equality implies positive duties and the State must co-operate actively with civil society both in the standard-setting process and in the implementation.[144] This active participation may redress some of the weaknesses of the majoritarian process by increasing the opportunities of disadvantaged groups to be heard. The participatory role of civil society increases chances that the adopted standards and that the implementation process promotes equality and reduces the need for individual complaints before the courts.

As seen above, the CRPD is based on a substantive diversity equality model to a larger extent than any of the UN human rights treaties adopted earlier. Also in regard to the participatory role of civil society, has the CRPD taken a step forward. For the first time in a UN human rights treaty, the CRPD has established a duty to cooperate with civil society both in the development and the implementation of the Convention:

> *"In the development and implementation of legislation and policies to implement the present Convention, and in other decision-making processes concerning issues relating to persons with disabilities, States Parties shall closely consult with and actively involve persons with disabilities, including children with disabilities, through their representative organizations."*[145]

In addition, the CRPD provides that States Parties must promote participation of persons with disabilities in non-governmental organisations in general and disabled persons organisations specifically under Article 29 on participation in political and public life.[146]

The Convention on the Rights of the Child and the International Convention on the Protection of the Rights of All Migrant Workers and Members of Their Families expressly envisage a role for *"other competent bodies"* in the work of their respective treaty bodies which in the case of the first two has been interpreted to mean NGOs.[147] However these treaties do not expressly envisage a role for civil

---

142 Fredman 2005b pp. 372.

143 Ibid.

144 Fredman 2005b, pp. 379–380.

145 CRPD Article 4(3) on general obligations.

146 CRPD Article 22(b)(i) and (ii).

147 CRC Article 45(1)(a) on the role of the Committee on the Rights of the Child. CRC 22(2) also obligates States to co-operate with NGOs in relation to refugee children. CRMW Article 74(4). See also "NGO participation in the activities of the Committee on Economic, Social and Cultural

society in the development of standards and their implementation in the way the CRPD does.

In sum, the position argued by *Fredman* that a duty for the State to involve civil society is inherent in the substantive diversity equality model is supported by the CRPD. The involvement of civil society in the conduct of State functions is especially relevant in relation to persons with disabilities who are presumably strongly under-represented in positions of power.

1.5.2. Involvement of Social Partners

The present Section deals with the question of the role of social partners in ensuring equality on the labour market for persons with disabilities. As mentioned above, social partners, i.e. trade unions and associations of employers have a special status because of their role as regulators of the labour market. While in some countries, such as Denmark, they have an almost exclusive power to regulate the labour market, this power is more restrained in other countries.

Trade unions work for an improvement of working conditions and thus for respect for core social and economic human rights, including fair wages, safe and healthy working conditions, and freedom from slavery as protected under the ICESCR and the ESC. Human rights law clearly recognises the importance of the social partners. The right to form and join trade unions and the right of trade unions to function freely with a minimum of limitations are expressly protected under the ICESCR and the ESC.[148] Also a clear manifestation of the positive perception of the social partners under human rights law is that the social partners have representation in the UN International Labour Organisations on a par with States. The International Labour Conference, which is the highest body of the International Labour Organisation and which crafts and adopts conventions and recommendations, consists of Member State delegations. Each delegation to the annual meeting of the International Labour Conference is made up of four delegates: two State representatives and two representatives of social partners – one on behalf of the workers and one on behalf of the employers. Each delegate may express him or herself freely and vote freely.[149]

However, the relationship between human rights law and the social partners is not completely unproblematic. Firstly, trade unions fight for a collective improvement of working conditions which may lead to disregard for the rights of individuals.

Rights" (E/C.12/2000/6) and the Guidelines for the participation of partners (NGOs and individual experts) in the pre-sessional working group of the Committee on the Rights of the Child (CRC/C/90, annex VIII).

148 ICESCR Article (1)(c) and ESC of 1996, Article 6 on the right to bargain collectively.

149 ILO Constitution of 1919 with latest amendment of 1972, Article 3.

Secondly, trade unions have the interests of their members at heart which may not necessarily be the same as the interests of all potential workers. This may lead to a conflict of interests between trade unions and persons who either do not wish to be members of trade unions in general or a specific trade union as well as persons who are marginalised in the labour market, such as women, ethnic minorities, immigrants and persons with disabilities. For example, trade unions in Iceland and Denmark were until recently permitted to enter into exclusive or closed-shop agreements with individual employers according to which only members of the trade union in question could be employed. This practice was found to be in violation of ECHR Article 11 on freedom of association in January 2006 by the ECtHR.[150] Other less direct practices of exclusion of non-members would include the adoption of working conditions which directly or indirectly creates barriers for entry into the labour market for certain groups of persons. For example it has been argued that trade unions with predominantly male members were partly responsible for upholding unequal wages for women in order to achieve higher wages for the majority of their members.[151] Similarly, it is possible that trade unions and employers have found it inconvenient to improve working conditions for other marginalised groups on the labour market such as persons with disabilities. Thirdly, the nature of the industrial relations system which builds on agreements entered into more or less freely between workers and employers' representatives sets limitations on the contents of the agreements. Agreements must be advantageous for both parties. Consequently, agreements on limitations in the managerial prerogative will be difficult to achieve. Fourthly and lastly, a system of regulation of the labour market based on agreements by the social partners leaves persons who are not covered by a collective agreement without protection. Thus the system of collective agreements may be founded on the principle that members enjoy special benefits which leaves non-members with a lower level of protection.

In conclusion, although social partners may play an important role in promoting human rights of persons on the labour market, there are several good reasons that the regulation of the labour market cannot be left to the social partners. In other words, the State must on the one hand enable the effective functioning of social partners. On the other hand, the State must still ensure that the rights of disadvantaged groups are not overlooked.

1.6. Conclusion

Based on the above analysis of the development of the models of equality and disability since the middle of the twentieth century under human rights law, it may

---

150 European Court of Human Rights, *Sørensen and Rasmussen v. Denmark,* Judgment of 11 January 2006, Application no. 52562/99 and 52620/66.

151 Edwards 2003, p. 29 and 427.

be concluded that the contemporary disability human rights approach is founded on the following principles and models:

- Principle of substantive diversity equality
  - General structures must reflect social diversity
  - Policies to redress inequality must be pro-active
  - Diversity policies must be mainstreamed into general policy
- Social universality model of disability
  - Social structures rather than impairment are main cause of exclusion
  - Disability is a universal feature of mankind – it is not limited to a certain group of persons
- Principle of participation of civil society in State functions
  - The State must be inclusive towards civil society in the exercise of its powers
  - The State must enable the effective functioning of social partners on the labour market without forgoing the rights of disadvantaged groups on the labour market.
- Individual rights support this process

As mentioned above under *Sub-Section 1.1. Methodology*, the contemporary disability human rights approach describes the model approach according to human rights law. Moreover, since the contemporary disability human rights approach is founded on the principle of equality, States Parties to the CRPD, for example, are legally bound to progressively seek to realise the contemporary disability human rights approach.

The precise implications of the contemporary human rights approach as regards persons with disabilities in the field of employment will be explored in detail in *Chapters IV-VII.* In Section 2 below, I provide an overview of the legal and political status of human rights of persons with disabilities in Denmark and Sweden.

2. Legal Status of Human Rights in Denmark and Sweden

In the above Section, I have examined the meaning of a contemporary disability human rights approach – what type of equality must States strive for under contemporary human rights law, how is disability perceived and what is the role of different actors on the labour market in achieving equality? In this Section, I examine the legal status of human rights in Denmark and Sweden. I also examine the national disability action plans from the perspective of the human rights approach. The aim of this Section is to provide an overview of the overall human rights framework of the situation of persons with disabilities in the labour market in Denmark and Sweden. The aim is not to provide an in-depth analysis of human rights protection in Denmark and Sweden which falls outside of the ambit of this thesis.

2.1. Human Rights Protection under Domestic Law

Constitutional human rights protection in Denmark and Sweden differ significantly. The Danish Constitution (Grundloven) was adopted in 1849 and has not been amended since 1953.[152] Although the Danish Constitution contains a short bill of rights with mostly civil and political rights, these rights are of little practical importance due to the fact that they have been overtaken by international human rights law.[153]

Contrary to the Danish Constitution, a new Swedish Constitution or *"Instrument of Government"* (Regeringsformen) was adopted first in 1719 and in a revised version in 1974 and it has been amended several times since then, lastly in 2002.[154] Whereas the Danish Constitution contains no prohibition on discrimination, the Swedish Instrument of Government contains three provisions on discrimination. Article 2 in Chapter 1 of the Swedish Instrument of Government provides that *"the public must prevent discrimination on the grounds of gender, skin colour, national or ethnic origin, language, religion, disability sexual orientation, age or any other grounds which concern the individual as a person."* However, it has not been considered to grant any justiciable individual rights. Article 16 of Chapter 2 of the Instrument of Government prohibits discrimination on the grounds of gender and Article 15 of Chapter 2 of the Instrument of Government provides that legal acts or other acts may not have a detrimental effect on any persons who are part of a minority group due to race, skin colour or ethnic origin. In contrast to the provision in Chapter 1 of the Instrument of Government, this provision, which does grant individual justiciable rights, does not include disability. A Commission on reform of the Instrument of Government, recommended in 2008 that sexual orientation be added to the list of grounds in Article 15 of Chapter 2, but did not touch on disability or age which are also only mentioned in Article 2 of Chapter 1.[155] In sum, while the

---

152 The Constitution of Denmark, Lov no. 169 of 5 june 1953. In Denmark, an amendment of the provision on the equal right of girls to the inheritance of the Royal throne was approved by a referendum on 7 June 2009. A full-text version of the Danish Constitution may be found at: www.folketinget.dk/pdf/constitutio.pdf. A full-text version of the Swedish Instrument of Government may be found at: www.riksdagen.se/templates/R_Page____6307.aspx.

153 Scheinin 2008, p. 140.

154 Instrument of Government (Regeringsformen), SFS 1974:152, lastly amended by SFS 2002:905. The Swedish Constitution refers explicitly to the Act on Freedom of the Press, the Fundamental Law on Freedom of Expression and the Act on incorporation of the ECHR and thereby gives them constitutional status.

155 Commission Report on a reform of the Instrument of Government, SOU 2008:125, "En Reformerad Grundlag", Stockholm 2008, p. 417.

constitutional protection against discrimination on the grounds of disability is quite weak in Sweden, it is non-existent in Denmark.

The question of the status of human rights treaties which have been incorporated into domestic law is examined in the present Sub-Section whereas the question of the status of human rights treaties which have not been incorporated into domestic law will be treated under *Sub-Section 2.2. Legal Status of International Human Rights Treaties* below. Both in Denmark and in Sweden, the only human rights treaty to have been incorporated into domestic law is the European Convention of Human Rights.[156] The ECHR enjoys a special status since the ECtHR to a certain extent acts as a fourth instance of appeal above the national Supreme Courts. The Swedish Instrument of Government includes a provision according to which laws and other regulations may not be enacted in contravention with Sweden's commitments under the ECHR.[157] The introduction of a provision in the Constitution, which prohibits violations of the ECHR, is taken to mean that any conflicts between Swedish legislation and the ECHR must be solved by setting aside domestic legislation.[158] The Danish Constitution does not contain such a provision.

The impact of the ECHR has been significant in both the Danish and the Swedish domestic legal orders. In a great number of cases, judgments have been founded on interpretations of domestic law in accordance with the ECHR and its incorporation act. In Denmark this had led to the setting aside of long-standing practices regarding the impartiality of judges.[159] Also it has led to strong limitations in the effect of legislation on compulsory repatriations of persons without Danish citizenship who commit criminal acts.[160] Although the effects of the interpretation of the ECHR was quite significant in the cases about compulsory repatriation of foreign citizens who had committed a crime, the Supreme Court cannot be said to have set aside domestic legislation since these interpretations were in accordance with the *wording* of legal provisions in question or their preparatory works which stated expressly that repatriations may only take place in accordance with ECHR.[161]

---

156 Danish incorporation act: Act no. 285 of 29 April 1992 on the European Convention on Human Rights (Lov om den europæiske menneskerettighedskonvention) with latest amendment by Act no. 538 af 8 June 2006. Swedish incorporation act: Act on the European Convention of Human Rights and Fundamental Freedoms (Lag om den europeiska konventionen angående skydd för de mänskliga rättigheterna och de grundläggande friheterna) SFS: 1994:1219 with latest amendment by SFS 2005:816.

157 Act SFS 1994:1469 amended Article 23 of the Instrument of Government.

158 Commission Report on a reform of the Instrument of Government, SOU 2008:125, "En Reformerad Grundlag", Stockholm 2008, p. 400.

159 UFR 1990.13H on the impartiality of judges.

160 UFR 1999.1394H on compulsory repatriation of foreign citizens who have committed a crime.

161 Spiermann 2002, p. 415. See also the discussion in Christoffersen 2000, p. 596 who finds that the interpretation of the provisions on compulsory repatriations were so significant that they amounted to setting aside domestic legislation.

In Sweden, there are also examples of interpretations of national law and practice in conformity with ECHR and its incorporation into national law. For example, the Swedish Supreme Court set aside a decision to imprison a reverend due to hate-speech against homosexuals because the Supreme Court found that imprisonment would be incompatible with the rights to freedom of religion and speech under ECHR.[162] Moreover, in at least in one case the Swedish Supreme Court has set aside the wording of a domestic legal provision with reference to ECHR. According to the Act on Compensation, compensation for non-economic loss could only be given in connection with certain specific situations which did not include a violation of the right to a fair trial under ECHR Article 6. The Swedish Supreme Court therefore chose to disregard the limitation in the national legislation and granted compensation with reference to ECHR Article 13 on effective remedies and the incorporation act.[163]

2.2. Legal Status of International Human Rights Treaties

Both Denmark and Sweden have a dualist tradition in relation to the implementation of international law in the national legal order. In the dualist tradition, international and domestic law are, in principle, viewed as two distinct legal systems.[164] Consequently, in a fully dualist system, an international rule does not have legal standing in the domestic legal system and cannot be relied on in a domestic or national court unless it has been incorporated into domestic law. In contrast, monist systems view international and domestic law as forming one whole. Thus, international standards, which are legally binding to the State in question, may be relied on in a domestic court on equal terms with domestic law.[165]

Dualist approaches may vary significantly from one country to another. At one end of the spectrum, one will find countries where courts disregard international rules and, at the other end, domestic courts that enforce international rules more seriously. Both Denmark and Sweden are relatively faithful to their international obligations. In both countries an *interpretation principle* entails that domestic law may be interpreted in accordance with international law.[166] Both Denmark and Sweden are to be found on the second end of the spectre and comply with international rules relatively faithfully. In fact, some scholars speak of a "*paradigm shift*" in relation to the legal status accorded to human rights treaties in the 1990s in Denmark and Sweden. In the 1970s, certain court rulings in Sweden denied the judicial

162 Denmark: UFR sagerne om udvisning. Sweden: the *Reverend Åke Green*-case, NJA 2005.89, see Nergelius 2008, p. 124 regarding this case.

163 NJA 2005.462. See also Åhman 2004, p. 172.

164 Shaw 1991, p. 101, Nergelius 1996, p. 174, Helgadottír 2009, p. 279, Spiermann 2006, p. 149.

165 Examples of European countries with monist legal systems are the Netherlands, Germany and France, Shaw, p. 124.

166 Spiermann 2006, p. 162, Nergelius, p. 151.

applicability of treaties as they were formally outside of the Swedish legal system. Sweden was more strictly dualist than Denmark.[167] However, since the 1990s, it is fully accepted in both Denmark and Sweden that Danish and Swedish courts not only have the competence, but the duty to apply international human rights in their adjudication.[168]

As mentioned above, the *interpretation principle* implies that Danish and Swedish courts must interpret domestic legislation in accordance with human rights treaties which they have ratified, even when the treaties in question have not been incorporated into Danish and Swedish law. However since it is an interpretation principle, the traditional assumption has been that a domestic rule could not be set aside where there is a conflict between a legally binding international rule and the wording of a domestic rule. Nevertheless, there is at least one example in Denmark of a case where the Danish Supreme Court considered whether a domestic rule was in accordance with international treaty obligations.[169] This would seem to imply that the Danish Supreme Court could not in advance exclude that it would set aside a domestic rule with reference to an international rule which had not been incorporated into Danish law.[170] In Sweden, there are several examples of cases where a certain interpretation of Swedish law has been justified with reference to international treaty obligations which had not been incorporated into Swedish law.[171] In conclusion, the actual usage of international human rights standards in especially Danish, but also in Swedish courts, brings Denmark and Sweden close to actually practising monist systems of law.[172]

In fact, the true hindrance for a stronger impact on Danish and Swedish law lies not in the lack of legal status of international human rights treaties, but rather with the tradition of a strong separation of powers between the legislative and the judiciary powers which is based on the supremacy of the Parliament. Due to this perception of the status of Parliament, neither Denmark nor Sweden have developed a strong tradition of constitutional review of legislation. The supremacy of Parliament means

167 Scheinin 2008, p. 140.

168 Scheinin 2008, p. 141. Christoffersen 2001, p. 142, argues that Denmark should adhere officially to the monist system as this would not in practice mean a great change from the present state of law. See for example a Swedish Supreme Court judgment which gives direct effect to ECHR by giving compensation for violation of ECHR Article 6 on the right to a fair trial with reference to ECHR Article 13, the *Lundgren*-case, NJA [Nytt Juridiskt Arkiv] 2005 p. 462. See also Nergelius 2008, p. 122 regarding this case.

169 UFR 2002.1789H where the Danish Supreme Court found that requirement of Danish citizenship to receive a permission to conduct a taxi company was not in violation of Danish international obligations.

170 Spiermann 2002, p. 418.

171 Supreme Administrative Court, 12 June 1991, Case No. 4642/1989, which made reference to the European Social Charter when it found that Russian asylum seekers could not be denied certain social security benefits.

172 Christoffersen 2001, p. 144.

that the judiciary is reluctant to pass judgments which will have too wide-reaching or political effect.[173] Thus, the responsibility for fulfilment of treaty obligations is believed to lie with the legislative power unless compliance can be achieved through minor interpretation adjustments of existing domestic law. The courts will as a rule remain relatively superficial in their examination of whether there is compliance with international law, if a conflict of rules would entail that the courts would take on what they perceive as political or legislative powers. Only where the international legal standards are very clear, will the courts be willing to make an exception to their perception of the division of powers between the judiciary and the legislators. An added consequence of this approach is that a high status is attached to the intention of the legislator. Thus, the preparatory works for proposals for new legislation before Parliament are considered to be highly authoritative sources of interpretation in Denmark and Sweden, as opposed to, for example, legal systems that place more importance on the aim of a legal act. This is described by *Nergelius* as a distinctly Nordic feature.[174]

In conclusion, although the legal systems in Denmark and Sweden are formally speaking dualistic in nature, both in Denmark and in Sweden international human rights are given increasing weight. However, both Denmark and Sweden have traditionally abided by a principle of Parliamentarian supremacy over the other State powers. Accordingly, the courts have traditionally been reluctant to pass judgments which they considered would amount to political decision-making. In sum, although the legal status of (international) human rights (law) is such that it may be given legal importance by the courts, the courts will be reluctant to make proactive interpretations of human rights standards if such interpretations do not concur with national law and policy.

Please find below in *Table 3* an overview of international human rights treaties and protocols of special relevance to disability employment law ratified by Denmark and Sweden respectively.

173 UFR 1990.181H on the long-standing practice of appointing staff from the Ministry of Justice as judges for a limited period of time as part of their training. The Supreme Court refrained from performing an in-depth interpretation of ECHR Article 6 with reference to "wide-reaching consequences that this could have for the organisation of the courts in this country". Spiermann 2002, p. 416 and Commission Report 1407/2001, Scheinin 2008, p. 149.

174 Nergelius 2008, p. 130.

Table 3. Overview of Danish and Swedish ratification status of human rights conventions of special relevance to disability employment policy

	Denmark		Sweden	
	Signed	Ratified	Signed	Ratified
ECHR, 1950	4 October 1950	13 April 1953	28 November 1950	4 February 1952
ECHR Protocol 12, 2000	–	–	–	–
European Social Charter, 1961	18 October 1961	3 March 1965	18 October 1961	17 December 1962
Revised European Social Charter, 1996	3 May 1996	–	3 May 1996	29 May 1998
Revised ESC Additional Protocol, 1995	9 November 1995	–	9 November 1995	29 May 1998
European Code of Social Security, 1964	16 April 1964	16 March 1973	16 April 1964	25 September 1965
ICCPR, 1966	20 March 1968	6 January 1972	29 September 1967	6 December 1971
ICCPR Optional Protocol, 1966	20 March 1968	6 January 1972	29 September 1967	6 December 1971
ICESCR, 1966	20 March 1968	6 January 1972	29 September 1967	6 December 1971
ICESCR Optional Protocol (opening September 2009)	20 March 1968	6 January 1972	29 September 1967	6 December 1971
CRPD, 2006	30 March 2007	24 July 2009	30 March 2007	15 December 2008
CRPD Optional Protocol	–	–	20 March 2007	15 December 2008
ILO Convention No. 111 (discrimination)	Yes	22 June 1960	Yes	20 June 1962
ILO Convention No. 159 (disabled persons)	yes	1 April 1985	Yes	12 June 1984

Table 3 shows that Denmark and Sweden have ratified all the main human rights instruments of relevance to disability employment law with the exception of the Revised European Social Charter of 1996 and the CRPD Optional Protocol on individual complaints to the Committee under the CRPD which have not been

ratified by Denmark. The unwillingness to ratify the European Social Charter of 1996 has been explained by the Government as a consequence of their adherence to the principle that the social partners should enjoy extensive freedom to regulate the labour market.[175] The Revised Social Charter of 1996 contains several provisions on rights of workers.[176] The unwillingness to ratify the CRPD Optional Protocol was explained in the following manner in the Proposal to Parliament to ratify the CRPD:

> *"The Government has found that it would be inappropriate to accede to the Optional Protocol and thereby give a possibility to individuals to complain directly to an international organ. The principle of gradual implementation means that the obligations of the States are difficult to define precisely. In addition, they will often have a distributive character. The [obligations under the] Convention are therefore not suitable to be determined through individual cases."*[177]

According to this statement by the Danish government, it would seem that disability human rights are still to a large extent viewed as concerning mainly welfare and compensation rights, rather than rights to inclusion and non-discrimination. This approach is also the foundation of Danish disability policy as it is described in the Danish Disability Action Plan described in the following Sub-Section.

2.3. National Disability Action Plans

The official Danish Disability Action Plan was formulated in a 25-page document in 2003 by the Ministry of Industry and Economy, which at the time was the leading Ministry on disability questions.[178] Apart from consultations with disability organisations and other Ministries, the Action Plan was not founded on a Commission Report nor did it spring from any thorough analysis of what is required in order to achieve equal opportunities for persons with disabilities. No new general national Action Plan on disability has been formulated since 2003. It is possible that the State Report under the CRPD, which is due at the end of the year 2011, will provide the Danish government with an opportunity to prepare a new action plan.

In Sweden, a comprehensive Disability Action Plan entitled *"From Patient to Citizen – A National Action Plan for the Disability Policy"* was adopted in 2000 and thorough and extensive follow-up plans have been regularly, lastly in 2009 with

175 See more on the monopoly of the social partners to regulate the labour market in Denmark in Chapter V Employers' Obligations.

176 Koch and others 2004, p. 59.

177 Reply by Minister for Social Affairs, Karen Ellemann to Question no. 2040 by Lise von Seelen, 29 April 2009, Tale no. 124.

178 Regeringen: *Handlingsplan for handicapområdet, 2003.*

new concrete goals.[179] Although reports do not in themselves lead to an improvement of the situation of persons with disabilities, thorough argumentation and preparation may ensure a more systematic approach to achieving the goals that have been set up. The Swedish Action Plan of 2009 underlines that the work with the Action Plans has created a more clear and result-oriented distribution of responsibilities.[180]

Even though both the Danish and the Swedish Action Plans state that they are based on the UN Standard Rules on Disability, it is clear that the contemporary disability human rights approach has had a stronger influence on the formulation of the Swedish Disability policy. The goals for the Swedish disability policy are threefold: 1) *"a society based on diversity"*, 2) a society *"shaped so that persons with disabilities of all ages may participate fully in social life"* and 3) *"equality in life conditions for girls and boys, women and men with disabilities"*.[181] In contrast, the Danish Action plan, being more brief, aims at achieving *"equal treatment – that all persons shall have possibilities for participating in social life irrespective of disability"*.[182] Thus, based on their wording, the Swedish Action Plans aims at achieving substantive diversity equality and the Danish Action Plans aims only at achieving 'substantive difference equality'.

The Swedish adherence to the contemporary disability human rights approach is reflected also in the main means for achieving the goals of the disability policies which are to: "identify and remove barriers for full participation", "prevent and fight discrimination against persons with disabilities" and "give children, youths and adults with disabilities the basis for independence and self-determination".[183]

Again in contrast to the Swedish Action Plan, the Danish means for achieving the goal of equality also reflect that the Danish policy is based on the substantive difference equality model rather than the substantive diversity equality model of the contemporary disability human rights approach. Thus, the Danish Action Plan

---

179 Original Plan: Handlingsplanen för handikappolitiken, Från patient till medborgare (Skrivelse 1999/2000:240). Three updates: *Uppföljning av den nationella handlingsplanen för handikappolitiken,* skrivelse 2002/03:25, Skrivelse 2005/06:110, Skrivelse 2009/10:166.

180 *Uppföljning av den nationella handlingsplanen för handikappolitiken,* Skrivelse 2009/10:166, p. 1.

181 *Uppföljning av den nationella handlingsplanen för handikappolitiken,* Skrivelse 2009/10:166, p. 6.

182 Regeringen: *Handlingsplan for handicapområdet, 2003, p. 5. See also a specific Disability in Employment Action Plan,* Beskæftigelsesministeriet, *Handicap og Job – En beskæftigelsesstrategi for personer med handicap,* 2004. Beskæftigelsesministeriet, *Initiativer,* 2006 (January and October). Beskæftigelsesministeriet, *Initiativer,* 2007. The proposed measures are either new compensation measures such as more personal assistance or new trials of new methods to assist persons with disabilities in finding employment. Anti-discrimination is only mentioned in passing. Employers are only targeted with soft-law measures information campaigns and a voluntary accessibility grading system.

183 *Uppföljning av den nationella handlingsplanen för handikappolitiken,* Skrivelse 2009/10:166.

states that the main instruments for achieving equality are firstly, *"compensation – that society helps persons with disabilities and offers benefits and assistive services to minimise the consequences of disability"* and secondly, *"sectoral responsibility"* or mainstreaming which means that *"all sectors must be involved in disability policy. Therefore the sector or authority which normally deals with an area also has the responsibility to take account of the situation of persons with disabilities"*. Although the Danish policy does acknowledge that general accessibility and mainstreaming are a prerequisite for equality, the strong focus on compensation as a founding principle indicates that the Danish official Disability Policy as it was formulated in 2003 sees disability as a difference which must be accommodated rather than a universal trait which general societal structures must take account of.

2.4. Conclusion

The above analysis of the legal status of human rights in Denmark and Sweden has made it clear that international human rights standards enjoy a strong legal status in both countries. Thus, in both countries the national courts will take account of international human rights standards in their adjudication. However, Denmark has shown more reluctance than Sweden to adopt new human rights obligations such as the Revised European Social Charter of 1996 and to be subjected to individual complaints before treaty bodies.

In relation to the national action plans on persons with disabilities, relatively striking differences were seen. Whereas the Swedish action plan on disability is based on substantive diversity equality and provides for relatively detailed means of achieving this goal, the Danish action plan is based on substantive difference equality and contains no comprehensive plan.

3. Conclusion

The protection of persons with disabilities has developed tremendously under human rights law from having been an issue of access to welfare services, to being a broader issue of equal treatment in relation to all human rights. Within the UN system, the new position of persons with disabilities under human rights has been given the strongest possible acknowledgement: a UN convention on the rights of persons with disabilities has been adopted. Within the European Council, both the European Committee on Social Rights and the ECtHR have interpreted the ESC and the ECHR in the light of the contemporary disability human rights approach. The 'contemporary disability human rights approach' describes the model approach according to human rights law, and States Parties to the CRPD for example are legally bound to progressively work towards the realisation of the contemporary disability human rights approach. It is based on three general principles or models:

Substantive diversity equality, the social universality model of disability and the principle of participation of civil society in the conduct of State functions. In the coming Chapters, I will flesh out the contemporary disability human rights approach in relation to different areas of law and policy and I will examine whether the EU as well as Denmark and Sweden are in line with the contemporary disability human rights approach in the area of employment.

Denmark and Sweden have both ratified the most important human rights instruments of special relevance to disability employment law with the exception of the Revised European Social Charter which Denmark has not ratified. Both countries have also adopted national disability action plans. Whereas the Danish national disability policy is based on substantive difference equality and has not been renewed since 2003, a highly detailed Swedish disability policy based on a contemporary human rights approach has been last renewed in 2009.

Part III

EU and Domestic Law and Policy

Chapter III
EU Law and Policy

1. Introduction

The present Chapter examines whether EU disability employment law and policy complies with the contemporary disability human rights approach.

This Chapter is structured so as to give an introduction to the development of EU disability policy and law and to analyse EU law and policy in the field of human rights law and in the areas of disability employment law and policy that are studied in the subsequent Chapters of the thesis. Thus, Section 2 deals with the development of EU disability policy and law. Sections 3, 4, 5, 6 and 7 correspond to Chapters II, IV, V, VI and VII of the thesis and examine EU law and policy in relation to human rights, equality law and policy, employers' obligations, employment promotion and income-replacement benefits. Since the contemporary disability human rights approach requires the inclusion of civil society in the conduct of State functions, I examine the co-operation of the EU with civil society in Section 8. Given that the strong role of the social partners is a key part of the Danish and Swedish labour market models, I also examine the position of social partners under EU law and policy in Section 8. Section 9 analyses the legal status of EU law in Denmark and Sweden. Finally, a conclusion is provided in Section 10.

2. Development of EU Disability Policies and Laws

The present Section gives an overview of the development of EU disability policies and laws from the perspective of the equality and disability models that were described in *Chapter II Human Rights*.

2.1. The Early Years from Treaty of Rome to the Mid-1970s

During this first stage, the EU was mostly silent on the issue of disability. It was only in the mid-1970s that the first disability Community Action Programme for the Vocational Rehabilitation of Handicapped Persons was adopted in 1974.[184] This Action Programme was the first Community regulation dealing specifically with

[184] Initial Community Action Programme for the Vocational Rehabilitation of Handicapped Persons 1974–1979, Council Resolution of 27 June 1974, *Official Journal* C 80, 9 July 1974, p. 30. Waddington 2006a, p. 6.

disability. It was a product of its time and clearly based on the medical model of disability. Thus, handicap was defined as:

> *"(...) any limitation, congenital or acquired, of a person's physical or mental ability which affects his daily activity and his work by reducing his social contribution, his employment prospects, his ability to use public services."*[185]

Being based on the medical model of disability, the aim of the Action Programme was to "*improve the opportunities for vocational rehabilitation available within the Community to the above persons*".[186]

2.2. Mid-1970s to the Treaty of Amsterdam

Until the 1990s, the mainstay of European Community disability policy continued to be Action Programmes rather than hard-law instruments.[187] In the late 1980s and early 1990s, the groundwork for a shift in disability policy away from paternalism and towards a rights-based approach was laid with the multi-annual disability Action Programmes called the Helios Programmes with Helios being an acronym for "*Handicapped People in the European Community Living Independently in an Open Society*".[188] The title of the Helios Programmes reflected that these new Action Programmes addressed far wider issues than merely employment-related rehabilitation which had been the topic of the first Action Programmes. The main activities under these programmes were support for dissemination of information through networks with Member State and civil society representatives.[189]

In July 1996, the Commission adopted a landmark Communication entitled *"Equality of Opportunity for People with Disabilities – A New European Community Disability Strategy"*.[190] This was the first comprehensive European Community Strategy on disability and was inspired by the UN Standard Rules on Equalization of Opportunities for Persons with Disabilities.[191] It formally embraced the social

185 Ibid. Section I. "Objectives – Definitions."

186 Ibid.

187 Waddington 2006a, p. 5.

188 HELIOS I Community Action Programme for Disabled People 1988–1991, *Official Journal* L 104, 23 April 1988, 38; HELIOS II Community Action Programme to assist Disabled People 1993–1996, Council Decision 93/136/EEC of 25 February 1993, OJ [2003] L 56/30. Waddington 2006a, p. 5.

189 Waddington 2006a, p. 7.

190 European Commission Communication COM (1996) 406 final of 30 July 1996. See also Council Recommendation 86/379 on the employment of disabled people in the Community. It established a guideline framework setting out examples of positive action to promote the employment and training of disabled persons.

191 Ibid. para. 27. UN Standard Rules on the Equalization of Opportunities for Persons with Disabilities adopted by the General Assembly on 20 December 1993 by its resolution 48/96.

model of disability and noted that *"the way in which society is organised serves to exclude disabled citizens"* and stated that *"the core value of equality – rendered here as equal opportunities – is now seen as the central benchmark against which economic and social structures must be assessed. It forms the essence of the rights-based approach to disability"*.[192] This Communication established, firstly, a High Level Group of Member States representatives for regular exchanges of information and best practices which continues to function today. Secondly, the Commission set up an inter-service working group to mainstream disability into its own internal processes including the legislative process which also continues to function today. And thirdly, the dialogue between the Commission and the disability NGOs was consolidated. This dialogue also continues to this day.[193] In December of 1996, the Council also adopted a Resolution on *"Equality of Opportunities for People with Disabilities"* which also reaffirmed the EU commitment to the principle of equality of opportunity and the social model of disability.[194]

Although the Commission Communication and Council Resolution from 1996 both represented a positive development towards a rights-based approach to disability within the EU based on the social model of disability, these documents were still a soft-law instruments with limited impact on the policies of Member States.

2.3. From the Amsterdam Treaty and Onwards

As regards disability policy and law specifically, large developments have taken place since the Amsterdam Treaty in 1997 which amended the Treaty of the European Union (TEU) and the Treaties Establishing the European Communities (TEC). The Amsterdam Treaty granted the European Community the authority to take action to combat discrimination on a number of grounds including disability in Article 13 TEC (now Article 19 of the Treaty on the Functioning of the European Union (TFEU)) which constituted the first mention ever of disability in the Treaty. Moreover, the Lisbon Treaty amends Article 3 TEC and extends the duty to mainstream gender equality to equality for all grounds mentioned in Article 19 TFEU. Thus the new Article 10 TFEU states the following: *"In defining and implementing its policies and activities, the Union shall aim to combat discrimination based on sex, racial or ethnic origin, religion or belief, disability, age or sexual orientation"*. The important question whether disability has in fact been mainstreamed into EU law and policy is examined immediately below.

192 Ibid., para. 2 and 18. Waddington 2006a, p. 18.

193 Quinn 2007, p. 238.

194 Resolution of the Council and of the Representatives of the Governments of the Member States meeting within the Council of 20 December 1996 on equality of opportunity for people with disabilities, OJ [1997] C12/01.

Important secondary law has been adopted on the basis of Article 13 of TEC / Article 19 TFEU. In the year 2000, the ground-breaking Employment Equality Directive addressing discrimination in the areas of employment and vocational training on the grounds, amongst others, of disability was adopted.[195] This Directive will be examined in detail below in *Section 4. Employment Equality Directive.* Moreover, the decision that the EU should formally conclude the CRPD was also based on Article 19 TFEU.[196] The importance of the EU's conclusion of the CRPD will be discussed below under *Section 2. Human Rights.*

Lastly, a new directive on discrimination on the grounds of disability outside of the field of employment has been proposed by the European Commission. If it is adopted, the *"Council Directive on implementing the principle of equal treatment between persons irrespective of religion or belief, disability, age or sexual orientation"* may extend the protection against discrimination on the grounds of disability to the areas of social protection, social advantages, health care, education and access to and supply of goods and services which are available to the public including housing and transport.[197]

As regards mainstreaming of disability into general laws and policies, there are several examples that this has taken place. Thus, disability has now been mainstreamed into a number of directives and regulations in the fields of transport, building infrastructure, public procurement, digital television and telecommunications. Some of these legal acts have their legal basis in Article 95 TEC (now Article 114 TFEU),[198] while others have their legal basis in Title V TEC

---

195 See also Council Resolution of 17 June 1999 on equal employment opportunities of people with disabilities, OJ [1999] C186/03.

196 The Council Decision regarding the confirmation of the CRPD uses the term 'conclusion' since this is the term used in Article 300 ECT. The term 'formal confirmation' is used in CRPD Article 43 as regards signatory regional integration organisations such as the European Union instead of 'ratification'. Council Decision 2010/48 of 26 November 2009 concerning the conclusion, by the European Community, of the United Nations Convention on the Rights of Persons with Disabilities, [2010] L23/35. The European Union "formally confirmed" its consent to be bound by the CRPD on 23 December 2010, cf. Article 43 of the CRPD.

197 Council Note from the Presidency, 15320/09, of 3 November 2009, Proposal for a Council Directive on implementing the principle of equal treatment between persons irrespective of religion or belief, disability, age or sexual orientation which revises Proposal for a Council Directive, COM(2008) 426 final, 2 July 2008.

198 Council Directive (EC) 2001/85 relating to special provisions for vehicles used for the carriage of passengers comprising more than eight seats in addition to the driver's seat, OJ [2002] L43/1; Council Directive (EC) 1995/16 on the approximation of the laws of the Member States relating to lifts, OJ [1995] L213/1 as amended; Council Directive (EC) 2004/17 coordinating the procurement procedures of entities operating in the water, energy, transport and postal services sectors, OJ [2004] L134/1; Council Directive (EC) 2004/18 on the coordination of procedures for the award of public works contracts, public supply contracts and public service contracts, OJ [2004] L134/114; Council Directive (EC) 2002/21 on a common regulatory framework for electronic communications networks and services, OJ [2002] L108/35; Council Directive (EC)

(now Title VI TFEU) on transport: Article 71 TEC (now Article 91 TFEU), which confers legislative powers on the Union to implement a common transport policy described in Article 70 TEC (now Article 90 TFEU), Article 80 TEC (now Article 100 TFEU) on rail, road and inland waterway transport as well as sea and air transport and Article 156 TEC (now Article 172 TFEU) on trans-European networks in the area of transport, telecommunications and energy infrastructure.[199]

In spite of the fact that we have only witnessed the first steps towards a full mainstreaming of disability into the policies of the EU, the inclusion of persons with disabilities into other legislations than non-discrimination legislation constitutes an important positive development. According to *Gerard Quinn*, this link between the non-discrimination agenda and the internal market in the field of disability may have positive implications for the European Social Model as such because of the potentially important effects of such a mainstreaming of social considerations.[200]

The spread of disability law and policy from equality law into different areas of the internal market has been supported by an active and conscious effort on the part of *inter alia* the Commission. Since its landmark Community Disability Strategy of 1996, it has on a regular basis adopted European Disability Strategies and Action Plans in relation to disability.[201] In its latest European Disability Strategy 2010–2020, the Commission aims at *"employer[ing] people with disabilities so that they*

2002/22 on universal service and users" rights relating to electronic communications networks and services, OJ [2002] L108/51. See also Council Directive (EC) 1999/5 on radio and telecommunications terminal equipment and the mutual recognition of their conformity, OJ [1999] L91/10.

199 Council Regulation (EC) 1107/2006 concerning the rights of disabled persons and persons with reduced mobility when travelling by air, OJ [2006] L204/1. Council Regulation (EC) 261/2004 establishing common rules on compensation and assistance to passengers in the event of denied boarding and of cancellation or long delay of flights, OJ [2004] L46/1; Council Directive (EC) 2003/24 amending Council Directive (EC) 98/18 on safety rules and standards for passenger ships, OJ [2003] L123/18; Council Directive (EC) 96/48 on the interoperability of the trans-European high-speed rail system, OJ [1996] L235/6 and Council Directive (EC) 2001/16 on the interoperability of the trans-European conventional rail system, OJ [2001] 110/01 as amended.

200 Gerard Quinn, 2007 as quoted by Waddington, 2009b, p. 125.

201 Commission Communication, COM (1996) 406 final of 30 July 1996 Equality of Opportunity for People with Disabilities – A New European Community Disability Strategy; Commission Communication COM (2000) 284 final of 12 May 2005 Towards a Barrier Free Europe for Persons with Disabilities; Commission Communication COM (2003) 650 final of 30 October 2003, Equal Opportunities for People with Disabilities: A European Action Plan; Commission Communication COM (2005) 604 final of 28 November 2005 on the Situation of disabled people in the enlarged European Union: the European Action Plan 2006–2007. COM (2007) 738 final, Communication from the Commission to the Council, the European Parliament, the European Economic and Social Committee and the Committee of the Regions, Situation of disabled people in the European Union: The European Action Plan 2008–2009.

can enjoy their full rights, and benefit fully from participating in society".[202] The strategy focuses on eliminating barriers under eight main areas for action, including accessibility, participation, equality and employment.[203] This emphasis on the removal of barriers is in line with the shift in EU policy and law towards a more substantive equality model which recognises that social structures and norms are not neutral, but place certain groups at a disadvantage. The contents of the European Disability Strategy in relation to employment specifically will be discussed below under *Section 5. Employers' Obligations, Section 6. Employment Promotion and Section 7. Income-Replacement Benefits.*

However, in spite of the obligation to mainstream disability into general policies and laws in the TFEU and the fact that some mainstreaming has taken place in for example the area of transportation, the *European Employment Strategy* does not pay much attention to disability. The European Employment Strategy is based on Guidelines for employment policies adopted by the Council as part of the broader economic strategy. Based on the Guidelines, a dialogue takes place between Member States and the Commission which also prepares annual Joint Employment Reports with recommendations for national employment policies. In the latest Guidelines for the employment policies of the Member States adopted in October 2010, the headlines of the four Guidelines on employment are:

> *"Increasing labour market participation of women and men, reducing structural unemployment and promoting job quality (Guideline No. 7); Developing a skilled workforce responding to labour market needs and promoting lifelong learning (Guideline No. 8); Improving the quality and performance of education and training systems at all levels and increasing participation in tertiary or equivalent education(Guideline No. 9); Promoting social inclusion and combating poverty(Guideline No. 10)."*[204]

Persons with disabilities are mentioned in both Guideline no. 7 on reducing structural unemployment and Guideline no. 10 on promoting social inclusion in the context of active labour market policies, making work pay and strengthening social protection systems. Thus, the approach to promoting employment of persons with disabilities in the Guidelines seems to address mainly shortcomings of persons with disabilities rather than shortcomings in general structures on the labour market: persons with disabilities must be given support to enter the labour market, they must be given economic incentives to do so and when they cannot enter the labour

---

202 COM (2010) 636 final, Communication from the Commission to the Council, the European Parliament, the European Economic and Social Committee and the Committee of the Regions, European Disability Strategy 2010:2020: A Renewed Commitment to a Barrier-Free Europe, p. 4.

203 Ibid.

204 Council Decision 707/2010 of 21 October 2010 on Guidelines for the Employment Policies of the Member States, OJ [2010] L308/46.

market, they must have access to social protection. Moreover, as will be discussed again under *Section 5. Employers' Obligations*, the guidelines promote the flexicurity model, which entails fewer obligations for employers towards employees with reduced working capacity and counters the creation of general structures on the labour market which are inclusive of persons with disabilities and reduced working capacity.

A more positive development away from formal equality and towards substantive equality has however taken place in the case law of the Court of Justice of the European Communities / European Union (ECJ/CJEU).[205] This is seen for example in the *Thibault*-case, where the ECJ underlined that *"the result pursued by the Directive [76/207] is substantive, not formal, equality"*.[206] Although this case did not concern equality of persons with disability, but gender equality, it is relevant because it gives insight into the concept of equality applied by the ECJ. The *Thibault*-case concerned an employer who deprived female employees on maternity leave of their right to have their work assessed annually. This meant that they were also deprived of the possibility of promotions when on maternity leave. The ECJ found that this constituted direct discrimination on the grounds of sex in violation of EU law and that the employer should not have treated maternity leave as an ordinary absence which would disqualify a woman from having an annual assessment of her work.

Although EU equality law on disability is by-and-large based on substantive equality, it is still based on substantive difference equality and a social minority model of disability rather than on the substantive diversity equality and a social universality model of disability of the contemporary disability human rights approach, cf. *Chapter II Human Rights*. As was explained in *Chapter II Human Rights*, the substantive diversity equality principle is characterised by the recognition that social structures must reflect social diversity. Proactive measures should no longer be just exceptions to the rule, but would be necessary in order to ensure the removal of barriers to full inclusion in social life. For example, the European Employment Strategy does not promote the removal of social barriers, but rather more focuses on compensation for lack of inclusion in the form of more support for entering the labour market. Interestingly, there are however signs that EU policy and law may be moving towards a contemporary disability human rights approach.

205 The "Court of Justice of the European Communities" was formally renamed the "Court of Justice of the European Union" in the Lisbon Treaty which entered into force on 1 December 2009, cf. Section 5 of TFEU. In the present text, the acronym "ECJ" refers to the European Court of Justice until 1 December 2009 and the acronym "CJEU" refers to the Court of Justice of the European Union after 1 December 2009.

206 ECJ C-136/95, *Thibault*, judgment of 30 April 2008. Council Directive 76/207/EEC of 9 February 1976 on the implementation of the principle of equal treatment for men and women as regards access to employment, vocational training and promotion, and working conditions. OJ [1979] L39/40. Barnard 2006, p. 337.

Especially the new proposal for a *"Council Directive on implementing the principle of equal treatment between persons irrespective of religion or belief, disability, age or sexual orientation"* shows signs hereof.[207] Thus the proposal for a new directive not only imposes a duty to provide reasonable accommodation and permits positive action, it also requires that:

> *"Member States shall take the necessary and appropriate measures to ensure accessibility for persons with disabilities, on an equal basis with others, within the areas set out in Article 3, unless this would impose a disproportionate burden. [...] Such measures shall include the identification and elimination of obstacles and barriers to accessibility, including with regard to the physical environment and to information and communication technology and systems."*[208]

The first Proposal by the Commission was even more explicit in imposing a positive obligation in that it specified that the duty to take measures for the promotion of accessibility was an *"anticipatory duty"* or a duty which did not require the existence of a specific individual complaint.[209] The negotiation and adoption of the new Directive is anticipated to be a drawn-out process, which means that it is not likely to be adopted in the near future.[210]

2.4. Conclusion

In conclusion, EU disability policy and law has undergone a tremendous development from the 1950s until today.

EU disability policy and law has progressed from being based on the medical model of disability to being founded on the social model of disability and from resulting only in soft-law to increasingly being reflected in hard-law. In addition, disability is increasingly being mainstreamed into policies and laws which are not disability-specific, for example in the areas of transportation and employment.

The strongest change in the disability policy and law of the EU took place in 1999 with the adoption of Article 13 TEC (now Article 19 TFEU) which gave the EU the competence to address disability discrimination. Prior to this inclusion of disability

---

207 Council Note from the Presidency 15320/09 of 3 November 2009, Proposal for a Council Directive on implementing the principle of equal treatment between persons irrespective of religion or belief, disability, age or sexual orientation which revises Proposal for a Council Directive, COM(2008) 426 final, 2 July 2008.

208 Ibid, Article 4.

209 See Proposal for a Council Directive, COM (2008) 426 final, Article 4(1) which also provides that anticipatory measures are required "in order to guarantee compliance with the principle of equal treatment". This sentence has been repeated in the proposal by the Swedish Presidency of November 2009.

210 Waddington 2009b, p. 140.

in the Treaty, disability had only been raised in non-binding resolutions and Action Programmes which aimed at informal information- exchanges. Since the adoption of Article 13 TEC (now Article 19 TFEU), the Framework Employment Directive which prohibits discrimination on the grounds of disability was adopted in the year 2000. In addition, a proposal for a new Directive, which will prohibit discrimination on the grounds of disability outside the field of employment, has been tabled by the Commission in 2008. Also, the right to equal treatment of persons with disabilities has been increasingly mainstreamed into policy and law adopted by the EU. Finally, the EU has adopted a Council Decision to formally confirm that the EU consents to be bound by the CRPD.[211]

On the whole, EU Disability law and policy has come a long way since its non-existence in the 1970s. However, there is, yet, room for improvement as regards for example the mainstreaming of disability issues into all relevant EU policies including the European Employment Guidelines. Finally, the present European promotion of labour markets based on the flexicurity model may in fact be countering the inclusion of persons with disabilities.

3. The EU and Human Rights Protection of Persons with Disabilities

The present Section seeks to give an overview of the protection of the human rights of persons with disabilities under EU law. This Section falls into two Sub-Sections: Sub-Section 3.1, which deals with general human rights instruments under EU law with a special focus on the EU Charter of Fundamental Rights of 2000. In Sub-Section 3.2, I examine the consequences on EU law and policy of the conclusion of the CRPD by the EU.

3.1. General Human Rights Instruments

The entry into force of the Lisbon Treaty on 1 December 2009 significantly strengthens the political and legal status of the principle of equality and human rights. Thus, the TEU now states that the EU is "founded on the values of respect for human dignity, freedom, democracy, equality, the rule of law and respect for human rights",[212] and that the aim of the EU "is to promote peace, its values and the well-being of its peoples"[213] and that the EU "shall combat social exclusion and

211 The term 'formal confirmation' is used in CRPD Article 43 as well as Council Decision 2010/48, of 26 November 2009 concerning the conclusion, by the European Community, of the United Nations Convention on the Rights of Persons with Disabilities, OJ [2010] L23/35, Article 3.

212 TEU Article 2.

213 TEU Article 3(1).

discrimination, and shall promote social justice and protection."[214] The TFEU has also been amended to reflect much stronger commitment to the principle of non-discrimination. Thus, a new provision, which now provides that "the Union shall aim to combat discrimination"[215] has been added to the TFEU. Finally, and most importantly from a legal perspective, the TFEU now provides that the rights, freedoms and principles set out in the Charter of Fundamental Rights of 2000 have *"the same legal value as the Treaties".*[216] Previously the Charter was not legally binding in itself, but it listed rights which were in themselves binding because they were guaranteed by the European Convention of Human Rights or *"result[ed] from the constitutional traditions common to the Member States"* and thus constituted *"general principles of the Community's law".*[217]

The EU Charter of Fundamental Rights contains several Articles of relevance for the present thesis. Firstly, it explicitly prohibits discrimination on the grounds of disability in Article 21. According to the texts of the explanations relating to the Charter, Article 21 of the Charter draws on Article 13 TEC (now Article 19 TFEU) and Article 14 of the ECHR.[218] There are however important differences between the formulation of Article 21 of the Charter and ECHR Article 14. Firstly, contrary to 14 ECHR, disability is an explicit non-discrimination ground from the outset. Secondly, the prohibition of discrimination in the Charter is not limited to the scope of application of the Charter or even the Treaties – as opposed to the prohibition of discrimination on the grounds of nationality contained in Article 21(2) of the Charter. Below, the CJEU's new interpretation of the principle of non-discrimination as an autonomous right under EU law is discussed in relation to the *Mangold* and *Kücükdevici*-judgments.[219]

In addition, Article 26 on the *"Integration of persons with disabilities"* provides that *"The Union recognises and respects the rights of persons with disabilities to benefit from measures designed to ensure their independence, social and occupational integration and participation in the life of the community."* According to the text of the explanations relating to the Charter, this provision is based inter

---

214 TEU Article 3(3).

215 TFEU Article 10.

216 TFEU Article 6(1).

217 TEU Article 6 and the Preamble of the Charter of Fundamental Rights and Freedoms of the European Union of 2000.

218 Note from the Praesidium, Text of the explanations relating to the complete text of the Charter as set out in CHARTE 4487/00 CONVENT 50, Brussels, 11 October 2000, CHARTE 4473/00, p. 23.

219 ECJ, Case C-144/04, Grand Chamber judgment of 22 November 2005, *Werner Mangold v. Rüdiger Helm*. CJEU Grand Chamber judgment of 19 January 2010, C-555/07, Seda Kücükdeveci v. Swedex GmbH & Co. KG.

alia on Article 23 of the Revised European Social Charter.[220] As shown in *Chapter II Human Rights*, the Revised European Social Charter is based on the principle of substantive diversity equality and on the contemporary disability human rights approach to persons with disabilities. Thus, from the point of view of persons with disabilities, Article 23 of the Revised Social Charter is a good basis for a provision on the rights of persons with disabilities in the EU Charter of Fundamental Rights.

Finally, Chapter IV on Solidarity of the EU Charter of Fundamental Rights contains several Articles, which touch upon issues that are relevant to the inclusion of persons with disabilities on the labour market including the *"Right of access to placement services"* in Article 29, the right to *"Protection in the event of unjustified dismissal"* in Article 30, the right to *"Fair and just working conditions"* in Article 31 and the right to *"Social security and social assistance"* in Article 34. According to the *"Text of the explanations relating to the Charter"*, these Articles are also based *inter alia* on the Revised European Social Charter.

Although these provisions in the EU Charter of Fundamental Rights may be seen as underpinning the development of EU policy to encompass not only strictly economic issues, it is quite difficult to assess the actual effect of these provisions on EU law and policy.[221] This is related to a number of facts: there may be tensions between other Union objectives such as economic development and integration which have been given priority over the protection of fundamental human rights; some human rights such as civil and political rights may be given higher priority than for example social rights; and the mainstreaming of human rights has been more successful in some areas of EU policy and law than in others.[222]

However, it seems that at least the right to non-discrimination, which is protected under the EU Charter of Fundamental Rights has now been given autonomous legal effect, in the sense that the CJEU performs an autonomous determination of the contents of the principle and has given it full direct effect to legal areas falling under EU law. Although the CJEU has not yet found that the principle of non-discrimination on the grounds of *disability* constitutes a general principle of EU law, there is no reason why it should not do so in the future. In 2005, the Grand Chamber of the ECJ handed down its judgment in the *Mangold*-case in which it stated that the principle of non-discrimination on the grounds of age is a general principle of EU law.[223] 'Age' is similar to 'disability' in that both grounds are new

220 Note from the Praesidium, Text of the explanations relating to the complete text of the Charter as set out in CHARTE 4487/00 CONVENT 50, Brussels, 11 October 2000, CHARTE 4473/00, p. 26.

221 McCrudden and Kountouros 2007, p. 115.

222 Ibid.

223 ECJ, Case C-144/04, Grand Chamber judgment of 22 November 2005, *Werner Mangold v. Rüdiger Helm*.

discrimination grounds and their legal basis in the Treaties is the same, namely Article 19 TFEU (previously Article 13 TEC). In addition, the EU Charter of Fundamental Rights prohibits discrimination on the grounds of *inter alia* age and disability in Article 21.

The *Mangold*-case concerned the adoption in Germany of legislation which permitted the employment of persons over 52 years of age under successive fixed-term contracts without objective justification, whereas such justification was required for persons under 52 years of age. The aim of this German legislation was to make it easier for persons over 52 years of age to obtain employment. The ECJ found that this differential treatment of persons over 52 years of age was in violation of EU law in spite of the fact that the period allowed for Germany to transpose the Employment Equality Directive had not yet expired. The ECJ noted firstly that Germany adopted the discriminatory legislation while it was exceptionally enjoying an extended period of two years for transposition of the Employment Equality Directive. It follows from Article 18 of the Employment Equality Directive that such States "*shall report annually to the Commission on the steps it is taking to tackle age... discrimination and on the progress it is making towards implementation*". The Court found that this obligation in Article 18 of the Employment Equality Directive would be rendered redundant if the Member States were "*to adopt measures incompatible with the objectives pursued by that act*".[224]

Secondly, *"and above all"*[225], the Court underlined that:

> *"Directive 2000/78 does not itself lay down the principle of equal treatment in the field of employment and occupation..., the source of the actual principle underlying the prohibition of those forms of discrimination being found, as is clear from the third and fourth recitals in the preamble to the directive, in various international instruments and in the constitutional traditions common to the Member States. The principle of non-discrimination on the grounds of age must thus be regarded as a general principle of EU law."*[226]

After finding that the principle of non-discrimination constitutes a general principle of EU law, the ECJ found that it was applicable in the case at hand because the discriminatory German law constituted a measure of implementation of another EU Directive and thus fell under EU law.[227] In conclusion, three very specific

224 Idem, para. 72.

225 Idem, para. 74.

226 Idem, para. 74 and 75.

227 Ibid. para. 76, The case concerned the implementation of Council Directive (EC) 1999/70 of 28 June 1999 concerning the framework agreement on fixed-term work concluded by ETUC, UNICE and CEEP, OJ [1999] L175/43. In the *Bartsch*-case from 2008, the ECJ refused to apply the prohibition of age discrimination as a community law principle because the contentious national legislation did not fall under community law. ECJ Judgment (Grand Chamber) of

circumstances played an important role in the argumentation of the court: firstly that Germany adopted this legislation during the period of extension that it had been given for implementing the Employment Equality Directive.[228] Secondly, the problematic German legislation was a measure of implementation of another EU Directive and thus fell under EU law and thirdly, that the prohibition of discrimination on the grounds of age constituted a general principle of EU law.

The reaction to the *Mangold*-judgment was relatively strong in academic literature because it appeared to further muddle the doctrine that Directives cannot (as a rule) have direct horizontal effect between private parties.[229] In this light, the subsequent judgment of the CJEU in the *Kücükdeveci*-case decided on 19 January 2010 was much awaited as it would give the CJEU the opportunity to clarify the legal status of Directives compared to the general principle of non-discrimination.[230] The case concerned the proceedings between Ms Kücükdeveci, a German national, and her former employer Swedex GmbH & Co. KG (Swedex), a privately held German company, regarding the calculation of the notice period applicable to her dismissal. According to German law, a person who had been employed for more than ten years was entitled to a longer notice period. However, German law also provided that any period of employment before the age of 25 years should not be taken into account. Since Ms Kücükdeveci was first employed at the age of 18 years, her first seven years of employment were not taken into account when calculating the length of her notice period.

The referring German Court had asked the CJEU to clarify whether the German legal act should be examined in relation to the general principle of EU-law which prohibits discrimination on the grounds of age or in relation to EC Directive 2000/78. According to Advocate General Bot, the German legal act should be examined in relation to the Employment Equality Directive on the grounds that conditions of dismissals fell within the scope of the Directive and that the period of time available to the Federal Republic of Germany for transposing the Directive had expired when Ms. Kücükdeveci was dismissed.[231] Advocate General Bot underlined that the Court would "*give an autonomous scope to the general principle of non-discrimination on grounds of age*" and "*deprive Directive 2000/78 of all useful effect*" if it were to examine the German legal act in relation to the EU principle of non-discrimination rather than the Directive.[232]

---

23 September 2008, C-427/06, Birgit Bartsch v. Bosch und Siemens Hausgeräte (BSH) Altersfürsorge GmbH, para. 24 and 25.

228 Tobler 2007, p. 1182.

229 Tobler 2007, p. 1182. Common Market Law Review Editorial 2006. Jans 2007.

230 CJEU Grand Chamber judgment of 19 January 2010, C-555/07, Seda Kücükdeveci v. Swedex GmbH & Co. KG.

231 Opinion of General Advocate Bot delivered on 7 July 2009, C-555/07, Seda Kücükdeveci v. Swedex GmbH & Co. KG, para. 30–31.

232 Idem, para. 34.

In its judgment, the CJEU did not follow the recommendation of the Advocate General, but stated instead that *"it is the general principle of European Union law prohibiting all discrimination on grounds of age, as given expression in Directive 2000/78, which must be the basis of the examination of whether European Union law precludes national legislation such as that at issue in the main proceedings."*[233] The CJEU recalled that the principle of non-discrimination on the grounds of age is a "*general principle of European Union law*" as it had in the *Mangold*-case and that "*Directive 2000/78 [merely] gives specific expression to that principle*".[234] Moreover, it underlined that "*Article 6(1) TEU provides that the Charter of Fundamental Rights of the European Union is to have the same legal value as the Treaties. Under Article 21(1) of the charter, '[a]ny discrimination based on ... age ... shall be prohibited'.*"[235] This reference to the Charter and its new legally binding status had not been made in the *Mangold*-case since the Treaty of Lisbon only entered into force on 1 December 2009 after the *Mangold*-judgment was handed down.

The fact that examination should be made on the basis of the general principle "*as given expression*" in the Directive seems to mean that CJEU will apply the Directive to give specific content to the general principle of EU law. Thus, the CJEU went on to examine the German legal act in relation to Article 6 of Directive 2000/78.[236] In other words, the Directive was not deprived of *all* useful effect as Advocate General Bot had feared. However, one must acknowledge that the recognition by the CJEU of the general EU principle of non-discrimination does deprive EC Directives of *some* useful effect as the reasoning implies that the CJEU will only give effect to Directives as far as the CJEU considers that the Directive in question expresses the content of the principle of non-discrimination. The CJEU's judgment in the *Association Belge des Consommateurs*-case, which was decided a year after the *Kücükdeveci*-case, illustrates this point poignantly.[237] The case concerning a Belgian law permitting that insurance companies operated with differentiation between men and women as regards insurance premiums paid by men and women on the grounds of actuarial factors. In this judgment, the CJEU went so far as to set aside a provision in Directive 2004/113 because "*a temporal limitation an exemption from the rule of unisex premiums and benefits, works against the achievement of the objective of equal treatment between men and women, which is the purpose of Directive 2004/113, and is incompatible with Articles 21 and 23 of the Charter.*"[238]

233 CJEU Grand Chamber judgment of 19 January 2010, C-555/07, Seda Kücükdeveci v. Swedex GmbH & Co. KG Idem, para. 27.

234 Idem, para. 21.

235 Idem, para. 22.

236 Idem, para. 33, 36 and 37.

237 CJEU Grand Chamber judgment of 1 March 2011, *Case C-236/09,* Association belge des Consommateurs Test-Achats ASBL v. Conseil des Ministres.

238 Idem, para. 32.

The CJEU's decision to declare a Directive to be invalid because it does not live up to the principle of non-discrimination sends a strong signal from the CJEU that it is performing an autonomous interpretation of the principle of non-discrimination and will not feel bound by Directives if these do not live up to the principle of non-discrimination. In relation to the Employment Equality Directive, this new strong-handed enforcement of the principle of non-discrimination by the CJEU will presumably mean that any derogations by the Member States of the armed forces from the scope of the Employment Equality Directive insofar as it relates to discrimination on the grounds of disability and age may be subject to an intensive scrutiny by the CJEU in spite of the express permission to derogate contained in Article 3(4) of the Directive. Another consequence of the new status of the principle of equal treatment may also be that the European Council will be faced with even more difficulties in reaching agreement on the proposal for a *"Council Directive on implementing the principle of equal treatment between persons irrespective of religion or belief, disability, age or sexual orientation"* since any limitations or derogations will not necessarily be upheld by the CJEU.[239]

In sum, with the *Kücükdeveci*-judgment the CJEU indicates a new beginning for the protection against discrimination as well as the EU Charter itself under EU law where even private parties may rely on the general principle of non-discrimination as expressed in the EU Charter in relation to other private parties. The only limitation is that the issue at hand will have to fall under secondary EU law before the general principle of non-discrimination applies between private parties.

3.2. CRPD

I now pass to the question of the consequences of the EU's formal confirmation to be bound by the CRPD, which took place on 23 December 2010.[240] Since the EU is not a State, but a *"regional integration organization"*, the CRPD uses the term 'formal confirmation'. The Council Decision uses both the term "conclusion" and "formal confirmation", but not ratification.[241] The EU's conclusion of the CRPD is historic, both because it strengthens the legal status of persons with disabilities under EU law and also because it is the first international human rights treaty

239 Council Note from the Presidency, 15320/09, of 3 November 2009, Proposal for a Council Directive on implementing the principle of equal treatment between persons irrespective of religion or belief, disability, age or sexual orientation which revises Proposal for a Council Directive, COM(2008) 426 final, 2 July 2008.

240 Council Decision 2010/48 of 26 November 2009 concerning the conclusion, by the European Community, of the United Nations Convention on the Rights of Persons with Disabilities, OJ [2010] L23/35. Signature by European Union took place on 30 March 2007 and ratification took place on 23 December 2010.

241 Council Decision 2010/48, title and Article 3.

concluded by the EU.[242] The legal basis for the Decision to conclude the CRPD is TEC Article 13 on action to combat discrimination on the grounds of *inter alia* disability, Article 95 on the approximation of laws for the functioning of the internal market and Article 300 on the procedure for concluding international agreements (now Articles 19, 114 and 218).[243] In the Commission Proposal for Decision on the conclusion of the CRPD, reference had also been made to numerous Articles which cover such areas as tariffs, self-employment, transport, State aid, common market and statistics.[244] The advantage of the longer list as proposed by the Commission would have been that the broad relevance of the CRPD to many different policy and law areas would have been stated explicitly. The advantage however of the shorter list opted for by the Council is that speculations on the importance of any left-out policy areas, such as the area of social policy, is avoided. Moreover the Appendix to the Decision contains a relatively comprehensive list of *"Community Acts which Refer to Matters Governed by the Convention".* The Appendix lists close to 70 different EU legal acts under headings such as 'accessibility', 'independent living, social inclusion, work and employment' as well as 'statistics and data collection'. In other words, the many different legal acts included in the appendix establish beyond doubt that the CRPD will be of relevance in many different law and policy areas of the EU.

The CRPD covers areas where the EU has exclusive competence, namely the areas of *"compatibility of state aid with the common market and the common custom tariff"*, as well as areas of shared competence.[245] In areas of exclusive EU competence, it will be less complicated for the Commission to promote the fulfilment of the CRPD since the Member States are not permitted to regulate these areas. However, in areas of mixed competence, which cover practically all areas of EU law and policy, the EU adopts laws and policy along side with Member States which adopt their own laws and policies. In these areas, it will be necessary for the Commission and the Member States to cooperate in order to ensure cohesion of national and EU policies in relation to persons with disabilities. The Council Decision on the conclusion of the CRPD envisages some coordination in areas of mixed competence, but at the same time it is assumed that the conclusion of the CRPD will not affect the distribution of competences of the Member States and the EU.[246]

---

242 Article 6 TEU provides that the ECHR shall also be concluded by the EU.

243 Council Decision 2010/48.

244 Reference had been made to Articles 26, 47(2), 55, 71(1), 80(2), 89, 93, 95 and 285 TEC (now Articles 31, 53, 62, 91, 100, 109, 113, 114, 338 TFEU), but not Article 300 TEC (now Article 218 TFEU).

245 Council Decision 2010/48, Annex II.

246 This is stated explicitly in Article 3 as regards the consequences of the designation of the Commission as focal point under the CRPD.

In sum, the EU's conclusion of the CRPD will presumably lead to stronger impetus within the EU for promoting the human rights of persons with disabilities. The development towards a higher degree of mainstreaming of disability issues in EU laws and policies will most probably be strengthened. Moreover, the cooperation between Member States and the Commission on reporting and monitoring under the CRPD may strengthen both national and EU policies of relevance for persons with disabilities.

3.3. Conclusion

In conclusion, a strong development is under way in relation to the protection of human rights of persons with disabilities under EU law with the recent conclusion of the CRPD and the awarding of legally binding status on the EU Charter of Fundamental Rights, which may lead to a stronger influence of the Charter on EU law and policy. Especially the conclusion of the CRPD could mean a stronger development towards more mainstreaming of the rights of persons with disabilities under EU law.

4. Employment Equality Directive

Council Directive 2000/78/EC of 27 November 2000 *"establishing a general framework for equal treatment in employment and occupation"* (the Employment Equality Directive) was adopted by the Council pursuant to Article 13 TEC (now Article 19 TFEU), which was introduced with the Amsterdam Treaty. It is *the* key piece of EU legislation for the promotion of equal opportunities of persons with disabilities in the field of employment. The present Section examines the main obligations under the Employment Equality Directive in relation to persons with disabilities. In *Chapter IV Equality Laws and Policies*, I examine whether the Danish and Swedish equality legislation comply with both the Employment Equality Directive and the contemporary disability human rights approach.

As a Framework Directive, the Employment Equality Directive defines *minimum* requirements for protection against discrimination on the grounds of *"religion or belief, disability, age or sexual orientation"*. Consequently, the Directive sets the floor and the Member States are free to provide a higher level of protection. The present examination of the Employment Equality Directive is an examination of minimum requirements in the EU and not an examination of the actual level of protection in the Member States.

The title of the Directive refers to *"equal treatment"* and Article 1 on the purpose of the Directive states that the Directive aims at putting into effect "the principle of equal treatment". The question arises whether this means that the Directive goes further than merely banning discrimination and also provides positive obligations to realise equality. In fact, the relationship between the two concepts of equality and discrimination has never been fully clarified in literature.[247] Equality and discrimination may be either seen as two sides of the same coin *or* the discrimination ban may be seen as enacting just some of the obligations ensuing from a more far-reaching concept of equality.

It seems that the Employment Equality Directive is based on the assumption that the prohibition against discrimination is a legal obligation ensuing from a more far-reaching concept of equality. Thus, while Article 2 of the Employment Equality Directive states that *"the principle of equal treatment shall mean that there shall be no direct or indirect discrimination",* Article 7 provides that positive action measures may be maintained or adopted *"with a view to ensuring full equality in practice*". In other words, the Employment Equality Directive is founded on the assumption that other measures than the prohibition against discrimination may be required to achieve equality.

Furthermore, the question is what type of equality the Employment Equality Directive seeks to achieve. Is the Directive based on a principle of formal or substantive difference or substantive universality equality? As explained in *Chapter II Human Rights*, substantive universality equality of the contemporary disability human rights approach is founded on the view that general structures should reflect diversity and that legally binding obligations should be imposed in order to achieve inclusive structures.

As mentioned above, according to Article 7 of the Employment Equality Directive, "*the principle of equal treatment shall not prevent any Member State from maintaining or adopting specific measures to prevent or compensate for disadvantages linked to any of the grounds*". This wording indicates that the Employment Equality Directive does not require the creation of inclusive general structures, but rather that it recognises the need for compensation for the disadvantages of the relevant groups in relation to existing general structures. In other words, the Employment Equality Directive would seem to be based on the principle of substantive difference equality rather than substantive diversity equality. This is also supported by the fact that the Directive prohibits indirect discrimination and imposes a duty to provide reasonable accommodation which would not be so, if the Employment Equality Directive was based on a formal equality concept.

Below, I examine the concept of disability (Sub-Section 4.1.), the definitions of direct discrimination (Sub-Section 4.2.), the definition of indirect discrimination

[247] Schiek 2009, p. 10.

(Sub-Section 4.3), reasonable accommodation (Sub-Section 4.4), harassment and instruction to discriminate (Sub-Section 4.5), Scope of application of the Employment Equality Directive (Sub-Section 4.6), the burden of proof (Sub-Section 4.7), positive action (Sub-Section 4.8), remedies (Sub-Section 4.9) and I conclude in Sub-Section 4.10.

4.1. Definition of Disability

In the present Sub-Section I examine the concept of disability under the Employment Equality Directive. I initially give a short overview of the concepts of disability in *Sub-Section 4.1.1. Models of Disability*. In *Sub-section 4.1.2 Delimitation of the Concept of Disability*, I examine the definition of the concept of disability with a special focus on the judgment of the ECJ in the *Chacón Navas*-case regarding the difference between sickness and disability. In *Sub-Section 4.1.3. Definition of Disability and the Causal-Link*, I discuss the implications of the Coleman-judgment on discrimination by association with disability for the coverage of the Employment Equality Directive. Finally, I conclude in *Sub-Section 4.1.4*.

4.1.1. Models of Disability

As described in *Chapter II Human Rights*, the definition of disability is central to the contemporary disability human rights approach. After having briefly summed up the definitions of the medical and social models of disability, I will in the present Section examine whether the definition of disability under the Directive is in accordance with the definition of disability of the contemporary disability human rights approach.

According to the *medical* model of disability the problems disabled persons face in their daily life are a natural and unavoidable consequence of the impairment itself, cf. *Sub-Section 1.2 of Chapter II Human Rights*. However, according to the *social* model of disability the problems arise in the interaction between the impairment and societal and environmental barriers outside of the individual disabled person, cf. *Sub-Sections 1.3. and 1.4. of Chapter II Human Rights*. Whereas measures to combat exclusion, which are based on the medical model of disability, will be aimed at reducing a person's impairments, measures to combat exclusion, which are based on the social model of disability, will primarily target social structures and attitudes. As mentioned above, the social model of disability falls into two sub-categories: the minority and the universality models of disability. Whereas the assumption under the *minority* model of disability is that persons with disabilities make up a discernable group of persons, the assumption under the *universality* model of disability is that all persons are at one time or another more or less disabled and that it does not make sense to speak of a discernable group of persons with disabilities.

A prohibition of discrimination on the grounds of disability is an acknowledgment that (at least some of) the problems facing persons with disabilities arise from the interaction of individuals with impairments with society. The assumption would therefore be that the Employment Equality Directive is based on this social model of disability. However, the Directive is silent on the definition of disability, leaving it up to the ECJ to set minimum standards for the scope of the definition of disability under the Directive. Since the definition of disability is crucial to the effective functioning of the prohibition of discrimination, the question of how to define disability, quickly became subject of a case before the ECJ. Unfortunately, as will be apparent from the text below, the ECJ judgment was rather disappointing. On a positive note, it was this unclear judgment from the ECJ, which is said to have been a turning point during the negotiations on whether or not to provide guidance on the meaning of the concept of disability in the UN CRPD.[248] Allegedly, the *Chacón Navas*-judgment led the European Commission to change its stance and stop opposing the inclusion of a definition of disability in the CRPD. As mentioned in *Chapter II Human Rights*, the CRPD Article 1 on the purpose of the Convention states that *"persons with disabilities include those who have long-term physical, mental, intellectual or sensory impairments which in interaction with various barriers may hinder their full and effective participation in society on an equal basis with others"*. Although this is not a formal definition of disability, the provision still provides guidance on the concept of disability under the CRPD.

4.1.2. Delimitation of the Concept of Disability

On 11 July 2006, the ECJ handed down its judgment in the *Chacón Navas*-case concerning whether 'sickness' could be subsumed under the discrimination ground 'disability' of the Employment Equality Directive.[249] The case before the national court concerned the dismissal of a woman effective from May 2004. A medical report ordered by the referring court in September 2004 stated that Ms. Chacón Navas had been *"unfit to work on the grounds of sickness"* as of October 2003 and *"that she was still unfit to work and that it was not envisaged that she would return to work in the short term"*.[250] The referring Court did not give information on the nature of the sickness. The main preliminary question was whether sickness fell under the concept of 'disability' of the Employment Equality Directive.

The ECJ established that the concept of disability for the purpose of Directive 2000/78 must be given an *"autonomous and uniform interpretation"* throughout the EU, having regard to the context of the provision and the objective pursued by the

248 Quinn 2007, p. 256.

249 ECJ judgment (Grand Chamber) of 11 July 2006, C-13/05, *Sonia Chacón Navas v. Eurest Colectividades SA*. See comments to the judgment in Waddington 2007 and Hoskins 2007.

250 Opinion of Advocate General Geelhoed delivered 16 March 2006, Case C-13/05, *Sonia Chacón Navas v. Eurest Colectividades SA*, para. 21–22.

legislation in question.[251] This reference by the ECJ to the need for a *"uniform interpretation"* is peculiar since the ECJ can only provide a minimum level of protection, it cannot prevent Member States from granting a higher level of protection if they so wish.[252]

With regard to the meaning of the concept of disability, the ECJ stated that:

> *"Directive 2000/78 aims to combat certain types of discrimination as regards employment and occupation. In that context, the concept of "disability" must be understood as referring to a limitation which results in particular from physical, mental or psychological impairments and which hinders the participation of the person concerned in professional life.*[253]

This definition is problematic from the perspective of the disability human rights approach because the definition requires limitations which result directly from an impairment. As such, the Court's definition is based on the out-dated medical model of disability.[254] This is a negation of the more contemporary social model of disability and the whole basis of the prohibition of discrimination which is to remove barriers to participation by altering attitudes and structures, as opposed to curing impairments. A definition based on the social model of disability would instead focus on the interaction between the individual and society.[255] For example, both past, future or presumed presence of an impairment could – in interaction with social barriers – hinder social participation and would be included if the definition were based on a social model of disability. I continue the discussion of the *Chacón Navas*-case below.

Given that the Court based itself on the medical model of disability rather than on the social model of disability in the *Chacón Navas* case, it was not surprising that the ECJ rejected that sickness was encompassed by the Employment Equality Directive. It stated:

> *"44. However, by using the concept of "disability" in Article 1 of that directive, the legislature deliberately chose a term which differs from "sickness". The two concepts cannot therefore simply be treated as being the same.*
> *45. Recital 16 in the preamble to Directive 2000/78 states that the "provision of measures to accommodate the needs of disabled people at the workplace plays an important role in combating discrimination on grounds of disability". The importance which the Community legislature attaches to measures for adapting the workplace to the disability demonstrates that it envisaged situations in which*

251 Judgment in case C-13/05, para. 42 and 40.
252 On the question of "uniformity" see Waddington 2007, p. 495.
253 Judgment in case C-13/05, para. 43.
254 Waddington 2007, p. 491.
255 Waddington 2007, p. 497.

participation in professional life is hindered over a long period of time. In order for the limitation to fall within the concept of "disability", it must therefore be probable that it will last for a long time.
46. There is nothing in Directive 2000/78 to suggest that workers are protected by the prohibition of discrimination on grounds of disability as soon as they develop any type of sickness.
47. It follows from the above considerations that a person who has been dismissed by his employer solely on account of sickness does not fall within the general framework laid down for combating discrimination on grounds of disability by Directive 2000/78."[256]

It is undoubtedly correct, as suggested by the Court, that the two concepts of sickness and disability cannot be treated as one and the same. However, it seems that the Court should have recognised that sickness and disability may in certain cases overlap, for example where a disease is progressive and has led to permanent impairments which will only become more and more serious. Had it done so, it could have avoided arguing in a contradictory manner in the *Coleman*-case compared to in the *Chacón Navas*-case. Thus, in paragraph 45 of the *Chacón Navas*-case quoted above, the Court refers to the duty to provide reasonable accommodation as a reason for limiting the persons covered by the protection of the Directive. However, in the *Coleman*-case, the Court underlined that the group of persons who have a right to accommodation are not necessarily the same as the group of persons who are entitled to protection against discrimination:

"the fact that Directive 2000/78 includes provisions designed to accommodate specifically the needs of disabled people does not lead to the conclusion that the principle of equal treatment enshrined in that directive must be interpreted strictly, that is, as prohibiting only direct discrimination on grounds of disability and relating exclusively to disabled persons."[257]

The Court concurred on several points with the General Advocate in its judgment in the *Chacón Navas*-case and even though the Court did not repeat the argumentation of the Advocate General in its judgment, it is likely that the ECJ may have been influenced by it. The Opinion of the Advocate General *Geelhoed* seems to have been guided to a large extent by a desire to restrain *"potentially far-reaching economic and financial consequences"* which would follow if the questions posed to the ECJ were answered affirmatively.[258] This reasoning stands in stark contrast both to the more common teleological method of interpretation of the Court which would have entailed giving precedence to ensuring an effective implementation of

[256] Judgment in case C-13/05, paras. 43–47.

[257] ECJ judgment (Grand Chamber) of 17 July 2008, C-303/06, S. *Coleman v. Attridge Law and Steve Law*, para. 43.

[258] Opinion of General Advocate Geelhoed of 16 March 2006, Case C-13/05 *Chacón Navas v. Eurest Collectividades SA*, para. 51. See also Quinn 2007, p. 255.

human rights (recitals 1–6 of the Directive) and *"providing a level playing field"* (recital 37) as the ECJ did in for example the *Coleman*-case.[259]

In the *Chacón Navas*-case, the ECJ did leave some possibility for interpreting "sickness" as falling within the Directive when it held that workers cannot be covered by the prohibition of discrimination *"as soon as they develop any type of sickness".*[260] The wording in for example French *"dès qu'une maladie quelconque se manifeste"* indicates that the Court used the word *any* in the meaning *any unspecified* rather than *any at all* and that it did not exclude that some sicknesses could in principle be seen as falling under the definition of disability. This would be in line with the opinion of the General Advocate who recognised that individuals who had sicknesses which caused long-term or permanent limitations should be regarded as disabled.[261] Thus, it is unfortunate the ECJ was not more elaborate on when such sickness might theoretically fall under the definition of disability.

4.1.3. Definition of Disability and the 'Causal Link'

In the Sub-Section above, it was seen that the ECJ had given a narrow definition of the concept of 'disability' of the Employment Equality Directive in the *Chacón Navas*-judgment. A later judgment by the ECJ in the *Coleman*-case raises the question whether this definition of disability could be broadened through a broad interpretation of the 'causal link'-requirement in *inter alia* the provision on direct discrimination of the Employment Equality Directive.[262] For example, discrimination on the grounds of future or presumed disability may not be encompassed under the definition of 'disability' as such, but may be protected under the Employment Equality Directive if the 'causal link' requirement is interpreted broadly. If the causal link requirement is interpreted broadly, it would not be a requirement that the victim himself or herself is discriminated due to his or her existing disability, but the victim could be discriminated due to his or her future or presumed disability as well as due to his or her association to a person with disability.

The *Coleman*-case, discussed above under *Sub-Section 4.2. Direct Discrimination*, concerns the question of discrimination by association related to the ground disability. Ms Coleman had allegedly been dismissed and harassed not on the

259 ECJ judgment (Grand Chamber) of 22 November 2005, Case C-144/04, *Werner Mangold v. Rüdiger Helm*. ECJ judgment (Grand Chamber) of 17 July 2008, C-303/06, S. *Coleman v. Attridge Law and Steve Law*.

260 Judgment in case C-13/05, paras. 46.

261 Opinion of General Advocate Geelhoed in Case C-13/05, para. 85. See also Waddington 2007, p. 493.

262 Judgment in C-303/06.

grounds of her own disability, but on the grounds of her son's disability. The ECJ stated that:

> *"the purpose of the directive, as regards employment and occupation, is to combat all forms of discrimination on grounds of disability. The principle of equal treatment enshrined in the directive in that area applies not to a particular category of person but by reference to the grounds mentioned in Article 1"*[263]

This quote shows that the Court sought to ensure that the Employment Equality Directive applies "*by reference to the ground*" and not *"to a particular category of person"*. By interpreting the Employment Equality Directive to provide protection against discrimination by association, the ECJ is significantly broadening the scope of protection of the Employment Equality Directive compared to the line it had set in the *Chacón Navas*-judgment. As explained above, the ECJ had based its definition of disability on a medical model of disability in the *Chacón Navas*-judgment, which implied that only persons with a specific type of impairment leading limitations in social participation, were entitled to protection under the Employment Equality Directive. Although the ECJ has not changed its definition of 'disability', which was based on the medical model of disability in the *Chacón Navas*-case, the ECJ has with the *Coleman*-judgment taken an important step towards ensuring effective protection against discrimination on the grounds of disability in line with the contemporary disability human rights approach.

In the *Coleman*-case, the ECJ applied the social model of disability when it recognised that not only persons who have a disability themselves may be subject to discrimination on the grounds of disability. According to the social model of disability, limitations do not result from the impairment itself, but from the interaction between impairment and social structures. The aim of anti-discrimination legislation is to remove discriminatory treatment and social structures which result in disability. In accordance herewith the focus in the *Coleman*-judgment was on the reason for the negative treatment of Ms. Coleman and not on whether or not Ms. Coleman herself had a disabling impairment. Interestingly, the *Coleman*-judgment was passed after the adoption of the CRPD and although the ECJ did not itself refer to the CRPD, the Advocate General did.[264]

I would argue that if the ECJ can find that the prohibition of direct discrimination covers differential treatment on the grounds of a *victim's child's disability*, then the Court could also find that the Employment Equality Directive applies when the differential treatment takes place on the grounds of the victim's own future or past disability.

---

263 Ibid. para. 38.

264 Opinion of Advocate General Poiares Maduro of 31 January 2008, C-303/06, Coleman v. Attridge Law and Steve Law, footnote 4.

Importantly, the reliance on the 'causal link' requirement to broaden the coverage of the prohibition of direct discrimination in stead of 'disability' itself means that the broadened coverage does not apply to the duty to provide reasonable accommodation or the right of Member States to adopt health and safety measures for the promotion of the integration of disabled persons into the working environment.[265] According to the wording of the Employment Equality Directive Article 5, the duty to provide reasonable accommodation concerns only 'persons with disabilities' and Article 7(2) on health and safety measures concerns only the integration of 'disabled persons'.[266] In line herewith the ECJ did in fact in the *Coleman*-judgment underline that these two provisions do only apply to disabled persons.[267] It remains unclear whether the ECJ will also interpret *"persons having a particular disability"* under the provision on indirect discrimination as excluding discrimination by association. On the one hand, the ECJ did not mention indirect discrimination when it noted that some provisions *"relate specifically to disabled persons"*, on the other hand the wording *"having a particular disability"* seems to point in the other direction. The question remains unresolved.[268]

4.1.4. Conclusion

In sum, although the first judgment of the ECJ on disability discrimination under the Employment Equality Directive was not in line the contemporary disability human rights approach, the second judgement seems to have moved the ECJ towards the contemporary disability human rights approach. Thus, in the *Chacón Navas-case,* the ECJ laid out a definition of disability based on the medical model of disability. However, the delimitation of the causal link requirement was in line with the social model of disability and the contemporary disability human rights approach in the *Coleman-judgment.*

4.2. Direct Discrimination

It follows from Article 2(2)(a) that *"direct discrimination shall be taken to occur where one person is treated less favourably than another is, has been or would be treated in a comparable situation, on any of the grounds referred to in Article 1",* including disability.

What is notable from this definition of discrimination is firstly that a person must have experienced a disadvantage (less favourable treatment), secondly that there must be a comparison to treatment of another person in a similar situation (than

265 Employment Equality Directive Articles 5 and 7(2).
266 Waddington 2009a, p. 675.
267 Judgment in C-303/06, paras. 39 and 40.
268 Waddington 2009a, p. 675.

another is, has been – or would have been treated), thirdly that there must be a direct causal link between the disadvantage and the discrimination ground and fourthly, that the prohibition of direct discrimination appears to be absolute.

The first question of whether or not there has been a disadvantage is relatively unproblematic. However, the other three issues, namely the comparison, the causal link and the fact that there is no justification, do raise special questions in relation to disability which I will look into in the present Sub-section.

The second requirement that a person who has allegedly been subject to discrimination be in a comparable situation with another person is of crucial importance because it amounts to a hidden justification clause to direct discrimination. If the alleged victim was not in a comparable situation with others then the disadvantage was not the result of direct discrimination. Moreover the comparability-test raises specific disability-related issues. The difficulty for persons with disabilities lies in finding the right comparison. There is a risk that a comparison between a person who is disabled and a person who is not disabled will result in the finding that their situations are not comparable and thus that there was no less favourable treatment. This comparison is by no means objective in the sense that it is independent of the subjective views of those performing the assessment. On the contrary, this assessment reflects subjective perceptions of what is just and unjust differential treatment and thus risks perpetuating inequalities in society.[269] If persons with disabilities are met with prejudices about their working capacity then it will be more unlikely that they be considered to be in a comparable situation with others without a disability.

The Employment Equality Directive does not provide a definition of 'comparable situation', but Recital 17 of the Preamble may be seen as providing some guidance in relation to the determination of when persons with disabilities are in a comparable situation with others. According to Recital 17:

> *"This Directive does not require the recruitment, promotion, maintenance in employment or training of an individual who is not competent, capable and available to perform the essential functions of the post concerned or to undergo the relevant training, without prejudice to the obligation to provide reasonable accommodation for people with disabilities."*

In the *Chacón Navas*-judgment, the ECJ stated that the Employment Equality Directive "precludes dismissal on grounds of disability which, in the light of the obligation to provide reasonable accommodation for people with disabilities, is not justified by the fact that the person concerned is not competent, capable and

269 Bell 2007, p. 205.

available to perform the essential functions of his post."[270] Presumably, this means that persons with disabilities are in a comparable situation with others when they are 'competent, capable and available' to a 'normal' degree after reasonable accommodation has been provided. However, reasonable accommodation will in many cases not lead to persons with disabilities to become for example available to the same degree as the majority of non-disabled employees. The accommodation of disabled persons with reduced working capacity could consist in reduced working hours, which would mean that would not be as available as most other employees. In conclusion, the definition of a 'comparable situation' is of crucial importance for the effective functioning of the prohibition of direct discrimination.

Secondly, the question of the *direct causal link* also raises disability-related questions. One interesting question in this regard concerns the situation when an employer does not fulfil a duty to provide reasonable accommodation. One may ask whether the lack of fulfilment of this duty amounts to differential treatment on the grounds of disability, and therefore potentially amounts to a form of direct discrimination, or whether the differential treatment occurs because neutral working conditions or physical environment places persons with a disability at a disadvantage. This question is interesting because the prohibition of direct discrimination is in principle stronger than the prohibition of indirect discrimination in that the prohibition of direct discrimination contains no explicit justification clause.[271]

However, the reference in Article 2(2)(ii) on indirect discrimination to reasonable accommodation indicates that it could have been the perception of the drafters that non-fulfilment of the duty to provide reasonable accommodation would amount to indirect rather than direct discrimination. According to Article 2(2)(ii), indirect differential treatment may be justified by providing reasonable accommodation. This provision is explained in more detail below under *Sub-Section 4.3. Indirect Discrimination.* At least, there is a risk that such a link is created by courts and practitioners due to the existence of Article 2(2)(ii). If non-fulfilment of the duty to provide reasonable accommodation is perceived as indirect discrimination the prohibition of direct discrimination on the grounds of disability will only rarely be applicable. In order to avoid that the prohibition of direct discrimination be watered down as regards disability, it is important to acknowledge that non-fulfilment of the duty to provide reasonable accommodation may constitute direct discrimination. If for example an employer intentionally disregards a duty to provide reasonable

---

270 Judgment in C-13/05, para. 51.

271 For an interesting analysis of the development in the ECJ's use of direct and indirect discrimination see Tobler and Waaldijk 2009, p. 735. According to Tobler and Waaldijk the judgment of the ECJ in the *Maruko*-case indicates that the ECJ is moving from a formal to a more substantive interpretation of direct discrimination. ECJ judgment of 1 April 2008, C-267/06, *Tadao Maruko v. Versorgungsanstalt der deutschen Bühnen.*

accommodation then the case should be treated as a case of direct rather than indirect discrimination. I will discuss this issue in more detail under *Section 4.4. Reasonable Accommodation* where it is also discussed whether lack of fulfilment of the duty to provide reasonable accommodation is a *sui generis* form of discrimination on a par with direct and indirect discrimination.

The requirement that there be a direct casual link between the disadvantage in question and the discrimination ground raises a second disability-specific question, namely the question whether the prohibition of discrimination covers also persons who have been discriminated on the grounds of their association with a person with disability. The question of discrimination by association is especially relevant in relation to disability because of the fact that family members without disabilities will often have caring duties towards family members with disabilities. Fortunately, one of the two cases decided by the ECJ on disability discrimination concerns this question. In the *Coleman*-case, the European Court of Justice examined the requirement that there be a link between a suffered disadvantage and disability. The Court was asked whether the alleged direct discrimination and harassment of an employee on the grounds that this employee was the primary carer of a disabled child, but was not disabled herself, constituted a sufficient causal link to disability. The Court stated the following:

> *"[...]the prohibition of direct discrimination laid down by those provisions is not limited only to people who are themselves disabled. Where an employer treats an employee who is not himself disabled less favourably than another employee is, has been or would be treated in a comparable situation, and it is established that the less favourable treatment of that employee is based on the disability of his child, whose care is provided primarily by that employee, such treatment is contrary to the prohibition of direct discrimination"*[272]

Thus, the ECJ has interpreted the Employment Equality Directive to protect family member of persons with disabilities from direct discrimination and harassment. In doing so, the ECJ underlined that this protection *"applies not to a particular category of person but by reference to the grounds mentioned in Article 1"*.[273] The question is whether the ECJ will only find that the Employment Equality Directive provides protection against discrimination by association when the relationship between the victim and the disabled person is of a very close nature, such as that between Ms. Coleman and her son for whom she was the primary caretaker, or whether the ECJ will find that the Employment Equality Directive also provides protection against discrimination by association with the disability of others even when the relationship between the victim and the disabled person is not very

272 Judgment in C-303/06, paras. 56.

273 Judgment in C-303/06, para. 50.

close.[274] This last possibility is supported by the proposal for a Council Directive on implementing the principle of equal treatment between persons irrespective of religion or belief, disability, age or sexual orientation, which states that discrimination by association occurs *"inter alia, when a person is treated less favourably, or harassed, because, in the view of the discriminator, he or she is associated with persons of a particular religion or belief, disability, age or sexual orientation, for instance through his or her family, friendships, employment or occupation."*[275] In my opinion, discrimination by association with a disabled person, who is not *closely* related to the victim of the discrimination, will probably only happen rarely. However, if it were to happen, it would be in line with the contemporary disability human rights approach to provide effective protection against the discrimination. I discuss the *Coleman*-case further especially under *Section 4.1 Definition of Disability.*

Finally, I will turn to the seemingly lack of a justification clause in case of direct discrimination on the grounds of disability. I write 'seemingly' because, as argued above, the comparability-test implies a justification test, which may be especially difficult for persons with disabilities to pass. In addition, two explicit exemptions apply: the "*public order and security*" and *"the occupational requirement"* clauses, which are both discussed below.

Article 2(5) provides that the protection afforded by the Directive

> *"shall be without prejudice to measures laid down by national law which, in a democratic society, are necessary for public security, for the maintenance of public order and the prevention of criminal offences, for the protection of health and for the protection of the rights and freedoms of others".*

This open-ended provision may in principle justify both direct and indirect differential treatment. This provision, which borrows its wording from the European Convention on Human Rights, was only inserted in the Directive late in its negotiations and its intended purpose is not immediately apparent.[276] However, it seems that the prevalent view is that this exemption clause may be used to dilute the absolute prohibition of direct discrimination on the grounds of disability. According to *Ellis*, the purpose was to ensure that *inter alia* people with dangerous physical and mental illnesses did not gain protection from the Directive.[277] Another author,

274 Waddington 2009a, p 672.

275 Council Note from the Presidency, 15320/09, of 3 November 2009, Proposal for a Council Directive on implementing the principle of equal treatment between persons irrespective of religion or belief, disability, age or sexual orientation which revises Proposal for a Council Directive, COM(2008) 426 final, 2 July 2008, Preamble 12a and Article 2(3a).

276 Bell 2002, p. 116.

277 Ellis 2005, p. 291.

Whittle, is also concerned that the provision creates an area of ambiguity and room for exploitation to the disadvantage of disabled people.[278] *Whittle* points out that the risk is *inter alia* that the *"protection of health"* element could be misused to reintroduce prejudice and ignorance about the capabilities of persons with disabilities which the Directive aims at eliminating.[279]

This *"public order and safety"* clause is problematic because it brings into question the absolute prohibition of direct discrimination. It is however possible that the provision will merely serve to re-enforce the *"objective justification clause"* which applies in the case of indirect discrimination. If this provision only serves to specify legitimate aims which may justify indirect differential treatment, then there could still be a risk that a less strict proportionality-test would apply when the "public order and safety" clause comes into play. In sum, this clause seems entirely unnecessary and may indicate that the drafters of the Directive were not entirely willing to fully embrace the rights-based approach as regards disability.

The second explicit exception to the prohibition of direct discrimination is provided in Article 4 according to which occupational requirements may justify differential treatment. According to its wording:

> *"Member States may provide that a difference of treatment which is based on a characteristic related to any of the grounds referred to in Article 1 shall not constitute discrimination where, by reason of the nature of the particular occupational activities concerned or of the context in which they are carried out, such a characteristic constitutes a genuine and determining occupational requirement, provided that the objective is legitimate and the requirement is proportionate."*

Disability-related occupational requirements could for example be *"not having a disability*" as in the case of airline pilots who are required to have good eye sight, but could also be "*having a specific disability"* as in the case of an organisation for persons with a specific disabilities which wants representation of persons with the specific disability among their staff. The occupational requirements that exclude persons with disabilities may have been set in place for safety reasons, which renders it more difficult to question the need for these occupational requirements. However, in order to ensure that persons with disabilities enjoy effective protection against discrimination it is necessary that also health and safety requirements be legitimate and proportionate. For example, a requirement that employees in certain

278 Whittle 2002, p. 317. The European Commission: Proposal for a Council Directive establishing a general framework for equal treatment in employment and occupation, COM (1999) 565 final, 25 November 1999 and the recitals of the Directive do not provide guidance as to its meaning. See in particular ECHR Article 8–11.

279 Whittle 2002, p. 318.

positions cannot have diabetes may be disproportionate because diabetes can be well under control and not pose a safety-risk or because reasonable accommodation could be provided by redistributing the most high-risk working tasks.

In conclusion, the protection against direct discrimination is somewhat incomplete and indicates a certain reticence as regards the social model of disability and the rights-based approach to disability. Firstly, the prohibition of direct discrimination is somewhat diluted by the explicit link between the duty to provide reasonable accommodation and the prohibition of indirect discrimination. Secondly, although the *"public order and security"* exception does not mention disability specifically, it is seen as weakening the protection against both direct and indirect discrimination on the grounds of disability. Thirdly, there is a risk that the 'comparability' and the 'causal link' requirements and the 'occupational requirement' exception may be interpreted in such a manner that they weaken the protection against direct discrimination on the grounds of disability. The ECJ has not yet had the opportunity to make judgments on the interpretation of the comparability requirement and the occupational requirement exception. However, in the *Coleman*-case the ECJ interpreted the causal link between a less favourable treatment and disability and it held that as long as the treatment took place on the grounds of disability then the victim him or herself does not have to be disabled. In other words, direct discrimination on the grounds of association with disability is covered by Employment Equality Directive. I now turn to the prohibition of indirect discrimination, which also raises specific issues in relation to disability.

4.3. Indirect Discrimination

According to Article 2(2)(b):

> *"indirect discrimination shall be taken to occur where an apparently neutral provision, criterion or practice would put persons having a particular religion or belief, a particular disability, a particular age, or a particular sexual orientation at a particular disadvantage compared with other persons [...]".*

This provision raises the following specific questions in relation to disability which I will discuss in the present Sub-Section: who may be seen as having a particular disability, when would they be seen as being at a particular disadvantage and thirdly how may the differential treatment which has led to a disadvantage be justified.

The reference to a 'person having a particular disability' seems to indicate that persons who are not themselves disabled at the specific time in question may not be covered by this provision. Please see below under *Section 4.1 Definition of Disability* where I discuss this question.

In relation to when a particular disadvantage shall be established, Recital 12 of the Preamble of the Employment Equality Directive stresses that

> *"The appreciation of the facts from which it may be inferred that there has been direct or indirect discrimination is a matter for national judicial or other competent bodies, in accordance with rules of national law or practice. Such rules may provide, in particular, for indirect discrimination to be established by any means including on the basis of statistical evidence."*

The recitals are not legally binding in themselves, but provide guidance as to the interpretation of the Directive and the obligations inferred on the Member States.

The wording of Recital 12 is based on ECJ case law concerning freedom of movement of workers.[280] This Recital indicates that the Member States are relatively free to decide on what grounds it may be established that a certain group has been placed at a particular disadvantage. Since indirect discrimination results from seemingly neutral provisions, criteria or practice, it is particularly important that a broad array of means are available to show that one group is put at a particular disadvantage. Especially for persons with disabilities, it will be difficult to prove a particular disadvantage by means of for example statistics since the group of persons with disabilities is so heterogeneous. The group of persons with a particular disability in a work place may be difficult to define for statistical purposes, which underlines the importance of ensuring that national courts are open to the use of different means for establishing that a group is placed at a particular disadvantage. From the perspective of persons with disabilities, it would have been preferable if the Employment Equality Directive had not left this important issue up to the Member States.

However, the Employment Equality Directive does provide minimum standards in relation to the establishment of differential treatment. Firstly, it follows from the wording of Article 2(2)(b) that Member States must ensure that it is sufficient to show that a person has experienced a disadvantage in relation not only to a specific person, but also to a hypothetical person.[281] Thus, it may be sufficient to show that a person with disability has most likely experienced a disadvantage due to the disability in question. Secondly, the reference to *"a particular disability"* rather than just *"disability"* indicates that the person or group that one compares with may be a person or group with another disability and must not be a person or group without a disability.[282] As discussed above under *Sub-Section 4.2. Direct*

---

280 European Commission: Proposal for a Council Directive establishing a general framework for equal treatment in employment and occupation, COM (1999) 565 final, 25 November 1999, p. 8 which refers to ECJ judgment of 23 May 1996, Case C-237/94, O'Flynn v Adjudication Officer.

281 Waddington and Hendriks 2002, p. 421.

282 Schiek 2002, p. 296. Wells 2003, p. 270. Whittle 2002, p. 306.

Discrimination, the choice of comparator is crucial when seeking to establish that a relevant disadvantage has occurred.

Once it has been established that an apparently neutral provision, criterion or practice would put persons having a particular disability at a particular disadvantage, the Employment Equality Directive Article 2(2)(b) provides two alternative defences to alleged indirect discrimination: the *"objective justification clause"* and the *"reasonable accommodation justification"*. The objective justification clause has the following wording:

> *"(i) that provision, criterion or practice is objectively justified by a legitimate aim and the means of achieving that aim are appropriate and necessary,"*

The objective justification test has been closely modelled on the Burden of Proof Directive stressing the need for a relatively strict standard of proportionality which in turn was modelled on ECJ case law on equal treatment of men and women.[283] In the leading *Bilka*-case concerning the justification of "employer-made" policies in the area of equal pay for men and women, the ECJ employed a strict proportionality test requiring that the differentiation in question was necessary to achieve an objective corresponding to a real business need. In the *Bilka*-case, the Court stressed that the differential treatment had to be *"based on objectively justified factors unrelated to any discrimination on grounds of sex."*[284] Thus the term *"objective"* would seem to entail that the justification must be entirely free of subjective opinions regarding the protected grounds, which would only amount to a re-introduction of the very prejudice that the Directive is aiming to remove.[285] The Commission's explanatory memorandum attached to the original proposal for the Employment Framework Directive also supports a rigorous interpretation of the objective justification clause: *"the aim [...] must deserve protection and must be sufficiently substantial to justify it taking precedence over the principle of equal treatment [...] [and] the means employed to achieve that aim must be appropriate and necessary."*[286] The "*objective justification clause*" does not in itself raise specific disability-related problems, although it may naturally be applied in a manner, which is inconsistent with optimal protection against disability discrimination. Rather it is the second justification clause, Article 2(2)(ii), which raises specific disability concerns and which is formulated in the following manner:

283 Council Directive (EC) 97/80 of 14 December 1997 on the wording of the burden of proof in cases of discrimination based on sex, OJ [1998] L14/8 – now replaced by Council Directive (EC) 2006/54 of 5 July 2006 on the implementation of the principle of equal opportunities and equal treatment of men and women in matters of employment and occupation which has kept the same justification clause in relation to indirect discrimination.

284 ECJ judgment of 13 May 1986, case 170/84, *Bilk*. Schiek 2002, p. 297.

285 Whittle 2002, p. 308.

286 European Commission: Proposal for a Council Directive establishing a general framework for equal treatment in employment and occupation, COM (1999) 565 final, 25 November 1999, p. 8.

"(ii) as regards persons with a particular disability, the employer or any person or organisation to whom this Directive applies, is obliged, under national legislation, to take appropriate measures in line with the principles contained in Article 5 in order to eliminate disadvantages entailed by such provision, criterion or practice."

According to the second justification clause, the respondent may retain the disputed provision, criterion or practice that is causing an adverse effect on persons with a particular disability when the respondent is under a legal obligation to provide the complainant with reasonable accommodation under Article 5, and does so. According to Article 5, the provision of reasonable accommodation entails making the appropriate adjustments to the working environment or working tasks to guarantee compliance with the principle of equal treatment. Measures which would impose a disproportionate burden on the employer are not required. The limitations on the duty to provide reasonable accommodation are analysed below under *Section 4.4.4. Limitations on the Duty to Provide Reasonable Accommodation.*

The *"reasonable accommodation justification clause"* has on the one hand been criticized as removing any group benefits that would have been accrued if only the "objective justification clause" applied. *Waddington and Hendriks* have illustrated this with an example concerning an employee using a wheelchair who cannot access his workplace. If the employer merely has to fulfil the duty to provide reasonable accommodation to the individual employee using a wheelchair, it will suffice that he provides one ramp to the entrance that this employee would use. However, if all disadvantages experienced by the group of persons using wheelchairs had to be removed, it would be necessary that the employer provide ramps at all entrances.[287] Although the reasonable accommodation duty is necessary and positive in itself, the present construction with a *"reasonable accommodation justification clause"* in fact allows Member States to exempt general barriers from the prohibition of discrimination.

In sum, the protection against indirect discrimination on the grounds of disability prescribed by the Employment Equality Directive is seriously flawed due to the fact that a *"reasonable accommodation justification clause"* has been introduced. If transposed into national law, it means that the prohibition of indirect discrimination risks being reduced to a duty to provide reasonable accommodation and that more general structural barriers are left untouched.

4.4. Reasonable Accommodation

From a disability perspective, one of the potentially most important provisions of the Directive is Article 5 which recognises the special position of persons with

[287] Waddington and Hendriks 2002, p. 415.

disabilities and requires that reasonable accommodation be provided by employers. Article 5 has the following wording:

> *"In order to guarantee compliance with the principle of equal treatment in relation to persons with disabilities, reasonable accommodation shall be provided. This means that employers shall take appropriate measures, where needed in a particular case, to enable a person with a disability to have access to, participate in, or advance in employment, or to undergo training, unless such measures would impose a disproportionate burden on the employer. This burden shall not be disproportionate when it is sufficiently remedied by measures existing within the framework of the disability policy of the Member State concerned."*

Recitals 16, 17, 20 and 21 of the Employment Equality Directive give guidance on the kinds of measures that would amount to reasonable accommodation and to when a measure would be considered disproportionate:

> *"(16) The provision of measures to accommodate the needs of disabled people at the workplace plays an important role in combating discrimination on the grounds of disability.*
> *(17) This Directive does not require the recruitment, promotion, maintenance in employment or training of an individual who is not competent, capable and available to perform the essential functions of the post concerned or to undergo the relevant training, without prejudice to the obligation to provide reasonable accommodation for people with disabilities. [...]*
> *(20) Appropriate measures should be provided, i.e. effective and practical measures to adapt the workplace to the disability, for example adapting premises and equipment, patterns of working time, the distribution of tasks or the provision of training or integration resources.*
> *(21) To determine whether the measures in question give rise to a disproportionate burden, account should be taken in particular of the financial and other costs entailed, the scale and financial resources of the organisation or undertaking and the possibility of obtaining public funding or any other assistance."*

As follows from the wording of Article 5 of the Employment Equality Directive, reasonable accommodation is a duty to provide accommodation of working conditions broadly speaking to ensure that persons with disabilities may have equal opportunities in the labour market. Below, I will discuss how this duty relates to the more well-known legal duties not to discriminate and positive action. In addition, I will discuss the extent of the duty to provide reasonable accommodation under the Employment Equality Directive.

The relative complexity of the concept of reasonable accommodation coupled with the brevity of the Directive and the lack of specific case law means that a number of questions remained still unanswered. However I will in the next Sub-Sections focus on the four main questions relating to reasonable accommodation, namely a) what are appropriate measures, b) who is entitled to reasonable accommodation and in which situations, c) when may an employer justifiably refuse to make 'reasonable accommodation' and d) how does the duty to provide reasonable accommodation fit into the non-discrimination framework?

4.4.1. What are "Appropriate Measures"?

According to the second sentence of Article 5, the duty to provide reasonable accommodation *"means that employers shall take appropriate measures, where needed in a particular case, to enable a person with a disability to have access to, participate in, or advance in employment or to undergo training, unless such measures would impose a disproportionate burden on the employer".*

Firstly, it may be considered whether *"appropriate measures"* are merely what would be sufficient to enable a person with a disability to have some access to participation, advancement and training. However, the qualification of *"appropriate measures"* in the second sentence of Article 5 according to which they should be *"needed in a particular case to enable a person with a disability to have access to, participate in, or advance in employment, or undergo training"* should be read in conjunction with the first sentence of Article 5 and recital 20. The first sentence of Article 5 underlines that the reasonable accommodation shall be provided "*in order to guarantee compliance with the principle of equal treatment".* Recital 20 of the preamble explains that appropriate measures are *"effective and practical measures to adapt the workplace to the disability".* Thus, measures are appropriate if they are effectively conducive to access, participation, advancement and training *on an equal footing* with persons without a disability.[288]

Secondly, one may ask what type of measures may constitute "*appropriate measures*". According to the wording of Article 5, it would seem that *any* measures which can be taken by the employer to "enable a person with a disability to have access to, participate in, or advance in employment, or undergo training" could be such "appropriate measures". This would also seem to be the view reflected by Recital 20, which mentions many different types of measures: *"for example adapting premises and equipment, patterns of working time, the distribution of tasks or the provision of training or integration resources".* However, in light of the fact that Article 5 on reasonable accommodation imposes a duty on employers and others, it would have been desirable that the Directive had been more explicit about the fact that all types of adaptations which may be made, are potentially "*appropriate*" under Article 5.

---

288 Waddington 2004, p. 63.

Thirdly, the identification of which measures will be appropriate will have to take place on the basis of an individualised assessment based on the specific job and the needs of the person with a disability. In addition, since the employer knows best what the essential functions of the position entail and what measures are at his disposal and since the disabled person knows best what type of accommodation, he or she needs, this process should be inter-active and participatory in order to be effective.[289]

In sum, the determination of what constitutes "*appropriate measures*" is central for the effective functioning of the duty to provide reasonable accommodation. The preamble of the Directive seems to acknowledge that a broad array of measures may be appropriate, but the Employment Equality Directive is still relatively open regarding the question and leaves it up to the Member States to define the contents of "*appropriate measures*".

4.4.2. Who is Entitled to Reasonable Accommodation and in Which Situations?

It follows from the wording of Article 5 that "*a person with a disability*" may be entitled to reasonable accommodation. This wording is different from the one in Articles 1, 2(1)(a) and 2(3) and 2(4) prohibiting direct discrimination, harassment and instruction to discrimination "*on the grounds of*" disability. The requirement that the person have a disability would seem to exclude persons whose need for accommodation arises from association with a person with a disability, e.g. persons with children with disabilities who may need to take time off to take care of their children more often than other parents. Also persons with past or future disabilities are presumably excluded from accommodation. This seems also to be the interpretation in the *Coleman*-case mentioned in *Section 4.1. Definition of Disability* above.[290]

It is clear from recital 17 of the Directive that the duty to provide reasonable accommodation shall not be regarded as a tool to require the employment of persons who are "*not competent, capable and available to perform the essential functions of the post concerned*". This was also acknowledged by the ECJ in the *Chacón Navas*-case where the ECJ stated that the Employment equality Directive precludes "*dismissal on grounds of disability which, in the light of the obligation to provide reasonable accommodation for people with disabilities, is not justified by the fact that the person concerned is not competent, capable and available to perform the essential functions of his post.*"[291]

---

289 Quinn 2007, p. 265.

290 ECJ judgment, C-303/06, S. *Coleman v. Attridge Law and Steve Law*, Grand Chamber judgment of 17 July 2008.

291 Ibid, para. 51.

This differentiation between persons who would and would not be able to perform "*essential functions of a post*" leads to questions regarding the definition of this concept. How narrowly should these functions be determined and when could accommodation consist in tailoring the functions of a post?[292] *Gerard Quinn* argues that adjudicatory bodies and courts should review how an employer defines the essential functions of a job and that over-conflation of the essential functions to avoid having to employ a person with disabilities would amount to at least indirect discrimination, which I agree with.[293]

4.4.3. Limitations on the Duty to Accommodate

According to Article 5, employers shall take appropriate measures *"unless such measures would impose a disproportionate burden on the employer"*. In this regard, recital 21 of the preamble states:

> *"To determine whether the measures in question give rise to a disproportionate burden, account should be taken in particular of the financial and other costs entailed, the scale and financial resources of the organisation or undertaking and the possibility of obtaining public funding or any other assistance."*

In view of the fact that Article 5 is opened with the words *"In order to guarantee compliance with the principle of equal treatment"*, the reference to discrimination in Recital 16 and especially due to the fact that indirect differential treatment may be justified if the duty to provide reasonable accommodation has been fulfilled, cf. Article 2, then it is important that the proportionality assessment must be similar to the one made in relation to indirect discrimination.[294] It should be acknowledged that a rejection of the duty to provide accommodation amounts to a negation of the principle of equality, cf. *Section 4.3. Indirect Discrimination* above.[295]

The assessment of whether an appropriate measure imposes a disproportionate burden necessitates first a delimitation of what can be classified as a burden. Naturally, direct costs associated with enacting an appropriate measure must be taken into account. It is more difficult to say whether indirect costs entailed by e.g. organisational restructuring, which reduces efficiency and non-economic burdens such as inconvenience of other staff members can be taken into account. However,

---

292 Waddington 2004, p. 45.

293 Quinn 2007, p. 264.

294 In addition, the provision on reasonable accommodation was a part of Article 2 in the first Directive proposal and was moved to Article 5 for purely technical drafting reasons, see Quinn 2007, p. 258.

295 Gijzen 2006, p. 400. The strict proportionality was developed in ECJ, Case C-170/84, *Bilka-Kaufhaus v. Weber von Hartz*. It was used in relation to the Employment Equality Directive in the *Mangold*-case, ECJ, Case C-144/04, Grand Chamber judgment of 22 November 2005, *Werner Mangold v. Rüdiger Helm*.

the fact that Recital 21 speaks of "*financial and other costs*" would seem to indicate that both direct and indirect disadvantages may be taken into account.

Secondly, the possibility of obtaining public funding or other assistance to help finance the costs of the measures should be examined. However, there is nothing to indicate that a duty to provide reasonable accommodation depends on whether or not full compensation can be obtained. The existence of sufficient public funding is just one situation among many others when the burden on the employer shall not be considered disproportionate.

Finally, Recital 21 states that "*the scale and financial resources of the organisation or undertaking must be taken into account*". Thus, a public employer with many employees or a multi-national undertaking with vast economic resources will be obliged to provide more costly and far-reaching accommodation than a small undertaking with few economic resources.

The ECJ did not provide guidance on how to perform the proportionality-test under the provision on reasonable accommodation in the *Chacón Navas*-case. However, Advocate General *Geelhoed* states in his Opinion that "*What is reasonable is also determined by the cost of appropriate resources, the proportionality of those costs if they are not reimbursed by the authorities, the reduction of or compensation for the disability thus made possible and the accessibility of the disabled person concerned to other occupation or forms of business where his disability will be no obstacle or far less of an obstacle.*" This reasoning by the Advocate General was not repeated by the Court. Advocate General *Geelhoed* seems to find that a broad array of considerations may be taken into account including both economic costs, reimbursement by the authorities and effectiveness of the accommodating measures. In addition, *Geelhoed* mentions a) *"the compensation for the disability thus made possible"* and b) *"the accessibility of the disabled person to other occupation or forms of business"*.

The reference to *"the reduction of or compensation of the disability"* seems to be a reference to the effectiveness of the accommodation according to which a measure which results in a large improvement of the disabled person's working capacity will be more likely to be considered proportionate as opposed to a measure which is not as effective.[296] Although the Employment Equality Directive does not mention the effectiveness-test in relation to the assessment of whether the accommodation constitutes a disproportionate burden, it seems logical that a more effective accommodation will be more likely to be found proportionate than a less effective accommodation.

---

296 Waddington 2007a, p. 727.

It is more surprising that *Geelhoed* also attaches importance to *"the accessibility of the disabled person to other occupation or forms of business"*. This requirement would mean that a person who could obtain employment in another field of occupation with less accommodation could more easily be turned down than others. If this concern were taken into consideration, one would also have to consider how much weight to give to the wishes of the individual and the actual possibilities that the individual would have for obtaining the other jobs. In my opinion, the Employment Equality Directive does not provide any authority for adding this extra requirement for obtaining accommodation, which in my view could result in upholding segregation of the labour market in positions for persons with certain disabilities and other positions for persons without disabilities. For example, a consequence could be that blind persons may be expected to hold jobs as masseurs or telephone operators which would only require a minimum of accommodation.

In sum, the wording of the Employment Equality Directive provides that the burden on the employer of a specific accommodation shall take account of both direct and other costs and possible reimbursement from the authorities. The economic and other resources of the employer shall also be taken into account.

4.4.4. Reasonable Accommodation, Direct and Indirect Discrimination and Positive Action

The question of whether failure to provide reasonable accommodation amounts to a violation of either direct or indirect discrimination or is in fact a *sui generis* form of discrimination is not answered by the text of the Employment Equality Directive. Article 5 on reasonable accommodation does state that reasonable accommodation must be provided *"in order to garantee compliance with the principle of equal treatment"* and in Article 2(1), *"the principle of equal treatment"* is defined as meaning *"that there shall be no direct or indirect discrimination"*. However the definition in Article 2(1) of equal treatment, which mentions only direct and indirect discrimination, cannot be read as excluding that other types of discrimination may also be recognised under the Employment Equality Directive since Article 2(3) provides that *"harassment shall be deemed a form of discrimination within the meaning of paragraph 1"*.[297]

The question remains however whether it would be possible under the Employment Equality Directive to argue that non-fulfilment of the duty to provide reasonable accommodation amounts to direct or indirect discrimination.

---

[297] Employment Equality Directive Article 2(3).

The first requirement under the provision on direct discrimination is that differential treatment has taken place on the basis of a forbidden ground.[298] In a situation where an employer rejects an application for a position because the applicant who is a wheelchair user would not be able to enter the premises of the employer's undertaking, one could either say that the decision is based on a neutral criterion, namely lack of accessibility. Or one could say that the employer rejected the application on the grounds of the employee's disability.

In cases of lack of adjustments for pregnancy, the ECJ has found that direct discrimination on the grounds of gender had been committed, but there are significant differences between pregnancy and disability.[299] The most important difference is that financial loss cannot justify differential treatment of pregnant women under the case law of the ECJ. This entails that there is no assessment of whether or not a certain type of adjustment of working conditions is reasonable or not. Even if the pregnant woman cannot work, she may not suffer any disadvantage. This is very different from the duty to provide accommodation for disability. This duty will not apply where it would entail unreasonable financial loss for the employer. The reason for this absolute duty to provide adjustments for pregnancy may be that pregnancy is per definition a time limited condition whereas disability will often be long-term. In addition, the principle of equal treatment of women and men on the labour market has a significantly longer history than that of equal treatment of persons with and without disability. This entails a greater awareness of the duties of employers towards women than towards persons with disability. In other words, since differential treatment of pregnant women, for example by refusing to make necessary adjustments of working conditions, cannot be justified with reference to financial loss, then it is unproblematic to equate it with direct discrimination. This is not the case as regards disability.

In addition, the Employment Equality Directive defines direct discrimination as less favourable treatment of two persons in a *comparable* situation. The question is whether one can say that a person who needs reasonable accommodation is in a comparable situation with others. One could argue that the whole point of reasonable accommodation is to place persons with disabilities in a comparable situation with others and thus that it is impossible to view persons with disabilities in a comparable situation before accommodation has taken place. However, one could also argue

298 Waddington 2007a, p. 741. Waddington and Hendriks 2002, p. 423.

299 Waddington and Hendriks 2002, p. 423; ECJ judgment of 8 November 1990, C-177/88, Elisabeth Johanna Pacifica Dekker v. Stichting Vormingscentrum voor Jong Volwassenen (VJV-Centrum) where the ECJ stated: "it should be observed that only women can be refused employment on grounds of pregnancy and such a refusal therefore constitutes direct discrimination on grounds of sex. A refusal of employment on account of the financial consequences of absence due to pregnancy must be regarded as based, essentially, on the fact of pregnancy. Such discrimination cannot be justified on grounds relating to the financial loss which an employer who appointed a pregnant woman would suffer for the duration of her maternity leave."

that persons with disabilities are comparable with others as long as they are competent, capable and available to perform the essential functions of a post provided that they are accommodated reasonably. In my opinion, both options are possible under the Directive.

However, as mentioned above under *Sub-Section 4.2. Direct Discrimination*, the real problem with equating non-fulfilment of the duty to provide reasonable accommodation with the prohibition of direct discrimination is in my opinion that direct discrimination does not – in principle at least – allow for a proportionality assessment. There is therefore a risk that an automatic link between the duty to provide reasonable accommodation and the prohibition of direct discrimination could lead to a more narrow interpretation of the duty to provide reasonable accommodation so that accommodation were only required in situations where it was self-evident and clear that accommodation would be proportionate and reasonable. Only in such cases, could one equate non-fulfilment of the duty to provide reasonable accommodation for disability with direct discrimination on the grounds of disability. However, equating non-fulfilment of the duty to provide reasonable accommodation with a violation of the prohibition of direct discrimination may also send a strong signal about the importance of the duty to provide reasonable accommodation, cf. *Chapter IV Equality Law and Policy* where it is described how Swedish law links reasonable accommodation with direct discrimination.

The fact that it may be problematic to equate a violation of the duty to provide reasonable accommodation with direct discrimination does not preclude that a violation of the duty to provide reasonable accommodation will not amount to direct discrimination in some cases. If for example, an employer categorically refuses to provide reasonable accommodation to persons with disabilities, then the employer may be guilty of direct discrimination on the grounds of disability.

The next question is whether non-fulfilment of the duty to provide reasonable accommodation could be perceived as indirect discrimination. The main problem in relation to subsuming lack of fulfilment of the duty to provide reasonable accommodation is that the provision on indirect discrimination is essentially oriented towards protecting the group of persons with disabilities or a specific disability whereas the duty to provide reasonable accommodation is very much an individual right. This means that not only would a person have to show that he or she needed accommodation in a specific situation "*to enable*" him or her "*to have access to participate in, or advance in employment*", but he or she would also have to show that lack of accommodation could be seen as an apparently neutral practice which would put persons with his or her particular disability at a particular disadvantage compared with other persons. In addition, it might also mean that the justification-clause for indirect discrimination, namely that "*the provision, criterion or practice is objectively justified by a legitimate aim and the means of achieving that aim are appropriate and necessary",* could be used as an additional means of justifying that accommodation is not made.[300]

In sum, although the Employment Equality Directive is not explicit about the issue, it seems that the least problematic solution is to view the non-fulfilment of the duty to provide reasonable accommodation as the violation of a *sui generis* form of discrimination and not as a violation of either direct or indirect discrimination. As will be seen in *Chapter IV Non-Discrimination*, Sweden has chosen to treat non-fulfilment as direct discrimination. Denmark seems to be treating the duty to provide reasonable accommodation as a *sui generis* form of non-discrimination.

Finally, it has in literature been discussed whether it would be more correct to view the duty to provide reasonable accommodation as a type of positive action rather than a duty necessary to prevent discrimination.[301] However, the Employment Equality Directive clearly does not view reasonable accommodation as a form of positive action. Firstly, reasonable accommodation is a legal duty under the Employment Equality Directive whereas there is no legal duty to enact positive action. Secondly, while reasonable accommodation aims at ensuring equality for an individual in a specific situation, positive action aims at improving opportunities for the disadvantaged group in general. Thirdly, while reasonable accommodation is not limited in time, positive action must be brought to an end once equality has been achieved.[302]

4.4.5. Conclusion on Reasonable Accommodation

Reasonable accommodation is of pivotal importance for the realisation of non-discrimination in relation to persons with disabilities. The fact that a duty to provide reasonable accommodation has been included in the Directive indicates that the Directive is founded on substantive difference equality according to which some relevant differences require different treatment. The Directive provides some guidance as to how this duty must be implemented by Member States, but the lack of ECJ case law on reasonable accommodation means that central issues such as the delimitation of which measures would be appropriate and the proportionality-test are as-of-yet left quite open.

---

300 Waddington 2007a, p. 743.

301 For an extensive description of the discussion of the relationship between reasonable accommodation and positive action see Waddington 2007a, p. 748.

302 Gijzen 2009. p. 397. Gijzen also mentions a fourth characteristic, which is that reasonable accommodation requires adaptation of the working environment.

4.5. Harassment and Instruction to Discriminate

The Employment Equality Directive prohibits two other forms of discrimination, namely harassment and instruction to discrimination. According to Article 2(3) of the Employment Equality Directive,

> *"harassment shall be deemed to be a form of discrimination within the meaning of paragraph 1, when unwanted conduct related to any of the grounds referred to in Article 1 takes place with the purpose or effect of violating the dignity of a person and of creating an intimidating, hostile, degrading, humiliating or offensive environment. In this context, the concept of harassment may be defined in accordance with the national laws and practice of the Member States."*

As persons with disabilities have a history of being subjected to demeaning language and treatment, protection against harassment is highly relevant to persons with disabilities. Demeaning language about persons with disabilities is so common that it has become part of the ordinary use of the language. For example, the expression "are you blind?" equates being blind with being stupid or not being able to grasp obvious things. Other examples are the use of words such as *"retarded"* and "*paranoid*" which commonly describe persons without impairments whose behaviour is simply annoying. This common use of impairments as negative words makes it easy to see how persons with such impairments can become the subject of demeaning language and behaviour. The ECJ has decided one case regarding harassment of persons with disabilities, namely the *Coleman*-case.[303] In this case, the ECJ confirmed that the Employment Equality Directive prohibits direct discrimination and harassment by association on the grounds of disability.

According to Article 2(4) of the Employment Equality Directive, *"An instruction to discriminate against persons on any of the grounds referred to in Article 1 shall be deemed to be discrimination within the meaning of paragraph 1."* In my opinion, this does not raise any specific disability-related issues.

4.6. Scope of Application

Article 3(1) defines the scope of application of the Employment Equality Directive as applying

> *"to all persons, as regards both the public and private sectors, including public bodies, in relation to:*
> *(a) conditions for access to employment, to self-employment or to occupation, including selection criteria and recruitment conditions, whatever the branch of activity and at all levels of the professional hierarchy, including promotion;*

303 ECJ judgment (Grand Chamber) of 17 July 2008, C-303/06, S. *Coleman v. Attridge Law and Steve Law.*

(b) access to all types and to all levels of vocational guidance, vocational training, advanced vocational training and retraining, including practical work experience;
(c) employment and working conditions, including dismissals and pay;
(d) membership of, and involvement in, an organisation of workers or employers, or any organisation whose members carry on a particular profession, including the benefits provided for by such organisations."

The scope of application of the Directive is the field of employment broadly defined, cf. litra a and c. It is more problematic exactly where the line should be drawn in regard to the field of vocational education, cf. litra b. The use of the terms *"vocational guidance, vocational training, advanced vocational training and retraining"* and the fact that "*education*" is listed in the Racial Equality Directive, but not the Employment Equality Directive, would seem to indicate that university education is not encompassed.[304] However in the *Vincent Blaizot*-case, University education was included within the definition of vocational training in Article 128 TEC (now Article 148 TFEU). According to the Court *"the only exception would be certain courses of study which, because of their particular nature, are intended for persons wishing to improve their general knowledge rather than prepare themselves for an occupation".*[305] Neither the Commission's Explanatory Memorandum to the Directive proposal nor the recitals of the Directive provide guidance in regard to the application of the Directive on university education.[306]

This relatively broad scope of application is however reduced with three exemptions, all of which have special relevance to persons with disabilities and are described below.

According to Article 3(2), *"the Directive does not cover differences in treatment based on nationality and is without prejudice to provisions and conditions relating to the entry into and residence of third-country nationals and stateless persons in the territory of Member States".* This caveat aims at ensuring that the Employment Equality Directive does not affect for example rules on the obtaining of work permits for third-country nationals in a Member State. However the conditions for obtaining work permits may well be indirectly discriminatory towards persons with disabilities who have reduced working capacity. For example, a full-time job could well be a condition for obtaining a work and residence permit. If such a requirement

304 Council Directive (EC) 2000/43 of 29 June 2000 implementing the principle of equal treatment between persons irrespective of racial or ethnic origin, OJ L 180/22, 19 July 2000, Article 3(1)(g).

305 ECJ judgment of 2 February 1988, Case 24/86, Vincent Blaizot v. University of Liège and others, para. 20.

306 European Commission: Proposal for a Council Directive establishing a general framework for equal treatment in employment and occupation, COM (1999) 565 final, 25 November 1999, p. 10.

is interpreted without consideration for reduced working capacity then it could result in indirect discrimination of persons with disabilities who may not be able to work full-time.

According to Article 3(3), the Employment Equality Directive does not apply to payments of any kinds made by state schemes, *"including state social security or social protection schemes"*.[307] Again this exemption is of high relevance, especially, to persons with disabilities, who have a high level of dependency on payments by state schemes in the form of both subsidies when in employment, and social security when not in employment. Especially the access to wage subsidies and other compensation schemes for persons who seek employment or are in employment, are of direct importance for access to employment. An example of a possible form of discrimination is the reservation of wage subsidies to persons with physical rather than intellectual disabilities. It is therefore highly unfortunate that the Employment Equality Directive allows Member States to exempt this area from the scope of application of the prohibition of discrimination. This is in line with the current approach of EU law and policy in the area of social security in general, where the Member States have held onto their sovereignty and rejected EU interference, cf. below *Section 7. Income Replacement-Benefits.*

Finally, Article 3(4) of the Employment Equality Directive contains a provision dealing specifically with age and disability according to which Member States may provide that the *"Directive, insofar as it relates to discrimination on the grounds of disability and age, shall not apply to the armed forces"*.[308] This provision allows Member States to exempt the armed forces from the prohibition of discrimination on the grounds of disability. This provision is in my view problematic from a human rights perspective since it undermines the human right not to be discriminated on the grounds of disability, which also applies in the armed forces. A consequence of this clash with the disability human rights approach is that the European Union was compelled to make a reservation to the CRPD with regard to the question of the application of the prohibition of discrimination to the armed forces.[309]

As stated in Recital 4 and confirmed by the ECJ in the *Mangold*-judgment, the Directive is not the source of the prohibition of discrimination, it simply provides a framework for its implementation. The fact is that the armed forces' exemption is not necessary since not having a disability would qualify as a genuine and determining occupational requirement in relation to most positions in the armed forces and differentiation on the grounds of disability would thus be permitted

307 Article 3(3).

308 Article 3(4).

309 Council Decision 2010/48 of 26 November 2009 concerning the conclusion, by the European Community, of the United Nations Convention on the Rights of Persons with Disabilities, [2010] L23/35, Article 2(2) and Annex III.

under Article 4 of the Employment Equality Directive. The recent judgment by the European Court of Human Rights in the *Glor*-case deals with the question of a penalty tax for persons who had not performed their compulsory military service. Although the European Court of Human Rights did acknowledge a broad margin of appreciation for Member States in organising their military service, it did recommend that Member States should ensure that Persons with Disabilities could carry out *"special types of military service [...] at the heart of the armed forces [which would] require lesser physical efforts"* or alternatively be permitted to carry out civil service.[310] Although the *Glor*-case concerned only compulsory military service and allowed to some extent, the segregation of persons with disabilities in civil service, it is my opinion that this case at least encourages States Parties to the ECHR, to protect persons with disabilities from discrimination also in the armed forces. The *Glor*-case is described in more detail in *Chapter II Human Rights.*

In conclusion, the scope of application of the Employment Equality Directive is on the one hand relatively broad in that it includes all types of employment and many types of further education, as these largely serve to prepare students for employment. On the other hand, three caveats make it possible for the Member States to reduce the scope of application in areas of importance for the employment opportunities of persons with disabilities: that the Directive does not cover conditions for entry into the territory of the Member States of third-country nationals, that it does not cover payments under State schemes and that Member States may exempt the armed forces from the area of application of the implementation legislation. The disability human rights approach is founded on the rights-based approach to disability and the prohibition of discrimination on the grounds of disability. The limitations to the scope of application thus prevent the Employment Equality Directive from living up to the disability human rights approach.

4.7. Burden of Proof

According to Article 10(1) of the Employment Equality Directive:

> *"Member States shall take such measures as are necessary, in accordance with their national judicial systems, to ensure that, when persons who consider themselves wronged because the principle of equal treatment has not been applied to them establish, before a court or other competent authority, facts from which it may be presumed that there has been direct or indirect discrimination, it shall be for the respondent to prove that there has been no breach of the principle of equal treatment."*

---

310 European Court of Human Rights, *Glor v. Switzerland,* Application no. 13444/04, judgment of 30 April 2009, para. 94–95.

Thus it follows from Article 10 that at least in cases regarding direct or indirect discrimination, the burden of proof will be shared between the plaintiff and the respondent. The question is whether the shared burden of proof also applies to cases of harassment, instruction to discriminate and failure to fulfil the duty to provide reasonable accommodation.

Both harassment and instruction to discriminate are deemed "*to be a form of discrimination within the meaning of paragraph 1*" according to which "the principle of equal treatment shall mean that there shall be no direct or indirect discrimination". Thus it would seem that once the plaintiff has established facts, from which it may be presumed that there has been harassment or instruction to discriminate, the respondent will have to prove that there has been no breach of the principle of equal treatment. Also in the context of the EU's own Staff Regulations, the Court of First Instance has partially reversed the burden of proof in cases concerning harassment.[311] In sum, the shared burden of proof should be applied in relation to harassment.

Article 5 on reasonable accommodation does not specify that failure to fulfil the duty to provide reasonable accommodation should be deemed to be a form of discrimination. However, Article 5 does state that reasonable accommodation shall be provided "in order to guarantee compliance with the principle of equal treatment" which according to Article 2(1) *"shall mean that there shall be no direct or indirect discrimination."* In addition Article 2(b)(ii) of the Employment Equality Directive states that indirect discrimination does not occur where the employer is obliged to provide reasonable accommodation under Article 5. On these grounds, it seems that the shared burden of proof should also apply to reasonable accommodation.

Presumably, however, victimisation under Article 11 does not qualify as a type of discrimination and the shared burden of proof will not apply.

4.8. Positive Action

Article 7 on positive action allows Member States to maintain and adopt positive action measures for the benefit of all protected groups under the Directive in Section (1), including disability, and a specific-disability related provision in Section (2):

> *"1. With a view to ensuring full equality in practice, the principle of equal treatment shall not prevent any Member State from maintaining or adopting specific measures*

311 Case T-242/97, Z v. European Parliament [1999] E.C.R. IA-77; II-401, paras. 104 and 107. Driessen-Reilly and Driessen 2003, p. 500 who agree that reversal of burden of proof applies in cases of harassment.

to prevent or compensate for disadvantages linked to any of the grounds referred to in Article 1.
2. With regard to disabled persons, the principle of equal treatment shall be without prejudice to the right of Member States to maintain or adopt provisions on the protection of health and safety at work or to measures aimed at creating or maintaining provisions or facilities for safeguarding or promoting their integration into the working environment."

Recital 26 provides information on the interpretation of this Article and states the following:

"The prohibition of discrimination should be without prejudice to the maintenance or adoption of measures intended to prevent or compensate for disadvantages suffered by a group of persons of a particular religion or belief, disability, age or sexual orientation, and such measures may permit organisations of persons of a particular religion or belief, disability, age or sexual orientation where their main object is the promotion of the special needs of those persons."

As mentioned above under the introductory part of *Section 4. Employment Equality Directive*, the Employment Equality Directive makes a distinction between the "*principle of equality*", on which the prohibition of discrimination and the duty to provide reasonable accommodation are based, and "*full equality in practice*" which can be achieved through positive action. Since the Directive does not impose a duty to provide positive action, but recognises the legitimate need for such actions, it would seem that the Directive is based on substantive difference equality rather than substantive diversity equality. If it were based on formal equality, it would not permit positive action.

Below, I will firstly discuss the general provision permitting positive action and the limitations to positive action as they have been defined in the case law of the ECJ. Secondly, I will analyse Section 7(2) on specific disability-related positive action. However, I will initially make a few remarks regarding the definition of positive action.

4.8.1. Definition of Positive Action

The definition of positive action may differ under different legal systems. However, for the purpose of this thesis, positive action will be defined as measures a) that are taken consciously and actively, b) that aim at achieving substantive equality, c) that target a certain discriminated group.[312]

[312] See the definition in the Employment Equality Directive above and the definition of UN Special Rapporteur Bossuyt in his final report on "the concept of affirmative action", UN doc E/CN.4/Sub.2/2002/21, 17 June 2002, para. 6.

Opinions differ regarding the degree to which positive action should lead to preferential treatment of the group in question. In order to analyse differences in this regard, *Olivier De Schutter* has proposed a categorisation of positive action measures into six types of measures in the employment field: a) "*Monitoring the composition of the workforce [...]*", b) *"Redefining the standard criterion on the basis of which employment or promotion is allocated (in general merit)",* c) *"Outreach measures, consisting in general measures targeting underrepresented groups, such as the provision of training [...]",* d) *"Outreach measures, consisting in individual measures such as the guarantee to members of underrepresented groups that they will be interviewed if they possess the relevant qualifications"*, e) *"Preferential treatment of equally qualified members of the underrepresented group, with or without exemption clause (also referred to as 'flexible quotas')"* and f) *"Strict quotas"*.[313] Whereas the first three types of measures a) to c) do not imply preferential treatment, the last three d) to f) do imply preferential treatment. The most far-reaching type of positive action is *"strict quotas"*, which imply that persons with a certain characteristic must be treated preferentially, irrespective of whether they are as qualified as other applicants. In other words, having a certain characteristic such as a disability gives an automatic right to preferential treatment under a system of *"strict quotas"*. *"Flexible quotas"* also give persons with a certain characteristic a right to preferential treatment, but only provided they are at least as qualified as other applicants. In other words, this preferential treatment is flexible because persons with the characteristic in question, for example disability, are not treated preferentially only on the basis of the characteristic (disability), but on the basis of characteristic *and* qualifications. In the Sections below, I seek to determine which of the six types of measures above are permitted under EU law.

4.8.2. ECJ Case Law on Positive Action

To date, ECJ case law on the limits of positive action has only dealt with sex and not yet with other grounds such as disability. Especially in light of Article 7(2) on disability-related positive action and the wide-spread use of positive action to promote employment of persons, it is possible that the ECJ will be more permissible in relation to disability than to other grounds. With this caveat in mind, I will now briefly describe the case law of the ECJ on positive action on the grounds of sex.

Interesting developments have taken place since the Amsterdam Treaty of 1997 both as regards hard law and in relation to ECJ case law.[314] Firstly, the TEC was amended to ensure that Member States be permitted to maintain or adopt positive action in the form of *"measures providing for specific advantages in order to make*

313 Waddington 2007a, p. 762.

314 See on positive treatment under EC law for example Gijzen 2006, p. 227, O'Cinneide 2006, p. 351. Barnard 2006, p. 417–431.

it easier for the underrepresented sex to pursue a vocational activity or to prevent or compensate for disadvantages in professional careers."[315] The wording "*specific advantages*" seems to indicate that also measures which imply preferential treatment will be permitted, but it is unclear whether also flexible and strict quotas would be permitted. Secondly, the case law of the ECJ has undergone a significant development since the Amsterdam Treaty.

As mentioned above, the case law of the Court concerns equal treatment of women and men and it predates the Recast Directive on Equal Treatment of men and women from 2006.[316] It therefore concerns the interpretation of Article 2(4) of the Equal Treatment Directive.[317] This case law is relevant since it sheds light on how the concept of positive action common to the different equality directives is interpreted by the ECJ.

In 1995, the ECJ handed down its first judgment regarding positive action in the renowned *Kalanke*-case, in which the Court found that a national rule, which gave *"absolute and unconditional priority"* for employment to women who were equally qualified with men in sectors where women were underrepresented, constituted discrimination of men in violation of EU law.[318] In a case from 1997, the *Marshall*-case, the Court found that a rule, which provided that priority for employment should be given to women who were equally qualified with men in sectors where women were underrepresented "unless reasons specific to an individual candidate tilt the balance in his favour", was in accordance with EU law.[319] Thus, it follows from this case law that type e) measures such as flexible quotas would be acceptable because they do not give automatic access to employment to persons from an underrepresented group.[320] However, type f) measures, namely strict quotas, would not be permitted.

This development has been cemented after the adoption of the Amsterdam Treaty, which established that outreach measures consisting in individual measures such as

315 Article 157 TFEU, Article 141 EC after the Amsterdam Treaty, Article 119 EC before the Amsterdam Treaty.

316 European Parliament and Council Directive (EC) 2000/54 of 5 July 2006 on the implementation of the principle of equal opportunities and equal treatment of men and women in matters of employment and occupation (recast), OJ[2006] L204/23.

317 Council Directive (EC) 1976/207 of 9 February 1976 on the implementation of the principle of equal treatment for men and women as regards access to employment, vocational training and promotion, and working conditions, OJ [1976] L39/40.

318 ECJ judgment of 17 October 1995, case C-450/93, *Kalanke v. Freie Hansestadt Bremen*, para. 22.

319 A Swedish rule giving automatic preference to women in competition for University chairs was found in violation of Community law was found in violation of Community law in ECJ case C-407/98, judgment of 6 July 2000, *Abrahammson and Anderson v. Fogelqvist.*

320 ECJ judgment of 11 November 1997, case C-409/95, *Marshall v. Land Nordrhein-Westfalen.*

the guarantee of job interviews (type d measures), would be acceptable too. Thus, in the *Badeck*-case, guaranties in relation to training places and job interviews were permitted.[321] Also in the *Lommers*-case, the ECJ permitted subsidised nursery facilities, which were reserved for children of female civil servants, but which could be made available to male civil servants who were single parents.[322]

The above shows that there has been a development from permitting only measures, which did not imply preferential treatment, to permitting certain types of measures implying preferential treatment. The position of the ECJ on positive action is important for determining the concept of equality that it adheres to. Presumably, the ECJ will strive towards using a similar concept of equality when interpreting the different equality directives. Article 7(2) of the Employment Equality Directive deals specifically with disability-related positive action and I examine below whether it reflects the recent development in the case law of the ECJ towards more acceptance of positive action.

4.8.3. Disability-Related Positive Action

Article 7(2) of the Employment Equality Directive deals specifically with disability and therefore deserves special consideration. It has the following wording:

> *"With regard to disabled persons, the principle of equal treatment shall be without prejudice to the right of Member States to maintain or adopt provisions on the protection of health and safety at work or to measures aimed at creating or maintaining provisions or facilities for safeguarding or promoting their integration into the working environment."*

Recital 27 gives the following guidance:

> *"In its Recommendation 86/379/EEC of 24 July 1986 on the employment of disabled people in the EU, the Council established a guideline framework setting out examples of positive action to promote the employment and training of disabled people, and in its Resolution of 17 June 1999 on equal employment opportunities for people with disabilities, affirmed the importance of giving specific attention inter alia to recruitment, retention, training and lifelong learning with regard to disabled persons."*

321 ECJ judgment of 28 March 2000, case C-158/97, *Badeck v. Hessischer Ministerprasident.*

322 ECJ judgment of 19 March 2002, case C-476/99, *Lommers v. Minister van Landbouw, Natuurbeheer en Visserij.* The ECJ also permitted preferential treatment of persons who had completed their military service in its judgment of 7 December 2000C-79/99, *Schnorbus.* However, it did not permit a service credit provided to female, but not to male civil servants in respect of each of their children for the purpose of calculating pension because it did not offset the disadvantages of women during their professional life, ECJ judgment of 8 March 2001, Case C-266/99, *Griesmar v. Ministre de l"Economie, des Finances et de l"Industrie.*

This provision was introduced into the Employment Equality Directive late in the drafting process. It was not contained in either the first proposal or the amended proposal for the Directive.[323] Thus, the Explanatory Memorandums do not provide guidance as to how this provision should be understood. It seems that this provision was added during Council negotiations.[324]

Quite out of place in Article 7 on positive action, it seems that the first part of Article 7(2) underlines that Member States may restrict opportunities of disabled persons on the grounds of health and safety.[325] If this is the correct understanding of this provision then it may be seen as in line with the problematic Article 2(5) which provides that the Directive shall be without prejudice to measures laid down by law and necessary for the protection of health in a democratic society, cf. above under *Section 4.2. Direct Discrimination.* According to *Gerard Quinn*, however, Article 7(2) was added in a positive spirit in order to underline that the Employment Equality Directive "does not contemplate health and safety law and policy as an obstacle to the achievement of a non-discriminatory and integrated work environment. Rather, it sees the non-discrimination principle as being complemented by health and safety law and especially by the latter's focus on adapting the workplace to suit the employee."[326] If this was the intention of the drafters, it is regretful that the provision was not formulated in clearer language.

The second part of Article 7(2) is less surprising in that it seems to permit the enactment of positive action in relation to persons with disabilities. Presumably this provision entails a greater leeway for Member States as regards positive action for the benefit of persons with disabilities than other groups. Thus, this provision seems to ensure that the widespread use of strict quotas (type f) measures), which do not necessarily comply with the principle of merit, may be in compliance with EU law. This assumption is also likely in view of the fact that Recital 27 refers to "*Council Recommendation on the employment of disabled persons in the Community*" which recommends the use of "*percentage targets*" for the promotion of employment of persons with disabilities.[327] The Employment Equality Directive hereby sets persons with disabilities in a special category as compared to other discriminated groups. In view of the development under human rights law, which increasingly recommends that such practices be rejected, and the broader margins for positive action under non-disability-specific case law of the ECJ, this provision is

323 Commission Proposal for a Council Directive establishing a general framework for equal treatment in employment and occupation, COM (1999) 565 final of 25 November 1999 and COM (2000) 652 final of 12 October 2000.

324 Quinn 2007, p. 272.

325 Barnard 2006, p. 430.

326 Quinn 2007, p. 272.

327 Council Recommendation (EEC) 89/379 of 24 July 1986 on the employment of disabled persons in the community, OJ [1986] L225/43, Article 2(b)(i).

unfortunate. The consequence of this provision may be that unnecessary segregation of the labour market will be upheld for longer time in relation to persons with disabilities that would otherwise be the case.

4.9. Remedies and Sanctions and Victimisation

Effective functioning of the Directive is dependent on an effective system of remedies, and sanctions, and protection against victimisation. Especially as regards persons with disabilities who are at risk of suffering indirect discrimination in the ordinary legal system, it is of crucial importance that effective complaints systems be available. Persons with disabilities may suffer indirect discrimination in the ordinary legal system, as they could be disadvantaged due to low incomes, low levels of education, lack of accessibility, lack of awareness of the needs of persons with disabilities and negative prejudice towards persons with disabilities.[328] It would seem that specialised equality bodies would be more likely to provide equal access to adjudication than ordinary courts since the specialised equality bodies would be set up with the aim of promoting equal rights for *inter alia* persons with disabilities.

As opposed to the Racial Equality Directive, the Employment Equality Directive does not require the establishment of a body for the promotion of equal treatment.[329] As pointed out by *Mark Bell,* this difference between the protection offered by the two Directives seems difficult to justify.[330] The Employment Equality Directive Article 9 (1) and (2) simply require that:

> *"Member States shall ensure that judicial and/or administrative procedures, including where they deem it appropriate conciliation procedures, for the enforcement of obligations under this Directive are available to all persons who consider themselves wronged by failure to apply the principle of equal treatment to them, even after the relationship in which the discrimination is alleged to have occurred has ended.*
> *Member States shall ensure that associations, organisations or other legal entities which have, in accordance with the criteria laid down by their national law, a legitimate interest in ensuring that the provisions of this Directive are complied with, may engage, either on behalf or in support of the complainant, with his or her approval, in any judicial and/or administrative procedure provided for the enforcement of obligations under this Directive."*

328 Clements and Read 2005, p. 23.

329 Council Directive (EC) 2000/43 of 29 June 2000 implementing the principle of equal treatment between persons irrespective of racial or ethnic origin, OJ [2000] L 180/22, Chapter III.

330 Bell 2002, p. 114.

As regards sanctions, Article 17 provides that:

> *"Member States shall lay down the rules on sanctions applicable to infringements of the national provisions adopted pursuant to this Directive and shall take all measures necessary to ensure that they are applied. The sanctions, which may comprise the payment of compensation to the victim, must be effective, proportionate and dissuasive."*

Recital 35 underlines that:

> *"Member States should provide for effective, proportionate and dissuasive sanctions in case of breaches of the obligations under this Directive."*

The ECJ has set out standards for the rules on sanctions in national law. As early as in 1984, the ECJ held that a compensation limited to a reimbursement of costs such as travelling expenses incurred did not satisfy the requirements in Article 6 of Directive 76/207 on the implementation of the principle of equal treatment for men and women as regards access to employment.[331] Similarly, the ECJ has held that the imposition of an upper limit on the amount of compensation received and the exclusion of an award of interest breached Article 6 of Directive 76/207.[332] A statutory presumption that the award should not exceed a ceiling of three months pay was however permitted when the employer could prove that the plaintiffs would not have been employed even if they had not been subject to discrimination.[333]

In addition, the obligation to provide an effective remedy includes protection against victimisation. Article 11 obligates Member States to:

> *"introduce into their national legal systems such measures as are necessary to protect employees against dismissal or other adverse treatment by the employer as a reaction to a complaint within the undertaking or to any legal proceedings aimed at enforcing compliance with the principle of equal treatment."*

As mentioned above under *Sub-Section 4.7. Burden of Proof*, victimisation is not a form of discrimination and the shared burden of proof therefore does not apply.[334]

---

331 ECJ judgment of 10 April 1984,, Case C-14/83, *Sabine von Colson and Elisabeth Kamann v Land Nordrhein-Westfalen*; ECJ judgment of 10 April 1984, Case C-79/83, *Dorit Harz v Deutsche Tradax GmbH*. Barnard 2006, p.437.

332 ECJ judgment of 2 August 1993, Case C-271/91, M. Helen Marshall v Southampton and South-West Hampshire Area Health Authority.

333 ECJ judgment of 22 April 1997, Case C-180/95, *Nils Draehmpaehl v Urania Immobilienservice OHG*.

334 Article 10.

4.10. Conclusion on Employment Equality Directive

The Employment Equality Directive is a key instrument in EU disability law and policy. It prohibits discrimination on the grounds of disability and it includes a duty to provide reasonable accommodation for disabled persons. Although this is a landmark Directive, several caveats and lacunas stand in the way of an optimal guarantee of equal treatment of persons with disabilities in the labour market. Firstly, the Directive only allows for, but does not obligate Member States to enact positive action in order to remove structural barriers to full equality. This means that the Directive is not based on the substantive diversity equality model. Secondly, the Directive does not contain a definition of disability and the definition set out by the ECJ was based on the medical model of disability and thus does not ensure full protection of persons with disabilities under the Directive. Thirdly, the Directive provides for special justifications in case of differential treatment on the grounds of disability namely the public security and health justifications which are both unnecessary and problematic. Finally, the scope of application of the Directive excludes payments of any kind by State schemes which are often a prerequisite for the participation of persons with disabilities on the labour market.

On a positive note, in its second judgment on disability discrimination under the Employment Equality Directive, the ECJ ruled that it provides protection against discrimination on the grounds of association with a disabled child. As a result, it seems that the Court has taken a small step towards the social model of disability.

5. Employers' Obligations

Whereas the last Section dealt with the Employment Equality Directive and the protection of persons with disabilities against discrimination, the present Section analyses the obligations of employers towards persons with disabilities and reduced working capacity under other areas of EU law and policy. Firstly, I examine whether employees with disabilities and reduced working capacity enjoy special protection against dismissal under EU law. Protection against dismissal due to disability would indirectly impose a positive duty on the employer to make adjustments for the employee who could otherwise have been dismissed. Secondly, the positive duties of the employer towards disabled employees with reduced working capacity under work environment law are examined. Such positive duties contained in employment protection legislation and work environment law would complement duties to make reasonable accommodation contained in anti-discrimination legislation.

5.1. Protection Against Dismissals

The topic of this Sub-section is the protection against dismissals of persons with disabilities under EU law, excluding that which follows from the prohibition of discrimination under the Employment Equality Directive. The question is whether EU law imposes a duty on Member States to limit the managerial prerogative of employers in connection with either collective dismissals or individual dismissals of persons with disabilities and/or reduced working capacity.

5.1.1. Hard-law on Protection Against Dismissals

EU law contains a number of legal acts providing for equal treatment of Union citizens in another country than his or her own and prohibiting discrimination on the grounds of for example gender, race, and disability.[335] It also provides an explicit prohibition of dismissals of pregnant women and women with newborns.[336] However, EU law does not establish a certain level of protection against dismissals due to reduced working capacity. This is still considered a question to be regulated by Member States. The legislation which comes closest to setting general employment protection standards stems from a concern in the 1970s that the Common Market had brought about increasing competition which had led to restructurings of companies and resulted in a rise in unemployment. In order to alleviate the negative effects of the Common Market, three Directives were adopted as a part of a Social Action Programme aimed at addressing the social consequences of economic change. These three Directives are: Directive 75/129 on collective redundancies, Directive 77/187 on employees' rights on transfer of undertakings and Directive 80/987 on insolvency.[337] None of these Directives set limitations on the right of employers to dismiss employees with disabilities and/or reduced working capacity.

---

335 European Parliament and Council Directive 2006/54 of 5 July 2006 on the implementation of the principle of equal opportunities and equal treatment of men and women in matters of employment and occupation (recast) OJ[2006] L204/23. Council Directive 2000/43 of 29 June 2000 implementing the principle of equal treatment between persons irrespective of racial or ethnic origin, OJ [2000] L180/22; Council Regulation (EC) 1612/68 on Free Movement of Workers, OJ [1968] Spec ed, L275/2 as amended by Reg 312/76/EEC, OJ [1976] L3/2 and Reg 2434/92/EEC, OJ [1992] L25/1. Employment Equality Directive as regards disability.

336 Council Directive (EEC) 92/85 of 19 October 1992 on the introduction of measures to encourage improvements in the safety and health at work of pregnant workers and workers who have recently given birth or are breastfeeding, OJ [1992] L348/1.

337 Council Directive (EEC) 75/129 on the approximation of the laws of the Member States relating to collective redundancies, OJ[1975] L48/29; Council Directive (EEC) 77/187 on the approximation of the laws of the Member States relating to the safeguarding of employees' rights in the event of transfers of undertakings, OJ [1977] L61/29 as amended by Dir 98/50/EC, OJ [1998] L210/88; and Council Directive 80/987 on the approximation of the laws of the Member States relating to the protection of employees in the event of the insolvency of their employer, OJ [1980] L283/23 as amended by Dir 87/164/EC, OJ [1987] L66/11.

5.1.2. Soft-law on Protection Against Dismissals

In soft-law and policy documents, a specific level of protection against dismissals has not been set out. However, the embracing of flexicurity policies in the European Employment Strategy suggests that the Union seeks to promote a flexible labour market, meaning a labour market which can hire or fire employees as it sees fit without (unnecessary) restrictions on employers' prerogatives. Thus, according to the European Employment Guidelines, *"Member States should integrate the flexicurity principles endorsed by the European Council into their labour market policies and apply them"*.[338] More specifically, *"Member States should therefore introduce a combination of flexible and reliable contractual arrangements, active labour market policies, effective lifelong learning, policies to promote labour mobility, and adequate social security systems to secure labour market transitions accompanied by clear rights and responsibilities for the unemployed to actively seek work"*.[339]

In the Commission Communication *"Towards Common Principles of Flexicurity: More and better jobs through flexibility and security"* from 2007, the Commission underlines that *"individuals increasingly need employment security rather than job security, as fewer have the same job for life"*.[340] Also according to this Communication, strict employment protection leads to increasing segmentation of the labour market because it decreases the entry rate from unemployment into work.[341] Although the Communication acknowledges that employment protection legislation encourages enterprises to invest in training of its employees, it seems that the Commission sees flexicurity as entailing a relatively *low level of protection against dismissals.* In sum, the European Employment Strategy promotes a relatively low level of protection against dismissals or *job* security with a view to creating more flexible labour markets.

5.2. Health and Safety

The present Section examines the extent of the positive duties of employers to make adaptations for the needs of employees with disabilities. As described above in *Section 4. Employment Equality Directive,* the duty to provide reasonable accommodation is a duty to make accommodations in order to ensure compliance with the principle of equal treatment. However, in addition to the duty to make reasonable accommodation contained in the anti-discrimination legislation, the duty

338 Council Decision 707/2010 of 21 October 2010 on Guidelines for the Employment Policies of the Member States, [2010] OJ L308/46, Guideline No. 7.

339 Ibid.

340 COM (2007) 359 final, p. 3.

341 Ibid., p. 6.

to make adaptations should also be reflected in the specialised field of health and safety in order to have full impact on the actual working conditions experienced by persons with disabilities. As I will discuss in more detail in *Chapter IV Equal Treatment and Chapter V Employers' Obligations*, the duty to provide reasonable accommodation in the anti-discrimination legislation should be seen as a back-stopper – as the minimum requirement to be fulfilled in order to avoid discrimination – and the health and safety legislation should reflect a positive and general duty to structure working conditions to the needs and capacity of the individual employee. The Commission has also recognised the link between reasonable accommodation and health and safety in its original proposal for the Employment Equality Directive.[342] The present Section falls into two Sub-Sections on hard-law and soft-law respectively.

5.2.1. Hard-law on Health and Safety

The Amsterdam Treaty of 1997 revised the wording of the new Article 137 TEC (now Article 153 TFEU), which provides for regulation by qualified majority voting on both health and safety matters and also on working conditions. According to Article 153 TFEU, *"The Union shall support and complement the activities of the Member States [...] [in the field of inter alia] improvement in particular of the working environment to protect workers' health and safety [...] and working conditions."* In addition, it should be noted that health and safety is mentioned in both the Community Charter of the Fundamental Social Rights of Workers and the EU Charter on Fundamental Rights that became legally binding with the adoption of the Treaty of Lisbon.[343] Article 31(1) of the EU Charter of Fundamental Rights provides that *"Every worker has the right to working conditions which respect his or her health, safety and dignity".*

The most important Directive on health and safety is the Framework Directive on Health and Safety 89/391, which has several more specific daughter Directives relating to health and safety at the workplace, equipment used by workers and dangerous agents as well as grand-daughter Directives relating to specific high-risk

342 The Commission recognised this link between reasonable accommodation and health and safety in its original proposal for the Employment Equality Directive, Commission Proposal for a Council Directive establishing a general framework for equal treatment in employment and occupation, COM (1999) 565 final of 25 November 1999, p. 9, which states: "This provision would supplement and reinforce the employer's obligation to adapt the workplace to disabled workers, as provided by framework Directive 89/391EC" of 12 June 1989 on the introduction of measures to encourage improvements in the health and safety of workers at work, OJ [1989] L183/1.

343 Community Charter of the Fundamental Rights of Workers of 9 December 1989, adopted by Declaration, Article 19. EU Charter of Fundamental Rights Article 31.

sectors or specific dangerous agents.[344] The Framework Directive on Health and Safety relies on broad and general principles of prevention and introduces measures to encourage improvement in health and safety rather than setting detailed technical requirements. The Directive applies to all sectors of activity, both public and private, but the self-employed are excluded from the personal scope of the Directive unless otherwise provided by national law.[345] According to Article 5(1), employers have a duty *"to ensure the health and safety of workers in every aspect related to the work."* Member States may however provide for *"the limitation of employer's responsibility where occurrences are due to unusual and unforeseeable circumstances, beyond the employer's control, or to exceptional events, the consequence of which could not have been avoided despite the exercise of all due care."*[346]

Article 6 fleshes out the obligations of the employer and of special interest in relation to persons with disabilities is the obligation in Article 6(2)(d) to adapt the work to the individual, especially as regards the design of the work places, the choice of work equipment and the choice of working and production methods with a view, in particular, to alleviating monotonous work and work at a predetermined work rate, thus reducing the effects on health.

In addition, Article 6(3)(b) requires that the employer, *"where he entrusts tasks to a worker, [shall] take into consideration the worker's capabilities as regards health and safety".* The principles laid out in the first six Articles of the Framework Directive must be implemented through five different types of activities on the part of the employer: "*awareness and evaluation*"; *"plan and take action"; "train and direct the workforce"; "inform and consult with workforce";* and finally *"report accidents to national authorities".*[347] Finally, it follows from Article 15 that *"Particularly sensitive risk groups must be protected against the dangers which specifically affect them."*

At first glance the reference in Article 6(2)(d) to adaptation of work to the individual seems to be an obligation to take account for example of an employee's reduced working capacity or disability. However, the fact that all the examples listed in the Article refer to generally strenuous work implies that the wording could just as well

344 Council Directive (EC) 89/391 on the introduction of measures to encourage the improvement of safety and health of workers at work, OJ [1989] L183/1 and the daughter Directives, which include: Council Directive (EC) 89/654 on the Minimum Safety and Health Requirements for the Workplace OJ [1989] L393/1; Council Directive (EC) 89/655 of 30 November 1989 concerning the Minimum Safety and Health Requirements for the Use of Work Equipment by Workers at Work, OJ [1989] L393/13.

345 Article 2 and 3.

346 Article 5(4).

347 Barnard 2006, p. 554.

have been *"adapt work to humans in general"*, which would imply that there would be no obligation to make accommodations for an individual worker's special needs. This interpretation is supported by the wording used in many of the other language versions of the Directive, which use the word "*human*" rather than "*individual*" (*l'homme, mensch, mens, uomo, homem, mennesket*).[348] In addition to the English version, at least the Spanish and the Swedish versions also use the word "*individual*" (*persona, enskilde*). Again the reference in Article 6(3)(b) to *"capabilities as regards health and safety"* could be taken to mean the individual's disability or weaknesses. However, this could also be understood as a reference to the worker's level of training as regards health and safety, which is again supported by many of the other language versions, for example the Spanish version speaks of professional capacity *(las capacidades profesionales)* and the Danish and Swedish versions use the term skills (*færdigheder, kunskaper*).[349]

The European Court of Justice has not yet had the opportunity to provide details on the interpretation of Article 6(2) on the duty to adapt the work to the individual, but it has been asked to assess whether the transposition into British national law of the related principle on employer's liability in Article 5 was satisfactory. The contested British Act provided that *"It shall be the duty of every employer to ensure, so far as is reasonably practicable, the health, safety and welfare at work of all his employees."*[350] The Court did not find that the disputed clause amounted to a violation of Article 5 of the Directive. The Court acknowledged that the UK had, with the insertion of the disputed clause, rejected a no-fault liability for employers. However, the Court did not find that the Commission had established *"to the requisite legal standard"* that this was in violation of the Directive.[351] This rejection by the Court of a no-fault liability supports a less strict interpretation of Article 6(2) and (3), which may contain a duty to provide accommodation for persons with disabilities.[352]

---

348 French, German, Dutch, Italian, Portuguese and Danish.

349 German: "eignung", French: "capacités", Italian: "capacità", Portuguese: "capacidades", Dutch: "gebied".

350 ECJ Case 127/05 *Commission v. United Kingdom* of 14 June 2007, para. 10.

351 Ibid., para. 51.

352 See also ECJ judgment of 15 June 2006, Case C-459/04, *Commission v. Sweden* on transposition of Article 7(8) of the Health and Safety Framework Directive on the definition by the Member State of capabilities of designated workers to carry out preventive health and safety activities. The case was dismissed by the Court. See also Commission Communication COM (2004) 62 final of 5 February 2002 on the practical implementation of the provisions of the Health and Safety at Work Directives 89/391 (Framework), 89/654 (Workplaces), 89/655 (Work Equipment), 89/656 (Personal Protective Equipment), 90/269 (Manual Handling of Loads) and 90/270 (Display Screen Equipment), p. 10, which lists lack of implementation of the principle of prevention as one of the main problems of implementation of the Framework Directive on Health and Safety.

In sum, the Health and Safety Framework Directive 89/391 is most probably not as far-reaching as regards accommodation to the needs of employees with disabilities as would appear from a first reading of the English version of the Directive. Naturally, a general duty to adapt work to human beings and to take account of vulnerable groups indicates that a certain minimum of adaptations to the needs of persons with disabilities is required under the Directive. However, the Directive does not establish a pro-active duty to ensure that working conditions are inclusive towards employees with disabilities or an explicit duty to make adaptations for employees who acquire a reduced working capacity. Although these duties could be inferred from the principle of preventive health and safety, it seems highly unlikely that this interpretation will either be required by the European Court of Justice or through national transposition laws due to the broad and general nature of the duty in the Directive.

The daughter Directive on Minimum Health and Safety Requirements for the Workplace does not mention the principle that adaptations of the workplace should be made to the individual's capacity. However, the Annexes to the Directive containing the technical requirements do provide that *"workplaces must be organized to take account of handicapped workers, if necessary. This provision applies in particular to [...] lavatories and workstations used or occupied directly by handicapped persons."*[353] It is not clear what the reference to necessity implies. Clearly, however, the Directive does not oblige employers to create accessible workplaces in general which would reduce the need for future individual adaptations. Adaptations are merely required when an individual employee with a disability must have his or her workplace adapted in order to carry out his or her work in a manner in accordance with the principles of preventive health and safety standards.

As mentioned above, working conditions are now also a part of the new Article 137 TFEU on health and safety. The most important and also the most controversial Directive adopted in this regard is the Working Time Directive 2003/88, which replaces the old Working Time Directive 94/104.[354] The Working Time Directive concerns all sectors of activity, both public and private with the exception of seafarers and the self-employed.[355] The Directive provides limits to weekly working time and night work, which the employer may not exceed, and entitlements to rest, which the worker may forgo. The general obligations of the Directive must be read in conjunction with *"the general principle of adapting work to the worker, with a view, in particular, to alleviating monotonous work and work at a pre-determined*

353 Council Directive (EC) 89/654 of 30 November 1989 concerning minimum safety and health requirements for the workplace, OJ [1989] L193/1, annex 1 on "workplaces used for the first time", Section 20, and annex 2 on "workplaces already in use", Section 15.

354 OJ [2003] L299/9; OJ [1993] L307/18.

355 Article 1 and 2.

work rate, depending on the type of activity, and of the health and safety requirements, especially as regards breaks during working time."[356] However, the Working Time Directive does not provide an obligation for employers to adapt working time to the individual worker's capacity. In other words, the Directive does not require that the employer reduce the working time of a worker with a reduced working capacity related to his or her disability. This lack of mainstreaming of the duty to make adaptations for the needs of persons with disabilities under the Working Time Directive echoes the lack of duty to make adaptations in the Health and Safety Framework Directive 89/391.

5.2.2. Soft-law on Health and Safety

In relation to soft-law and policy, it is quite surprising that health and safety did not feature in the European Employment Strategy as adopted by the Lisbon Council in March 2000 in spite of the fact that the aim of the strategy was to promote *"better jobs"*. In the 2001 and 2003 employment guidelines, health and safety came in at the behest of the Commission.[357] In both 2005, 2008 and 2010, the Council Guidelines also mention health and safety.[358] According to Guideline No. 7,

> *"The quality of jobs and employment conditions should be addressed. Member States should combat in-work poverty and promote occupational health and safety."*[359]

In its *"Community Strategy 2007–2012 on health and safety at work"*, the European Commission put forward that *"we should be aiming at a situation in which work enhances a person's health and wellbeing and in which being able to find and retain a job improves the general health of the population."*[360] This is an ambitious and broad goal for health and safety legislation in employment, but the strategy does not seem to be reflected in the plans for health and safety legislation on employees with disabilities. Thus the Strategy does not include plans for imposing a general duty to make adaptations for the employees with disabilities. Instead disability is only mentioned explicitly in relation to the need for more extensive rehabilitation following occupational illnesses and accidents at work. However in relation to *"social and demographic change"* in the EU, it is underlined that policies on health and safety can help to meet the challenge of an ageing population and the need for

356 Article 13.

357 Council Decision (EC) 2001/53, OJ [2001] L22/18, Council Decision (EC) 2003/578, OJ [2003] L197/13. Barnard 2006, p. 546–7.

358 Council Decision (EC) 2005/600, OJ [2005] L205/21. Council Decision (EC) 2008/618 of 15 July 2008 on guidelines for the employment policies of the Member States, OJ [2008] L198/47.

359 Council Decision 707/2010 of 21 October 2010 on Guidelines for the Employment Policies of the Member States, [2010] OJ L308/46.

360 European Commission Communication, COM (2007) 62 final, on Improving quality and productivity at work: Community Strategy 2007–2012 on health and safety at work, p. 3.

more women and ethnic minorities in employment *"by tailoring the workplace more effectively to individual needs"*. Although not mentioned specifically, a duty to adapt to individual needs would also benefit persons with disabilities. The Strategy does not propose new regulations in this regard, but invites the European Agency for Health and Safety at Work to identify measures which are essential.[361]

In conclusion, relatively detailed European legislation has been adopted in the field of health and safety. This legislation is based on the principle of prevention and underlines that employers must take account of the needs of vulnerable groups which include persons with disabilities. However, although a duty to provide reasonable accommodation for persons with disabilities may be inferred from this legislation, this duty is so vaguely formulated that it is unlikely to have a strong impact on the legal order of Member States. The lack of focus on disability is also reflected in soft-law and policy documents which do not promote employers' obligations to make adaptations for disabled employees.

5.3. Conclusion on Employers' Obligations

In conclusion, the Lisbon Strategy and the employment guidelines stress that Europe should strive for better jobs which entails that working conditions should be improved. However, a closer look at the existing EU legislation shows that it is relatively weak at least when it comes to imposing a duty on employers to create working conditions, which are inclusive towards persons with disabilities. This would require both proactive duties to create inclusive working conditions and duties to make adaptations for individuals with disabilities. The existing EU regulations do not impose such duties. Instead, the Employment Guidelines recommend the *flexicurity* model, which at least according to the European Commission entails relatively weak job protection legislation. The Employment Equality Directive may lead to increased protection against dismissals on the grounds of disability-related reduced working capacity under national employment protection law, but this requires that the ECJ ensures a strong interpretation of the Employment Equality Directive, *cf. Chapter V Employers' Obligations*.

6. Employment Promotion

The purpose of the present Section is to give an overview of EU law and policy on employment promotion of persons with disabilities. Employment promotion is here

361 Ibid., p. 10. See also European Commission Communication COM (2006) 571 final of 12 October 2006 on The demographic future of Europe – from challenge to opportunity, which focuses on ageing populations, rise in immigration from outside the European Union and the need for more women in the labour market, but not the need for more persons with disabilities in the labour market.

understood broadly as including legally binding (hard-law) obligations on employers to improve employment opportunities for persons with disabilities as well as non-binding policies (soft-law) aiming at encouraging employers to improve employment opportunities for persons with disabilities. In addition, employment promotion covers also activities undertaken by public employment services that address unemployed persons with disabilities in order to improve their employment opportunities. In *Sub-Section 6.1.,* I examine whether EU law obliges States to take certain measures to promote employment of persons with disabilities and whether EU law imposes limitations to these measures. Since the limitations for positive treatment have been examined in *Section 4. Employment Equality Directive*, I will concentrate here on the limitations contained in State Aid legislation. In *Sub-Section 6.2*, I examine whether EU *policy* makes recommendations to Member States to adopt a certain policy in relation to State employment promotion.

6.1. Hard-law on Employment Promotion

The goal of a *"high level of employment"* has been given a prominent place in Article 3 TEU. However, the EU has only been conferred with limited powers to harmonise public employment services and employment policies in the Member States. Thus, Title IX TFEU on "*Employment*" merely provides that the EU shall "work towards developing a coordinated strategy for employment". Instead the limited powers to regulate public employment services and employment policies must be found in Title X TFEU on "*Social Policy*". According to Article 153 TFEU of Title X, the Union shall support and complement the activities of the Member States *inter alia* in the field of "integration of persons excluded from the labour market" and to this end, the European Parliament and the Council may adopt "*minimum requirements for gradual implementation*" by means of directives. In practice, the EU has not adopted directives harmonising employment promotion. Consequently, the European Employment Strategy and the OMC are the main instruments for achieving such a coordination of policies. They will be examined in *Sub-Section 6.2. EU soft-law on employment promotion.*

However, in spite of the lack of EU secondary legislation harmonising employment promotion, the fundamental principles of the internal market still apply to this area of law and policy. Thus, EU law relating to the internal market sets limitations on and influences the development of law and policy on employment promotion at Member State level. The two main areas of the internal market influencing the organisation and development of employment promotion are the freedom of movement of workers and the principle of fair competition. The effective functioning of employment promotion services is relevant when seeking to ensure equal opportunities for workers from other EU Member States. The principle of fair competition is relevant as for example employment promotion in the form of wage subvention may distort competition in favour of the undertakings hiring personnel with wage subvention. The freedom of movement of workers aims at the creation of an internal EU market for employment and it entails *inter alia* the abolition of all discrimination on the grounds of nationality between workers of the EU.[362] The "close co-operation of employment promotion services" is mentioned explicitly in TFEU Article 46 as an area where the EU Parliament and Council may adopt Directives or Regulations in order to bring about freedom of workers. In relation to state aid, it follows from Article 107 TFEU that:

> *"aid granted by a Member State or through State resources in any form whatsoever which distorts or threatens to distort competition by favouring certain undertakings or the production of certain goods shall, insofar as it affects trade between Member States, be incompatible with the internal market."*

Article 107 TFEU sets limitations to the amount of subsidies payable to individual undertakings, including subsidies in the form of wage subventions for employees with disabilities and reduced working capacity. However, exemptions have been made for support given to promote the employment of disabled workers which shows that the state aid legislation is not merely governed by economic interests, but also takes account of social policy. The Commission's General Block Exemption Regulation describes certain types of state aid which may be granted without prior notification to the Commission.[363] The General Block Exemption Regulation for example provides in Article 41 that *"aid for the employment of disabled workers in the form of wage subsidies"* shall be permitted provided that *"the aid intensity shall not exceed 75% of the eligible costs"* understood as *"wage costs over any given period during which the disabled worker is employed."*[364] However, it follows from Article 6 of the General Block Exemption Regulation that individual notification to the Commission regarding aid schemes will be necessary in all cases where *"aid for the employment of disabled workers in the form of wage costs"* or *"additional costs of employing disabled workers"* exceeds 10 million euro per undertaking per year.[365] The Commission has published a Communication which describes the *"Criteria for the analysis of the compatibility of State aid for the employment of disadvantaged and disabled workers subject to individual notification"*.[366] According to this Communication, the Commission will take into account whether state aid is an *"appropriate policy instrument"*, *"incentive effect and necessity of*

362 TFEU Chapter 1 "Workers" of Title IV on "Freedom of Movement of Persons, Services and Capital".

363 Commission Regulation (EC) No. 800/2008 of 6 August 2008 declaring certain categories of aid compatible with the common market in application of Article 87 and 88 of the Treaty, OJ [2008] L 214/3.

364 Ibid. Article 2(20) and (21).

365 Ibid. Article 6(1)(i) and (j).

366 Commission Communication, "Criteria for the analysis of the compatibility of State aid for the employment of disadvantaged and disabled workers subject to individual notification", OJ [2009] C188/02.

the aid" and *"proportionality of the aid"*, as well as whether or not the state aid is likely to have negative effects in the form of distortions of competition.[367] The Communication underlines that *"In any case, aid intensities must never exceed those laid down in Articles 40 (2) and 41 (3) of Regulation (EC) No 800/2008."*[368] In other words, state aid may never exceed the limits in intensities provided in the General Block Exemption Regulation, but it may in specific situations exceed the limit of 10 million euro to one undertaking per year set in Article 6 of the General Block Exemption Regulation.

The General Block Exemption Regulation from 2008 raised the limit for permitted wage subsidies from 60% of eligible costs in the 2002-Regulation.[369] The question of Danish and Swedish compliance with EU law will discussed in *Chapter VII Employment Promotion.*

Although the fundamental principles of freedom of movement of workers and fair competition, which stem from the internal market ideal, have not led to harmonisation of national employment services, it seems that they have influenced national employment services towards "*economisation*" and "*privatisation*". *Freedland et al* define "*economisation*" as a *"transition to regulation of a given sphere of activity as an economic or market activity rather than as a social one"* and *"privatisation*" as the *"dynamic towards situations in which a service which was often one of public monopoly will increasingly be provided by a combination of competition and cooperation between public and private providers*".[370]

One of the clearest examples of EU competition law influencing national employment services towards privatisation and economisation is the *Höfner*-case from 1990 in which the ECJ found that the German Federal Employment Office was not entitled to maintain a monopoly over employment placement services and that it was abusing a dominant position contrary to Articles 82 and 86 TEC (now Articles 102 and 106 TFEU) because the statutory service was *"manifestly incapable of meeting demand"* and the activities of private recruitment agents were prohibited.[371] The same conclusion was reached by the ECJ in the *Job Centre*-case of 1997.[372]

---

367 Ibid. Paras. 5–13.

368 Ibid., para. 13.

369 Commission Regulation (EC) No. 2204/2002 of 12 December 2002 on the application of Articles 87 and 88 of the EC Treaty to State aid for employment, OJ [2002] L337/3, Article 5(2).

370 Freedland, Craig, Jacqueson and Koutouris 2007, p. 356 and 357.

371 ECJ judgment of 23 April 1991, Case C-41/90 *Höfner and Elser v. Macroton*,.

372 ECJ judgment of 11 December 1997., Case C-55/96 *Job Centre Coop. arl,* See also Barnard 2006, p. 36.

As pointed out by *Barnard*, there may be social interests behind refraining from privatising employment services.[373] For example, there may be a risk that employment services, which are increasingly economised and privatised, are forced to concentrate on stronger and cheaper job seekers rather than weaker and more expensive job seekers such as for example some job seekers with disabilities. However, these concerns were not taken up by the ECJ in the *Höfner*- and *Job Centre*-cases.[374]

6.2. Soft-law on Employment Promotion

As mentioned above under *Sub-Section 7.1. Hard law on Employment Promotion*, the EU mainly seeks to influence employment promotion through the development and application of the European Employment Strategy in the OMC. As was the case with hard-law, this soft-law process supports the dynamic of privatization and economization of public employment services as well as an orientation towards policies and practices based upon active labour market policies, 'making work pay' (meaning that there must be economic incentives for starting to work) and contracting out employment services.[375] Thus, according to the Council Employment Guidelines from October 2010, Member States should introduce *"active labour market policies [...] policies to promote labour mobility, and adequate social security systems to secure labour market transitions accompanied by clear rights and responsibilities for the unemployed to actively seek work."*[376] At the same time, strong employment promotion is a component of the flexicurity model promoted by the European Employment Strategy, thus is it also underlined that *"Employment services play an important role in activation and matching and they should therefore be strengthened with personalised services and active and preventive labour market measures at an early stage."*[377] These tendencies are also clear in the Joint Employment Report 2008/09 where it was underlined to be of particular importance in the short and medium term that the Member States promote *"active labour market policies: Prioritise integrating better active and passive labour market policies"*.[378]

---

373 Barnard 2006, p. 36.

374 ECJ judgment of 23 April 1991, Case 41/90 *Höfner and Elser v. Macroton,*; ECJ judgment of 11 December 1997, Case C-55/96, *Job Centre Coop. arl,*.

375 Freedland, Craig, Jacqueson and Koutouris 2007, p. 360.

376 Council Decision 707/2010 of 21 October 2010 on Guidelines for the Employment Policies of the Member States, [2010] OJ L308/46, Guideline No. 7.

377 Ibid.

378 Council (Employment, Social Policy, Health and Consumer Affairs) 7435/09 of 9 March 2009, p. 8 and 9.

6.3. Conclusion on Employment Promotion

The two main areas of EU hard-law influencing the organisation and development of employment promotion are the freedom of movement of workers and the principle of fair competition. These areas *inter alia* entail limitations on use of wage subsidies for promoting employment of persons with disabilities. The case law of the ECJ in relation to freedom of movement of workers and the principle of fair competition, push national employment services towards an increased economisation and privatisation of employment promotion services. In addition, EU soft-law and the European Employment Strategy push Member States into the direction of active labour market policies which entails both strengthened employment promotion services as well as higher focus on the duties of the unemployed to be available for the labour market. The European Employment Strategy also recommends strengthened employment services as part of the flexicurity model which promotes employment security rather than job security.

In sum, it is somewhat complicated to assess the effects of the employment promotion policies promoted by the European Union in relation to persons with disabilities. On the one hand, stronger focus on employment services may benefit unemployed persons with disabilities. On the other hand however, increased focus on costs and duties of unemployed persons may place unemployed persons with disabilities because they may need more costly support to obtain employment than others.

7. Income-Replacement Benefits

The purpose of the present Section is to give an overview of EU law and policy on income-replacement benefits for persons with disabilities outside of the labour market, as well as persons with disabilities who are at risk of being excluded from the labour market. Therefore, the main focus will be on long-term income-replacement benefits for permanently disabled persons and on short-term income-replacement benefits for persons who have a reduced working capacity for a limited time. As explained in the introductory Chapter, the reason for examining these benefits in particular, is that the conditions attached to and size of income-replacement benefits is seen as influencing the motivation for labour market participation and thereby *actual* labour market participation. I will start with an analysis of hard law and subsequently, I will examine soft-law and policy in this area.

7.1. Hard Law on Income-Replacement Benefits

It follows from the EU Charter of Fundamental Rights that "*The Union recognises and respects the entitlement to income-replacement benefits and social services providing protection in cases such as maternity, illness, industrial accidents, dependency or old age, and in the case of loss of employment, in accordance with the rules laid down by Community law and national laws and practices.*" This provision is formulated in a relatively broad manner and the extent of the obligation seems limited to existing rules laid down by existing EU and national law. Moreover, even though the EU Charter of Fundamental Rights purports to build on constitutional traditions and international obligations common and binding on the Member States, the Charter has only recently become legally binding and the effect of this provision on EU law and policy is – as of yet – minimal.

Furthermore, the main legal basis for adopting EU laws and policies on income-replacement benefits is Article 48 TFEU according to which, *"The European Parliament and the Council shall [...] adopt such measures in the field of social security as are necessary to provide freedom of movement for workers"* and Articles *137 TEC according to which the "Union shall support and complement the activities of the Member States in the following fields: [...] (c) social security and social protection of workers; (d) protection of workers where their employment contract is terminated."*

In addition, Article 156 TFEU provides that *"the Commission shall encourage cooperation between the Member States and facilitate the coordination of their action in all social policy fields under this chapter"*. However, although both Articles 48 and 153 TFEU envisage the adoption of legally binding minimum standards, they provide for a sort of veto for Member States who may declare that a legal act would *"affect important aspects of its social security system"* or require unanimity in the Council.[379] In addition, Article 48 TFEU aims at ensuring freedom of movement of workers and not harmonization of social security and Article 153(4) TFEU underlines that provisions adopted *"shall not affect the right of Member States to define the fundamental principles of their social security systems and must not significantly affect the financial equilibrium thereof"*.

All in all, the TFEU allows for the adoption of European laws and policies in the field of social security taking into account the limitations that result from a strong defensiveness on the part of States to maintain their sovereignty in this policy field and the related fact that both traditions and resources vary significantly among States.

---

[379] Article 48 TFEU and Article 153(2) TFEU.

The consequence of the limited legal basis on income-replacement benefits in the treaty is that secondary legislation builds on the principles of non-discrimination, the single-state-rule, aggregation of benefits and exportability, but does not seek to harmonise benefits through the imposition of minimum standards on Member States. The prohibition of discrimination covers firstly discrimination on the grounds of nationality, but also other grounds, which will be examined in more detail below.

Regulation 883/2004 on the application of social security schemes to employed persons and their families moving within the Union codifies the above-mentioned principles of non-discrimination, the single-State-rule, aggregation of benefits and exportability.[380] According to Article 18 TFEU and as fleshed out in Regulations 883/2004, both direct and indirect discrimination on the grounds of nationality are prohibited.[381] The single-State-rule implies that only one State's social benefit system covers each migrant worker and the starting point is that the state of employment is the relevant State. Regulation 883/2004 provides detailed rules on the choice of social benefit system.[382] The principle of aggregation ensures that the host Member State takes account of periods of insurance completed in other Member States.[383] Finally, the principle of exportability means that some long-term benefits such as disability pensions may be retained irrespective of place of residence as long as the beneficiary resides in an EU Member State.[384] However, the principle of exportability does not apply to "special non-contributory benefits", which migrant workers can therefore not take with them to other Member States.[385] According to Regulation 883/2004 these special non-contributory benefits include those *"solely specific protection for the disabled, closely linked to the said person's social environment in the Member State concerned"*. These benefits include for example personal assistance and benefits to cover costs of assistive devices, which may be of crucial importance for persons with disabilities in their daily lives.

The fact that these benefits are not exportable means that persons with disabilities will be dependent on the legislation of the Member State that he or she is moving to, for these benefits. This lack of exportability in practice, ties persons with disabilities to the Member State, which provides them with this assistance, and limits the mobility of persons with disabilities. This limitation in the principle of exportability is most probably a consequence of the fact that the European States wish to retain a

380 Regulation (EC) No 883/2004 of the European Parliament and of the Council on the coordination of social security systems Regulation, [2004] OJ L166/1; (EC) No 987/2009 of the European Parliament and of the Council of 16 September 2009 laying down the procedure for implementing Regulation (EC) No 883/2004 on the coordination of social security systems, [2009] OJ L284/1.

381 Articles 4 and 5 of Regulation 883/2004.

382 Title II of Regulation 883/2004.

383 Article 6 of Regulation 883/2004.

384 Article 7 of Regulation 883/2004.

385 Article 70 of Regulation 883/2004 and Annex 2a.

high degree of self-determination in the area of social security combined with a lack of sensitivity towards the needs of persons with disabilities.

In addition to the prohibition of discrimination on the grounds of nationality mentioned above, the EU has also introduced prohibitions of discrimination on the grounds of gender and race in the field of social security. Thus, Directive 79/7 on equal treatment of men and women in matters of social security covers *Statutory* social security schemes as regards persons in the labour force and the Recast Directive on equal opportunities and equal treatment of men and women encompasses *occupational* social security schemes.[386] While State social security schemes are covered by Directive 79/7, the Recast Directive covers schemes not governed by Directive 79/7 *"whose purpose it is to provide workers [...] with benefits intended to supplement the benefits provided by statutory social security schemes or to replace them, whether membership is compulsory or optional"*.[387] Both Directives apply to social security schemes which provide protection against sickness, disability and accidents at work and occupational disease. Both Directives prohibit discrimination as regards the scope of schemes, conditions of access, contributions and calculation of benefits.[388] Directive 79/7 allows for exceptions and derogations with the most important one being *"the determination of pensionable age for granting old-age and retirement benefits"*, but the Recast Directive does cover pensionable age and mentions the fixing of different retirement ages as an example of discrimination.[389] However in spite of exceptions and derogations, the protection against discrimination on the grounds of gender in relation to social security is relatively comprehensive and the European Court of Justice has in several cases upheld the principle of equal treatment between men and women.[390] Interestingly, the case law of the Court shows that a weaker test of objective justification applies in the area of discrimination and social benefits than in respect of employment discrimination and that the Court gives a wider deference to national systems in cases concerning social security.[391] The Racial Equality Directive also covers social protection, including social security and healthcare.[392] No case has

386 Council Directive (EEC) 79/7 of 19 December 1978 on the progressive implementation of the principle of equal treatment for men and women in matters of social security (OJ[1979] L6/1); European Parliament and Council Directive 2006/54 of 5 July 2006 on the implementation of the principle of equal opportunities and equal treatment of men and women in matters of employment and occupation (recast) OJ[2006] L204/23.

387 Directive (EEC) 79/7 Article 3(1) and Recast Directive Article 2(1)(f).

388 Directive (EEC) 79/7 Article 4 and Recast Directive Article 5.

389 Directive (EEC) 79/7 Article 7(1)(a) and Recast Directive Article 9(1)(f).

390 ECJ C-384/85, judgment of 24 June 1987, Jean Borrie Clarke v Chief Adjudication Officer; ECJ C-102/88, judgment of 13 December 1989, Ruzius-Wilbrink v. Bedrijfsvereniging voor Overheidsdiensten.

391 ECJ C-280/94 Posthuma-van Damme. ECJ C-8/94, judgment of 1 February 1996, Laperre v. Bestuurcommissie beroepszaken in de provincie Zuid-Holland. Barnard 2006, p. 498.

392 Council Directive (EC) 2000/43 of 29 June 2000 implementing the principle of equal treatment between persons irrespective of racial or ethnic origin OJ [2000] L180/22, Article 3(1)(e).

been brought before the European Court of Justice regarding the interpretation hereof.

As regards disability discrimination, the Employment Equality Directive, discussed above in Section 3 above, which covers discrimination on the grounds of religion or belief, disability, age and sexual orientation, expressly excludes income-replacement benefits from its scope of application: *"This Directive does not apply to payments of any kind made by state schemes or similar, including state social security or social protection schemes".*[393] This exclusion of the area of social security was remarkable in light of the fact that the Employment Equality Directive constituted part of an anti-discrimination package based on Article 13 TEC (now Article 19 TFEU) together with the Racial Equality Directive, which already from the first proposal from the Commission, applied to social security.[394] In contrast, in the first Commission Proposal for the Employment Equality Directive, social protection and social security were not mentioned under Article 3 which defines the scope of the Directive.[395] Under the final negotiations in the Council, the explicit exclusion of social security schemes was added to the final text of the Directive.[396] The reason for the reluctance to adopt a prohibition of discrimination on the grounds of disability in the area of social security was most probably that Member States feared that this would result in a significant limitation of their sovereignty. As opposed to 'race', 'sexual orientation' or (for the most part) 'gender', 'disability' is in itself a criterion, that used to define eligibility to social benefits. For example, persons with severe impairments may be eligible to compensation for additional costs of living. In this light, a prohibition of discrimination on the grounds of disability in the area of social benefits would be more likely to lead to a certain degree of harmonisation of eligibility for social benefits among Member States than the introduction of bans against discrimination on other grounds. For example, it might lead to a prohibition of differentiations between intellectual and physical impairments in legislation on social benefits.

---

393 Article 3(3).

394 Commission proposal for a Council Directive implementing the principle of equal treatment between persons irrespective of racial or ethnic origin, COM (1999) 566 final of 25 November 1999, p. 16.

395 Commission Proposal for a Council Directive establishing a general framework for equal treatment in employment and occupation, COM (1999) 565 final of 25 November 1999, p. 20.

396 The amended Commission Proposal does not contain the final Article 3(3) text, COM (2000) 652 final of 12 October 2000, p. 10. The press release from the Council Meeting Employment and Social Policy, Luxembourg 17 October 2000, PRES/00/378 of 4 December 2000, where the political agreement on the proposal for the Directive was reached states that the agreement was reached after "difficult negotiations" and "on the basis of a compromise text which accommodated the difficulties encountered by certain Member States." Social security is not mentioned explicitly.

The new proposal for a Council Directive implementing the principle of equal treatment between persons irrespective of religion or belief, disability, age or sexual orientation of 2 July 2008 does cover social security.[397] However, as mentioned above under *Sub-Section 2.3 From the Amsterdam Treaty and onward*, prolonged negotiations are expected before the adoption of the Directive. According to a 'Progress Report' from the Belgian Presidency, which was adopted by the Council Meeting on Employment, Social Policy, Health and Consumer Affairs in December 2010, *"there is a clear need for extensive further work on the proposal"*.[398] Provided that the level of protection in the Directive is not reduced, the adoption of this Directive will rectify the lack of legally binding protection against discrimination on the grounds of disability in the area of social security and bring this protection up to level with the protection against discrimination on the grounds of race and gender.

The overview above of legally binding instruments shows that the protection of persons with disabilities in relation to social security is relatively weak: persons with disabilities do not enjoy a right to exportability of some important disability-specific benefits and persons with disabilities still are not protected against discrimination in the field of social security. However, social policy is a policy area where non-legally binding instruments are used to a high extent. These will be looked at below.

7.2. Soft-law on Income-Replacement Benefits

As explained above under *Sub-Section 6.2 Soft-law on Employment Promotion*, the Council Employment Guidelines from October 2010 promote the flexicurity model which entails on the one hand that Member States should ensure *"adequate social security systems to secure labour market transitions"* and that income-replacement benefits should encourage *"participation in society and in the labour market."*[399] And *"be accompanied by clear rights and responsibilities for the unemployed to actively seek work.'*[400]

The Commission's Proposal for a Joint Report on Social Protection and Social Inclusion of 2010 also underlines the double focus on ensuring income support whilst promoting participation:

397 COM (2008) 426 final, p. 8.

398 Report from the Presidency to the Permanent Representatives Committee (Part I)/ Council EPSCO, 16335/10, 19 November 2010.

399 Ibid, Guideline No. 10.

400 Council Decision 707/2010 of 21 October 2010 on Guidelines for the Employment Policies of the Member States, [2010] OJ L308/46, Guideline No. 7.

> *"Adequate income support is crucial for people in time of need, but policies must also help them to participate in the labour market. Both spending and participation in active labour market measures, including life long learning, have improved overall in recent years. [...]Modern social security policies are an important tool to prevent people moving on to long-term sickness and disability benefits, or early retirement schemes.'*[401]

Although the description of EU policy in the field of social benefits remains relatively general, it is clear that the EU policy in this area goes into the direction of using social benefits as an integrated part of an active labour market policy. In other words, the policies relating to social benefits must be aimed at employment while ensuring adequate support for those who cannot work. When social benefits are increasingly linked with an active labour market policy there is a risk that groups which are marginalised on the labour market, such as some persons with disabilities, may lose necessary social benefits and become socially marginalised. On the positive side, more focus on active support may also lead to more support for returning to the labour market for persons with disabilities on long-term income-replacement benefits. I will discuss the consequences for persons with disabilities of linking social benefits to an active labour market policy more in *Chapter VII Income-Replacement Benefits.*

7.3. Conclusion on Income-Replacement Benefits

In sum, the EU has not adopted minimum standards or harmonising secondary legislation in the area of social security. Instead, general cross-cutting rules such as the principle of freedom of movement and prohibition of discrimination on the grounds of nationality apply. This means that it is up to Member States to ensure that persons with disabilities have access to necessary social benefits. EU *policy* on social security is based on the flexicurity model and promotes social benefits as an integrated part of active labour market policy, which may both be detrimental and positive for persons with disabilities who are dependent on income-replacement benefits and need support to return to the labour market.

8. Involvement of Civil Society and Social Partners

In *Chapter II Human Rights*, I described how the contemporary disability human rights approach entails that civil society are involved when the State carries out its functions. In addition, since the social partners play such a strong role in regulating the labour market in both Denmark and Sweden, it is of interest to examine the

[401] Draft Joint Report on Social Protection and Social Inclusion submitted to the European Council (EPSCO) on 15 February 2010, 6500/10, Communication from the Commission COM (2010) 25 final, Proposal for the Joint Report on Social Protection and Social Inclusion.

inclusion of social partners in EU law and policy. In *Sub-Sections 8.1 Civil Society* and *8.2. Social Partners*, I give an overview of the involvement of civil society and social partners in the EU law and policy areas dealt with above. Sub-Section 8.3 contains a conclusion.

8.1. Civil Society

As explained in *Chapter II Human Rights,* the involvement of civil society in State functions is a central component of the contemporary disability human rights approach. It is crucial, therefore, to examine the involvement of civil society in the EU's law and policy-making.

After the 1992 Maastricht Treaty, a critical debate on the EU's democratic legitimacy led the Commission, in particular, to seek to involve civil society in its law and policy-making. This culminated in the *White Paper on European Governance of 2001,* which formally recognised that civil society holds *"a key function in the implementation of good governance by openness, participation, accountability, effectiveness and coherence."* The aim of the involvement of civil society was both to enhance democratic legitimacy and to improve the quality of laws and policies of the EU.[402] During the decade following the White Paper of 2001, the Commission has continued to enhance its policy of involvement of civil society.[403] Moreover, with the entry into force of the Lisbon Treaty, an explicit duty of direct consultations with civil society is now contained in the Treaties. Thus, the TFEU now provides that:

> *"The institutions shall maintain an open, transparent and regular dialogue with representative associations and civil society" and "The European Commission shall carry out broad consultations with parties concerned in order to ensure that the Union's actions are coherent and transparent."*[404]

However, a formalised platform for consultations with representatives of non-public interests has existed since the Treaty of Rome of 1957 in the form of the European

---

402 Kohler-Koch and Finke 2007, p 206. Finke 2007, p. 3.

403 Commission Communication 'European Transparency Initiative, A framework for relations with interest representatives (Register and Code of Conduct)' of 27 May 2008, COM(2008)323 final. Commission Communication 'General principles and minimum standards for consultation of interested parties by the Commission' of 11 December 2002, COM(2002)704.

404 Article 11(2) and (3) of TEU. Before the adoption of the Lisbon Treaty, Protocol No 7 on the application of the principles of subsidiarity and proportionality, annexed to the Amsterdam Treaty stipulated that "the Commission should [.] consult widely before proposing legislation, and, wherever appropriate, publish consultation documents." This Protocol is now No. 2 annexed to the TFEU.

Economic and Social Committee (EESC).[405] The EESC shall be consulted as a part of the legislative procedure in several different areas including the freedom of movement of workers, health and safety, exclusion of persons from the labour market and social security of workers.[406] It follows from the TFEU that the *"Economic and Social Committee shall consist of representatives of organisations of employers, of the employed, and of other parties representative of civil society, notably in socioeconomic, civic, professional and cultural areas.'*[407] The EESC has maximum 345 members, which are appointed by the Council on the basis of lists drawn up by the Member States. Out of the present 343 members of the EESC, less than five members are representatives of disability organisations.[408] In March 2010 the EESC adopted an opinion on "*People with Disabilities: Employment and Accessibility*" which calls *inter alia* for ratification by the EU of the CRPD, stronger mainstreaming of disability in the EU 2020 Strategy, the Employment Guidelines and the Social Agenda and recommends the adoption of a "*European Disability Pact*" so that "*a variant of the OMC would be applied to disability*".[409] The recommendations of this EESC opinion seem to be entirely in line with the policy of the policy of European Disability Forum, which is the biggest European disability umbrella organisation.[410]

Literature on the inclusion of civil society in EU decision-making has pointed out that civil society representation in European decision-making is in many cases not representative in a democratic sense.[411] The impact of civil society depends firstly on the organisation capacity of the civil society organisations in question.[412] Whereas disability organisations are no doubt able to send a strong and clear message to the policymakers in the central areas of concern such as specialised legislation on disability, it is more doubtful that the disability organisations have the necessary capacity to influence policy-makers into mainstreaming disability into general policies and laws. In addition, the receptiveness of the EU policy-makers

405 Treaty of Rome of 1957, Article 193 ("representatives of various categories of economic and social activity"), ECT Article 297 as introduced by the Treaty of Nice of 2000, "various economic and social components of organised civil society".

406 TFEU Articles 46 and 153.

407 TFEU Article.

408 Http://memberspage.eesc.europa.eu/Result.aspx (December 2010).

409 European Economic and Social Committee, Opinion on "People with disabilities: employment and accessibility by stages for people with disabilities in the EU. Post-2010 Lisbon Strategy" of 17 March 2010, SOC/363, Sections 3.1 and 3.3.

410 The homepage of European Disability Forum mentions the EU ratification of the CRPD and a 'European Disability Pact' as among its Top Five Campains. The other Top Five Campains (comprehensive disability specific legislation, European e-accessibility legislation and disabled air passenger rights) are also mentioned in the EESC opinion sections 3.6.2.3, 1.12 and 5.12.

411 Tömmel 2010, p. 4.

412 Ibid and Friedrich 2007, p. 19.

towards input from civil society seems to be limited to the Commission and to the Parliament whereas the Council seems less approachable for civil society.[413]

In sum, the EU has increasingly sought to include civil society in its policy and law-making, which is reflected in both the treaties and adopted policies by the Commission. However, significant problems still remain in practice. The actual influence of civil society on law and policymaking varies across areas, institutions and depends to a large extent on the capacities of the civil society organisations in question.

8.2. Social Partners

The question of the position of social partners under EU law and policy is quite complex. On the one hand, the Union gives high priority to strengthening the dialogue with social partners both at the European and the national level. On the other hand, any attempt at regulation of the labour market by the EU, runs the risk of becoming a stick in the wheel of national industrial relations. Member States have therefore been careful to limit legal competence of the EU in this area and the EU institutions share a strong respect for industrial relations. However, in practice it has however been impossible to ignore that EU law and actions influence industrial relations at the national level. In this Section, I give a brief overview of the conflicting interests governing EU law and policy on social partners.

In the Treaties, the dialogue with the social partners has also been given high priority. Accordingly Article 151 TFEU, which sets out the aim with the social policy of the Union, states that the Union and the Member States shall have *"dialogue between management and labour"* as one of their objectives. In addition, the dialogue with the social partners at the European level has been given a formal legal basis in the treaties. Thus, Article 154(2) TFEU requires that the Commission shall consult with social partners before submitting proposals in the social policy field and Article 155(2) TFEU provides that the agreements of the European social partners may be given *erga omnes* effect through a Council decision on a proposal from the Commission.[414] Directives of general interest adopted by the contractual method include the Parental Leave Directive, the directives on Part-time Work and Fixed-term Work.[415] In addition to the dialogue on issues of general interest, sectoral social dialogues have been organised by the European Commission in more than 30 different sectors between the European social partners. These general and

413 Friedrich 2007, p. 19.

414 These provisions were first introduced in Social Policy Protocol of the Maastricht Treaty and incorporated into the Treaty with the Amsterdam Treaty.

415 Council Dir. 96/34/EC as amended by 97/75/EC; Council Dir. 97/81/EC as amended by 98/23/EC; Council Dir. 99/70/EC respectively. Freedland and others 2007, p. 87.

sectoral dialogues play a growing role in influencing the European Commission not just through Framework Agreements between the social partners, but also through more soft consultations and joint actions.[416]

In recognition of the fact that the Member States have different traditions as regards the organisation of industrial relations, Article 153(5) TFEU expressly exempts the *"right of association, the right to strike or the right to impose lock-outs"* from the legal basis to regulate the field of social policy. This restriction in the competence of the EU means that the EU has had to concentrate its regulative efforts in limited areas in spite of the importance accorded to the industrial relations by the EU. One example of the difficulties in adopting legislation in this field concerns a Directive on the involvement of workers in corporate decision-making, which could have implications for existing modes of worker and union involvement in Member States. Although the Commission sought to introduce an institutionalised right to employee-participation in corporate decision-making since the beginning of the 1970s, it was not until 1994 that the European Works Council Directive was adopted.[417]

In spite of the fact that the rights of association and collective action have been exempted from the legal competence of the EU, these rights are recognised as fundamental rights in the EU Charter of Fundamental Rights. As a result the Charter contains Article 12 on the freedom of assembly and of association, Article 27 on *"Workers' right to information and consultation within the undertaking"*, and Article 28 on the right to *"collective bargaining and action"*. However, as mentioned above under *Section 2 EU and Human Rights*, the EU Charter on Fundamental Rights does not confer legal competence on the Union. The Charter serves to limit the Union's actions as well as action by Member States in the EU sphere. In practice, the inclusion in the Charter may nevertheless be decisive as it serves to counter-balance the fundamental principles associated with the creation of the internal market. However, in the *Laval*- and *Viking*-cases, the ECJ limited the right of unions to enact collective actions where they were used to undermine fundamental EU freedoms of establishment of undertakings and of provision of services.[418]

---

416 Barnard 2006, p. 103. Commission Decision 98/500/EC of 20 May 1998 on the Establishment of Sectoral Dialogue Committees Promoting the Dialogue between the Social Partners at the European Level, OJ [1998] L225/28.

417 Council Directive (EC) 1994/45 of 22 September 1994 on the establishment of a European Works Council or a procedure in Community-scale undertakings and Community-scale groups of undertakings for the purposes of informing and consulting employees, OJ [1994] L254/64.

418 ECJ Judgment of 18 December 2007, C-341/05, Laval un Partneri Ltd v. Svenska Byggnadsarbetareförbundet; ECJ judgment of 11 December 2007, C-438/05, International Transport Workers" Federation v. Viking Line Abp.

EU policies also place significant weight on strengthening the social dialogue between employers and trade unions both at national and European levels. The social dialogue is seen as the cornerstone of corporate governance designed to create a European labour market based on high skill, high effort and high trust which now lies at the core of the European Employment Strategy.[419] Thus, the dialogue with social partners runs as a red thread through the Guidelines for the Employment Policies of the Member States for 2008–2010.[420] According to the introduction to the Guidelines, Member States shall implement the objectives and priorities specified in the Guidelines *"in cooperation with the social partners"*. In addition, "*an integrated flexicurity approach is essential*" to achieve full employment. This includes flexible labour relations. Finally, it is also stated that "*European and national social partners should play a central role*" in ensuring good governance of employment and social policies.[421]

As regards disability, the European social partners have made a declaration for the European Year of People with Disabilities on the promotion of equal opportunities and access to employment for people with disabilities in 2003.[422] In their work programme for 2006–2008, the social partners have indicated that they may negotiate an autonomous framework agreement on the integration of disadvantaged groups on the labour market.[423] Such an agreement was not reached. However, the Work Programme of the European Social Partners 2009–2010 states that the European social partners will carry on negotiating and implementing a "*framework agreement on inclusive labour markets.*"[424]

In sum, the EU and the social partners have a complex relationship. Above, it has become clear that the EU values the dialogue between the social partners highly, which is underlined by the fact the formal role given to the social partners in the Treaties. On top of this, the EU has worked to strengthen the social dialogue within Member States through secondary legislation and policies on the labour market.

419 Barnard 2006, p. 702.

420 Council Decision 2008/618 of 15 July 2008, OJ [2008] L198/47.

421 Ibid., Annex p. 1.

422 Joint declaration by European Trade Union Confederation (ETUC), Union of Industrial and Employers' Confederations of Europe (UNICE), European Association of Craft Small and Medium-Sized Enterprises (UEAPME), European Centre of Enterprises with Public Participation and Enterprises of General Economic Interest, 20 January 2003. See also a Statement by Uni-Europa Commerce and EuroCommerce on "promoting employment and integration of disabled people in the European distribution sector of 28 May 2004.

423 UNICE, CEEP, UEAPME: Work Programme of the European Social Partners 2006–2008, para. 3.

424 ETUC, BusinessEurope, CEEP and UEAPME: Work Programme of the European Social Partners 2009–2010, p. 3.

8.3. Conclusion

In conclusion, the EU actively involves both civil society in accordance with the contemporary disability human rights approach. Naturally, there is still room for improvement. In relation to the involvement of civil society organisations, it seems that the dialogue is still largely informal and that possibilities for influence vary significantly across different policy areas and depend to a large extent on the resources of the civil society organisations in question rather than on democratic representativeness. Moreover, the EU also involves social partners actively in the development and implementation of EU law and policy. In contrast to the involvement of civil society, the involvement of social partners is more structured, but limited by the in-built conflicts of interests between the EU, which pull in the direction of regulation of the labour market and the Member States and social partners who often pull in the direction of non-interference.

9. Legal Status of Denmark and Sweden under EU Law

The present sub-section will firstly give a brief overview of the legal status of Denmark and Sweden under EU law. In addition, I will look briefly at how EU law has influenced the Danish and Swedish labour market models which are characterised by a high degree of regulation by collective agreements rather than by legislation (especially in Denmark). The Danish and Swedish labour market models are described in more detail in *Chapter I Introduction*. The examination of how EU law and policy has influenced Danish and Swedish *material* law will be examined in the respective Chapters IV to VII on equal treatment, employer's duties, public employment services and social benefits.

Denmark joined the European Communities on 1 January 1973 following a referendum held in 1972. In 1992, a majority of voters in Denmark rejected the Maastricht Treaty which was only ratified by Denmark following the adoption in December 1992 of a "*Decision of the Heads and State and Government, Meeting within the European Council, Concerning Certain Problems Raised by Denmark concerning the Treaty of the European Union*". In 1997, when the Amsterdam Treaty was adopted, a "*Protocol no. 5 on the position of Denmark*" was annexed to the Treaty Establishing the European Community. This Protocol provides that Denmark shall not take part in the adoption of legal acts, and will not be bound by legal acts in the areas of union citizenship and justice and home affairs, defined as measures pursuant to Title IV of the TEC. Title IV of the TEC covers *"visas, asylum, immigration and other policies related to free movement of persons"*. In addition, Denmark does not participate fully in the European cooperation in the area of defence. According to Article 7 of the Protocol, Denmark may at any time choose to disapply the protocol and participate fully in the EU cooperation. The Danish protocol does not cause any significant limitations in the Danish obligations with regards to European disability law and policy as described in the present Chapter. Only persons with disabilities who are third-country nationals may not have the same right to social security in Denmark as in other EU Member States.[425] Denmark ratified the Lisbon Treaty on 29 May 2008.

Sweden joined the European Communities on 1 January 1995 following a referendum held in 1994. A referendum held in 2003 led to the rejection of Swedish participation in the Euro. Sweden is thus fully bound by European Disability policy as described in the present Chapter. On 10 December 2008, Sweden ratified the Lisbon Treaty.

When Denmark and Sweden became members of the European Communities the question of the influence of EC law on the Danish and Swedish "*labour market model*" was considered of central importance to both the Danish and the Swedish governments.[426] However, several developments now indicate that the initial perception in Denmark and Sweden that *status quo* in the regulation of the Danish and Swedish labour markets would remain untouched has proven wrong.

Firstly, it has not been possible to implement EU Directives merely through collective agreements since persons who were not covered by a collective agreement would not enjoy the protection of the Directive in question. This has resulted in a need for more national legislation regulating issues, which would previously have been regulated by collective agreement. Thus, both in Sweden and in Denmark, there has been a significant rise in the amount of labour laws that have been passed since the 1990s compared to previous years.[427] On the one hand, Sweden has simply implemented Directives using legislation only. Denmark, on the other hand, has used a mix of legislation and collective agreements to implement Directives. The *subsidiary*- method has been the most common. According to this method, legislation is given a subsidiary status to collective agreements provided that these comply with the Directive. In addition, the *erga-omnes*-method has also been used. According to this method a collective agreement implementing EU legislation is made to apply to all persons on the labour market through a law.[428] The Danish social partners have had an interest in using collective agreements to implement Directives because the Danish Labour Court and other collective conflict resolution

425 Council Regulation (EC) 859/2003 of 14 May 2003 extending the provisions of Regulation (EEC) No 1408/71 and Regulation (EEC) 574/72 to nationals of third countries who are not already covered by those provisions solely on the ground of their nationality which was adopted with reference to Article 63(4) in Title IV ECT does not apply to Denmark, OJ [2003] 124/1.

426 Swedish Proposition for Parliamentary Decision on Swedish Membership of the European Union, Regeringens Proposition 1994/95:19 *Sveriges Medlemskab i Europeiska Unionen,* p. 218 and 227.

427 Bruun and Malmberg 2005, p. 17. Nielsen and Roseberry 2008, p. 36.

428 Nielsen 2006, p. 66. Council Directive 93/104/EC of 23 November 1993 *concerning certain aspects of the organization of working time* was implemented by using the *erga-omnes* method.

systems can only be used if the issue of contention is based on a collective agreement. Issues concerning the interpretation of laws must be resolved in the ordinary court system. This is not the case in Sweden where all disagreements between employers and employees must be resolved by the labour court as long as the parties are bound by the same collective agreement.[429]

In sum, it is clear that the labour market systems of Denmark and Sweden are 'Europeanised' in the sense that the regulation of the labour markets in Denmark and Sweden is increasingly shared between the State and the social partners. At the same time however, both the treaties and the legislation adopted in the EU as well as the jurisprudence of the ECJ show a high degree of respect for the Danish and Swedish labour market models.[430] In line herewith, the *Laval*-judgment should not be seen as indicating a lack of appreciation for the Danish and Swedish labour market models by the ECJ. On the contrary, the judgment merely applies fundamental EU principles of freedom of movement of workers, and non-discrimination of nationals of other Member States to collective agreements in the same way that these principles would apply to legislation.

10. Conclusions

In conclusion, EU law and policy has undergone significant developments since the 1950s. EU law and policy has progressed from being founded on the principle of formal equality, to being based on the principle of substantive equality, to the point where they now even show signs of moving towards the substantive diversity equality model. As regards disability more specifically, EU law and policy has moved from ignoring the trend towards the adoption of a disability policy, which, at least according to the description in the Disability Strategy, is in conformity with a contemporary human rights approach.

An analysis of EU law and policy in the areas of employment and social benefits, however, reveals a more complex reality. On the one hand, the EU has adopted a landmark equal treatment directive in the area of employment, and a proposal for a new equal treatment directive outside of the area of employment has been tabled. On the other hand, persons with disability still seem to be an under-protected group

---

429 Bruun and Malberg 2005, p. 29.

430 Examples include Article 137(5) EC on the regulation of the labour market which states that Article 137 "shall not apply to pay, the right of association, the right to strike or the right to impose lock-outs." The Charter of Fundamental Rights also protects the Right of collective bargaining and action in Article 28. Numerous Directives expressly allow for implementation through collective agreements. See for example Article 18 of European Parliament and Council Directive (EC) 2003/88 of the of 4 November 2003 concerning certain aspects of the organisation of working time, OJ [1983] L299/9.

and the interests of persons with disabilities have not been taken into account as yet in all EU employment laws and policies.

The Employment Equality Directive is a key piece of legislation as regards equal treatment of persons with disabilities in the EU. It establishes a right to non-discrimination on the grounds of disability in employment and a duty to provide reasonable accommodation. However, several exceptions and caveats relating specifically to disability significantly reduce the level of protection provided to persons with disabilities. In addition, the ECJ has provided an inadequate definition of disability based on the medical model of disability, which could seriously hamper the effective implementation of the Directive.

In the area of employers' obligations, relatively detailed legal acts on health and safety, only few obligations are imposed to ensure that working environment becomes inclusive towards persons with disabilities. Moreover, the EU policy is based on the flexicurity model, which promotes more flexibility for employers to dismiss employees. Few employers' obligations towards employees with reduced working capacity mean that employees with disabilities are at a risk of exclusion from the labour market and delay the creation of inclusive general structures on the labour market.

In the area of employment promotion, little secondary legislation has been adopted, but in line with the flexicurity model, the EU promotes economisation of employment promotion services as well as active labour market policies. On the one hand, more focus on employment promotion may benefit unemployed persons with disabilities and on the other hand, there is a risk that more focus on economisation of employment services may disadvantage vulnerable groups on the labour market such as persons with disabilities.

As regards income-replacement benefits, little EU legislation has been adopted with a view to achieving a harmonisation of social security policies and laws in the Member States. Instead, cross-cutting principles such as the principle of freedom of movement and the right to non-discrimination apply. However, persons with disabilities have to a certain extent been carved out of these general rules. As mentioned above, the EU promotes active labour market policies and the flexicurity-model which is also of relevance in relation to income-replacement benefits. Similarly to above, more support for returning to the labour market may benefit persons with disabilities who receive income-replacement benefits. However, more focus on incentives for seeking work may also place persons with disabilities at risk of losing necessary income-replacement benefits.

Finally, although there is room, yet, for improvement, the EU actively involves both civil society and social partners in its law and policymaking in accordance with the contemporary disability human rights approach.

In the following Chapters, I will compare Danish and Swedish law in the light of the contemporary disability human rights approach and examine in which direction EU law and policy is influencing Danish and Swedish law and policy.

Chapter IV
Equality Law and Policy

1. Introduction

In the present Chapter, I explore what the disability human rights approach entails with regard to equality in employment and whether Danish and Swedish laws and policies are based on the contemporary disability human rights approach in this respect. Finally, I assess whether the two States have fulfilled their duties under the European Employment Equality Directive.

After an introduction of the laws and their enforcement in Denmark and Sweden in Section 3, I focus on the definition of disability (Section 4), on the protection against direct and indirect discrimination (Sections 5 and 6), Reasonable accommodation (Section 7), the material scope of protection of the ban against discrimination (Section 8), and Positive action (Section 9). A conclusion is contained in Section 10.

2. Contemporary Disability Human Rights Approach

In the present Section, I explore what the contemporary disability human rights approach entails as regards equality law and policy. I start out with examining the relationship between the right to protection against discrimination and the principle of equality (Section 2.1.) and I then examine more closely the contemporary disability human rights approach in relation to the specific elements of protection against discrimination, including the definition of disability (Section 2.2) and positive action (Section 2.3).

2.1. Non-Discrimination and Equality

The ban against discrimination on the grounds of disability is seen as the cornerstone of the contemporary disability human rights approach which seeks to abolish society's unequal treatment of persons with disabilities rather than seeking to 'cure' persons with disabilities. This has been reflected in all contemporary human rights instruments such as the European Social Charter, the European Charter of Fundamental Freedoms and Rights and the CRPD.[431] In the CRPD,

[431] The European Social Committee "emphasises the importance of the non-discrimination norm in the disability context and finds that this forms an integral part of Article 15", European Social Committee, Conclusions 2003, Statement of Interpretation on article 15, p. 10. European Charter of Fundamental Freedoms and Rights of 2000, contains a ban against discrimination on the grounds of disability in Article 21(1). See also European Court of Human Rights, *Glor v.*

"*non-discrimination*" is listed as one of the general principles on which the CRPD is founded. In addition, the CRPD states that:

> *"discrimination against any person on the basis of disability is a violation of the inherent dignity and worth of the human person" and that the purpose of the CRPD is the "full and equal enjoyment of all human rights and fundamental freedoms by all persons with disabilities, and to promote respect for their inherent dignity".*[432]

As discussed under *Chapter II Human Rights*, the protection provided under a prohibition of 'discrimination' will be based on a specific form of equality. A prohibition of discrimination based on formal equality model will for example not provide protection against indirect discrimination whereas this is the case for a prohibition of discrimination based on substantive equality.

As explained in *Chapter II Human Rights*, the fact that the contemporary disability human rights approach is based on the substantive diversity equality principle means that positive measures to eliminate or reduce disadvantage between different groups in society are not seen as an exception to the rule of equal treatment. This model of equality is forward-looking and aims at changing general structures in society so that they reflect the equal rights of different groups in society. Thus, according to the substantive diversity equality model, society is diverse and general structures must reflect this. A prohibition of discrimination founded on the substantive diversity equality model will be interpreted so as to provide maximum protection against both direct and indirect discrimination. In addition, the duty to provide reasonable accommodation for persons with disabilities will be strongly established.

The CRPD does not specify how the ban against direct and indirect discrimination should be defined, but it does provide that *"all forms of discrimination, including denial of reasonable accommodation",* shall be prohibited and it defines disability discrimination as *"distinction, exclusion or restriction on the basis of disability which has the purpose or effect of impairing or nullifying [...]".*[433] Thus not only direct discrimination on the grounds of disability, but also indirect discrimination on apparently neutral grounds, which has the effect of placing persons with disability at a disadvantage must be encompassed. 'Denial of reasonable accommodation' is defined as a form of discrimination and presumably other forms of discrimination such as harassment are also encompassed since 'all forms of discrimination' are included.[434] Other questions of importance for the effective

---

Switzerland, Application no. 13444/04, judgment of 30 April 2009, where the ECHR finds discrimination on the grounds of disability.

432 Preamble (h) and Article 1.

433 CRPD Article 2.

434 CRPD Article 2.

functioning of a ban against discrimination are also not mentioned specifically, such as the question of burden of proof.

In relation to the scope of application of the ban against discrimination on the grounds of disability, it follows from Article 4(2) of the CRPD that a general ban against discrimination must be introduced by all States Parties: *"States Parties shall prohibit all discrimination on the basis of disability and guarantee to persons with disabilities equal and effective legal protection against discrimination on all grounds."* In other words, a prohibition should cover as a minimum all the areas that covered by the CRPD. In relation to the field of employment, the CRPD specifies that the prohibition of discrimination must apply *"with regard to all matters concerning all forms of employment, including conditions of recruitment, hiring and employment, continuance of employment, career advancement and safe and healthy working conditions"*.[435] Other areas of relevance for the possibility of persons with disabilities to take fully part in the labour market include for example the field of education, where the CRPD specifically mentions the right to protection against discrimination.[436]

The importance of the prohibition of discrimination on the grounds of disability has also been established for example by the European Committee on Social Rights, which interprets Article 1(2) on the duty of States to *"protect effectively the right of the worker to earn his living in an occupation freely entered upon"* and Article 15(2) on the duty of States Parties to *"undertake measures for the placing of disabled persons in employment"* of the ESC of 1961 as requiring the adoption of a prohibition of discrimination on the grounds of disability in the field of employment:

> *"The Committee considers that under Article 1§2 legislation should prohibit discrimination in employment at least on grounds of race, ethnic origin, religion, disability, age, sexual orientation and political opinion. Where a state party has accepted Article 15§2 of the Charter the Committee will examine legislation prohibiting discrimination on grounds of disability under this provision."*[437]

Moreover, the Committee on Social Rights has in two cases found discrimination on the grounds of disability in violation of the Revised European Social Charter due to lack of access to education for children with intellectual disabilities.[438] As explained in *Chapter II Human Rights, Section 1.3. From the 1970s until 2000s*, the

435 CRPD Article 27.

436 CRPD Article 24 on education.

437 European Committee of Social Rights, Conclusions XVIII-1 – Austria, Article 1, p. 27.

438 European Committee of Social Rights, Complaint No. 13/2002 by Autism-France v. France of 4 November 2003 and Complaint No. 41/2007 by Mental Disability Advocacy Centre v. Bulgaria of 3 June 2008.

European Committee on Social Rights interpreted the prohibition of discrimination and the right to education as entailing a right to access an educational system with inclusive general structures. The European Committee on Social Rights found that the systematic absence of persons with disabilities from the mainstream educational system in Bulgaria constituted a violation of the ESC.[439] In other words, it seems that the European Committee on Social Rights interpreted the prohibition of discrimination in line with the 'substantive diversity equality' model.

In sum, it follows firstly that the prohibition of discrimination on the grounds of disability is of central importance under the contemporary disability human rights approach. Secondly, the ban against discrimination on the grounds of disability must be interpreted in line with the substantive diversity equality model as requiring the alteration of general structures so that they are inclusive to persons with disabilities. I return to the question of positive action measures in the *Section 2.3 Positive Action* below.

2.2. Definition of Disability

In *Chapter II Human Rights*, I discuss the definition of disability under the contemporary disability human rights approach. As opposed to under the minority model of disability, persons with disabilities are not considered to be a specific insular minority under the universality model of disability. Instead, the definition of disability under the universality model of disability should not necessarily target the disabled persons-minority group, but it should reflect the aims and purposes of the legislation in question. Thus in relation to non-discrimination legislation, the focus should be on whether or not the differential treatment took place on the grounds of disability. The focus should not be on whether or not the alleged victim is sufficiently disabled to be perceived as part of the disabled persons minority group and thus to qualify for protection. However, disability still needs to be defined in order to determine whether a certain treatment was based on such grounds or not. The severity of a person's disability should not be decisive since discrimination may take place both on the grounds of minor and major disabilities and be equally objectionable. Moreover it should not be relevant, whether or not a person has experienced limitations in his or her social life since this will to a large extent depend on whether or not that person has met with inclusive design and attitudes. Again, persons who have to date not experienced limitations in their social life due to their impairment, may well have the same impairments as others who have and be equally as prone to be subjected to discrimination on the grounds of disability.

---

439 European Committee on Social Rights, Complaint No. 41/2007 by Mental Disability Advocacy Centre of 3 June 2008, para. 35 and 37.

Nonetheless, it seems that it is necessary to require the presence (in the past, present or future) of long-lasting impairments in order to differentiate disability from illness. Thus, the CRPD Article 1 on the purpose of the CRPD states that "*persons with disabilities include those who have long-term physical, mental, intellectual or sensory impairments*". Also, the ECJ states the following: "*The importance which the Community legislature attaches to measures for adapting the workplace to the disability demonstrates that it envisaged situations in which participation in professional life is hindered over a long period of time. In order for the limitation to fall within the concept of 'disability', it must therefore be probable that it will last for a long time.*"[440]

Moreover, since the heart of the matter concerns the grounds on which the differential treatment has taken place, it follows that a person who is mistakenly perceived as having an impairment, who has previously had an impairment or who is developing an impairment may also be subjected to discrimination on the grounds of disability. It follows also that a family member's impairment may be grounds for discrimination.

In sum, the definition of 'disability' under the disability human rights approach varies according to the context of the definition in question. In relation to legislation providing protection against discrimination on the grounds of disability, 'disability' should relate to the reason for the differential treatment in question and not the impairment of the alleged victim. Although 'disability' may be defined as excluding for example short-term impairments, the key is that all persons may obtain protection if the grounds for the differential treatment were related to disability.

2.3. Positive Action

As described in *Chapter III Human Rights, Section 1.4. Current Trends*, positive action is an essential characteristic of substantive diversity equality on which the CRPD is based. The main characteristics of substantive diversity equality is that claims-led non-discrimination approach is complemented with a proactive approach according to which general structures must be changed to become inclusive. The role of the State is to ensure equality and participation as opposed to merely refraining from interferences with the individual. CRPD Article 3 explicitly states that the Convention is based on "*equality of opportunity*" which means that formal equality is not sufficient. Moreover, the proactive approach aims at altering general structures in society so that they become inclusive towards persons with disabilities and runs as a thread through the articles of the Convention.[441]

---

440 ECJ judgment (Grand Chamber) of 11 July 2006, Case C-13/05, *Sonia Chacón Navas v. Eurest Colectividades SA*, para. 45.

441 Kayess and French 2008, p. 20.

The present Section will explore firstly whether positive action is required or merely permitted under human rights law and secondly whether specific positive action measures such as strict quotas, which grant preferential treatment to persons who may be less qualified than others, are permitted or required under human rights law. Special focus will be on the CRPD since this convention represents the newest and most specific UN convention on disability. In addition, the CEDAW Committee has issued a General Recommendation which also sheds light on the possible interpretation of the CRPD. The European Committee on Social Rights has examined the use of positive action measures in order to promote employment of persons with disabilities and is thus of special interest. In contrast, the European Court of Human Rights has permitted the use of positive action measures, but its case law consists of only one judgment which is not of special interest to the issue at hand.[442]

As mentioned in *Chapter III EU Law and Policy*, positive action may be understood as measures that are taken consciously and actively in order to promote substantive equality for a certain disadvantaged group.[443] The types of measures that fall under the definition of positive action, are very broad ranging from very soft measures to strict quotas. However, as explained by the CEDAW-Committee, not all measures favourable to the disadvantaged group amount to positive action. According to the Committee: *"The provision of general conditions in order to guarantee the civil, political, economic, social and cultural rights of women and the girl child, designed to ensure them a life of dignity and non-discrimination cannot be called temporary special measures"*[444] (which is the terminology used in the CEDAW convention for positive action).

According to CRPD Article 5(4) *"Specific measures which are necessary to accelerate or achieve de facto equality of persons with disabilities shall not be considered discrimination under the terms of the present Convention."*

As opposed to the CEDAW conventions the CRPD does not explicitly distinguish between 'temporary special measures' and 'special measures', which are not temporary.[445] According to CEDAW Article 4(2), *"Adoption by States Parties of special measures, including those measures contained in the present Convention,*

442 In ECHR judgment (Grand Chamber) of 12 April 2006, Stec and Others v. the United Kingdom, Application No. 65731/01, the Court found that positive differential treatment of women did not constitute discrimination of men because of the "disadvantaged situation of women", para. 66.

443 See the definition in the Employment Equality Directive above and the definition of UN Special Rapporteur Bossuyt in his final report on "the concept of affirmative action", UN doc E/CN.4/Sub.2/2002/21, 17 June 2002, para. 6.

444 UN Committee on the Elimination of All Discrimination Against Women, General Recommendation No. 25, 2004, para. 19.

445 CEDAW Article 4(1) and 4(2).

aimed at protecting maternity shall not be considered discriminatory." In its General Recommendation, the CEDAW-Committee explains that the aim of the 'temporary special measures' is to *"correct past current forms and effects of discrimination against women"* as opposed to special measures relating to maternity, which consists in *"non-identical treatment of women and men due to their biological differences. [...] These measures are of a permanent nature, at least until such a time as the scientific and technological knowledge [...] would warrant a review.'*[446]

The fact that the CRPD has left out the word 'temporary' indicates that the drafters of the convention sought to cover both types of special measures: temporary special measures aiming at overcoming effects of discrimination and permanent special measures necessary due to biological differences between persons with disabilities and persons without disabilities. An example of permanent special measures could be the provision of personal assistants to persons with disabilities in need hereof.

The fact that measures must be 'necessary' indicates on the one hand that the specific measures must be proportional with the aim of 'accelerating or achieving de facto equality'. In addition, this wording also underlines that specific measures may be required in order to accelerate or achieve de facto equality. As stressed by the CEDAW Committee, *"temporary special measures are part of a necessary strategy"* and *"States Parties are obliged to adopt and implement temporary special measures in relation to any of these articles if such measures can be shown to be necessary and appropriate in order to achieve the overall, or a specific goal of, women's de facto or substantive equality.'*[447] In sum, positive action measures may be required if they are necessary in order to achieve substantive equality. This is however a relatively vague definition of when the enactment of positive action measures is required since substantive equality will only rarely have been fully achieved.

The next question is whether all types of positive measures are allowed or even required or whether only some are. The guidance obtained from the CRPD is not precise when it comes to permitted types of positive action measures. CRPD Article 27 regarding Work and Employment states that employment in the private sector shall be promoted *"through appropriate policies and measures, which may include affirmative action programmes, incentives and other measures"*.[448] This could at

446 UN Committee on the Elimination of All Discrimination Against Women, General Recommendation No. 25, 2004, paras. 15 and 16.

447 UN Committee on the Elimination of All Discrimination against Women, General Recommendation No. 25, 2004, paras. 18 and 24. In para. 24 reference is made to all substantive provisions of the CEDAW convention which oblige Member States to "take all appropriate measures".

448 CRPD Article 27(1)(h).

least in principle include, for example, strict quotas which provide a right to preferential treatment to applicants with disabilities even if these are not equally qualified with other applicants as long as the quotas are considered 'necessary'.

Similarly, the CEDAW Committee has also stated that special measures such as strict quotas which set aside the merit principle may be necessary:

> *"The adoption and implementation of temporary special measures may lead to a discussion of qualifications and merit of the group or individuals so targeted, and an argument against preferences for allegedly lesser-qualified women over men in areas such as politics, education and employment. As temporary special measures aim at accelerating achievement of de facto or substantive equality, questions of qualification and merit, in particular in the area of employment in the public and private sectors, need to be reviewed carefully for gender bias as they are normatively and culturally determined. For appointment, selection or election to public and political office, factors other than qualification and merit, including the application of the principles of democratic fairness and electoral choice, may also have to play a role."*[449]

Similarly, the European Social Committee also does not exclude the use of strict quotas as such. Thus in its conclusions on the implementation of both the European Social Charter of 1961, the Committee underlines that *"The Committee recalls that Article 15§2 does not require the introduction of quotas but, when such a system is applied, the Committee examines its effectiveness when assessing conformity with Article 15§2."*[450] The fact that the European Social Committee concentrates on the 'effectiveness' of quotas rather than for example whether the quotas require that only persons with disabilities who are equally qualified with others receive preferential treatment, indicates that also strict quotas are permitted under both the European Social Charter and the Revised European Social Charter. An example of the issues which the European Social Committee examines in relation to quotas is:

> *"the number of persons with disabilities actually employed under the quota system, the number of employers subject to the quota, the number of employers who have not met the requirements of the quota and have been subject to additional taxation, and whether the quota system applies in the public sector."*[451]

In conclusion, positive action measures are a crucial component of substantive diversity equality. The CRPD is based on substantive diversity equality and

449 General Recommendation No. 25, para. 23.

450 Council of Europe, European Committee of Social Rights, *Conclusions XVIII-2, 2007,* ***Germany,*** *p. 152. (European Social Charter of 1961), Conclusions 2008 –* ***Armenia****, Article 15, p. 58 (Revised European Social Charter of 1996).*

451 Council of Europe, European Committee of Social Rights, Conclusions XIX-1 Slovakia Article 15, 2008, p. 375.

consequently it not only permits, but requires the use of positive action measures in order to accelerate and achieve substantive equality for persons with disabilities. However, it is still left up to States to decide which positive action measures will be appropriate. Similarly under both the CEDAW convention and the European Social Charter, the choice of positive action measures is considered to fall within the realm of the States parties of the different conventions as long as the measures in question do promote equality.

2.4. Conclusion

In conclusion, the enactment of an effective ban against discrimination on the grounds of disability is of central importance under the contemporary disability human rights approach. The definition of disability must reflect the aim of the non-discrimination legislation to provide protection against discrimination and the duty to provide reasonable accommodation must be recognised. Finally, the contemporary disability human rights approach is based on the substantive diversity approach which means that positive action for the promotion of equality is essential. In the following sub-section, I examine whether Denmark and Sweden have embraced the contemporary disability human rights approach.

3. Overview of Danish and Swedish Equality Law

The present Section gives an overview of the legal acts in place to promote equality of persons with disabilities through protection against discrimination and duties to enact positive action. In addition, a short presentation is made of the administrative complaints mechanisms which have been set up in Denmark and Sweden to promote equality of persons with disabilities.

In Denmark, the adoption of a ban against discrimination on the grounds of disability took place once Denmark was required to do so under the European Employment Equal Treatment Directive.[452] Initially, it was attempted to implement the provisions on disability and age of the Employment Equality Directive through agreement between the social partners, which would be complemented with a legal act, but no general agreement could be reached between the social partners.[453] On

452 Council Directive 2000/78/EC of 27 November 2000 establishing a general framework for equal treatment in employment and occupation. The deadline for national implementation of the provisions regarding disability was 2 December 2003, which could be extended to 2 December 2006, cf. Article 18.

453 The Government and social partners discussed the implementation of the Employment Equality Directive in the so-called implementation committee which comprises both representatives of government and the social partners. Only Protocol of 2 October 2004 between Danish Employers (DA) and CO-Industri succeeded in reaching agreement on the implementation of the

22 December 2004, the existing Act Prohibiting Differential Treatment on the Labour Market was amended to cover also age and disability.[454]

Today, the Danish Act Prohibiting Differential Treatment on the Labour Market covers discrimination on the grounds of disability, as well as religion or belief, political opinion, sexual orientation and age. Discrimination on the grounds of race, skin colour and national, social or ethnic origin is prohibited by the Act on Ethnic Equal Treatment and discrimination on the grounds of gender is prohibited by the Act on Equal Treatment of Men and Women in Employment, the Act on Equal Pay for Men and Women and the Act on Equality between Men and Women.[455]

In Denmark, an Equal Treatment Board which considers individual complaints over discrimination on the grounds of disability as well as gender, race, skin colour, religion or belief, political opinion, sexual orientation, age and national, social or ethnic origin was established in 2009.[456] The Equal Treatment Board is presided over by three judges and there are nine ordinary members of the Board who are appointed by the Ministry of Employment. Ordinarily, one judge and two ordinary members decide each case. The decisions of the Board are legally binding, but the parties to a case may bring the case to the courts for a new judgment if they wish. During 2009, the Board made 64 decisions in total and 2 decisions regarding disability, and during 2010, the Board made 7 decisions regarding disability.[457]

Employment Equality Directive. See DA's comments to the proposed amendment to the Act Prohibiting Differential Treatment on the Labour Market (Arbejdsmarkedsudvalgets Betænkning af 8. December 2004 til L92, bilag 1).

454 Act amending Act Prohibiting Differential Treatment on the Labour Market (Lov om ændring af lov om forbud mod forskelsbehandling på arbejdsmarkedet m.v.), L 1417 of 22 December 2004. Latest version of Act Prohibiting Differential Treatment on the Labour Market, LBK 1310 of 16 December 2008.

455 Act no. 734 of 28 June 2006 on Equal Treatment of Men and Women in Employment (Lov om Ligebehandling af Mænd og Kvinder i Beskæftigelse m.v.), Act no. 899 of 5 September 2008 on Equal Pay for Men and Women (Lov om Ligeløn til Mænd og Kvinder), Act no. 1095 of 19 September 2007 on Gender Equality with latest amendment by Act no. 484 of 12 June 2009 (Lov om Ligestilling mellem Mænd og Kvinder).

456 Act no. 387 of 27 May 2008 on the Equal Treatment Board, which entered into force on 1 January 2009 (Lov om ligebehandlingsnævnet). Link to Equal Treatment Board: www.ligebehandlingsnaevnet.dk/.

457 Decision of Equal Treatment Board, Case 35/2009 of 23 September 2009 regarding a police officer who could no longer take part in trips to abroad due to a reduced working capacity and who could therefore no longer receive a pay supplement linked to participation in trips. The Board did not consider this to be in violation with the ban against indirect discrimination because the differential treatment was found to be justified. In Case 64/2009 of 16 December 2009 a man with a 'permanent psychological fragility' had been turned down for a position which required experience with administrative work. Since the plaintiff did not have such experience, the Equal Treatment Board found that he had not been subjected to direct or indirect discrimination due to disability. The Board did not take a stand on whether or not 'permanent

Before 2009, there was no administrative complaints system for persons who had been subjected to discrimination on the grounds of disability. Since 1993, a Centre for Equal Treatment of Disabled Persons has promoted equal treatment of persons with disability, but the Centre has not been mandated to hear individual complaints.[458] The Danish Institute for Human Rights has sought to raise awareness on the human rights of persons with disabilities, but has not had a specific mandate to consider complaints on the grounds of disability discrimination.[459]

In Sweden, the *"Prohibition of Discrimination in Working Life on the Grounds of Disability Act"* was introduced in 1999 making Sweden the first Continental European country to prohibit discrimination on the grounds of disability.[460] Already in 1992, a Commission Report on Disability recommended the adoption of a ban against discrimination on the grounds of disability in the field of employment.[461] However, it was not until after the adoption of UK and US statutes prohibiting discrimination on the grounds of disability, that the Swedish Government presented a proposal in its list of planned legislation in 1996.[462] This proposal met with strong criticism from disability organisations, employers' organisations as well as academia because it was either considered too lenient or too strict on employers.[463] An amended version of this proposal was adopted in 1999 and only minor changes were made in 2003 and 2005 to ensure full compliance with the Employment Equal Treatment Directive.[464] On 1 January 2009, a new Discrimination Act which covers 'sex, transgender identity or expression, ethnicity, religion or other belief, disability, sexual orientation or age' was adopted.[465] The Discrimination Act is not limited to

---

psychological fragility' qualified as disability. Ligebehandlingsnævnets Årsberetning 2009, p. 3.

458 Centre on Equal Treatment of Persons with Disabilities established by Parliamentary Decision B43 of 2 April 1993.

459 Act on the Establishment of the Danish Centre for International Studies and Human Rights, Act no. 411 of 6 June 2002 (Lov om Etablering af det Danske Center for International Studier og Menneskerettigheder).

460 Act prohibiting discrimination in working life on the grounds of impairment, SFS 1999:132, (Lagen om förbud mot diskriminering i arbetslivet på grund av funktionshinder). The UK Disability Discrimination Act of 1995 was the first act prohibiting discrimination on the grounds of disability in Europe.

461 SOU 1992:52 Handicapputredning.

462 Departementspromemoria DS 1996:56, 'Förbud mot diskriminering i arbetslivet av personer med funktionshinder'. Inghammar 2007, p. 279. Americans with Disabilities Act of 1990 inspired the UK Disability Discrimination Act of 1995.

463 Academics such as Numhauser-Henning and Sveneus, Claesson-Wästberg criticised the proposal in the Press: Sydsvenska Dagbladet, 27 October 1996, and Dagens Nyheter, 18 January 1997. Inghammar 2007, p. 279.

464 Acts amending Act prohibiting discrimination in working life on the grounds of impairment, SFS 2003:309 and SFS 2005:478 (Lagener om ändring af lagen om förbud mot diskriminering i arbetslivet av personer med funktionshinder).

465 Discrimination Act, SFS 2008:567 with latest amendment by SFS 2009:526, (Diskrimineringslag), Chapter 1, Section 1.

"working life" as was the 1999-Act, but covers also *"education"*, which was previously covered by the Act on Equal Treatment of Students at Universities Act and *new* areas as regards disability including *"goods, services and housing", "health and medical care and social services etc", "social insurance system, unemployment insurance and financial aid for studies"*.[466]

In 1994, a Handicap Ombudsman to prevent discrimination on the grounds of impairments was established in Sweden.[467] The Handicap Ombudsman was established with reference to the UN Standard Rules on Disability.[468] As of 1 January 2009, a Discrimination Ombudsman replaced the four previous specialised Ombudsmen and was given a mandate to prevent discrimination and promote equal rights and opportunities for all irrespective of sex, transgender identity or expression, ethnicity, religion or other belief, impairment, sexual orientation or age.[469] The Discrimination Ombudsman may seek to obtain a settlement between the parties or to bring the case before the courts. The Discrimination Ombudsman cannot make decisions regarding complaints which are binding on the parties of the case. During 2009, the Discrimination Ombudsman received almost 2.600 complaints, which is 20% more than the four specialised Ombudsmen received in total in 2008. Of these complaints, 900 concerned discrimination on the grounds of impairment. During 2009, the Ombudsman received 785 complaints regarding discrimination in the field of employment on all grounds. Almost 700 cases were ended in 2009. Of these 700 cases, 7 cases were decided by the Labour Court and 20 were settled by the parties of the case with assistance from the Disability Ombudsman.[470]

In sum, both Denmark and Sweden have a ban against discrimination on the grounds of disability in the field of employment. The Swedish ban dates back to 1999 and is now contained in a Discrimination Act which covers all protected grounds in Sweden as well as having a broad scope of application. The Danish ban against discrimination on the grounds of disability was only introduced in 2004 in one of the three Danish legal acts which prohibit discrimination on the labour market. Both Denmark and Sweden have either an administrative complaints board or an Ombudsman which consider or provide assistance in case of complaints over discrimination on all protected grounds both inside and outside the labour market. The protection against discrimination on the grounds of disability in the labour

---

466 Discrimination Act, Chapter 2, Sections 12, 13 and 14.

467 Act on Disability Ombudsman, SFS 1994:749, (Lag om Handikappombudsmannen).

468 Preparatory Works to the Act on the Disability Ombudsman, Prop. 1993/94:219, p. 1.

469 Act on Discrimination Ombudsman, SFS 2008:568 without amendments, (Lag om Diskrimineringsombudsmannen). The previous four specialised Ombudsmen sought to promote equal rights irrespective of gender, ethnicity and race, sexual orientation and disability. Link to Discrimination Ombudsman: www.do.se.

470 None of these cases concerned discrimination on the grounds of impairment, Discrimination Ombudsman Annual Report 2009, p. 35.

market is examined in detail below in relation both the obligations of Denmark and Sweden under the European Equal Treatment Directive and under human rights law.

4. Definition of Disability

The definition of the concept of disability under the legal acts protecting against discrimination is of crucial importance for ensuring effective protection against discrimination on the grounds of disability. In this Section, the definitions of disability under the Danish and Swedish Acts are compared and analysed in the light of the disability human rights approach and EU law.

4.1. Danish Definition of disability

The Danish Act on Differential Treatment on the Labour Market does not provide a definition of 'disability', and the Preparatory Works give an unclear picture of the intended coverage of the term. The Preparatory Works explain that the concept of disability must be understood as *"physical, psychological or intellectual impairment [which] must be compensated in order for that person to function on an equal footing with other citizens in a similar situation."* However, the meaning of *"compensation"* is not provided although it is mentioned that *"it is not a requirement for protection against differential treatment on the grounds of disability that there is a specific need for compensation.'*[471]

In other words, it seems that the Preparatory Works have set up a two-pronged definition. Firstly, there must be a physical, psychological or intellectual impairment and secondly, there must be *"a need for compensation"*.[472] Presumably, the use of the word *compensation* is a reference to the Danish principle of compensation on which the Danish disability policy is founded, cf. *Chapter II Human Rights, Section 2.3 National Disability Action Plans*. According to the Danish National Action Plan, compensation entails *"that society helps persons with disabilities and offers benefits and assistive services to minimize the consequences of disability"*.[473] In other words, compensation may be understood as public benefits and assistance provided to persons with disabilities such as e.g. personal assistance and wage subvention for employment on the open labour market.[474] The fact that the Preparatory Works state that *"it is not a requirement for protection against differential treatment on the*

---

471 Danish Preparatory Works, Proposal L92 of 11 November 2004, '4.1. Handicapkriteriet' and 'Bemærkninger til de enkelte bestemmelser', 'Til no. 2'.

472 Ibid.

473 Regeringen: *Handlingsplan for handicapområdet, 2003.*

474 See *Chapter VII on Social Benefits* and *Chapter VI on State Measures* (for the promotion of employment of persons with disabilities).

grounds of disability that there is a specific need for compensation" presumably indicates that the provision of compensation in relation to the specific employment position in question was not intended to be a requirement to qualify as having a disability under the Danish Act on Differential Treatment on the Labour Market.[475] The Preparatory Works do not mention how long the impairment in question is required to last, in order to be covered by the concept of disability under the Danish Act on Differential Treatment on the Labour Market.

I now turn to Danish case law on the concept of disability under the Act on Differential Treatment on the Labour Market. In the first two cases decided by a High Court, the Western High Court found that two women who had multiple sclerosis and post-traumatic stress syndrome respectively were not disabled under the Act on Differential Treatment on the Labour Market.[476] Both women were employed in 'flexjob'-positions, which means that the employees worked reduced hours and that special consideration had to be shown for their reduced working capacity while the employers received a reimbursement of part of their salary.[477] In both cases, the Western High Court held firstly that the presence of a disability in the sense of the Act on Differential Treatment requires a *"physical, mental or intellectual impairment, which results in a need for compensation in order for the person in question to be able to function on an equal footing with other citizens in a similar life situation."* The Western High Court then explained that *"Section 2a of the Act on Differential Treatment on the Labour Market [...] provides that employers of a person with a disability under certain circumstances have an obligation to fulfil the need for compensation which follows from an impairment"*. Finally the Court concluded that *"it was proven that A's illness, especially on account of the tiredness, sensory disorders and memory problems, had led to an impairment, but the High Court did not find that the impairment, which at the time of the dismissal only required additional compensation in the form of a further reduction of her working time, could be seen as a disability in the sense of the Act on Differential Treatment on the Labour Market.'"*[478]

In sum, in these first two High Court judgments on the definition of disability, it was established that a disability in the sense of the Act on Differential Treatment required both an impairment and a reduced working capacity, which entailed a far-

475 Danish Preparatory Works, Proposal L92 of 11 November 2004, '4.1. Handicapkriteriet' and 'Bemærkninger til de enkelte bestemmelser', 'Til no. 2'.

476 Danish Western High Court Judgment of 11 October 2007, published in UFR2008.306V (multiple schlerosis). Danish Western High Court Judgment of 11 October 2007, No. B-2722–06, unpublished (post traumatic stress syndrome).

477 See more on the flexjob scheme in Chapter VI Employment Promotion.

478 Danish Western High Court Judgment of 11 October 2007, published in UFR2008.306V (multiple schlerosis). The reasoning of the Court was almost identical in the Danish Western High Court Judgment of 11 October 2007, No. B-2722–06, unpublished (post traumatic stress syndrome). See a critical analysis of these two judgments in Justesen 2008.

reaching need for compensation. Interestingly, it was not sufficient to receive substantial compensation in the form of a special employment contract with reduced working hours, special consideration for low productivity, and wage subvention from the State, i.e. 'flexjob'-positions. It is unclear what the Court required in addition to the already present compensation in the form of employment under special working conditions. It is possible that the Court either required that the persons in question should be in need of significant technical aids or personal assistance in order for the Court to consider them as disabled.

However, in more recent judgments from 2010, neither the Western High Court nor the Eastern High Court seem to agree with the definition applied by the Western High Court in 2007. Thus, in a judgment from 12 March 2010, the Western High Court found that a woman who had suffered a fractured skull and brain damage, which meant that she had memory problems and problems concentrating, was disabled in the sense of the Act on Differential Treatment. She had been hired in a 'flexjob'-position and could only work reduced hours with specific simple tasks, but she did not need assistive devices or personal assistance in her daily life or in her work.[479] In a case decided on 5 May 2010, the Eastern High Court found that a man with epilepsy who was hired in a so-called 'flexjob' position with two-thirds public wage subsidy was found to have a disability in sense of the Act on Differential Treatment because he had a *"permanent impairment which gave rise to a need for compensation in the form of reduced working hours, special consideration in order to avoid stress, repetitive work, dangerous work and the handling of machines"*.[480]

Similarly to the findings in the newer judgments by the Western High Court and the Eastern High Court, the Danish Equal Treatment Board also does not stipulate that a person fulfills a need for special assistive devices or personal assistance in order to be 'disabled' in the sense of the Danish Act on Differential Treatment. In a case decided in September 2009, the Danish Equal Treatment Board found that a policeman who had a longer-lasting reduced mobility and pain in one shoulder and who could no longer undertake operative tasks was disabled in the sense of the Act on Differential Treatment on the Labour Market. The Board stated that *"disability or a person with disability requires the presence of a physical, psychological or intellectual impairment, which gives rise to a need for compensation in order to allow the person in question to function on an equal footing with other citizens in a similar life situation.'*[481] Four out of five members of the Board found that the plaintiff had a disability. In two other cases decided in 2010, the Equal Treatment Board found again that persons whose impairment did not entail a need for special

479 Western High Court Judgment of 12 March 2010, 14. Section, No. B-1904–08 (unpublished).
480 Danish Eastern High Court Judgment of 5 May 2010, 18. Afd., no. B-2215–09 (unpublished).
481 Danish Equal Treatment Board, Case no. 35/2009 of 23 September 2009.

assistive devices or personal assistants were disabled in the sense of the Employment Equality Directive.[482]

In sum, it would seem that a definition of disability in the sense of the Danish Act on Differential Treatment has crystallised in Danish case law according to which a person with a permanent impairment which entails a need for significant compensation is disabled. It is not necessary that the person need specific assistive devices or personal assistance.

Nevertheless, in May 2010, the Danish Supreme Court decided to refer the question of a need for assistive devices to the ECJ for preliminary ruling. The referral to the ECJ regarding the definition of disability will take place from the Maritime and Commercial Court which is a specialised Court at the same level as the Eastern and Western High Courts. The Maritime and Commercial Court handles cases regarding employment law if the case is considered of fundamental importance and one party in the case requests that the City Court make a referral of the case to the Maritime and Commercial Court. In cases regarding employment law, two of the three judges will be experts appointed by Employers' and Employees' Organisations respectively.[483] On 24 August 2009, the Maritime and Commercial Court found that two women who both had severe back and shoulder problems respectively were both disabled under the Act on Differential Treatment on the Labour Market.[484] The first case concerned a woman employed in a company, which rents out apartments. She handled client contacts mainly over the telephone. She had to have an operation of her back, after which she had to be on sick leave for three months in order to carry out rehabilitative training. After the rehabilitation period she applied for reduced hours of work because of continued back pains. The second case concerned a receptionist who had shoulder and neck problems following a car accident and she had also applied for reduced working hours. In these cases, the Maritime and Commercial Court found that both women were disabled in the sense of the Danish Act on Differential Treatment in spite of the fact that neither of the two plaintiffs needed assistive devices or personal assistance. The Maritime and Commercial Court stated the following: *"The problems, which are to be considered of a permanent or at least of long-lasting character, lead to an impairment in relation to her work tasks with her employer and resulted in a need for compensation in order for her to function on an equal footing with others in a similar situation."*[485]

482 Danish Equal Treatment Board, Case no. 46/2010 of 30 June 2010 and Case 105/2010 of 1 December 2010.

483 The Justice of Administration Act, LBK 1053 of 29 October 2009, Sections 94(1) and 227(1).

484 Danish Maritime and Commercial Court, Decision of 24 August 2009, F-19–06 and Danish Maritime and Commercial Court, Decision of 24 August 2009, F-13–06.

485 Danish Maritime and Commercial Court, Decision of 24 August 2009, F-13–06 and Commercial Court, Decision of 24 August 2009, F-19–06. The Court decided to send two questions for preliminary adjudication by the European Court of Justice regarding the 120-days rule and reasonable accommodation, cf. *Section 8 Reasonable Accommodation.*

Due to disagreement on the formulation of two questions to be referred to the ECJ, the ruling of the Maritime and Commercial Court went to the Danish Supreme Court.[486] On 7 May 2010, the Danish Supreme Court found that a referral should be made to the ECJ regarding the question whether:

> *"a permanent impairment, which does not imply a need for special assistive devices or the like, and which only means that the person in question is not able to work full time, shall be found to be disabled in the sense of the Employment Equality Directive."*[487]

In my opinion, it is highly unlikely that the ECJ will state that a disability in the sense of the Employment Equality Directive requires the need for special assistive devices or personal assistance. In the *Chacón Navas*-case, which concerned the differentiation between sickness and disability, the ECJ stated that *"The concept of "disability" must be understood as referring to a limitation which results in particular from physical, mental or psychological impairments and which hinders the participation of the person concerned in professional life."*[488] Thus, in the *Chacón Navas*-case the ECJ did not require that the limitations resulting from the impairment were of a specific type. In accordance with the social model of disability, the need for compensation is a result of the existence of barriers for participation. In other words, a person with a specific impairment might need an assistive device where working procedures are not inclusive, but might not need an assistive device in an inclusive setting. Consequently, requiring the need for special assistive devices or personal assistance would be to ignore the role of social barriers in relation to disability and would introduce a problematic arbitrariness in the definition of disability under the Employment Equality Directive. Although the ECJ has been criticised for applying a medical as opposed to a social model of disability in the *Chacón Navas*-case, the ECJ did take a step in the direction of recognising the social model of disability in the *Coleman*-case. It is therefore unlikely that the ECJ would apply a medical model of disability in the definition of disability and find a disability presupposes the need for special assistive devices.[489]

Although the definition of disability applied by the Western and Eastern High Courts in 2010 and the Equal Treatment Board implies a less far-reaching need for

---

486 As will be discussed more under *Sub-Section 8 Reasonable Accommodation*, the Maritime and Commercial Court decided to ask the ECJ whether reduced working hours may fall under the duty of employers to provide reasonable accommodation.

487 Danish Supreme Court Decision of 7 May 2010, case 283/2009 Dansk Arbejdsgiverforening som mandatar for Pro Display A/S under konkurs mod HK Danmark som mandatar for A, and case 284/2009 Dansk Almennyttigt Boligselskab – DAB mod HK Danmark som mandatar for B.

488 ECJ judgment (Grand Chamber) of 11 July 2006, Case C-13/05, *Sonia Chacón Navas v. Eurest Colectividades SA*, para. 43.

489 ECJ judgment (Grand Chamber) of 17 July 2008, C-303/06, S. *Coleman v. Attridge Law and Steve Law*. See also Chapter III EU Law and Policy, Section 4 Employment Equality Directive.

compensation than the definition applied by the Western high Court in 2007, they do still require a need for compensation in the form of e.g. reduced working hours or employment in a 'flexjob' with public wage subvention. This new definition may be in accordance with the Employment Equality Directive, but the definition does not comply with the contemporary disability human rights approach. The contemporary disability human rights approach encompasses all degrees of impairment as long as they are long-lasting. Also minor impairments, which do not give rise to a need for compensation, may in interaction with social barriers result in a disability. For example a person with a missing finger would be considered disabled under the contemporary disability human rights approach, but would be unlikely to be disabled under the Danish Act on Differential Treatment.

As mentioned above, the Danish Preparatory Works do not mention the question of the duration of an impairment and whether it is a requirement that the impairment in question be longer-lasting or even permanent.[490] In several cases decided by the Western High Court, the Maritime and Commercial Court and the Danish Equal Treatment Board, it has been found that temporary impairments such as reduced mobility in a shoulder, which lasted around one year, could not qualify as a disability in the sense of the Danish Act on Differential Treatment on the Labour Market because of their temporary nature.[491] Moreover, in at least three other cases, the Danish High Courts have stated that disability results from a *"permanent impairment"*.[492] However, no case has been tried where it could be assessed whether the Danish courts would consider a longer-lasting, but not permanent impairment, as falling under the definition of disability under the Act on Differential Treatment on the Labour Market.

In the *Chacón Navas*-case, the ECJ stated that it must be probable that the limitation lasts a long time:

490 Danish Preparatory Works, Proposal L92 of 11 November 2004, '4.1. Handicapkriteriet' and 'Bemærkninger til de enkelte bestemmelser', 'Til no. 2'.

491 Danish Western High Court Judgment of 20 March 2009 where the Western High Court stated that a person who had suffered a shoulder injury with a good prognosis for full recovery was not disabled because the impairment in question was temporary in nature, UFR 2009.1966V. Danish Equal Treatment Board Case 105/2010 of 1 December 2010 concerning a person who was expected to recover fully from a shoulder-injury within one year and Case 19/2010 of 24 March 2010 concerning a person with epilepsy who had only had one attack and was expected not to suffer any more attacks. Since epilepsy is a permanent condition, it seems peculiar that the Equal Treatment Board found his impairment to be of temporary nature. Danish Maritime and Commercial Court, judgment of 24 August 2009, F-45–06 which concerned a woman who had suffered a work-related injury to her shoulder and who had a new full-time position at the time of the judgment.

492 Danish Eastern High Court Judgment of 5 May 2010, 18. Afd., no. B-2215–09 (unpublished). Danish Eastern High Court Judgment of 26 August 2010, 11. Afdeling, B-644–09, unpublished. Danish Western High Court Judgment of 12 March 2010, 14. Section, No. B-1904–08, unpublished.

> *"The importance which the Community legislature attaches to measures for adapting the workplace to the disability demonstrates that it envisaged situations in which participation in professional life is hindered over a long period of time. In order for the limitation to fall within the concept of "disability", it must therefore be probable that it will last for a long time."*[493]

As explained in *Chapter III EU Law and Policy, Section 4 Employment Equality Directive*, the Employment Equality Directive as it is interpreted by the ECJ sets a minimum threshold for the protection which Member States must provide. It follows, that Member States cannot limit the definition of disability only to permanent limitations or impairments. As long as they are longer lasting in duration, they must be encompassed by the concept of disability. This interpretation of the concept of disability is also in accordance with the guidance provided on the concept of disability in CRPD Article 1 on the purpose of the Convention which states that *"Persons with disabilities include those who have long-term physical, mental, intellectual or sensory impairments [...]."*

4.2. Swedish Definition of Disability

In contrast to in Denmark, the situation in Sweden is clear and the coverage is broad. As opposed to in Denmark, the Swedish Discrimination Act prohibits discrimination on the grounds of *impairment* not *disability*. The use of the word *impairment* rather than *disability* presumably serves to underline that the limitation in functional capacities is not required to have become a disability, which would require limitations in participation. The concept is defined in the Discrimination Act as *"a long-lasting physical, psychological or mental limitation of a person's functional capacities which follows from an injury or a disease, which existed at birth, occurred later in life or may be expected to occur"*.[494] The concept is unchanged since it was introduced in the first Act Prohibiting Discrimination in Working Life on the Grounds of Impairment in 1999.[495] The Preparatory Works from 1999, explain that the:

> *"Government agrees with the preparatory commission's assessment that the delimitation of the persons covered by the Act should be broad. [...] The purpose of the Act is to prevent an employer from taking into consideration a person's impairment when this is not a relevant consideration. As pointed out by the preparatory Commission, there are no grounds for considering discrimination of a person with a less pronounced disability as less serious than discrimination of*

---

493 Case C-13/05, Sonia Chacón Navas v. Eurest Colectividades SA, Grand Chamber judgment of 11 July 2006, para. 45.

494 Swedish Discrimination Act, Chapter 1, Section 5.

495 Swedish title: Lag om förbud mot diskriminering i arbetslivet av personer med funktionshinder, SFS 1999:132.

> *person with a pronounced disability. All forms of discrimination on the grounds of impairment must therefore be prohibited. It is not the degree of impairment, but the impairment itself, which should be decisive. On these grounds the Government rejects that 'limitations in daily life' should not be an additional requirement for protection under the Act as was proposed in two hearing statements regarding the proposal.'*[496]

In addition, the Preparatory Works also specify that:

> *"illnesses which may be expected to lead to limitations in a person's functional capacities shall also be encompassed by the protection under the Act as soon as the illness has been diagnosed".*[497]

In the Preparatory Works to the Discrimination Act adopted in 2008, examples of such illnesses with a progressive development were HIV, cancer and Multiple Sclerosis.[498] Finally, the Discrimination Act adopted in 2008 covers also situations where a person is mistakenly assumed to have a disability.[499]

In sum, the only qualifying requirement seems to be that the impairment in question must be long-lasting or expected to be long-lasting. Thus, it would seem that only impairments which are expected to last a relatively short period of time are excluded from protection. Examples given in the Preparatory Works of such impairments are those associated with a broken arm or leg or persons who are expected to recover after a period of convalescence or rehabilitation.[500]

The broadness of the definition under Swedish law has been confirmed in the few cases decided on discrimination on the grounds of impairment by the Swedish Labour Court. In two cases concerning two men with diabetes and multiple sclerosis respectively, the illnesses had not resulted in reduced working capacities, but the Court underlined that the definition of 'impairment' encompasses *"persons who are carriers of an illness, which does not limit the person's functional capacities, but which may in the future have such effects".*[501] A third case concerned a man who had a food-allergy which was well under control and was nevertheless considered to have an impairment. The plaintiff had not in five years had an allergic reaction and he expected that he would be able to avoid future allergic reactions by avoiding the

---

496 Swedish Preparatory Works, Prop. 1997/98:179, p. 33.

497 Swedish Preparatory Works, Prop. 1997/98:179, p. 34.

498 Swedish Preparatory Works, Prop. 2007/08:95, p. 123. The Discrimination Act does not encompass genetic predispositions for a certain illness, which may lead to a disability.

499 Swedish Preparatory Works, Prop. 2007/08:95, p. 123. As opposed to Swedish Preparatory Works, Prop. 1997/98:179, p. 33.

500 Swedish Preparatory Works, Prop. 1997/98:179, p. 33.

501 Swedish Labour Court judgment, AD 2003 no. 47, Svenska Metallindustriarbetareförbundet v. Skandinaviska Raffinaderi Aktiebolag Scanraff, p. 5. Swedish Labour Court judgment, AD 2005 no. 32, Sveriges Civilingenjörsförbund v. T. & N. Management AB, p. 15.

food that he was allergic to.[502] This food comprised a limited number of vegetables, nuts and mango-fruit. The allergic reaction he could get if he did eat these products was not life-threatening. Here again, the Court made reference to the fact that not only illnesses which resulted in limitations in a person's functional capacities were encompassed, but also where limitations may be expected to arise in the future was an illness encompassed provided that the limitations were long-lasting. The last case concerned a prison guard who had suffered a shoulder and neck injury in a car accident, which had lead to a reduced working capacity in that the prison guard had been on full-time or part-time sick leave during the three years after the accident and until the case was tried by the Court. The question whether the effects of the injury might be bettered over time was not discussed in this case. Instead, it was taken for granted by the parties and the Court that the plaintiff had a disability in the sense of the Act on Differential Treatment on the Labour Market.[503]

Altogether the Swedish definition of *impairment* is very broad encompassing any more or less severe long-lasting physical, psychological or mental limitation of a person's functional capacities, which follows from an injury or a disease, which existed at birth, occurred later in life or may be expected to occur. Also the situation where discrimination takes place where a person is mistakenly assumed to have an impairment is covered.

The Swedish definition is significantly broader than the definition of disability which was established by the European Court of Justice in the *Chacón Navas*-case since the Swedish definition does not require a limitation *"which hinders the participation of the person concerned in professional life."*[504] As mentioned in Chapter III, Section 3.4. Definition of Disability, the European Court of Justice stated that the concept of disability must be given an *"autonomous and uniform interpretation"* throughout the Community.[505] The reference by the ECJ to the need for a *"uniform interpretation"* is peculiar since the Employment Equality Directive is a framework directive which means that the ECJ can only define the minimum level of protection to be provided in all Member States.[506] The ECJ cannot prevent Member States from granting a higher level of protection than the protection against disability discrimination under the Employment Equality Directive.[507]

502 Swedish Labour Court judgment, AD 2006 no. 97, Malmö Lokala Samorganisation av Sveriges Arbetares Centralorganisation v. Svenska Kyrkan, p. 16.

503 Swedish Labour Court judgment, AD 2003 no. 76, SEKO – Facket för Service och Kommunikation v. Staten genom Kriminalvårdsstyrelsen.

504 ECJ judgment (Grand Chamber) of 11 July 2006, Case C-13/05, *Sonia Chacón Navas v. Eurest Colectividades SA*,.

505 Ibid. para. 42 and 40.

506 On the question of "uniformity" see Waddington 2007b, p. 495.

507 Recital 28 of the Preamble of the Employment Equality Directive provides: "(28) This Directive lays down minimum requirements, thus giving the Member States the option of introducing or maintaining more favourable provisions."

4.3. Conclusion

In conclusion, Denmark and Sweden have adopted very different approaches as regards the definitions of the central concept of disability. Firstly, the Danish Act does not provide an explicit definition whereas the Swedish Act does. Secondly and most importantly, the Danish concept of disability has been interpreted relatively narrowly while the contrary is the case for Sweden. In Denmark, the Danish Supreme Court has referred the question of the severity of the impairment in question to the ECJ for a preliminary ruling. While the Eastern High Court, the Maritime and Commercial Court and the Equal Treatment Board require the presence of an impairment which gives rise to a need for compensation in the form of for example reduced working hours and employment with wage subvention, the Western High Court has required the specific need for assistive devices and personal assistance. Moreover, the impairment in question must be permanent. In contrast, the Swedish Discrimination Act defines 'impairment' as any more or less severe long-lasting physical, psychological or mental limitation of a person's functional capacities. Thirdly, Danish definition of disability does not cover past, future or perceived disability whereas Swedish law does.

As described in *Chapter II Human Rights* and in *Section 2 Contemporary Disability Human Rights Approach* above, the definition of disability in a given discrimination law reflects the equality and disability model that the legislation is based on. The Danish legislation seems to be based on the minority model of disability since it focuses to a large extent on determining whether an alleged victim qualifies for protection under the Act on Differential Treatment on the Labour Market. The alleged victim must show that he or she was part of the insulated disabled persons-minority group in order to qualify for protection against discrimination. Only persons who have severe impairments which have resulted in reduced working capacities will be encompassed by the protection under the Act.

In contrast, the Swedish definition of disability is based on the universality model of disability and thus embraces the contemporary disability human rights approach. The Swedish legislation focuses on the motive for the treatment in question as opposed to focussing on the health status of the alleged victim. Consequently, discrimination on the grounds of impairment is prohibited regardless of whether the impairment – in interaction with various barriers – has resulted in a disability. Not only severe impairments, but also minor impairments as well as perceived, past and future impairments are covered.

5. Direct Discrimination

In the present Sub-section, I will compare Danish and Swedish definitions of direct discrimination on the grounds of disability as well as examine whether the protection offered in Denmark and Sweden lives up to the obligations under EU law and human rights law.

Similarly to *Chapter II EU Law and Policy, Section 4.2. Direct discrimination*, the present Section compares Danish and Swedish law in relation to four different aspects of protection against direct discrimination: less favourable treatment (Sub-Section 5.1), a comparable situation (Sub-Section 5.2), causal link to disability (Sub-Section 5.3) and possible justifications and exceptions to direct discrimination (Sub-Section 5.4). A conclusion and analysis from a human rights perspective is provided in Sub-Section 5.5. The assessment of compliance between EU law and Swedish/Danish law is discussed where there may be cause to question compliance.

According to the Employment Equality Directive:

> *"Direct discrimination shall be taken to occur where one person is treated less favourably than another is, has been or would have been treated in a comparable situation, on any grounds referred to in Article 1 [including disability]".*

In Denmark, the Act on Differential Treatment on the Labour Market defines direct discrimination in the following manner:

> *"Direct discrimination will be taken to occur when a person is treated worse than another is, has been or would have been treated in a similar situation on the grounds of race, skin colour, religion or belief, political opinion, sexual orientation, age, disability or national, social or ethnic origin."*[508]

In Sweden, the Discrimination Act which entered into force on 1 January 2009 defines direct discrimination in the following manner:

> *"Direct discrimination: that someone is disadvantaged by being treated worse than someone else is treated, has been treated or would have been treated in a comparable situation, if this disadvantaging is associated with sex, transgender identity or expression, ethnicity, religion or other belief, disability, sexual orientation or age."*[509]

---

508 Danish Act on Differential Treatment on the Labour Market, L253 of 7 April 2004, Section 1(2). (my own translation).

509 Discrimination Act, Chapter 2, Section 4(1). (my own translation based on official translation).

The wordings of both the Danish and the Swedish definitions are very similar to one another as well as to that of the Employment Equality Directive. I examine below whether the interpretation of the concept of discrimination by the Danish and Swedish courts are equally similar.

5.1. Less favourable treatment

One of the few differences between the three definitions of direct discrimination contained in the Employment Equality Directive, the Danish and the Swedish legal acts is that the Danish and Swedish Acts require "*worse treatment*" whereas the Employment Equality Directive requires "*less favourable treatment*".

However there are no indications in the Preparatory Works of the Danish Act or in existing case law that the intention with the wording "*worse*" rather than "*less favourable*" has been to limit the coverage of the ban against discrimination.[510]

The Swedish legislation has used the wording "*worse treatment*" since the implementation of the Employment Equality Directive in 2003. However the Preparatory Works specify that the wording is used in order to simplify the language of the legal act and that no change in meaning was intended with the change of words from "*less favourable treatment*" to "*worse treatment*".[511]

In sum, it would seem that both under the Danish and the Swedish legislation, all less favourable treatment will potentially qualify as a form of direct discrimination.

5.2. Comparable Situation

As explained in *Chapter II EU Law and Policy, Section 4.2. Direct Discrimination*, the requirement that the alleged victim of direct discrimination is in a comparable situation to another person is of crucial importance because the assessment of whether or not two situations are comparable, amounts to an implicit justification clause. If the alleged victim was not in a comparable situation to others, then the worse treatment may be justified and may not amount to direct discrimination. Moreover, the requirement that the alleged victim be in a comparable situation with another raises certain disability-specific issues since the assessment reflects subjective perceptions of what is just and unjust differential treatment and thus risks perpetuating inequalities in society.[512] According to Recital 17 of the Employment

510 Danish Preparatory Works, LF 40 2003/1 Forslag til lov om ændring af lov om forbud mod forskelsbehandling på arbejdsmarkedet, 22 October 2003, Bemærkninger til Lovforslagets enkelte bestemmelser, til no. 2, til stk. 2.

511 Swedish Preparatory Works, Prop. 2002/03:65, p.87.

512 Bell 2007, p. 205.

Equality Directive, the duty to provide reasonable accommodation should be taken into account when performing the comparability-test, but the person subject to the test must be *"competent, capable and available to perform the essential functions of the post concerned or to undergo the relevant training"*.[513] In sum, the definition of "*essential functions*" and the extent of the duty to provide reasonable accommodation are important in relation to determining when a person with a disability is in a comparable situation with others. If these concepts are not defined in a clear manner conducive to the aim of preventing discrimination, then persons with disabilities will not enjoy full protection against direct discrimination.

Both the Danish and the Swedish implementing laws have almost word-by-word renditions of the wording of the Directive on comparability-test. Both the Danish and Swedish Acts use the word 'another'/ 'someone else' as does the Employment Equality Directive. The reference to "*another*" / "*someone else*" indicates that it is not a requirement that the comparator be a person without a disability. It could be e.g. a person with another disability or even a person without an association to a person with a disability.

Prior to the implementation of the Employment Equality Directive, the Swedish Act on Discrimination in Working Life on the Grounds of Impairment prescribed a comparison with a person *"without such an impairment"*.[514] In 2003, the reference to a comparator *"without such an impairment"* was removed in order to broaden the scope of application of the prohibition of discrimination. According to the Preparatory Works from 2003, the reference to a comparator 'without such an impairment' presupposed that the victim himself or herself had an impairment and it thereby excluded discrimination by association with a person with an impairment. In order to avoid implicitly limiting the scope of protection to persons who have an impairment themselves, the Act on Discrimination in Working Life on the Grounds of Impairment was amended to refer merely to "*another*" without specifying that this should be a person without such an impairment.[515]

Importantly, the reference to "*is treated, has been treated or would have been treated in a comparable situation*" in the Swedish provision establishes that a comparison may be made to a hypothetical other person. It is not necessary to compare with a person who is currently or has already been subjected to better treatment. The Swedish Preparatory Works confirm this interpretation.[516] Although the Danish Preparatory Works are once again silent, there are no indications that

513 See also ECJ judgment (Grand Chamber) of 11 July 2006, Case C-13/05, *Sonia Chacón Navas v. Eurest Colectividades SA*, para. 49–51.

514 Swedish Act on Discrimination in Working Life on the Grounds of Impairment, SFS 1999:132, Section 3(1) before amendment by SFS 2003:309 of 5 June 2003.

515 Swedish Preparatory Works, Prop. 2002/03:65, p.89.

516 Swedish Preparatory Works, Prop. 2002/03:65, p.88.

this should not also be the understanding of the Danish Act on Differential Treatment on the Labour Market.[517]

Moreover, the treatment must have occurred in a "*similar situation*" (tilsvarende) in the Danish and a "*comparable situation*" (jämförbar) in the Swedish legal acts. In Denmark, the use of the concept of "*similar situation*" (tilsvarende) gives rise to question whether this is intended as more narrow concept than "*comparable*". Once again however the wording of the Danish version of the Employment Equality Directive differs from the English, Swedish, French and German versions and the Danish Preparatory Works do not explain the meaning of the different wording.[518]

The question is whether persons with disabilities will be more unlikely than others to be considered *"competent, capable and available to perform the essential functions of the post concerned or to undergo the relevant training"* as required under the comparability-test. The Danish Preparatory Works do not specify how this comparison should be carried out. Since the comparability-test amounts to a test of whether a differential treatment was justified, the question will be whether a certain differential treatment was justified under general employment law. If, on the one hand, it is justified under general employment law to dismiss an employee with reduced working capacity then he or she will not have been in a comparable situation to a person without reduced working capacity when he or she was dismissed. If on the other hand, it is not justified to dismiss the employee with a reduced working capacity, then the employee was in a comparable situation with others without reduced working capacity and a differential treatment based on the reduced working capacity could amount to direct discrimination.

As will be explored in *Chapter V Employers' Obligations*, longer-lasting reduced working capacity will as a rule warrant dismissals in Denmark. This could entail a reluctance to consider persons with reduced working capacity in a comparable situation with others under the Danish discrimination law.

Case law from the Eastern High Court shows that the Court has taken three different approaches in three cases concerning dismissals where an explicit reference was made to the disability of the employee as well as a seemingly neutral criterion. The first case was decided by the Eastern High Court in 2008 and concerned the dismissal of an architect with reduced eye-sight with reference to his disability, the need for economic cut-backs and his relative lack of flexibility.[519] The Court

517 Danish Preparatory Works: L40 of 22 October 2003.

518 Danish: tilsvarende, Swedish: jämförbar, German: vergleichbar, French: comparable. The Spanish wording (anàloga) is also more narrow than the Swedish, German, French and English wordings.

519 Eastern High Court Judgment of 5 March 2008, 6. Section, No. B-413–07, Arkitektforbundet mod Kulturarvsstyrelsen.

acknowledged the need for economic cut-backs and rejected that the criterion flexibility amounted to indirect discrimination. The Court did not assess the case in relation to the prohibition of direct discrimination.

The second case decided on 5 May 2010, concerned a man with epilepsy who was dismissed after he had an epileptic attack while driving during working hours.[520] The dismissal was made with reference to his disability and his safety. The Eastern High Court stated that *"did not constitute a necessary and appropriate measure and that there were other possibilities, which would not impose a disproportionate burden on the employer, cf. Section 2a* [on reasonable accommodation] *of the Act on Differential Treatment on the Labour Market".* In other words, the Court implied that the case was considered in relation to the prohibition of indirect discrimination as opposed to direct discrimination. In conclusion however, the Court found a violation of Section 2(1) defining the scope of the Act to encompass dismissals and Section 1(1) listing the protected grounds.

The third case concerned a lawyer with Multiple Sclerosis who was dismissed with reference to her disability and the need for economic cut-backs as well as the fact that she generated an economic loss for the employer.[521] The Court did not find that the employer could lift his burden of proof that he had a need for economic cut-backs and that she generated a loss. On these grounds, the Court found that the dismissal constituted both direct and indirect discrimination.

The above cases confirm the assumption that a person who needs significant accommodation, will as a starting point, not be considered in a comparable situation with others. Consequently, a dismissal based on disability and a neutral ground such as lack of flexibility, safety concerns, economic cut-backs will as a rule not lead the Courts to consider the dismissal as direct discrimination as long as there is a significant need for reasonable accommodation. Only in the last case, where the Court rejected the neutral ground, namely the need for economic cut-backs, and the employer already provided extensive accommodation to the employee, did the Court consider that there was a comparable situation and that there consequently had been a violation of the ban against direct (as well as indirect) discrimination.

In Sweden, in contrast to in Denmark, the concept of "*comparable situation*" is defined significantly broader. Firstly, in Sweden, it is clearly established that the assessment of whether or not a person with a disability is in a comparable situation with another requires that the duty to provide reasonable accommodation be taken into account. Thus, Section 2 of Chapter 2 of the Discrimination Act provides that:

---

520 Eastern High Court Judgment of 5 May 2010, 18. Afdeling, B-2215–09, unpublished.

521 Eastern High Court Judgment of 26 August 2010, 11. Afdeling, B-644–09, unpublished.

"the prohibition of discrimination also applies in cases where the employer, by taking reasonable support and accommodation measures, can see to it that an employee, a job-applicant or a trainee with a disability is put in a comparable situation to people without such a disability."[522]

A judgment from March 2003 by the Swedish Labour Court illustrates how the Swedish comparability assessment is performed. The case concerned a small company with less than ten employees, who performed customer surveys on demand. One of the staff members was diagnosed with Multiple Sclerosis on 2 October 2003. On 10 October 2003, he informed his employer of his illness. During the month of October he was off on sick leave for two weeks and he worked half-time during the last two weeks of the month. In November he worked full-time and in December and January his working hours were reduced with 25%. On 16 January 2004, he was laid off with reference to the fact that the company needed to cut down due to a significant decline in turnover. The Swedish regulations on lay-offs, which will be described in *Chapter V Employers Duties*, set up rules for identifying who will be laid off in cases of cut backs. According to these rules, the persons who have been hired last must be laid off first. If two persons have been hired at the same time, the youngest of these must be laid off. In order to provide small companies with less than ten employees with more freedom in this process, two key staff may be preserved. It was uncontended in this case that the company needed to cut back staff. The question was however whether the company had chosen to preserve two staff members who were not key-staff in order for the calculus to select the disabled person for redundancy. In view of the fact that the two persons who were pointed out as key staff members had no special qualifications, had relatively little experience and had only been hired recently, the Court found that they did not qualify as key personnel. On these grounds, the Court found that the employer had committed direct discrimination with a connection to impairment. As regards the comparability assessment, the Court stated the following:

"It has not been alleged that the disability has influenced the working capacity of MK. It is uncontended that he had sufficient qualifications for a continued employment if one takes such factors as education and experience into consideration. It is also uncontended that he had been employed for the same period of time or longer than anyone else employed with the company. According to the Court, the conditions have in this case been so that it is reasonable and natural to consider that MK and the others in the company were in a comparable situation."[523]

---

522 Discrimination Act of 5 June 2008 Chapter 2, Section 1, (my own translation based on official translation).

523 Swedish Labour Court judgment, AD, 2005 no. 32 Sveriges Civilingenjörsförbund v. T. & N. Management AB, p. 17.

The above case illustrates that the Swedish Labour Court focused on the qualifications for continued employment of the employee in question. One may ask why the employer did not contend that the reduced working hours sustained by the employee amounted to reduced working capacity and meant that the employee was not in a comparable situation with others. The answer is most probably that dismissals due to illness and reduced working capacity are as a rule not permitted in Sweden. Thus, even if the employee's working capacity was reduced, he would still have been in a comparable situation with others.

In conclusion, it seems that the Danish "*similar situation*" requirement renders it significantly more difficult for persons with disabilities to obtain protection against direct discrimination than the *"comparable situation"* requirement under Swedish law. This is based on an unwillingness by the Courts to consider that a person who has been subjected to differential treatment on the grounds of his or her disability was in a comparable situation with others as long as there was a need for reasonable accommodation.

5.3. Causal Link Between Disability and the Differential Treatment

The question of the causal link between disability and the differential treatment raises in particular the following two questions: firstly, whether it is necessary that the differential treatment took place mainly on the grounds of disability or whether it is sufficient that disability only constituted one of several grounds for the differential treatment. Secondly, whether it is necessary that the person who is subjected to the differential treatment is himself disabled or whether discrimination on the grounds of association to disability is encompassed by the national legislations.

The definition of direct discrimination in Section 1(2) of the Danish Act on Differential Treatment on the Labour Market requires that the differential treatment has taken place *"on the grounds of disability"* (på grund af handicap). In the Swedish legal Acts the disadvantage must "*be connected to impairment*" (missgynnandet har samband med funktionshinder). Both the Danish and Swedish wording on the causal link was introduced in order to implement the Employment Equality Directive.[524]

The Danish Preparatory Works are silent on the issue of whether it is sufficient that the differential treatment is founded only partially on the disability in order to find direct discrimination. Based on the case law of the Eastern High Court, which mentioned in the above *Section 5.2 Comparable Situation that* direct discrimination

524 Denmark: L253 of 7 April 2004. Sweden: SFS 1999:132 amended by SFS 2003:309; SFS 2003:307, Section 3(1), and SFS 2001:1286, Section 7 amended by SFS 2003:311.

will seemingly not be found where differential treatment took place on the grounds of disability as well as neutral ground.[525]

As regards Sweden, it follows from the ordinary meaning of the word 'connected to' that the causal link between disability and the differential treatment need not be very strong. In addition, the Swedes have taken a clear stand in the Preparatory Works to encompass also disadvantages founded partially on disability.[526] Moreover, the Swedish Labour Court has made it clear that that it is sufficient that disability is one of several grounds for the differential treatment:

> *"For discrimination to be taken to occur, it follows from the Preparatory Works that it is not a requirement that the discrimination be intentional, but that there must be a connection between the disadvantage and the employee's or applicant's disability. It will be a case of discrimination even where the disability is just one of several grounds for the behaviour of the employer."*[527]

The Swedish Labour Court has had the opportunity to try one case where the question was whether there was a causal link between a demotion and disability. The case concerned a prison guard who had his supervising functions taken away a year after he had suffered a neck and shoulder injury in a car accident. After the injury, the prison guard was on sick leave a significant amount of time and mostly only worked part-time. The employer argued that a decision to change the job-description of the guards with supervisory functions was taken with effect for all existing staff. Also, the persons in charge of selecting staff for filling the new positions had not been given information on the plaintiff's disability. On these grounds, the Court did not find that it had been made probable that the disability of the prison guard had any connection what so ever on the decision to demote him and the Court rejected that he had been discriminated on the grounds of disability.[528] In conclusion and in contrast to Denmark, it is clear in Sweden that the ban against discrimination on the grounds of disability applies also when disability is only one among several grounds for the differential treatment although the Swedish Court did not find that discrimination on the grounds of disability had taken place in the concrete case.

---

525 Eastern High Court Judgment of 5 March 2008, 6. Section, No. B-413–07, Arkitektforbundet mod Kulturarvsstyrelsen. Eastern High Court Judgment of 5 May 2010, 18. Afdeling, B-2215–09, unpublished. Eastern High Court Judgment of 26 August 2010, 11. Afdeling, B-644–09, unpublished.

526 Prop. 2002/03/65 p. 90, prop. This was also the case according to the Act of 1999, cf. prop. 1997/98/179 p. 42.

527 Swedish Labour Court judgment, AD 2005 no. 32, Mål nr A 77/04, Sveriges Civilingenjörsförbund v. T. & N. Management AB, p. 15.

528 Swedish Labour Court judgment, AD 2003 no. 76, SEKO – Facket för Service och Kommunikation v. Staten genom Kriminalvårdsstyrelsen, judgment of 8 October 2005.

In relation to discrimination on the grounds of association with disability, the *Coleman* judgment of the European Court of Justice has established that the Employment Equality Directive provides protection at least in some cases.[529] The *Coleman* case concerned a woman who did not have a disability, but who was allegedly harassed and subjected to direct discrimination because her son was disabled. In this judgment, the ECJ held that a person could be subject to discrimination on the grounds of association with a person who is disabled. Thus, it is no longer entirely up to Member States to determine whether or not discrimination on the grounds of association with a person with a disability is encompassed at the level of national legislation implementing the Employment Equality Directive. As regards Denmark, the Danish Act on Differential Treatment does not mention discrimination by association in contrast to the Danish Act on Ethnic Equal Treatment which was amended at the same time as the prohibition against discrimination on the grounds of disability was introduced into the Danish Act on Differential Treatment.[530] Moreover, discrimination on the grounds of association to disability is not mentioned in the Preparatory Works to the Danish Act on Differential Treatment. However, in judgment of 22 June 2010, the Western High Court found that a woman who had been discriminated on the grounds of her son's disability was protected under the Danish Act on Differential Treatment.[531]

In contrast, the Swedish have provided protection against discrimination on the grounds of association since 2003. Thus, the Swedish Preparatory Works state that the protection also applies *"when a person is discriminated on the grounds of his or her association to another person's (...) disability."*[532]

Finally, it is unresolved under Danish law whether the protection against discrimination in the Act on Differential Treatment on the Labour Market extends to discrimination on the grounds of a wrongful assumption that a person has a disability. The wording of Section 1(1) on direct discrimination does allow for this possibility by requiring only differential treatment 'on the grounds of' disability rather than differential treatment of persons 'with' a disability. In contrast, the Swedish Preparatory Works underline that differential treatment on the grounds of

529 ECJ (Grand Chamber), judgment of 17 July 2008, Case C-303/06, Coleman v Attridge Law. See also Chapter III EU Law and Policy, Section 3 Employment Equality Directive.

530 L374 af 28 May 2003, Section 3.

531 Danish Western High Court judgment of 22 June 2010, 12. Section, Case No. B-2040–09, Kristelig Arbejdsgiverforening som mandatar for Anpartsselskabet Rødbo *mod* HK/Danmark som mandatar for F. No direct reference was made to the Coleman-case in the reasoning of the Western High Court or in the City Court judgment of first instance.

532 Swedish Preparatory Works, Prop. 2002/03/65 p. 91. Discrimination on the grounds of association with disability is not mentioned in the Preparatory Works to the Act SFS 1999:132, prop. 1997/98/179 p. 42.

a wrongful assumption that someone has a disability would be differential treatment "*connected to*" an impairment.[533]

In conclusion, the little existing case law in Denmark indicates that the finding of direct discrimination requires a strong causal link between the differential treatment and the disability. In fact, it would seem that as long as the differential treatment has also taken place both on the grounds of disability and a neutral ground (e.g. economic cut-backs) then the causal link will not be strong enough to find direct discrimination. In Sweden, the causal link is more lax and thereby ensures a wider protection against direct discrimination than under Danish law. In Denmark, the Courts have confirmed that discrimination on the grounds of association with a person with disability is prohibited under Danish law. In Sweden, the preparatory works, established that discrimination on the grounds of association with disability was covered by the Act.

5.4. Exceptions

Finally, I turn to the justification clauses in case of direct discrimination on the grounds of disability. Firstly, there is the comparability-test, which was discussed above under *5.2 Comparable Situation.* Secondly and thirdly, the Employment Equality Directive includes two other exemptions: the *"public order and security"* and *"the occupational requirement"* clauses, which are both discussed below.

Neither the Danish nor the Swedish legal Acts contain a provision equivalent to Article 2(5) of the Employment Equality Directive, which states that the *"Directive shall be without prejudice to measures laid down by national law which, in a democratic society are necessary for public security [...] and for the protection of the rights and freedoms of others."* Presumably, the reason that neither Danish nor Swedish law mentions this provision is that it is clear under both Swedish and Danish law that the ban against discrimination on the grounds of disability does not mean that, for example, public security or the rights and freedoms of others shall be set aside.

In a case decided by the Danish Eastern High Court on 5 May 2010, a workman was dismissed with reference to safety concerns after he had an epilepsy-attack while driving a car during working hours. The epilepsy-attach resulted in a collision with two other cars. The Eastern High Court stated the following: *"In spite of the fact that the dismissal took place with reference to safety concerns, the High Court finds that a dismissal immediately after the accident did not constitute a necessary and appropriate measure and that there were other possibilities, which would not impose a disproportionate burden on the employer, cf. Section 2a of the Act on*

533 Swedish Preparatory Works, Prop. 2002/03:65, p. 91.

Differential Treatment on the Labour Market".[534] The use of the wording *"in spite of"* shows that safety concerns can as a rule justify decisions by an employer. However, in the specific situation, the Danish High Court considered that the employer could prevent any safety concerns by providing the employee with reasonable accommodation to minimise the risk that he would have new epileptic attacks in dangerous situations.

Similarly, the Swedish Labour Court has acknowledged that differential treatment would be permitted if it was necessary in order to protect the health of other staff or the person with a disability. In a case before the Swedish Labour Court, the employer had argued that the reason for the differential treatment of the person with a disability had been that the disability entailed a health risk for other employees as well as for the disabled person himself. The case concerned a man with diabetes who had been rejected for a position as a production operator in an oil refinery. The Swedish Labour Court stated that the central question was whether *"the disability actually influenced the working capacity of the employee or applicant so that he or she was not objectively qualified for the position at hand".*[535] In addition, the Court stated that *"in principle an employer is not guilty of discrimination if he refrains from hiring a person who due to his disability may rightly be assumed to undertake a risk to his own health by performing the job-function in question."*[536] Importantly however, the Court underlined that an individual assessment of a person's working capacity and the health risk that a position implied would have to be done and that it was not possible to make these assessments on the basis of general information on specific disabilities. After an individual assessment of the plaintiff, the Court came to the conclusion that his condition did not constitute a sufficient risk to others or himself in order to warrant the rejection of his application.[537] In spite of the fact that the Court found that he had been victim of direct discrimination, the Court also acknowledged that it would have been justified to reject the application for a position if the applicant's disability would have entailed a risk for himself or others.

Both the Danish Act on Differential Treatment on the Labour Market and the Swedish Discrimination Act exempt differential treatment on the grounds of genuine and determining occupational requirements from the protection against

---

534 Eastern High Court Judgment of 5 May 2010, 18. Afdeling, B-2215–09, unpublished.

535 Swedish Labour Court judgment, AD 2003 no. 47, Svenska Metallindustriarbetareförbundet v. Skandinaviska Raffinaderi Aktiebolag Scanraff, p. 5.

536 Swedish Labour Court judgment, AD 2003 no. 47, Svenska Metallindustriarbetareförbundet v. Skandinaviska Raffinaderi Aktiebolag Scanraff. See also Swedish Labour Court judgment, AD 2006 no. 97, Malmö Lokala Samorganisation av Sveriges Arbetares Centralorganisation v. Svenska Kyrkan, p. 15.

537 Swedish Labour Court judgment, AD 2003 no. 47, Svenska Metallindustriarbetareförbundet v. Skandinaviska Raffinaderi Aktiebolag Scanraff, p. 8.

direct and indirect discrimination, cf. Article 4 of the Employment Equality Directive.[538]

In sum, neither Danish nor Swedish legislators have found that it was required to include a justification clause regarding the rights and freedoms of others, which is positive in relation to compliance with the contemporary disability human rights approach. As illustrated by the Danish and Swedish case law, this naturally does not mean that it is unjustified to treat differentially to protect the rights and freedoms of others. Both Danish and Swedish legislation contain an exemption where disability is a 'genuine occupational requirement'.

5.5. Conclusion

In conclusion, Danish protection against direct discrimination is narrower than the Swedish protection: Firstly, it is more unlikely that a person with a disability will be considered in a comparable situation with others under Danish law, and secondly, it also seems that the causal link between disability and the differential treatment must be stronger under Danish law than under Swedish law. There are no significant differences in relation to the *"rights and freedoms of others"*-exemption and the *"genuine occupational requirement"*-requirement. The narrow interpretation of the comparability and the need for a stronger causal link under Danish law mean that the prohibition of direct discrimination is only rarely applied under Danish law. This is problematic in relation to the contemporary disability human rights approach because of the central importance of protection against direct discrimination.

6. Indirect Discrimination

This Section examines the concept of indirect discrimination in Denmark and Sweden, beginning with the requirements for finding indirect differential treatment (Section 6.1). Since the Employment Equality Directive provides that indirect differential treatment may either be justified under the 'objective justification clause' described above or the 'reasonable accommodation clause', the implementation of these two clauses in Danish and Swedish law will be examined subsequently in Section 6.2 on the objective justification clause and Section 6.3 on the reasonable accommodation clause. In addition to comparing Danish and Swedish protection against indirect discrimination, I will also examine whether Danish and Swedish protection comply with EU law and live up to the disability human rights approach.

---

538 Danish Act on Differential Treatment on the Labour Market, Section 6(2). Swedish Discrimination Act, Chapter 2, Section 2(1).

According to the Danish Act on Differential Treatment on the Labour Market:

> *"Indirect discrimination shall be taken to occur where an apparently neutral provision, criterion or practice would put persons having a particular race, skin colour, religion or belief, political opinion, sexual orientation or national, social or ethnic origin or having a particular age or with a disability at a disadvantage compared with other persons unless the provision, criterion or practice is objectively justified by a legitimate aim and the means of achieving it are appropriate and necessary, cf. however Section 2 a."*[539]

According to the Swedish Discrimination Act:

> *"Indirect discrimination: that someone is disadvantaged by the application of a provision, a criterion or a procedure that appears neutral, but that may put people of a particular sex, a particular transgender identity or expression, a particular ethnicity, a particular religion or other belief, a particular disability, a particular sexual orientation or a particular age at a particular disadvantage, unless the provision, criterion or procedure has a legitimate purpose and the means that are used are appropriate and necessary to achieve that purpose."*[540]

6.1. Indirect Differential Treatment

Although the Employment Equality Directive does not use this concept, I define 'indirect differential treatment' as the treatment which occurs *"where an apparently neutral provision, criterion or practice would put persons having [...] a particular disability [...] at a particular disadvantage compared with others"* which may either be justified and legal or not justified and constitute indirect discrimination. In this Sub-section, I examine when indirect differential treatment will be taken to occur under Danish and Swedish law. The Danish definition of when indirect differential treatment may be taken to occur was introduced in 2004 and is in line with the definition in the Employment Equality Directive. Both according to the wording of the provision and the Preparatory Works, it is sufficient that the criterion or practice would typically put certain groups at a disadvantage.[541] In other words, it is not a requirement that the disadvantage has occurred. Similarly, the Swedish legal text and Preparatory Works do not require that the person in question has already been disadvantaged. It is sufficient that the criterion or practice "*may put people [...] at a particular disadvantage*"[542] The Swedish definition of indirect discrimination was amended with the adoption in June 2008 of the Discrimination Act. In sum, the requirements in relation to when indirect differential treatment occurs are relatively

---

539 Section 1(3) of Act on Differential Treatment on the Labour Market.

540 Swedish Discrimination Act Chapter 1, Section 4(2).

541 Act on Differential Treatment on the Labour Market, Section 3 and proposition L40 of 22 October 2003, 'Til de enkelte Bestemmelser', 'Til no. 3'.

542 Swedish Preparatory Works: Prop. 2007/08:95, p. 103.

similar in Denmark and Sweden and in line with the Employment Equality Directive.

6.2. Objective Justification Clause

Once it has been established that indirect differential treatment has taken place then the question arises whether this treatment was justified either under the *objective justification clause* which will be discussed in this section or under the *reasonable accommodation clause* which will be discussed in the next section. The formulations of the objective justification clauses in both the Danish and Swedish legislations are almost word-for-word renditions of the wording of the Employment Equality Directive except that the Swedish provision does not contain the word "*objective*". However, instead of including the word "*objective*", the Swedish Preparatory Works underline that the aim of a certain provision, criterion or belief *"must not be discriminatory and that the assessment must be objective in the sense that it must not be based on any inappropriate considerations"*. The Danish Preparatory Works are silent on the question of how to perform the objective justification test.[543]

However, although Danish and Sweden law would appear to provide similar protection against indirect discrimination, the existing case law indicates that this is not so. The Danish High Courts have decided three cases regarding indirect discrimination on the grounds of disability. The first case from 2008 gave the impression that the objective justification test was performed in a perfunctory manner.[544] The case, which has also been mentioned above, concerned an architect with reduced eye-sight who was dismissed after 29 years of employment with the Danish Heritage Agency when economic cut-backs had to be made. He was singled out for redundancy because the management considered him to be less flexible than others due to his reduced eye-sight. Two out of the three High Court judges found that the use of the flexibility criteria was objectively justified. They argued that inspections of buildings constituted a significant part of the work of the employed architects, that it had been decided by management that the plaintiff could not conduct inspections on his own and that the decision that he could not conduct inspections on his own was justified on objective considerations for the efficient and correct handling of cases. Also the judges stressed that it had not been shown that the plaintiff could have obtained public wage subvention to hire a personal assistant who could provide assistance for carrying out professional tasks. The conclusion was that the two judges could not find grounds for criticising that the Danish Heritage Agency had given priority to members of staff who could carry out all working tasks on their own and who thus were fully flexible.

---

543 Swedish Preparatory Works: Prop. 2007/08:95, p. 104. Danish Preparatory Works: L40 of 22 October 2003, "Til no. 2, til stk. 3".

544 Eastern High Court Judgment of 5 March 2008, 6. Section, No. B-413–07.

In contrast, the third judge found that the dismissal had violated the equal treatment principle. The dissenting judge underlined that the Heritage Agency had referred to the plaintiff's reduced eye-sight as a reason for dismissing him, that the heritage Agency had not substantiated that the Agency's future work would be changed to consist essentially of inspections and that the Agency had not fulfilled its duty to show that accommodating measures would either have been inappropriate or constitute a disproportionate burden on the Agency.

When one holds up the argumentation of majority against that of the dissenting judge, the leniency of the justification test applied by the majority stands out. The majority judges seem to simply examine whether one may find objective grounds for the treatment imposed on the plaintiff. In contrast, the dissenting judge required that such objective grounds be sufficiently strong to warrant setting aside the equality principle.[545]

In the subsequent two cases decided by the Eastern High Court on indirect discrimination on the grounds of disability, the Court gave more weight to the employers' obligation to show that the dismissal was appropriate and necessary and that he had fulfilled his duty to provide reasonable accommodation and found a violation in both cases. In the case decided on 5 May 2010 by the Eastern High Court concerning a workman who was dismissed following a epileptic-attack which had resulted in a car accident, the Court stated the following: *"In spite of the fact that the dismissal took place with reference to safety concerns, the High Court finds that a dismissal immediately after the accident did not constitute a necessary and appropriate measure and that there were other possibilities, which would not impose a disproportionate burden on the employer, cf. Section 2a of the Act on Differential Treatment on the Labour Market"*.[546] In other words, the Court found that the employer had neither shown that the dismissal was necessary and appropriate nor that accommodation would impose a disproportionate burden on the employer. Although the Court used the wording *"necessary and appropriate measure"* from the provision on indirect discrimination in Section 1(3) of the Danish Act on Differential Treatment on the Labour Market, the Court concluded that there had been a violation of Section 2(1), which defines the scope of application of the Act to encompass dismissals, in conjunction with Section 1(1) which lists the protected grounds.

In the third case decided by the Eastern High Court on 26 August 2010 regarding indirect discrimination on the grounds of disability, the Court found a violation of Section 2(1) of the Danish Act on Differential Treatment on the Labour Market, which defines the scope of application of the Act to encompass dismissals, in

545 Roseberry 2004, p. 189. Jacobsen 2005, p. 301.

546 Eastern High Court Judgment of 5 May 2010, 18. Afdeling, B-2215–09, unpublished.

conjunction with Section 1(2) on direct discrimination and Section 1(3) on indirect discrimination.[547] The case, which has also been mentioned above, concerned the dismissal of a lawyer with reference to the need for economic cut-backs and her Multiple Sclerosis. Also in this case, Eastern High Court referred both the objective justification clause (using the word "*necessary*") and duty to provide reasonable accommodation. It stated the following:

> *"In spite of the need to adjust the expenses of the company, the Court does not consider that it was necessary to dismiss the plaintiff or that it has been shown that the employer could not have provided reasonable accommodation or that the plaintiff generated an economic loss".*

In sum, although the first judgment on indirect discrimination on the grounds of disability from 2008 gave the impression that the Danish Courts would apply a very lenient proportionality and necessity-test in relation to the objective justification clause, the two judgments from 2010 show that the High Court has been willing to apply to apply a relatively strict necessity-test.

In Sweden, the Swedish Labour Court has made no judgments regarding indirect discrimination on the grounds of disability, but the Court has in several cases shown that it will perform a strict test of scrutiny of the justifiability of any differential treatment based on disability. Thus, the judgment regarding the rejection of an application for a position as production operator due to the applicant's diabetes, which is described above under *Section 5 Direct Discrimination* above, is an example of the strictness of scrutiny applied by the Swedish Labour Court.[548]

In conclusion, although the Danish High Court applied a very lenient test in relation to the objective justification clause in its first case on indirect discrimination on the grounds of disability, it has applied a stricter test in two cases in 2010. It is expected that the Swedish Labour Court will also apply a strict test in relation to the objective justification clause.

6.3. Reasonable Accommodation Clause

As mentioned above, the Employment Equality Directive provides that indirect differential treatment may either be justified under the 'objective justification clause' described above or the 'reasonable accommodation clause'. The present Section analyses how Denmark and Sweden have implemented this clause into their respective national discrimination laws.

---

547 Eastern High Court Judgment of 26 August 2010, 11. Afdeling, B-644–09, unpublished.

548 Swedish Labour Court judgment, AD 2003 no. 47, Svenska Metallindustriarbetareförbundet v. Skandinaviska Raffinaderi Aktiebolag Scanraff.

As argued under *Chapter III EU Law and Policy, Section 5.3. Indirect Discrimination* the *reasonable accommodation justification clause* is problematic because it risks removing any group benefits that would have been accrued if only the *objective justification clause* applied. Interestingly, Denmark and Sweden have adopted different approaches in regard to this clause. The Danes have followed the example set by the Employment Equality Directive and have made a reference to the provision on reasonable accommodation in the provision on indirect discrimination.[549]

In the three cases decided by the Danish Eastern High Court regarding indirect discrimination on the grounds of disability, which were mentioned above *Sub-Section 6.2. Objective Justification Clause*, the Eastern High Court examined both whether the indirect differential treatment was justified under the objective justification clause and whether the employer had fulfilled his duty to provide reasonable accommodation.[550]

In contrast, the Swedes have adopted an approach, which differs both from that of the Employment Equality Directive and Danish law. Thus, as explained under *Section 5 Direct Discrimination* above, the duty to provide reasonable accommodation is linked with the ban against direct discrimination. The Swedish Discrimination Act provides that the prohibition of direct discrimination applies in cases where an employee, a job-applicant or a trainee with a disability is put in a comparable situation to people without such a disability if he or she is reasonably accommodated.[551] As explained above, under Swedish law, lack of reasonable accommodation is seen as direct rather than indirect discrimination. The Preparatory Works explain that *"it follows from the definitions of indirect discrimination in the EC Directive and the Swedish discrimination laws that it is not possible to make a link to reasonable accommodation"*.[552] The reason for the impossibility of finding either finding that lack of reasonable accommodation amounts to indirect discrimination or that indirect differential treatment may be justified by providing reasonable accommodation is not explained in the Preparatory Works. However, the reason must be the relatively wide causal link between differential treatment and disability under the provision on direct discrimination and the link between the comparability-test under direct discrimination and the duty to provide reasonable accommodation. According to the Swedish provision on

---

549 Section 1(3) of the Act on Differential Treatment on the Labour Market ends with a reference to Section 5a on reasonable accommodation.

550 Eastern High Court Judgment of 5 March 2008, 6. Section, No. B-413–07, Arkitektforbundet mod Kulturarvsstyrelsen. Eastern High Court Judgment of 5 May 2010, 18. Afdeling, B-2215–09, unpublished. Eastern High Court Judgment of 26 August 2010, 11. Afdeling, B-644–09, unpublished.

551 Discrimination Act of 5 June 2008 Chapter 2, Section 1.

552 SOU 2002:43, p. 285.

direct discrimination, any differential treatment *"connected with disability"* must be assessed under this provision rather than the provision on indirect discrimination. For example, when a person with a disability has been rejected due to a reduced working capacity which is connected to his or her disability, the treatment must be assessed under the provision on direct discrimination. In order to determine whether the differential treatment amounts to direct discrimination, it examined whether the person with the disability is in a *"comparable situation"* with others. The provision on direct discrimination provides that this comparability-test must take account of the duty to provide reasonable accommodation.

The Swedish approach is positive from a human rights' perspective for two reasons: first of all it provides important guidance in relation to the comparability test under the provision on direct discrimination. Secondly, it ensures that the ban against indirect discrimination remains group-oriented. Under the Swedish legislation, an indirectly discriminatory provision, measure or procedure, which places a group of persons with a particular disability at a disadvantage, will be not be allowed if the provision of reasonable accommodation to one individual with a disability is made.

6.4. Conclusion

In conclusion, the Danish approach seems to be in line with the Employment Equality Directive by operating with two justification clauses to indirect differential treatment whereas the Swedish approach is different. Thus, the Swedish legislation does not permit justification of indirect discrimination through the provision of reasonable accommodation. In other words, the Swedish law provides considerably stronger protection against indirect discrimination on the grounds of disability than Danish law and the minimum protection required under Employment Equality Directive. In conclusion, the protection against indirect discrimination offered under Swedish law is more in line with the contemporary disability human rights approach than the protection offered under Danish law.

7. Reasonable Accommodation

As discussed in *Chapter II Human Rights*, the duty to accommodate persons with disabilities is a key aspect of a human rights-based approach to non-discrimination. Without access to reasonable accommodation, persons with disabilities can be excluded from full participation on the labour market due to lack of accessibility and adjustment for their needs. However the duty to provide reasonable accommodation also sets limitations on employers' prerogatives to hire and fire as they wish and to organise work as they see fit. As will be explored further in *Chapter V Employers' Obligations*, Denmark has imposed relatively few limitations on employers' prerogatives under general employment law and health and safety law while the opposite is the case in Sweden. The duty to provide reasonable accommodation in discrimination law must be analysed with this difference in mind.

The following questions will shed light on how far-reaching the duties to provide reasonable accommodation are in Denmark and Sweden and whether they comply with obligations under EU law and the contemporary disability human rights approach: What is understood by reasonable accommodation (Section 8.1), who is entitled to claim a reasonable accommodation and in which situations (Section 8.2), when may an employer justifiably refuse to make a reasonable accommodation (Section 8.3) and how does reasonable accommodation fit with the prohibitions against direct and indirect discrimination and possible duties to take positive action (Section 8.4).[553]

Denmark has chosen to implement Article 5 of the Employment Equality Directive in a shortened version which leaves out the first sentence of Article 5. This means that the Danish provision contains no reference to the principle of equal treatment and that it does not mention the concept of reasonable accommodation. According to the Danish Act on Differential Treatment on the Labour Market, Section 2 a:

> *"The employer shall take measures which are appropriate to the particular needs of a person with a disability in order to enable this person to have access to, participate or advance in employment or to undergo training. This does not apply if such measures would impose a disproportionate burden on the employer. If the burden is remedied by public measures, the burden will not be deemed disproportionate."*

In contrast to the Danish provision, the Swedish provision does mention the limitations on the extent of the duties to provide reasonable accommodation. Section 1 of Chapter 2 of the Discrimination Act provides the following:

> *"The prohibition of discrimination also applies where the employer, through the provision of reasonable support and accommodation, can see to it that an employee, a job-applicant or a trainee with an impairment is put in a comparable situation with persons without such an impairment."*

7.1. Meaning of "Reasonable Accommodation"

The present Sub-Section examines firstly what conditions need to be satisfied for an accommodation to be regarded as "*reasonable*".

---

553 See Chapter III EU Law and Policy, Section 4 regarding the duty to provide reasonable accommodation under the Employment Equality Directive.

As described by *Waddington*, the term "*reasonable*" may refer either to an *effective* accommodation or it may refer to the fact that the accommodation must *not result in excessive difficulties* for the employer. In addition, the term may mean an accommodation which is both effective and does not result in excessive difficulties for the employer.[554] Below, I examine whether "*reasonable*" under Danish and Swedish law refers to effective accommodation and/or accommodation which does not result in excessive difficulties.

As mentioned above, the Danish Act on Differential Treatment on the Labour Market does not use the word "*reasonable*" in the legal text. Instead the legal text states firstly that the measures must be "appropriate" and it then provides that the measures must not impose a disproportionate burden to the employer. This shows that the Danish legislation provides for a two-stepped test whereby it must be established firstly which measures would be effective and then whether taking these measures would result in excessive difficulties for the employer.

In Sweden, the legal text does not mention the proportionality-test explicitly. Instead employers are obliged to provide *"reasonable accommodation"* in order to ensure that persons with disabilities are placed in comparable situation with others. Thus, it would seem from the formulation of the Swedish provision that "*reasonable*" means effective. However, since limitations on the duty to provide reasonable accommodation also exist under Swedish law, it is possible that "*reasonable*" also means accommodation which does not result in excessive difficulties. Nevertheless, according to the wording of the Swedish provision, the weight is on providing a right to effective accommodation.

In sum, the meanings of "*reasonable accommodation*" in Danish and Swedish law seem to be slightly different. According to the Danish provision, "*reasonable*" means both effective and proportionate. Whereas in Sweden, the wording of the provision on "*reasonable accommodation*" only underlines that the accommodation must be effective. The limitations on the obligation to provide reasonable accommodation are discussed below in *Sub-Section 7.4 Limitations on Duty to Provide Reasonable Accommodation.*

7.2. What are "Appropriate Measures"?

The present Section examines what types of measures may be considered "*appropriate*" under Danish and Swedish law.

In relation to the type of measures, which may be required, the Danish Preparatory Works refer to the Employment Equality Directive on the one hand and to Danish

554 Waddington 2007a, p. 665.

legislation on public promotional measures such as wage subvention and support to employers for technical aids to employees with a disability on the other hand. Thus the Preparatory Works state that *"the aim with this provision is to establish the duty of employers to make accommodations that are appropriate in relation to the specific needs of a person with disabilities in order to enable that person to gain access to the labour market, stay employed and develop in his or her position, as is the case for colleagues who are not disabled."*[555] In addition, the Danish preparatory Works make reference to Recital 20 of the Preamble of the Employment Equality Directive and underline that the accommodating measures should be *"effective and practical"* and list the examples contained in Recital 20: *"adapting premises and equipment, patterns of working time, the distribution of tasks and the provision of training and integration resources"*.[556] Moreover, it is underlined in the Preparatory Works that the costs of personal assistance and adapting equipment may be covered by public authorities under the legislation on public employment promotion. This indicates that these types of accommodating measures may also be required under the provision on reasonable accommodation.

The Danish case law on appropriate measures is once again quite unclear. On the one hand, the Eastern High Court has in two cases from 2010 found that reduced working hours, personal assistance, special consideration in the design of the working place, special consideration in organising work to avoid stress, repetitive work, handling of machines and dangerous work, as well as communication to take into account a low level of intelligence and a need for clear and concrete directions were all considered to be appropriate measures.[557] In contrast, the Danish Supreme Court agreed in May 2010 to refer a question regarding appropriate measures to the CJEU for a preliminary ruling. According to the decision by the Supreme Court, one of the questions to the CJEU will be the following:

> *"If an employee is otherwise competent, capable and available to carry out his working task, but due to disability, he or she is only able to carry out the work during fewer hours than full time, would reduced working hours then be among the measures encompassed by Article 5 of Council Directive 2000/78/EC?"*[558]

---

555 Danish Preparatory Works, L92 of 11 November 2004, 'Til de enkelte bestemmelser', 'Til no. 11'.

556 Ibid.

557 Eastern High Court Judgment of 5 May 2010, 18. Afdeling, B-2215–09, unpublished. Eastern High Court Judgment of 26 August 2010, 11. Afdeling, B-644–09, unpublished., In a judgment by the Danish Maritime and Commercial Court of 2 April 2009, F26/07, the provision of personal assistance was considered to be an appropriate measure, but it was found to impose a disproportionate burden on the employer.

558 Danish Maritime and Commercial Court, Decision of 24 August 2009, F-19–06 and Danish Maritime and Commercial Court, Decision of 24 August 2009, F-13–06. See also the Decision by the Supreme Court of 7 May 2010 mentioned above in Section 4.1. Danish Definition of Disability whereby the Maritime and Commercial Court will also refer a question on the definition of disability to the ECJ in the same cases.

The fact that the Danish Supreme Court has agreed that this question be referred to the CJEU for a preliminary ruling shows firstly that the state of law is unclear under Danish law and secondly that the Supreme Court wished on the one hand to ensure compliance with the Employment Equality Directive and on the other that the Court did not wish to impose duties on employers which would go further than the minimum imposed by the Employment Equality Directive.

In Sweden, the Preparatory Works also make reference to Recital 20 of the Employment Equality Directive when seeking to describe the types of measures which may be required. The Preparatory Works clearly envisage both measures which target the organisation of work (pattern of work, distribution of tasks) as well as measures which target the physical accessibility of the working place. In contrast to the Danish Preparatory Works, the Swedish Preparatory Works do not mention legislation on public promotional measures such as economic support to employers of persons with disabilities for technical aids or personal assistance. Instead, the Swedish Preparatory Works focus on the relationship between the duties of employers under the Health and Safety Act and under the provision on reasonable accommodation in the Discrimination Act. Interestingly, the Preparatory Works state that *"there are no reasons to expect that an employer who lives up to his responsibilities under the Health and Safety Act and the Employment Insurance Act should need to consider additional measures with reference to the Discrimination Act."*[559] However, the Preparatory Works do specify that the Health and Safety Act does not apply as regards job applicants, which means that the duty to provide reasonable accommodation does introduce new duties for the employer at least in relation to job applicants. As will be seen in *Chapter V Employers' Obligations*, the Swedish Health and Safety Act imposes far-reaching duties on employers also as regards accommodation for individual needs. Consequently, the reference to the Health and Safety Act does not amount to a limitation of the duties to provide reasonable accommodation under the Discrimination Act. Rather it is a consequence of the fact that the duty to provide reasonable accommodation has been mainstreamed into the health and safety legislation in Sweden. As will be discussed in more detail in *Chapter V Employers' Obligations*, this approach has the advantage that the duties of employers towards all employees are regulated in one legal act, namely the legislation on health and safety. In addition, the Act on Health and Safety is forward-looking in that it provides duties on employers based on the needs of employees without requiring that differential treatment has already taken place.[560]

In sum, both Danish and Swedish provisions on reasonable accommodation stress that the measures in question must be effective. While the Danish Eastern High Court has defined appropriate measure quite broadly, the Danish Supreme Court

559 Swedish Preparatory Works, Prop. 2007/08:95, p. 154.
560 Ibid.

has agreed that a question concerning appropriate measures be referred to the CJEU for a preliminary ruling. The question to be referred to the CJEU is whether reduced working hours may constitute appropriate measures and shows a reluctance on the part of some Danish Courts to ensure effective accommodation. In contrast, the Swedish provision on reasonable accommodation does not mention the proportionality test explicitly. Moreover, the duty to provide reasonable accommodation complements existing and far-reaching duties to provide adjustments for individual needs under Swedish health and safety law.

7.3. Who is Entitled to Reasonable Accommodation and in Which Situations?

According to the Danish provision on reasonable accommodation, only *"persons with disabilities"* make up the category of potential claimants of this right. As described above, the Danish Courts have interpreted the category of people who are entitled to protection under the Act on Differential Treatment on the Labour Market in a narrow manner to comprise only persons who presently have a long-lasting and serious impairment and who need compensation. In addition, the *Coleman*-judgment means that also persons who have an association with persons with disabilities may obtain protection from discrimination on the grounds of disability. However, the ECJ specified in this case that the duty to provide reasonable accommodation only applies to disabled people and not to persons who may need accommodation due to their association with a person with disability.[561] For example a mother with a disabled child could well need more flexible working hours due to her caring duties. Thus, in light of the Directive, the Danish Courts can only be expected to allow persons with disabilities to qualify for reasonable accommodation.

Similarly to the Danish Act on Differential Treatment on the Labour Market, the Swedish Discrimination Act only provides for a right to reasonable accommodation to *"employees, job applicants and trainees with an impairment"*.[562] Thus, the wording of the provision would seem to exclude persons with an association to disability from qualifying for reasonable accommodation.[563] However the link between the provision on reasonable accommodation and the prohibition of direct discrimination may open a possibility that employers could have a duty to provide reasonable accommodation to persons in need hereof due to their association with disability. The question has still not been decided by the Swedish Courts.

561 ECJ judgment (Grand Chamber) of 17 July 2008, Case C-303/06, Coleman v Attridge Law, para 39.

562 Section 1 of Chapter 2 of Swedish Discrimination Act.

563 Prop. 2002/03:65, p.89 which led to Lag (2003:309) om ändring i lagen (1999:130) om förbud mot diskriminering i arbetslivet av personer med funktionshinder, which entered into force on 1 July 2003.

The next question concerns the requirements that must be met by an individual with a disability who would like to be accommodated. Since the aim of the reasonable accommodation duty is to ensure that barriers to equal participation of persons with disabilities are removed, only persons who qualify for the position or training in question should receive accommodation. In the *Chaçon Navas*-judgment, the ECJ stated that

> *"the prohibition, as regards dismissal, of discrimination on the grounds of disability contained in Articles 2(1) and 3(1) (c) of Directive 2000/78 precludes the dismissal on grounds of disability which, in the light of the obligation to provide reasonable accommodation for people with disabilities, is not justified by the fact that the person concerned is not competent, capable or available to perform the essential functions of his post."*[564]

The requirement that a person be *"competent, capable or available to perform the essential functions of his post"* was taken from Recital 17 of the Employment Equality Directive and is thus of critical importance for determining when accommodation may be required. The *Chaçon Navas*-judgment did not provide guidance on the meaning of "*essential functions*".[565]

In Denmark, the Preparatory Works state that the *"duty to provide reasonable accommodation will only be relevant in cases where the person with a disability has the necessary qualifications to carry out the position in question after he or she has been accommodated"*. Thus, the Danish Preparatory Works do not mention the concept of "*essential functions of the post*", but merely state that he or she must be qualified to carry out "*the position in question*".

Out of the three judgments of the Danish Eastern High Court which concerned the duty to provide reasonable accommodation, the concept of "*important functions*" was considered explicitly in only one case.[566] The case, which has been mentioned several times above, concerned an architect with reduced eye-sight who was dismissed after 28 years of employment with the Danish Heritage Agency. The majority of the judges noted that "*inspections constitute an important part of the work of architects in the Heritage Agency"*. On the grounds that accommodation in the form of a personal assistant to help the plaintiff carry out inspections would cause a disproportionate burden to the employer, the Court found that the dismissal did not violate the Act on Differential Treatment on the Labour Market. Surprisingly, the Court did not assess whether it would have been reasonable to accommodate the

564 ECJ Judgment (Grand Chamber) of 11 July 2006, Case C-13/05, *Sonia Chacón Navas v. Eurest Colectividades SA*,.

565 Waddington 2007a, p. 705.

566 Mentioned by dissenting judge in Eastern High Court Judgment of 5 March 2008, 6. Section, No. B-413–07 on dismissal of architect with reduced eye-sight.

plaintiff by giving him other working tasks than inspections even though the Agency had done so on its accord until around one year before the dismissal. In contrast, the dissenting judge found that *"The Heritage Agency has not shown that the future working tasks in the Agency will mainly be made up of inspections or that the tasks that the plaintiff has carried out to date will fall away as a consequence of reductions"*. Thus, the dissenting judge did not use the "*essential functions*" criterion explicitly, but she also did make an assessment of what the work would mainly consist of. In sum, although the judges did not use the concept of "*essential functions*", they seem to have made an assessment of what the position would mainly consist of. However the majority of the judges seem to have applied a relatively lenient scrutiny to the description by the employer of what would constitute 'important part of the position' in the future.

In one other case decided by the Danish Eastern High Court, the Court implicitly made a decision on essential functions.[567] The case, which has also been mentioned above, concerned the dismissal of a lawyer with Multiple Sclerosis who was dismissed after she informed her employer that she no longer had the strength to represent clients in court proceedings. The High Court did not touch upon the question of essential or important functions in its reasoning.

Similarly to in Denmark, the Swedish Preparatory Works do not mention the concept of *"essential functions of the post"* in relation to reasonable accommodation. However, the Swedish Labour Court has established that the concept of *"essential functions of the post"* will be used in the assessment of whether a person is in a comparable situation with another. *"A comparable situation"* is both required in relation to the duty to provide reasonable accommodation and the ban against direct discrimination. In its case law on direct discrimination, the Swedish Labour Court has explained that:

> *"the assessment of whether there is a comparable situation entails firstly an assessment of whether the impaired person can perform the most essential functions of the position. If the impairment does not reduce his or her capacity for the work in question and the persons in question have similar working tasks, education and experience then there is a similar situation and differential treatment may constitute discrimination."*[568]

In sum, the concept of *"essential functions"* is used in both Danish and Swedish case law in spite of the fact that neither legal Acts mention the concept.

567 Eastern High Court Judgment of 26 August 2010, 11. Afdeling, B-644–09, unpublished.

568 Swedish Labour Court, judgment no. 47/03, Mål no. A-127–2002, Svenska Metallindustriarbetareförbundet v. Skandinaviska Raffinaderi Aktiebolag Scanraff, p. 5.

Finally, the question is whether the employee has a duty to inform the employer of his or her disability before the employer is under a duty to carry out reasonable accommodation or whether the employer carries the risk of not knowing that he or she should have made accommodations.

The Danish Preparatory Works do not mention the question of knowledge presumably because it is unlikely that an employer would not realise that a person is disabled and in need of accommodation since the Danish definition of disability requires a serious impairment with a need for compensation. In addition, it seems unresolved whether the employee with a disability must make requests for accommodation or whether the employer has a duty to inquire about the need for accommodation. In the judgment by the High Court regarding the dismissal of an architect with reduced eye-sight, the fact that the employer had not examined the possibilities for reasonable accommodation did not lead the Court to find that the duty to provide reasonable accommodation had been violated.[569] Thus, lack of examination of possibilities for accommodation was not in itself sufficient to amount to a violation of the duty to provide reasonable accommodation.

The Danish Maritime and Commercial Court came to the opposite conclusion in a case regarding the dismissal of an employee with a disability.[570] The Court found that the employer did not have sufficient grounds to reject making accommodation and thus that the employer had violated the provision on reasonable accommodation of the Act on Differential Treatment in Employment. It should be underlined however that in the Maritime and Commercial Court judgment it was highly likely that the employee could have received appropriate compensation by the authorities whereas this was not the case in the High Court case. In other words, it may not necessarily be a problem that the employer has refrained from examining the possibilities for accommodation if it turns out that none would have been possible or that they would have been disproportionate.

In contrast, the Swedish Preparatory Works stress that the employee must inform his employer of the disability. However, once the employer has been informed of the disability, it is the employer's responsibility to examine whether there is a need for accommodation. Thus, the Swedish Preparatory Works note that

> *"It is self-evident that an employer cannot stay passive and await information from the employee. An employer with knowledge that an employee has an impairment should take the initiative to have a dialogue with the employee and examine whether supporting and accommodating measures are possible to eliminate or reduce the limitations that the impairment results in."*[571]

569 Eastern High Court Judgment of 5 March 2008, 6. Section, No. B-413–07.

570 Danish Maritime and Commercial Court, judgment of 2 April 2009, F26/07.

571 Swedish Preparatory Works: Prop. 2007/08:95, p. 153.

In sum, Danish preparatory works are less clear than Swedish preparatory works in relation to the concept of essential functions in relation to the duty to provide reasonable accommodation and the duty of the employer to examine whether or not reasonable accommodation is called for. In spite hereof, it seems that both Danish and Swedish Courts do perform assessments of essential functions and require that employers examine possibilities for accommodation as soon as they should be aware that such a need may exist.

7.4. Limitations on the Duty to Accommodate

In the present Sub-Section, the considerations which must be taken into account when determining whether an accommodation will impose a disproportionate burden on the employer, will be discussed. In order to compare the extent of the duties imposed on employers in Denmark and Sweden respectively, the importance granted to availability of public support for accommodating measures is analysed. In addition, the question of the extent of the duty to provide reasonable accommodation compared to employer's duties to provide adjustments for individual needs under health and safety law is examined.

As stated in *Chapter III EU Law and Policy*, the wording of the Employment Equality Directive provides that the burden on the employer of a specific accommodation shall take account of both direct and other costs and possible reimbursement from the authorities. The economic and other resources of the employer shall also be taken into account.

In Denmark, the Preparatory Works merely quote Recital 21 of the Employment Equality Directive and do not provide additional guidance on how to perform the proportionality-test under the provision on reasonable accommodation. However, the Preparatory Works do in this context provide information on the possibilities for publicly-funded accommodation measures under the Act on an Active Employment Effort. The relative importance granted to the legislation on public support for accommodating measures in the Preparatory Works indicates that the possibility for public support will be important for the assessment of proportionality of a given accommodating measure.

In fact, the possibility for obtaining public support does seem to play an important role also in the Danish case law regarding the duty to provide reasonable accommodation. In two Danish judgments by the Maritime and Commercial Court where employers were found to have violated his duty to provide reasonable accommodation, the employers had turned down the authorities when they offered to examine the possibilities for reimbursing accommodating measures.[572] The fact

572 Danish Maritime and Commercial Court, Judgment of 2 April 2009, F26/07.

that the employer turned down the offer amounted to refraining from examining whether the accommodating measures would be disproportionate and the Maritime and Commercial Court concluded that the employer had violated his duty under the provision on reasonable accommodation. Also, in the judgment by the Eastern High Court concerning the dismissal of an architect with reduced eye-sight, the Court placed significant importance on the fact that the Court considered it unlikely that he would be entitled to personal assistance to carry out his working tasks.[573]

In three other cases where the Danish High Courts found that employers had not fulfilled their obligations to provide reasonable accommodation, it is interesting to note that the employees were all hired in 'flexjob'-positions with wage subsidies amounting to two-thirds of their wages.[574] When a person is hired in a 'flexjob'-position with wage subvention, the employer agrees to reduced working hours, to show special consideration to the needs associated with the employees disability and to accept that he or she has lower productivity than others. In other words, almost any accommodation required for persons with 'flexjob' is subsidised and in principle agreed to by the employer. See for example the judgment by the Western High Court of 12 March 2010 concerning a legal secretary who was employed in a 'flexjob'-position.[575] She had worked for more than thirty years with the same employer. She suffered a serious head injury in a car accident, which resulted in loss of memory, loss of capacity to concentrate and tiredness. Although the employer had agreed to hire her under a 'flexjob'-contract, the Western High Court found that the employer had not fulfilled its duty to provide reasonable accommodation because the employer gave her too much work and should not have given her new types of working tasks which she had difficulties in learning.

In sum, it seems that public support is of significant importance when examining the proportionality of accommodating measures. Although employers are required to carry some of the costs themselves, it will no doubt be difficult for persons with disabilities to obtain accommodation, which is not to a significant degree reimbursed or subsidised by the authorities. The tradition in Denmark that the public authorities and not the employer shall carry the burden of disability, no doubt influences the assessment of when an accommodation is proportionate.

In addition to stressing access to public support when assessing whether an accommodation will result in a disproportionate burden on the employer, the Danish Preparatory Works also mention health and safety law according to which *"consideration must be made for persons with disabilities in the design of*

573 Eastern High Court Judgment of 5 March 2008, 6. Section, No. B-413–07.

574 Western High Court Judgment of 12 March 2010, 14. Section, No. B-1904–08, unpublished. Eastern High Court Judgment of 5 May 2010, 18. Afdeling, B-2215–09, unpublished. Eastern High Court Judgment of 26 August 2010, 11. Afdeling, B-644–09, unpublished.

575 Western High Court Judgment of 12 March 2010, 14. Section, No. B-1904–08.

permanent places of work. The duty to provide reasonable accommodation thus entails a more far-reaching duty for the employer [than is required under the Health and Safety Act]."[576] It is interesting to note that the duty to provide reasonable accommodation under Act on Differential Treatment on the Labour Market is explicitly described as more far-reaching than the duties under the Health and Safety Act. A full mainstreaming of the rights of persons with disabilities to reasonable accommodation requires that health and safety law reflects the duty to provide individual adjustments for persons with disabilities. The duties of employers under the Health and Safety Act are discussed in more detail in *Chapter V Employers' Obligations.*

In Sweden, the Preparatory Works state "*The proportionality assessment must be done with special consideration for the employer's economic and other capacities, the type and the degree of impairment and the type of employment and how long the employment is intended to last.*"[577] In other words, the Swedish Preparatory Works point to four different types of considerations: a) the economic capacity of the employer, b) the type of impairment and c) the type of employment and d) length of employment. The reference to economic capacity of the employer follows directly from the Employment Equality Directive, which mentions *"scale and financial resources of the organisation or undertaking"* in Recital 21. However, it is not clear what is meant with the reference to the *"type of impairment"*. It could be a reference to the degree of effectiveness of an accommodating measure or it could be a reference to the individual's need for accommodation. The Preparatory Works to the previous Swedish Act on the Prohibition of Discrimination in Working Life of Persons with Impairments also mentions effectiveness of the accommodation as a relevant parameter in the proportionality assessment which could indicate that this is the meaning of *"type of impairment"* under the Discrimination Act.[578] The introduction of this parameter in the proportionality assessment could be problematic in relation to the Employment Equality Directive, which does not mention the degree of effectiveness of a measure in relation to the proportionality assessment. However, one could argue that it would be difficult not to take account of a measure's effectiveness when assessing whether it would impose a disproportionate burden on the employer.

In addition, the Swedish Preparatory Works refer to the *"type of employment"*. The Preparatory Works explain that *"the employer's duties in relation to support and accommodating measures for trainees will typically be less far-reaching than for employees since a traineeship does not entail the same type of relationship as an*

576 Danish Preparatory Works, L92 of 11 November 2004, 'Til de enkelte bestemmelser', 'Til no. 11'.

577 Swedish Preparatory Works to the Discrimination Act, Prop. 2007/08:95, p. 152.

578 Swedish Preparatory Works to the Act on the Prohibition of Discrimination in Working Life on the Grounds of Impairment, Prop. 1997/98:179, p. 55.

employment."[579] Finally, the Preparatory Works also mention that length of employment may be taken into consideration. Type and length of employment are not mentioned in the Employment Equality Directive, but it seems reasonable to take into account whether the person in question will be hired as a trainee or as an employee and how long the person with a disability will be working for the employer although this should not mean that accommodation should be reserved for full-time permanent employees. If the trainee or employee has only been hired for a very brief period of time, it will not be possible for the employer to spread out the costs over several years whereas this would as a rule be the case with employees who have permanent contracts.

In contrast to both the Danish Discrimination Act and the Employment Equality Directive, the Swedish Discrimination Act does not mention explicitly that the burden to the employer may be remedied by public measures. In fact, the Preparatory Works of the first Swedish Act on the Prohibition of Discrimination in Working Life on the Grounds of Impairment of 1999 underline that the employer may only take account of public support if the support has been granted when the employer is assessing whether or not to provide reasonable accommodation.[580] If the public authorities have not taken a stand regarding the possibility for public support then this parameter shall be disregarded in the proportionality assessment. In line herewith, the Preparatory Works to the Discrimination Act of 2008 do not view the duty to the employer to provide reasonable accommodation as complementing the support given by public authorities for accommodating measures. Rather, the duty to provide reasonable accommodation is seen as overlapping and complementing the duty of employers under the Health and Safety Act and the General Insurance Act. As mentioned above under *Sub-Section 8.1. Meaning of Reasonable Accommodation*, the Swedish Preparatory Works state that *"there are no reasons to expect that an employer who lives up to his responsibilities under the Health and Safety Act and the Employment Insurance Act should need to consider additional measures with reference to the Discrimination Act."*[581] Thus, as opposed to in Denmark, the Swedish Preparatory Works stress that the duty to provide reasonable accommodation has essentially been mainstreamed into health and safety law.

The question of limitations applicable to the duty to provide reasonable accommodation in Sweden has been tried explicitly in only one case decided on 17 February 2010.[582] The case concerns a woman with severely reduced eye-sight who applied for a position with the Public Insurance Authority as a case worker.

579 Swedish Preparatory Works to the Discrimination Act, Prop. 2007/08:95, p. 153.

580 Swedish Preparatory Works to the Act on the Prohibition of Discrimination in Working Life on the Grounds of Impairment, Prop. 1997/98:179, p. 55. Inghammar 2007, p. 295.

581 Swedish Preparatory Works, Prop. 2007/08:95, p. 154.

582 Swedish Labour Court judgment, AD 2010 no. 13 of 17 February 2010, Diskrimineringsombudsmannen v. Staten genom Försäkringskassan.

The question was whether it was reasonable to require that the Public Insurance Authority should undertake a re-programming of the database system, which was an important working tool, in order to enable her to read text on the computer screen. This reprogramming would be very costly and amount to approximately 20,000 hours of work for software specialists and would still not have enabled the plaintiff to navigate without help in the database. In addition it would still have been necessary to provide the plaintiff with a personal assistant to help her read all the hand-written documents in the cases that she would have to deal with. The Labour Court stated that the reprogramming of the database *"would have been too time consuming and substantial"* and that the disabled employee would still have needed personal assistance to make use of the reprogrammed database. On these grounds, the Labour Court concluded that it would not have been reasonable to require the accommodation for her reduced eye-sight. In my opinion, even though the Labour Court came to the conclusion that accommodation could not reasonably be required, the case still illustrates how thoroughly the Court examines whether or not accommodation is required.

As a consequence of the fact that the duty to provide reasonable accommodation will as a rule not be as far-reaching as the duties under the health and safety law, cases regarding the need for individual adjustment will as a rule be tried under the Act on Employment Protection in combination with the Health and Safety Act and the General Insurance Act rather than the Discrimination Act.[583] An example among several, which are described in *Chapter V Employers' Obligations,* concerns the dismissal of a welder who had developed pains in his shoulders after approximately 13 years employment. The employee had a permanently reduced working capacity due to the pain in his shoulders and thus had an 'impairment' in the sense of the Discrimination Act, but the plaintiff did not refer to the Discrimination Act. In relation to the Employment Protection Act, the Court stated the following:

> *"As mentioned above, the employer is obliged to make a thorough examination of the possibilities for rehabilitation and accommodation measures. It follows from the employers' rehabilitation duties that the employer must take all reasonable measures necessary to uphold the employment. In the present case, the Court does not find that it has been established that the employee cannot continue to work for the employer. In the Labour Court's opinion, there have not been any satisfying reasons why the employer has not examined the working capacity of the plaintiff as a welder and whether he could have benefitted from the use of technical aids in order to continue to work for the employer."*

[583] See for example Swedish Labour Court Judgment, AD 2006 nr 90, Industrifacket Metall v Teknikarbetsgivarna och P.T. Rostfria o Mek Aktiebolag i Ramlösa.

On these grounds, the Labour Court concluded that the dismissal violated the Employment Protection Act.

In conclusion, the limitations on the duty to provide reasonable accommodation under Danish and Swedish law respectively is coloured by the existing traditions regarding employers' obligations to provide accommodation for employees' disabilities. The extent of the duties of employers under Health and Safety law will be examined in *Chapter V Employers' Obligations* and it will be seen that the duties of Swedish employers are significantly more far-reaching than those of Danish employers. Similarly, the duty to provide reasonable accommodation is also interpreted in a more restrictive manner under Danish law than under Swedish law. Moreover, the weight given to the possibility for public reimbursement of accommodation measures is significantly higher in Denmark than in Sweden. Whereas this seems to be a decisive factor under Danish law, the Swedish Preparatory Works underline that the wide-reaching duties of employers under the Health and Safety Act will be guiding when assessing the proportionality of a possible measure under the Discrimination Act. Again, the Danish Courts seem reluctant to impose too far-reaching duties on employers.

7.5. Reasonable Accommodation, Direct and Indirect Discrimination and Positive Action

As described in *Chapter III EU Law and Policy, Section 4.4. Reasonable Accommodation*, the duty to provide reasonable accommodation falls within the non-discrimination rather than the positive action framework of the Employment Equality Directive. In addition, it seems that the reasonable accommodation duty is treated as a *sui generis* form of non-discrimination rather than as an aspect of either direct or indirect discrimination.

In Denmark, similarly to the Employment Equality Directive, reasonable accommodation is also treated as a part of the non-discrimination framework rather than as a form of positive action. Thus, positive action is merely a voluntary measure, which employers may chose to take, and not an individual right, which an individual with disabilities may claim.[584] However, the legal text of the Act on Differential Treatment on the Labour Market and the Preparatory Works are less clear when it comes to how the duty to accommodate relates to the non-discrimination framework. In addition, the Danish courts have adopted different approaches in the judgments where they have found violations of the duty to provide reasonable accommodation. Thus in three judgments by both the Eastern High Court, the Western High Court and the Maritime and Commercial Court, the courts find a violation of the duty to provide reasonable accommodation without also

[584] Act on Differential Treatment on the Labour Market, Section 9(2).

finding a violation of the prohibition of direct or indirect discrimination.[585] In these cases, the Courts seem to view lack of fulfilment of the duty to provide reasonable accommodation as a sui generis form of discrimination. For example in the judgment by the Maritime and Commercial Court, which concerned the dismissal of a man who had severe back-problems after many years of hard physical work as a sales person in a building market, the Court simply stated that *"it was not shown that the employer had fulfilled his duty to take appropriate accommodating measures under Section 2a of the Act on Differential Treatment on the Labour Market."*[586] Subsequently, the Court went directly to the question of compensation and did not examine whether the violation of the duty to provide reasonable accommodation also amounted to direct or indirect discrimination.

In another judgment by the Eastern High Court, the Court stated that the employer had not shown that he had fulfilled his duty to provide reasonable accommodation, but the question of reasonable accommodation was only raised as part of the assessment of whether the indirect differential treatment was justified.[587]

In sum, it would seem that lack of fulfilment of the duty to provide reasonable accommodation is considered a *sui generis* form of discrimination under Danish case law.

In Sweden, the situation is different in that non-fulfilment of the duty to provide reasonable accommodation has since 1999, when the duty was first introduced, been perceived as a part of the duty not to commit direct discrimination.[588] Thus, the wording of the provision clearly states firstly that reasonable accommodation is necessary to respect the *"The prohibition of discrimination"* and secondly that an accommodation is made to ensure that *"an employee, a job-applicant or a trainee with a disability is put in a comparable situation with persons without such a disability."*[589] According to the Preparatory Works, *"the question of a comparable situation only has relevance in relation to direct discrimination. Therefore non-fulfilment of the duty to provide support and accommodating measures cannot be deemed to be indirect discrimination"*.[590]

585 Danish Maritime and Commercial Court, Judgment of 2 April 2009, F26/07. Western High Court Judgment of 12 March 2010, 14. Section, No. B-1904–08. Eastern High Court Judgment of 5 May 2010, 18. Afd., no. B-2215–09 (unpublished).

586 Danish Maritime and Commercial Court, Judgment of 2 April 2009, F26/07.

587 Danish Eastern High Court Judgment of 26 August 2010, 11. Afdeling, B-644–09, unpublished.

588 Act prohibiting discrimination in employment on the grounds of disability, SFS 1999:132 Lagen om förbud mot diskriminering i arbetslivet på grund av funktionshinder.

589 Swedish Discrimination Act, Chapter 2, Section 1(4).

590 Swedish Preparatory Works, Prop. 2007/08:95, p. 150.

The close link between the duty to provide reasonable accommodation and the prohibition of direct discrimination is evidenced in one case before the Swedish Labour Court. In this case where the Swedish Labour Court had found direct discrimination on the grounds of discrimination, the question of reasonable accommodation was implicitly relevant because the case concerned the dismissal of an employee who needed an accommodation. The case is described in detail above under *Section 5 Direct Discrimination* and it concerns the dismissal of an employee with multiple sclerosis allegedly due to economic cut-backs. The employer claimed that the dismissal had nothing to do with the employee's impairment and had not alleged that the working capacity of the dismissed employee with multiple sclerosis had been so reduced that he was no longer in a comparable situation with others. Presumably, the reason for this was firstly, that the employer was arguing that the impairment had not influenced him and secondly, that it was self-evident that the employer would have to accommodate the employee for the reduced working capacity connected to his multiple sclerosis. In fact, the employee was already working only 75% of full time at the time of his dismissal because he was weakened by his multiple sclerosis so the employer was already providing accommodation for his impairment. It seems that the Swedish Labour Court took it for granted that accommodation should have to be provided for the employee with reduced working capacity. In relation to the question of comparability, the Swedish Labour Court stated the following:

> *"It has not been alleged that the disability has influenced the working capacity of MK. It is uncontended that he had sufficient qualifications for a continued employment if one takes such factors as education and experience into consideration. It is also uncontended that he had been employed for the same period of time or longer than anyone else employed with the company. According to the Court, the conditions have in this case been so that it is reasonable and natural to consider that MK and the others in the company were in a comparable situation."*[591]

In other words, the Court did not find it necessary to examine whether it would be reasonable to provide accommodation for the employee with reduced working capacity due to his multiple sclerosis since he was evidently in a comparable situation with others due to his working tasks, education and experience. It was taken for granted that it would have fallen within the duties of the employer to provide reasonable accommodation for the employee with multiple sclerosis for example in the form of reduced working hours. This far-reaching duty to provide reasonable accommodation is linked with the fact that employers in Sweden are under extensive duties to make accommodations for employees with reduced working capacity under Swedish health and safety legislation and employment protection legislation, cf. *Chapter V Employers' Obligations*.

---

591 Swedish Labour Court judgment, AD 2005 no. 32, Mål nr A 77/04, Sveriges Civilingenjörsförbund v. T. & N. Management AB, p. 17.

In *Chapter II EU Law and Policy, Section 5.4. Reasonable Accommodation*, I raised the concern that a link between the prohibition of direct discrimination and reasonable accommodation could lead to a more narrow interpretation of the duty to provide reasonable accommodation than would be the case if the duty to provide reasonable accommodation were seen as a self-standing duty. However, in Sweden, the link between the prohibition of direct discrimination and the duty to provide reasonable accommodation has not led to such a weakening of the duty to provide reasonable accommodation. As mentioned above, it seems likely that Sweden is a special case because the duties of the employers to make adjustments for disabled employees do not mainly stem from the duty to provide reasonable accommodation in the non-discrimination framework, but rather from the health and safety legislation and employment law. The duties of employers under this legislation are examined in *Chapter V Employers' Obligations*.

7.6. Conclusion

In conclusion, both Danish and Swedish law provides a right to reasonable accommodation within the non-discrimination framework. There are however significant differences between the contents of this duty in the two countries and the way in which the duty fits in the non-discrimination framework and existing duties to provide accommodation for disabled employees under health and safety law and employment law. In Denmark, employers have relatively few duties to make adjustments for persons with disabilities under health and safety law and employment law. This means that the duty to provide reasonable accommodation under non-discrimination law entails new duties for employers. In Sweden, employers have significant duties to make adjustments under health and safety law and employment law, which means that the duty to provide reasonable accommodation only adds new duties in relation to (potential) job applicants. In Denmark, the duty to provide reasonable accommodation has been implemented in such a way as to impose only minimum duties on employers: the group of persons potentially eligible for accommodation is defined narrowly, the types of accommodating measures that may be required is still unresolved and the Courts seem to place a great deal of importance on public subventions when assessing whether or not accommodation would impose a disproportionate burden on an employer. In contrast, Swedish law defines the group of persons eligible for accommodation broadly, accommodating measures are defined broadly and the proportionality assessment is strict.

8. Scope of Application

The present Section examines the scope of application of the prohibition of discrimination under Danish and Swedish law, with special focus on the areas of relevance to the field of employment, including the employer-employee relationship, membership of workers' or employers' organisations, armed forces, self-employment, education and training as well as related areas of transport, infrastructure and social security.

The delimitation of the scopes of application of the different legal acts providing protection against discrimination on the grounds of disability is also important in relation to the question whether the protection in the two countries epitomizes the contemporary disability human rights approach. As discussed in *Chapter II Human Rights*, a human rights approach to non-discrimination in employment and occupation requires that the protection against discrimination on the grounds of disability applies in all areas of the employment and labour market. In addition, one may argue that the disability human rights approach requires protection against discrimination on the grounds of disability also in areas which are related to the field of employment and labour market, such as education, transport, infrastructure and social security.

8.1. Employer-Employee Relationship

The employer-employee relationship is covered in Denmark by the Act on Differential Treatment on the Labour Market first adopted in 1996, which provides in Section 2 (1) that *"An employer may not subject employees or applicants to vacant positions to differential treatment in relation to recruitment, dismissal, transfer, promotion, pay and working conditions."*[592] In addition, Section 3 provides that *"An employer may not subject employees to differential treatment as regards access to vocational guidance, vocational training and vocational retraining."*[593]

In Sweden, Section 1 of Chapter 2 of the Discrimination Act adopted in 2008 has the heading "Working Life" and provides that:

> *"An employer may not discriminate against a person who, with respect to the employer, 1) is an employee, 2) is enquiring about or applying for work, 3) is applying for or carrying out a traineeship, or 4) is available to perform work or is performing work as temporary or borrowed labour."*[594]

Whereas the Danish legislation follows the example set by the Employment Equality Directive and enumerates the different conditions and situations in which the prohibition of discrimination applies, the Swedish Discrimination Act uses a different method. Thus, the Swedish Discrimination Act lists instead the persons

592 Unchanged since the Act no. 459 of 12 June 1996.

593 Unchanged since the Act no. 459 of 12 June 1996.

594 Swedish Discrimination Act, SFS 2008:567 of 5 June 2008.

whom the employer may not discriminate against. According to the Preparatory Works, the reason for this new approach was to avoid delimitation problems and to avoid including a long and complex list of conditions or situations, which had been growing since its introduction in the 1999 legal acts prohibiting discrimination.[595] In addition, the Preparatory Works underline that the *"the aim is that the ban against discrimination shall apply in all situations which may arise between an employer and a job-applicant or an employer or at all in relation to employment."*[596]

One area where the Danish Act on Differential Treatment may provide less coverage than the Swedish Discrimination Act concerns sheltered employment for persons with disabilities. Sheltered employment is understood as work for employers who practically do not employ others than persons with severely reduced working capacity typically in a segregated environment without collegial contact to persons without severely reduced working capacities.[597] As described in *Chapter VI Employment Promotion*, persons with disabilities working in sheltered workshops enjoy relatively different coverage under general labour law in Denmark compared to in Sweden. In a case from September 2009, the Western High Court overturned a city court judgment and concluded that persons working in sheltered employment were not employees in the sense of the Act on Sickness Benefit or the Act on Employment Contracts.[598] In this case, the Court also stated that:

> *"Sheltered employment is as mentioned considered a social measure and it therefore does not amount to a violation of the Employment Equality Directive that the plaintiff is not entitled to receive sickness benefits."*

Thus, it seems that the Western High Court found that sheltered employment amounted to *"payments of any kind made by state schemes or similar, including state social security or social protection schemes"*, which are not encompassed by the Employment Equality Directive, cf. Article 3(3).

In contrast, in Sweden, persons working in sheltered employment (Samhall) receive pay and are for the most part covered by collective agreements.[599] Persons working in sheltered employment in Sweden are therefore undoubtedly covered by the Swedish Discrimination Act. This has also been the position of the previous Swedish Handicap Ombudsman who considered persons working in sheltered

---

595 Swedish Preparatory Works, Prop. 2007/08:95, p. 138.

596 Swedish Preparatory Works, Prop. 2007/08:95, p. 139.

597 See more on sheltered employment in *Chapter VI Employment Promotion.*

598 Western High Court Judgment of 23 September 2009, 7. Section, No: B-0796–08.

599 Swedish Labour Court judgment, AD 2005 no. 43, W. i Bollstabruk v. Samhall Midland AB, p. 22. Although persons working with Samhall are not covered by the Act on Employment Protection, they are covered by the principles governing the Act.

employment to be covered under the Act on Discrimination in Working Life on the grounds of impairment.[600]

Another difference between the coverage of the Danish and Swedish Acts is the limitation under the Danish Act on Differential Treatment on the Labour Market to "*applicants to vacant positions*" where the Swedish Discrimination Act both persons who are "*enquiring about*" and persons who are "*applying for work*". According to the Swedish Preparatory Works, the reason for this is that it not uncommon for discrimination to occur when persons inquire about the possibility of applying for a position. Presumably, persons making enquiries about work would be covered by the Employment Equality Directive under *"conditions for access to employment"*, which is not limited to applicants for work.[601]

Also as regards the employer-employee relationship, the question of coverage of chief executive officers has been discussed in Denmark. The Danish Federation of Employers (DA) has in its commentary to the Act on Differential Treatment on the Labour Market stipulated that the Act does not cover Chief Executives who are not considered to be employees in the strict sense of the word.[602] However the fact that Section 5a (1) specifically covers individual contracts would seem to exclude this restrictive interpretation of the scope of application of the Act. Also there is nothing in the Preparatory Works or the wording of the Danish Act to suggest that it was the intention of the Danish legislators to exclude this group from protection. Chief executives must be presumed to be covered by the scope of application of the Employment Equality Directive, cf. the reference to *"at all levels of the professional hierarchy"* in Article 3(1) (a). There are no indications in Swedish literature that this would also be an issue in Sweden so presumably, chief executives are covered by the Swedish Discrimination Act.

Although the Danish Act on Differential Treatment does not explicitly mention trainees, the Danish courts have found that the Act applies to such individuals.[603] In Sweden, the Discrimination Act explicitly covers persons who *"seek or carry out traineeships"*.[604]

8.2. Membership of Workers' or Employers' Organisations

In accordance with the Employment Equality Directive Section 3(1) (d), both the Danish and the Swedish acts cover membership of and involvement in an

600 Information provided by Head of the Legal Department of the Handicap Ombudsman, Torbjörn Andersson, 17/11/2006. The cases have all been settled through mediation.

601 Employment Equality Directive Article 3(1)(a).

602 Bardenfleth and Madsen 2005, p. 24.

603 Danish Eastern High Court judgment of 10 August 2010, UFR 2000.2350Ø.

604 Swedish Discrimination Act, Chapter 2, Section 1(3).

organisation of workers or employers as well as benefits provided for by such organisations.[605]

8.3. Armed Forces

It follows from Article 3(4) of the Employment Equality Directive that *"Member States may provide that this Directive, insofar as it relates to discrimination on the grounds of disability (...) shall not apply to the armed forces"*. When the prohibition of discrimination on the grounds of disability was implemented in Denmark, it was provided that the Minister of Defence may exempt the armed forces in active service from fulfilling the ban against differential treatment on the grounds of disability.[606] The Minister of Defence may only decide to do so after hearing the relevant organisations of employees. The Danish Minister of Defence has not however made use of the possibility to exempt the armed forces as regards differential treatment on the grounds of disability.

In contrast, Sweden has chosen to explicitly prohibit discrimination *"in connection with enrolment inspection, admission tests or other examinations of personal circumstances under the National Total Defence Service Act and in connection with enlistments for and during the performance of national military service or civilian service."*[607]

In sum, the prohibition of discrimination on the grounds of disability presently applies in both Denmark and Sweden, although the Danish Act provides that the Danish Minister for Defence may choose to exempt the armed forces in active service.

8.4. Self-Employment

The Danish Act on Differential Treatment on the Labour Market provides that *"the prohibition of differential treatment applies also to anyone who sets conditions and makes decisions regarding the access to self-employment or occupation."*[608] It is not resolved under Danish case law whether the Act would apply in relation to the conditions under which the self-employed work, but it would seem likely that *"access to self-employment or occupation"* covers also conditions, which apply after the initial permission to start working has been given. The Swedish Discrimination Act explicitly covers both 'starting and running a business and

605 Danish Act on Differential Treatment on the Labour Market, Section 3(4). Swedish Discrimination Act, Chapter 2, Section 11.

606 Danish Act on Differential Treatment on the Labour Market Section 1a.

607 Swedish Discrimination Act, Chapter 2, Section 15.

608 Danish Act on Differential Treatment on the Labour Market Section 3(3).

professional recognition'.[609] In sum, it would seem that both access to and conditions which apply after the initial access-phase of self-employment and occupation are covered under both the Danish and Swedish Acts.

8.5. Education and Training

In relation to vocational training, the Danish Act on Differential Treatment in Working Life specifies that *"the employer may not treat employees differentially in access to vocational guidance, vocational education, vocational adult further education and retraining"*.[610] In addition, it is stipulated, that *"the prohibition of differential treatment applies also to those who provide guidance and training"*.[611] The Danish Act on Differential Treatment on the Labour Market does not apply to primary or secondary school and it is unresolved whether it would apply to university education, which is not perceived as vocational training in the same manner as the more technically oriented schools, which are covered. As argued in Chapter III EU Law and Policy, it seems that the Employment Equality Directive covers universities, in which case Denmark may not be fulfilling its implementation obligations under the Directive.

The situation is different in Sweden where the Discrimination Act is not limited to the labour Market. Thus, it covers not only employer's decisions or treatment in relation to access to training, but also all forms of education and training, including primary school, secondary school, universities and vocational training.[612]

8.6. Related Areas of Transport, Infrastructure and Social Security

The Danish Act on Differential Treatment on the Labour Market does not cover the related areas of transport, infrastructure, housing or social benefits since the Act only imposes duties on employers, providers of vocational training, organisations of employers and employees and those who make decisions regarding access to self-employment and occupation. In contrast, the Swedish Discrimination Act covers *"labour market policy activities and employment services not under public contract"*, *"goods, services and housing supplied to the general public"*, *"health and medical care and social services"*, *"social insurance system, unemployment*

609 Swedish Discrimination Act, Chapter 2, Section 10.

610 Danish Act on Differential Treatment on the Labour Market Section 3(1).

611 Danish Act on Differential Treatment on the Labour Market Section 3(1) and (2). See also UFR 2001, p. 207, judgment by Western High Court which applied to Act on Differential Treatment on the Labour Market in relation to differential treatment committed in an Adult- and Further Education Centre which provided technically oriented training for unskilled workers.

612 Swedish Discrimination Act Chapter 2, Sections 5–8.

insurance and financial aid for studies".[613] The prohibition of discrimination in access to goods, services and housing covers for example restaurants refusing to serve persons with disabilities. However, the Preparatory Works specify that this provision *"does not provide protection against disadvantage suffered by persons with disabilities due to lack of accessibility. Thus, it is not discrimination in violation of this provision that access to goods, services or housing is difficult for persons with disabilities because a shop or a building lacks lifts or other assistive devices."*[614]

Since the prohibition of discrimination on the grounds of disability is a central part of the contemporary disability human rights approach and since equal access to related areas transport, infrastructure and social security are of great importance for the realisation of substantive equality on the labour market, both Denmark and Sweden should prohibit discrimination on the grounds of disability in these areas in order to meet the requirements of the contemporary disability human rights approach.

8.7. Conclusion

In conclusion, the differences as regards scope of application in relation to the implementation of the Employment Equality Directive are not many, although the Swedish Discrimination Act provides wider coverage with respect to, for example, sheltered employment and university education. However, the difference is striking between Denmark and Sweden when one compares coverage that goes beyond the scope of the Employment Equality Directive. Where Danish law provides no protection against discrimination outside the scope of the Employment Equality Directive, Sweden ensures protection also as regards goods, services, housing, health and social security. In spite of providing broad coverage, the Swedish Discrimination Act does not cover the important areas of accessibility to infrastructures and transport. In sum, although the coverage provided by Sweden is far more in compliance with the contemporary disability human rights approach, even the Swedish coverage too, needs to be broadened, if it is to fully embody the contemporary disability human rights approach.

9. Positive Action

The present section examines whether or not employers have a *duty* to implement measures for the promotion of employment opportunities of persons with disabilities.

---

613 Swedish Discrimination Act, Chapter 2, Sections 9, 12, 13 and 14.

614 Swedish Preparatory Works, Prop. 2007/08:95, p. 519.

As mentioned in *Chapter III EU Law and Policy, Section 4.8 Positive Action*, definitions of positive action may differ under different legal systems. However, for the purpose of this thesis, positive action will be defined as measures that are taken consciously and actively with the view to promoting substantive equality for a certain disadvantaged group.[615] Thus, these measures differ from the duty to provide reasonable accommodation for specific needs of individuals with disabilities contained in non-discrimination legislation. The duty to provide accommodation targets the disadvantage of a specific individual in relation to specific barriers, which hinder that person in relation to a specific situation, e.g. the performance of working tasks or taking part in a training course. In contrast, positive action is general in nature and aims at improving employment opportunities of employees or jobseekers with disabilities as a group. Positive action may also entail measures consisting in individual measures such as the guarantee of a job-interview of persons from a disadvantaged group who have the relevant qualifications. However these measures are only individual in that they give an individual a specific advantage, such as for example an invitation to a job interview. They are not individual in the sense of reasonable accommodation where the measure in question is tailored to the needs of an individual.

Also as described in *Chapter III EU Law and Policy, De Schutter* has categorised positive action into six types of measures in order to perform a more qualified comparison of different regulations of positive action.[616] Types a) to c) include monitoring of the composition of the workforce, redefining standard criteria on the basis of which employment or promotion is allocated and general outreach measures. Types a) to c) measures do not entail preferential treatment of members of the targeted group. In contrast, measures d) to f) do entail preferential treatment and include d) outreach measures consisting in e.g. the guarantee of job-interviews, e) flexible quotas according to which preferential treatment is granted to members of the group provided that they possess the relevant qualifications and f) strict quotas which do not require the possession of relevant qualifications. Below, I seek to determine which of these types of active measures are required or permitted in Denmark and Sweden. I first examine the obligations of *public employers (Sub-Section 9.1)* and I then examine the obligations of *private employers (Sub-Section 9.2)*.

As explained above in *Chapter II Human Rights*, formal equality is based on the assumption that all persons are equal and it therefore does not recognise the need for positive action. In contrast, substantive difference equality recognises that differences may in some exceptional circumstances warrant differential treatment

615 See the definition in the Employment Equality Directive above and the definition of UN Special Rapporteur Bossuyt in his final report on "the concept of affirmative action", UN doc E/CN.4/Sub.2/2002/21, 17 June 2002, para. 6.

616 Waddington 2007a, p. 762.

and thus positive action. Finally, substantive diversity equality is based on the assumption that diversity is a fact of life and that positive action will be necessary to achieve full substantive equality. Therefore the use of positive action in relation to persons with disabilities in Denmark and Sweden is important in relation to the determination of whether or not Danish and Swedish equality law and policy is based on substantive diversity equality and thus in line with the contemporary disability human rights approach.

Both in Denmark and in Sweden, the starting point is that employers are free to decide whom they want to hire. The anti-discrimination laws set certain limitations to the employer's freedom to choose between different applicants.[617] In addition, in Sweden, the Employment Protection Act provides that persons who have been dismissed within nine months due to work shortage have a preferential right to be hired by the company in question, provided that they possess the relevant qualifications.[618] The question of interest here is whether the employer may choose to enact positive action measures to promote the employment opportunities of persons with disabilities. Both Danish and Swedish legislation on discrimination *permit* the voluntary use of positive action measures by employers, which does not entail preferential treatment, provided that an advantage is not given to a person with a disability who is less qualified than another without disability, (type a) to e) measures).[619] The differences between the legislation in Denmark and Sweden concern the *duties* of employers to enact positive measures rather than the rules on voluntary positive action. The following Sub-Sections therefore concentrate on the question of duties of employers to enact positive action.

9.1. Public Employers

In Denmark, the government has not set targets for the share of employees with disabilities. However, a priority right for employment of persons with disabilities in the public sector has been adopted. According to Section 3 of the Act on Compensation of Persons with Disabilities in Employment, *"A person, who has difficulties in obtaining employment on the open labour market due to a disability, has priority for vacant positions with public employers, applications for stalls etc,*

617 Swedish Discrimination Act, Chapter 2.

618 Section 25 of Swedish Act on Employment Protection, (Lag om Anställningskydd), originally SFS 1982:80.

619 Denmark: Section 9(3) in Act on ban against Discrimination in the field of Employment. Although the wording of the definition of direct discrimination of Chapter 1, Section 2, indicates that it grants protection also to persons without disabilities, it follows from the Preparatory Works that preferential treatment of persons with disabilities is not encompassed by the ban against discrimination because the ban only protects persons with disabilities, cf. Prop. 2 07/08:95, p. 218. See also SOU 1998:107, Främjandelagen – en oversyn, p. 42–43 regarding public employers.

and permission for taxi driving, if the applicant has the same qualifications as other applicants.'[620] It follows that a public employer must call a person with a disability for an interview if the applicant requests that the priority right be used or if the Employment Services makes such a request. Only if the applicant does not fulfil formal educational requirements may the employer deny calling him or her for an interview.[621] In addition, if the public employer decides not to hire the applicant with a disability, the employer may not fill the position before the employer has provided the Employment Service with a written explanation and has negotiated with the Employment Service about whether the disabled applicant could be hired.[622] No data is available on how often this priority right is used. However, research shows that very few potential users of the priority right to public employment know of its existence. Only 8% of persons with disabilities who were registered as job applicants and had applied for work during the last year had heard of this right in 2006.[623] Also a relatively small study from the year 2000 involving 34 municipal and state employers showed that only 17% had ever been requested to give priority to a disabled applicant for a position.[624] In sum, although the public authorities have a duty to give persons with disabilities access to job-interviews, the duty is only rarely used in practice.

In Sweden, the Instrument of Government, which is one of four fundamental laws, provides that *"public authorities shall seek to promote inclusion and equality in society. Public authorities shall prevent discrimination of persons on the grounds of [...] impairment [...] or other personal characteristics"*.[625] Also the Act on State Authorities' Responsibility for the Realisation of the Disability Policy provides that State authorities shall promote full participation of persons with disabilities in social life.[626]According to this Act, State authorities are obliged to promote accessibility to their localities and services. In addition they should prepare annual plans for the fulfilment of these goals. However, no general targets have been set for the employment of persons with disabilities by public employers. The Swedish Agency

620 Section 3(1) of Act no. 727 of 7 July 2009 on compensation of persons with disabilities in employment, (Lov om kompensation til handicappede i erhverv).

621 Section 6(1) and (2) of Executive Order on Compensation for Persons with Disabilities in Employment, BEK no. 179 of 13 March 2008, (Bekendtgørelse om compensation til handicappede i erhverv).

622 Ibid.

623 Larsen, Schademan and Høgelund 2008, p. 131.

624 Center for Ligebehandling af Handicappede, *Offentlige Myndigheders Personalepolitik,* Februar 2000.

625 Instrument of Government (Regeringsformen), Section 2 of Chapter 1 and Act on Public Recruitment (Lag om offentlig anställning), SFS 1994:260, Section 4.

626 SFS 2001:526, (Förordning om de statliga myndigheternas ansvar för genomförandet av handikappolitiken).

for Disability Policy Coordination has prepared guidelines for inclusive employment policies for State employers.[627]

In sum, while Denmark has not set targets for hiring a certain number of persons with disabilities in the public sector, it has enacted individual priority rights for persons with disabilities who apply for positions in the public sector. However, this right is rarely used in practice. In contrast, Sweden has neither enacted targets for hiring persons with disabilities in the public sector nor adopted individual priority rights for applicants for positions in the public sector.

9.2. Private Employers

In Denmark, private employers do not have a legal obligation to give preferential treatment to applicants with disabilities although they are, as mentioned above, permitted to undertake such measures.

Similarly, in Sweden, the Discrimination Act, which entered into force on 1 January 2009 does not impose a duty to undertake positive action for the promotion of equal rights and opportunities of persons with impairments.[628] The Commission, which prepared the Discrimination Act of 2008 had recommended that the Discrimination Act should widen the duty to undertake positive measures to encompass not only existing grounds of gender, ethnicity, religion or belief, but also new grounds including impairment.[629] Nevertheless, the Government decided against adding 'impairment' to the list of grounds in the Chapter on positive measures of the Discrimination Act of 2008. The Government argued that it was still not established that duties to undertake positive measures had an effect on the treatment of discriminated groups and that the extent of the duties imposed on employers needed to be made more clear.[630] A new Commission report on positive action for the promotion of equal rights and opportunities, which was published in February 2010, also recommends that employers be obliged to promote equal rights and opportunities for all covered groups under the Swedish Discrimination Act, including persons with impairments.[631] According to this Commission Report, the current Discrimination Act sends out a wrong signal when it only imposes a duty to take positive action in relation to some discrimination grounds. The Commission

---

627 Handisam: *Riktlinjer för tillgänglighet,* 2007, pp. 31–36.

628 Chapter 3 on Active Measures of Discrimination Act, SFS 2008:567 of 5 June 2008, Diskrimineringslag.

629 Commission Report, Section 1 of Chapter 2 on Working Life, SOU 2006:22 p. 73, A Unified Discrimination Legislation, "En Sammanhållen Diskrimineringslagstiftning".

630 Preparatory Works to Discrimination Act, Prop. 2007/08:95, p. 318–19.

631 Commission Report SOU 2010:7 of February 2010 on active measures to promote equal rights and opportunities, "Aktiva Åtgärder for at främja lika rettigheter och möjlikheter", p. 53.

Report stresses that employers should be motivated to promote equal rights and opportunities for all discriminated groups through a legal obligation to do so.[632]

However another Swedish legal act imposes a duty on employers to promote the employment of persons with *"reduced working capacity"* – not *"impairment"*, which is a much broader concept under Swedish law. The Act on Certain Promotional Employment Measures of 1974 provides duties on employers to cooperate with the public employment service to promote the employment of employees with reduced working capacity and elderly persons.[633] The adoption of the Act took place as a reaction to the fact that persons with reduced working capacity were increasingly experiencing difficulties in finding and holding on to employment in the open labour market and it was hoped that the new duties on employers to cooperate with the public employment service could alleviate any unwanted exclusionary effect of the Act on Employment Protection, which was being strengthened at the same time.[634] The Act on Certain Promotional Employment Measures aimed at promoting employment on the open labour market.[635] The use of quotas had been discussed by the Commission preparing the Act on Certain Promotional Employment Measures, but was rejected for three reasons: that it would be technically difficult to implement, that it would not be effective in promoting employment of the group of employees with the most reduced working capacity and that it would be in contradiction to the principle of co-operation between *inter alia* employers and authorities, which was believed to be the most effective tool to promote employment.[636]

According to the Act on Certain Promotional Employment Measures of 1974, the Employment Service may impose relatively far-reaching obligations on employers to promote the continued employment and hiring of persons with reduced working capacity.[637] The Act is however founded on the principle of three-way voluntary co-operation between the employers, the social partners and the Employment Service.[638] The Employment Service may *"to the extent that it considers that it is required"* impose a duty on employers to give information about the composition of staff as regards age, gender, nationality, reduced working capacity as well as

632 Ibid.

633 The provisions in the Act on Promotional Employment Measures on promotional measures are modeled on similar provisions contained in the Act on Certain Measures for the Promotion of Employment of Elderly Employees on the Open Field of Employment from 1971. Lagen om vissa åtgärder för att främja sysselsättning av äldre arbetstagare på den öppna arbetsmarknaden, SFS 1971: 202.

634 Preparatory Works to Act on Promotional Employment Measures, p. 82 and 96, Prop. 1973:129.

635 Preparatory Works to Act on Promotional Employment Measures, p. 96, Prop. 1973:129.

636 Preparatory Works to Act on Promotional Employment Measures, p. 103, Prop. 1973:129.

637 Sections 7–13 of Act on Promotional Employment Measures, Lag om vissa anställningsfrämjande åtgärder, SFS 1974:13 with latest amendment of SFS 2007:401.

638 Commission Report, SOU 1998:107, "Främjandelagen – en oversyn", p. 106.

working tasks and forthcoming changes, such as resignations, dismissals, redeployments and vacant positions.[639] In addition, the Employment Services may, on the grounds of the information provided by the employer, impose a duty on employers to take part in a dialogue with the Employment Service.[640] Employees' and employers' organisations will also be invited to take part.[641] Moreover, the Employment Service may also *"If it finds that there are grounds to do so, [...] give guidelines on measures to be taken for the improvement of employment possibilities of employees of old age or employees with reduced working capacity"*.[642] Finally and only as a last resort, the Employment Service may decide that employers can only hire employees who have been assigned or approved by the Employment Service if *"the employer has not abided by the guidelines that were given by the Employment Service [...] and it is clear from the circumstances of the case that compliance cannot be achieved by other means."*[643] If the employer does not comply with the duty to provide information on staff or refuses to take part in dialogue meetings the Employment Service may impose a fine.[644]

Since their introduction more than 30 years ago, only one study carried out in 1992 has been made to determine the practical use of the Swedish rules. The study shows that the local Employment Service offices have been very reluctant to use the instruments set up under the Act on Certain Promotional Employment Measures. The Employment Service had at that point never made use of forced assignments or approvals of new recruits.[645] Nevertheless, both the central and the local offices of the Employment Service agreed that the provisions on promotional measures had a positive effect. Even though the Employment Service did not use the formal instruments under the Act, reference was made to the Act under more informal contacts with the companies.[646]

9.3. Conclusion

In conclusion, Denmark has imposed legal obligations on public employers to give preferential treatment to jobseekers with disabilities and Sweden has adopted general obligations on the State authorities to promote inclusion of persons with disabilities in social life. No specific targets for the employment of persons with disabilities have been adopted in Sweden or Denmark. As regards private employers, Denmark has not imposed legal obligations to give preferential treatment. Similarly,

639 Section 7 of Act on Promotional Employment Measures.
640 Section 8 of Act on Promotional Employment Measures.
641 Section 8 of Act on Promotional Employment Measures.
642 Section 9 of Act on Promotional Employment Measures.
643 Section 12 of Act on Promotional Employment Measures.
644 Sections 7(2) and 8 (2) of Act on Promotional Employment Measures.
645 Swedish Commission Report, SOU 1998:107, p. 69–70.
646 Ibid., p. 72.

Sweden has refrained from imposing a duty on employers to undertake positive action to promote equal rights and opportunities for persons with disabilities on the labour market even though such a duty has been imposed as regards gender, ethnic origin, religion or other belief.[647] Sweden has however adopted legislation, according to which, the Public Employment Service may impose duties on private employers to give preferential treatment to jobseekers with reduced working capacity. But in practice, the possibility of imposing positive duties on employers is only rarely used in Sweden.

In light of the traditional Danish reluctance to adopt regulations which interfere with the self-regulation of the labour market by employers' and employees' organisation, it is not surprising that no duties to undertake positive action have been adopted in Denmark. It is in my opinion more surprising that Sweden has not imposed duties on private employers to promote equal rights and opportunities of persons with disabilities on the labour market when the Swedish Discrimination Act was adopted in 2008 since Swedish employers are already under significant obligations to ensure that working conditions are inclusive towards persons with disabilities, cf. *Chapter VI Employer's Obligations*. In addition, the Swedish Discrimination Act imposes duties to undertake positive action as regards some discrimination grounds such as gender and ethnicity and not others, which seems to defy the aim of a unified legislation for all grounds. Finally, the Swedish legislation on Promotional Employment Measures does impose duties on employers to enter into a dialogue with Swedish Employment Services regarding possible positive action for the promotion of employment of persons with reduced working capacity.

In sum, duties to enact positive action are practically not used in either Denmark or Sweden. As explained in *Chapter II Human Rights Law*, the existence or not of duties to enact positive action is crucial in relation to determining whether a State has adopted a human rights approach which actively promotes equal opportunities for persons with disabilities. According to the contemporary disability human rights approach based on substantive diversity equality, the State should not only permit some forms of positive action, it should also establish legally binding duties to promote equality of opportunities through positive action.

10. Conclusion

Whereas Danish protection against discrimination on the grounds of disability was only introduced when the obligation arose under EU law and then only as a minimum protection characterised by a reluctance to limit the freedom of employers, the Swedish protection against discrimination on the grounds of disability was

[647] Swedish Discrimination Act Chapter 3, Section 1.

introduced long before Sweden was obliged to do so under EU law. In line with the strong protection of persons with disabilities under employment protection and health and safety legislation, the Swedish protection against discrimination is relatively strong.

The comparison in this chapter has made it clear that the Swedish protection against direct discrimination is stronger than the Danish protection. The definition of "*impairment*" under Swedish law is significantly broader than the definition of "*disability*" under Danish law. Danish law requires the existence of a long-lasting and possibly permanent impairment which results in a need for compensation. Under Swedish law all longer-lasting impairments are encompassed. Contrary to the Danish definition, the Swedish definition of "*impairment*" covers also past, future and perceived impairments. In addition, persons with disabilities are more likely to be considered in a 'comparable situation' with others under Swedish law and because the causal link between the disability and the differential treatment need not be as strong under Swedish law as compared to Danish law. In addition, the protection against indirect discrimination is stronger under Swedish law because Swedish law does not provide a reasonable accommodation justification. The scope of application of the ban against discrimination is broader in Sweden than in Denmark since it covers for example all levels of education. The duty to provide reasonable accommodation is a more far-reaching duty under Swedish law where employers are also under far-reaching duties to provide accommodation for persons with impairments under Swedish health and safety law. In sum, the Swedish protection against discrimination on the grounds of disability is more in line with the contemporary disability human rights approach than the Danish protection.

However, as regards positive action, neither Denmark nor Sweden has fully implemented a contemporary disability human rights approach. Whereas both countries permit the use of voluntary positive action by private employers, neither of the two countries have enacted duties for employers to enact positive action for the promotion of equality of opportunities for persons with disabilities. As a result, neither the Danish nor the Swedish equality legislation, can be said to be fully based on substantive diversity equality of the contemporary disability human rights approach. Finally, neither Denmark nor Sweden prohibit discrimination on the grounds of disability in the related and important area of accessibility to buildings open to the public and Denmark does not prohibit discrimination on the grounds of disability in the related areas of transport, housing or social benefits.

Chapter V
Employers' Obligations

1. Introduction

As explained in *Chapter I Introduction*, persons with disabilities *without* reduced working capacity enjoy the same high rates of employment as persons without disabilities. It is persons with disabilities *and* reduced working capacity who suffer exclusion from the labour market in especially Denmark where only 26% compared to 50% in Sweden are in employment. The exclusion of persons with disabilities and reduced working capacity points to the importance of examining the obligations of employers towards employees with disabilities and reduced working capacity under general legislation on the labour market such as employment protection legislation and health and safety legislation. Employment protection legislation provides more or less strong protection for persons with disability and disability-related reduced working capacity, and health and safety legislation imposes more or less far-reaching duties on employers to create accessible work places and make adjustments for employees with disabilities and employees with disability-related reduced working capacity.

In *Chapter IV Equality Laws and Policies,* the main subject was protection against discrimination on the grounds of disability and the promotion of equality through the imposition of positive action measures on employers. The present Chapter examines how the duties to promote inclusive general structures and provide protection against discrimination on the grounds of disability, including the duty to provide reasonable accommodation have been reflected and mainstreamed into general labour laws in Denmark and Sweden.

As will be explained in more detail below in Section 2, the contemporary disability human rights approach requires that general structures are inclusive to persons with disabilities. General labour laws form part of the general structures on the labour market and define the minimum standards which as a starting point apply to everyone on the labour market, contrary to anti-discrimination legislation which only applies if disability came into play and only if differential treatment has taken place. Moreover, especially health and safety laws may impose relatively specific duties on employers to create accessible work places and prepare for the event that at least some employees do lose working capacity at some point in time. Ideally, the present Chapter should also examine the duties to create generally accessible work places under building regulations, but this Chapter is limited to labour laws regulating the relationship between employers and employees.

In Section 2, I provide an overview of the obligations of employers towards employees with disabilities and disability-related reduced working capacity under the contemporary disability human rights approach. In Section 3, I examine the protection against dismissals on the grounds of disability and disability-related reduced working capacity under employment protection legislation. In Section 4, I examine the obligations of employers under health and safety legislation to make adjustments and create inclusive work places for persons with disabilities and disability-related reduced working capacity. In Section 5, I examine the question whether any specific protective measures have been adopted to protect persons with disabilities and disability-related reduced working capacity from dismissals due to work shortage. Section 6 discusses EU law and policy in relation to the findings on Danish and Swedish law and policy. Section 7 provides a conclusion.

2. Contemporary Disability Human Rights Approach

In the present Section, I examine the obligations of employers in relation to persons with disabilities and disability-related reduced working capacity under the contemporary disability human rights approach. This Section will focus on the following three questions: In Sub-Section 2.1., I examine whether limitations should be imposed on the right of employers to dismiss persons with disability-related reduced working capacity (protection against dismissals on the ground of disability as such is only provided in anti-discrimination legislation) and whether obligations to make adjustments and create generally inclusive work places for persons with disabilities and disability-related reduced working capacity should be imposed on employers under health and safety laws. In Sub-Section 2.2., I examine whether all employees on the labour market should be covered by protection against unfair dismissals, and in Sub-Section 2.3, whether persons with disabilities and disability-related reduced working capacity should be entitled to special protection when dismissals take place due to shortage of work.

As explained in *Chapter II Human Rights, Section 1.5. Involvement of Civil Society and Social Partners,* the conduct of State functions in line with the contemporary disability human rights approach requires the involvement of civil society. Moreover, it is a fundamental principle of the contemporary disability human rights approach that equality on the labour market should as far as possible be promoted and ensured through enforceable rights and obligations.

2.1. Employers' Obligations Towards Employees with Disabilities and Disability-Related Reduced Working Capacity

As was seen in *Chapter II Human Rights*, the CRPD is founded on the principle of substantive diversity equality and requires the creation of inclusive general structures on the labour market. Thus, CRPD Article 27(1) on "*Work and Employment*" states that persons with disabilities have a right to employment in an inclusive labour market and work environment:

> *"States Parties recognize the right of persons with disabilities to work, on an equal basis with others; this includes the right to the opportunity to gain a living by work freely chosen or accepted in a labour market and work environment that is open, inclusive and accessible to persons with disabilities."*[648]

It is however a little disappointing from the perspective of the contemporary disability human rights approach that Article 27 of the CRPD on Work and Employment does not specify more clearly how one should achieve a labour market and work environment that is inclusive. Instead, the drafters chose to focus mainly on anti-discrimination. It was agreed at the Sixth Session of the Ad-Hoc Committee, which drafted the CRPD, that the CRPD should *"take a rights-based approach to this article"*.[649] This could have meant that a rights-based approach should be taken to ensure that general structures become inclusive, but it seems that it was interpreted to mean that the prohibition of discrimination is the key to realising the right of persons with disabilities to equal participation on the labour market. Consequently, litra (a) of Article 27(2), which deals with the concrete measures to realise the principles set out in the Chapeau of the Article, underlines the right to protection against discrimination on the grounds of disability on the labour market.[650] Only in litra (b) of Article 27(2) is it underlined that persons with disabilities should have access to *"just and favourable conditions of work [...] and safe and healthy working conditions"*, and it is not specified what is meant with just, favourable, safe and healthy conditions of work.

In contrast, Article 24 of the CRPD on education reflects that it is founded on the principle of substantive diversity equality in a significantly clearer manner. Thus, Paragraph 2 (b) of Article 24, which explains how the right to education should be realised, starts by establishing that States Parties shall ensure that *"Persons with disabilities can access an inclusive, quality and free primary education and secondary education on an equal basis with others in the communities in which they live"*. Only later is it also underlined that persons with disabilities have a right to reasonable accommodation in education.

In sum, although Article 27 on the right to work could have contained more clear designs on how to achieve its goal, there is no doubt that it requires the creation of a labour market which is *"open, inclusive and accessible to persons with*

648 UN CRPD Article 27(1).

649 Travaux préparatoires, Report of the Sixth session of the Ad-hoc committee to the General Assembly on Draft Article 22, para. 95, A/60/266 of 17 August 2005.

650 Ibid. para. 98.

disabilities".[651] Article 27(2), which explains how the goal of an open, inclusive and accessible labour market should be achieved, provides that Member States must prohibit discrimination on the grounds of disability and ensure just and favourable conditions of work.

The reference to *"just and favourable conditions of work"* presumably means that both health and safety legislation, which govern the working environment in work places, and employment protection legislation, which governs working conditions more broadly, namely when an employee may be dismissed, must ensure that persons with disabilities may work on an equal basis with others. It follows that health and safety legislation should impose duties on employers to create accessible work places and make adjustments for employees with disabilities and disability-related reduced working capacities. In accordance with the duty to provide reasonable accommodation under the contemporary disability human rights approach, the duty to provide adjustments and disability-related reduced working capacity only applies when the person in question will become able to perform essential functions of the job in question.

In relation to protection against dismissals on the grounds of disability, anti-discrimination legislation should provide protection against dismissals founded on disability as such. There is no need to prohibit dismissals on the grounds of disability in employment protection legislation as well. However employment protection legislation should provide protection against dismissals on the grounds of disability-related reduced working capacity while taking account of the employers' obligations to make adjustments and the employee's capacity to perform essential functions of the job in question.

It is important to underline that the above-described duties to limit the right of employers to dismiss on the grounds of disability-related reduced working capacity and to introduce duties to create inclusive work places and make adjustments for disability and reduced working capacity under health and safety laws do not merely require that national anti-discrimination law be mainstreamed into these general labour laws. Thus, there is an independent obligation on States to ensure that employment protection and health and safety laws reflect the right of persons with disabilities to inclusion on the labour market. An inadequate level of protection under national anti-discrimination law, for example due to a too narrow definition of disability, will make it even more pertinent that the level of protection under general labour laws is adequate.

As explained in *Chapter II Human Rights, Section 1.4 Current Trends*, the definition of disability under the contemporary disability human rights approach is broad.

---

651 CRPD Article 27(1).

Thus, disabilities may arise as a consequence of interaction between long-term impairments and social barriers. It is not a requirement that the impairments in question be severe. The specific meaning of *"long-term"*, which was used in Article 1 of CRPD, is not clear. The impairment should be sufficiently long-term to distinguish it from sickness, but some sicknesses will entail long-term impairments and disabilities and so the distinction is not absolute. Presumably, a long-term impairment is not necessarily expected to last indefinitely or be permanent, and is expected to last longer than for example one year, but it is not possible to give an exact expected duration. The concept should however be interpreted and understood with the social universality model of disability in mind. According to this model of disability, disability is not a characteristic, which differentiates one part of humanity from another part. It is a condition of life of each person and of human diversity. In light of the aim of imposing limitations on the right of employers to dismiss on the grounds of disability-related working capacity, it is interesting to keep in mind that the burden of limitations on the employer will presumably be smaller if a working capacity is not clearly long-term and thus disability-related. Where the reduced working capacity is clearly long-term and disability-related then the burden of limitations concerning the right to dismiss the employee in question, will presumably be greater on the employer. This means that law-makers and employers should not be too concerned with the definition of when a working capacity is sufficiently long-term to be disability-related. In practice, employment protection legislation will probably already limit the right of employers to dismiss due to short-term reduced working capacity because it is not proportional. This means that a change in employment protection legislation will most probably have the greatest practical impact on the treatment of persons with long-term reduced working capacity who are not considered disabled under national anti-discrimination law.

Employment protection laws may not always operate with a distinction between reduced working capacity and disability-related reduced working capacity. Thus, one may ask whether the contemporary disability human rights approach obligates States to limit the right of employer to dismiss on the grounds of all types of reduced working capacity including reduced working capacity, which is not related to disability, such as for example drug-abuse or social problems. However, the contemporary disability human rights approach is limited to disability policy and law. It follows that it cannot obligate Member States to impose limitations on the rights of employers to dismiss on the grounds of reduced working capacity when it is unrelated to disability and to impose duties. It is nevertheless possible that the consequence of employment protection laws and policies in accordance with the contemporary disability human rights approach will in practice lead to stronger protection of all persons with reduced working capacity irrespective of the reasons for the reduced working capacity. In sum, the CRPD requires that health and safety legislation and employment protection legislation impose duties on employers both with regard to disability and with regard to reduced working capacity when it is associated with disability. The CRPD cannot impose obligations as regards reduced working capacity which is not related to disability.

Similarly to the CRPD, Article 15 of the Revised European Social Charter of 1996 which provides that policies must aim at inclusion and that Member States shall undertake: *"to promote their access to employment through all measures tending to encourage employers to hire and keep in employment persons with disabilities in the ordinary working environment and to adjust the working conditions to the needs of the disabled."*[652] In order to comply with this provision, Member States are obliged to prohibit discrimination on the grounds of disability on the labour market and

> *"to prohibit dismissals on the basis of disability. In addition, there must be obligations on the employer to take steps in accordance with the requirement of reasonable accommodation to ensure effective access to employment and to keep in employment persons with disabilities, in particular persons who have become disabled while in their employment as a result of an industrial accident or occupational disease."*[653]

In other words, the European Committee on Social Rights recognises that inclusion on the labour market requires that legislation on employment protection and health and safety legislation, which regulates the work environment, should impose obligations on employers with regard to employees with disabilities. The reference to the duty to provide reasonable accommodation shows that employment protection legislation and health and safety legislation should also ensure protection and obligations to create inclusive structures and make adjustments for employees with disabilities and reduced working capacity. Moreover, the quotation shows that the European Committee on Social Rights imposes especially far-reaching obligations as regards disability which results from industrial accidents or occupational diseases.

ILO Convention No. 159 Vocational Training and Employment of Persons with Disabilities of 1983 is founded on the medical model of disability and does not fully recognise the importance of social barriers for inclusion and participation of persons with disabilities on the labour market. Although the Convention does aim at *"equality of opportunity [...] for employment in the community"*, it recommends vocational rehabilitation and employment services for persons with disabilities as the means for achieving this goal. The importance of inclusive general structures is not recognised by this Convention. However, the ILO Code of Practice on Managing Disability in the Workplace from 2001, which is not a legally binding document, recommends that:

---

652 Revised European Social Charter Article 15(2).

653 Digest of the Case law of the European Committee on Social Rights, 1 September 2008, p. 113.

> *"The competent authorities should periodically review all rules and regulations governing employment, job retention and return to work in the public and private sectors, to ensure that they do not contain elements of discrimination against people with disabilities".*

In other words, although this ILO Code of Practice recognises that general rules and regulations governing employment must not discriminate against persons with disabilities, it does not specify that the duty to provide accommodation for disability and reduced working capacity should amount to limitations on the rights of employers to dismiss on the grounds of reduced working capacity, and employers' obligations to make adjustments for disability and reduced working capacity in health and safety legislation. In sum, ILO hard-law and soft-law does not concur with the contemporary disability human rights approach described above.

In conclusion, it follows from the principle of substantive diversity equality as well as the principles of inclusion, mainstreaming and the rights-based approach that general legislation on the labour market such as employment protection legislation and health and safety legislation should reflect the duty to provide reasonable accommodation for reduced working capacity related to disability. Firstly, employment protection law should therefore limit the right of employers to dismiss on the grounds of reduced working capacity related to disability. In this regards, it is important to keep in mind that disability is understood as a broad concept under the contemporary disability human rights approach to encompass all long-term impairments, which in interaction with social barriers may lead to a disability. Secondly, health and safety law should reflect the duty to create accessible and inclusive working conditions and to make adjustments for both disability and reduced working capacity related to disability. Working conditions should be understood broadly as encompassing not only the physical environment, but also working hours and the organisation of work as well as attitudes among colleagues.

2.2. Protection Against Unfair Dismissals

Whereas the previous Sub-Section examined whether disability-specific obligations should be contained in employment protection and health and safety legislation, the present Sub-Section examines whether human rights law has imposed a duty on States to ensure that all employees on the labour market enjoy minimum protection against unfair dismissals in line with the rights-based approach. Protection against unfair dismissals is a prerequisite for the enjoyment of protection against dismissals on the grounds of disability and disability-related reduced working capacity.

Both ILO and ICESR provide a right to protection against unfair dismissals. ILO Convention No. 158 *"Termination of Employment"* of 1982 provides that *"The employment of a worker shall not be terminated unless there is a valid reason for such termination connected with the capacity or conduct of the worker or based on the operational requirements of the undertaking, establishment or service."*

Moreover, Article 6 of the UN International Covenant on Economic, Social and Cultural Rights (ICESCR) states that the right to work in Article 6 of the Covenant *"includes the right of everyone to the opportunity to gain his living by work which he freely chooses or accepts"*. According to the General Comment of the Committee on Economic, Social and Cultural Rights, this includes the right not to be deprived of work unfairly.[654]

The Revised European Social Charter of 1996 Article 24(1) goes even further than the UN instruments mentioned above in that it specifies that only small groups of employees on the labour market should be without protection. Thus, the Revised European Social Charter Article 24(1), which was based in part on ILO Convention No. 158, states that employers shall recognise:

> *"the right of all workers not to have their employment terminated without valid reasons for such termination connected with their capacity or conduct or based on the operational requirements of the undertaking, establishment or service".*

The European Committee on Social Rights has specified that States Parties have a duty to prohibit unfair dismissals and the Committee has made it clear that it will only accept the exceptions listed in the Appendix to the Revised European Social Charter:

> *"The Committee recalls that under the Appendix to Article 24 of the Revised Charter only workers engaged for a specified period of time or a specified task, undergoing a period of probation or engaged on a casual basis may be excluded from protection against termination of employment."*[655]

This has lead the Committee to find that employment protection legislation which excludes persons who have been employed for less than six months with the same employer is prohibited, as violating the Revised European Social Charter Article 24.[656] Moreover, the Committee may accept that the prohibition of unfair dismissal has not been adopted by law, but it will in such cases require that Member State demonstrate that all employees are protected on the basis of for example established case law: *"In the absence of any explicit statutory ban, states must be able to show*

654 UN Committee on Economic, Social and Cultural Rights, General Comment No. 18 on the Right to Work adopted on 24 November 2005, E/C.12/GC/18, para. 4.

655 European Committee on Social Rights, Conclusions 2003 on Revised European Social Charter, volume 1, p. 320 (Italy).

656 Ibid., European Committee on Social Rights, Conclusions 2005 on Revised European Social Charter, volume 1, p. 111 (Cyprus).

how national legislation conforms to the requirements of the Charter." This was also underlined in the Preparatory Works to the European Social Charter of 1996 which state that protection against unfair dismissals shall apply to all employed persons with a few exceptions and that the protection shall, *"insofar as they are not made effective by means of collective agreements, arbitration awards or court decisions or in such other manner as may be consistent with national practice, be given effect by laws or regulations."*[657]

Moreover, the European Committee on Social Rights has specified that persons working in sheltered employment should enjoy the usual labour rights at least when the main activity is production work.[658] In other words, persons in sheltered employment should not be deprived of basic protection against unfair dismissals simply with reference to the fact that they are in sheltered employment.

Based in part on the Revised European Social Charter, the European Union Charter on Fundamental Rights also provides a right to protection against unfair dismissals.[659] According to Article 30, *"Every worker has the right to protection against unjustified dismissal, in accordance with Community law and national laws and practices."*

In sum, ILO-Convention No. 158, ICESCR, the Revised European Social Charter and the European Union Charter on Fundamental Rights all provide that employees have a right to protection from unfair dismissals. As argued above under *Sub-Section 2.1. Employers' Obligations towards Employees with Disabilities and Disability-Related Reduced Working Capacity*, such protection should limit the right of employers to dismiss employees with reduced working capacity. Only by limiting the right of employers to dismiss employees with reduced working capacity will the general structures of the labour market become inclusive towards persons with disabilities and reduced working capacity in line with the contemporary disability human rights approach.

2.3. Dismissals Due to Shortage of Work

The question examined under the present Sub-section is whether persons with disabilities and disability-related reduced working capacity should be entitled to special protection against dismissals due to shortage of work under the contemporary disability human rights approach. The rationale would be that persons with

657 Ibid. Articles 1 and 2.

658 Council of Europe, European Committee of Social Rights, *European Social Charter (revised), Conclusions 2007, vol. 1, Estonia, 2005, p. 387.*

659 Text of the explanations relating to the complete text of the Charter as set out in CHARTE 4487/00 CONVENT 50, 11 October 2000, Explanations to Article 30.

disabilities have lower labour market participation and thus are at a higher risk of exclusion from the labour market than many other employees if they lose their employment. Such a protection would qualify as positive action treatment since it would amount to preferential treatment of persons with disabilities and disability-related reduced working capacity.

Neither the CRPD, the European Social Charter nor the European Union Charter of Fundamental Rights mentions this type of preferential treatment specifically. However, as described in *Chapter II Human Rights, Section 1.4. Current Trends*, positive action is an essential characteristic of substantive diversity equality and the CRPD imposes a duty on States Parties to promote equal employment of persons with disabilities. Furthermore, the CRPD mentions *"affirmative action programmes"*, which are synonymous with positive action measures, as a means of promotion of equality. Moreover, the CRPD specifically requires the promotion of job-retention programmes which could include obligations on the part of employers to retain employees with disabilities in situations of dismissals due to a shortage of work. Similarly, the European Committee on Social Rights recommends the use of positive action measures for promoting employment of persons with disabilities and it does not require the imposition of specific positive action measures.[660]

In sum, positive action measures in the form of obligations on employers to refrain from dismissing persons with disabilities in situations of shortage of work are not required under contemporary disability human rights approach. However, such positive action measures would be in line with the contemporary disability human rights approach.

2.4. Conclusion

In conclusion, it follows from the principle of substantive diversity equality as well as the principles of inclusion and mainstreaming that general legislation on the labour market such as employment protection legislation and health and safety legislation should reflect the duty to provide reasonable accommodation for reduced working capacity related to disability. Firstly, employment protection law should therefore limit the right of employers to dismiss on the grounds of reduced working capacity related to disability. In this regard, it is important to keep in mind that disability is understood as a broad concept under the contemporary disability human rights approach to result from the inter-action of long-term impairments and social barriers. Secondly, health and safety law should reflect the duty to create accessible and inclusive working conditions and to make adjustments for both disability and disability-related reduced working capacity. Working conditions should be understood broadly as encompassing not only the physical environment,

660 Digest of the Case law of the European Committee on Social Rights, 1 September 2008, p. 113.

but also working hours and the organisation of work as well as attitudes among colleagues.

The contemporary disability human rights approach also requires the adoption of employment protection legislation which covers practically all employees on the labour market.

Moreover, it is an essential characteristic of the substantive diversity equality concept on which the contemporary disability human rights approach is based that positive action measures should be undertaken to promote equality. Moreover, the CRPD specifically requires the promotion of job retention programmes. Thus, although special protection against dismissal for persons with disabilities and reduced working capacity in situations of shortage of work is not specifically required, they are in accordance with the contemporary disability human rights approach.

Finally, the contemporary disability human rights approach requires the involvement of civil society in the conduct of State functions such as the regulation of the labour market, and that a rights-based approach be applied where this is possible.

In Section 3 below, it is examined whether Danish and Swedish employment law limit the right of employers to dismiss employees with disability-related reduced working capacity. In Section 4, the obligations of employers under health and safety law towards employees with disability and employees with disability-related reduced working capacity are examined.

3. Dismissal Due to Disability-Related Reduced Working Capacity

It follows from the contemporary disability human rights approach that limitations on the right of employers to dismiss due to disability must be mainstreamed into general employment protection legislation. As explained above, the main question is whether employment protection law imposes limitations on the right of employers to dismiss employees due to disability-related reduced working capacity. *"Disability"* should be understood broadly to encompass disability, which may arise as a result of interaction between all long term impairments and social barriers.

As was seen in *Chapter IV Equality Law and Policy, Sub-Section 4.1 Definition of Disability*, the definition of disability under Danish anti-discrimination law is narrower than the definition of disability under the contemporary disability human rights approach. The Danish definition of disability under anti-discrimination law covers only disabilities which arise from severe and permanent impairments. In other words, any limitations on the right of employers to dismiss employees with disabilities related to minor impairments, which are long-term as well as severe impairments, which are not permanent, must therefore stem from Danish employment protection legislation. As was seen in *Chapter IV Equality Law and Policy, Sub-Section 4.1 Definition of Disability*, the definition of disability under Swedish anti-discrimination legislation is in accordance with the contemporary disability human rights approach. Thus, the question is whether the existing prohibition of discrimination and duty to provide reasonable accommodation under Swedish anti-discrimination law has been mainstreamed into Swedish employment protection law.

In *Sub-Section 3.1. Material Limitations* below, I examine the limitations which apply under employment protection law on the right of employers to dismiss employees due to disability-related reduced working capacity. I*n Sub-Section 3.2. Protection Against Unfair Dismissals*, I examine when employees are protected against unfair dismissals under either employment protection legislation or collective agreements.

3.1. Material Limitations

In the present Sub-Section, I examine the material limitations which apply under employment protection law on the right of employers to dismiss employees due to their disability-related reduced working capacity. The main questions are to what degree employers must continue to employ employees who have a disability-related reduced working capacity and when it is legal for employers to dismiss employees due to their disability-related reduced working capacity.

3.1.1. Denmark

In Denmark, it is considered a cornerstone of the much-praised flexicurity model that employers enjoy extensive freedom to dismiss employees.[661] The regulation of the employment market is to a large extent based on the assumption that in the long run, it is in the best interest of both employers and employees that the only limitations on the managerial prerogatives of the employer are a result of free negotiations between employers and employees on a collective and an individual basis. Interference from the State in this balance of interest is seen as detrimental to an economically sound employment market. As a consequence, contractual principles dominate the thinking on limitations on the employer's right to dismiss his employees. In each case, a concrete assessment is made of whether it is reasonable that the employee be dismissed due to his sickness or reduction in working capacity. The dominance of contractual principles means that the employer

661 Barbier, Colomb and Kongshøj Madsen 2009, p. 6.

may as a rule expect from the employee that he or she delivers the initially agreed working performance.

In Denmark, employment protection legislation does not distinguish dismissals on the grounds of reduced working capacity on the grounds of short-term impairments related to for example sickness and dismissals on the grounds of reduced working capacity related to long-term impairments. Instead all reduced working capacity related to impairments, which are not perceived as permanent and severe, are treated as relating to sickness even when the sickness entails long-term impairments and thus qualifies as disability under the contemporary disability human rights approach (but not Danish anti-discrimination law). Due to the lack of differentiation under Danish employment protection law, I initially examine the level of protection against dismissals related to sickness as it is understood under Danish law. Subsequently, I will attempt to determine the level of protection in relation to disability-related reduced working capacity specifically.

In Denmark, a short period of sickness is not a sufficient justification for dismissal. In other words, absence over a certain period of time is necessary to justify a dismissal. The disruption and inconvenience caused by the absence due to sickness may be sufficient to dismiss an employee. It is not a requirement that the sickness is chronic in nature or that the employee is unable to perform any work before a dismissal is warranted. A concrete assessment of the proportionality of a dismissal must be performed in each case. Criteria to be taken into account in assessing proportionality of a dismissal include length of absence, number of periods of absence, whether the employee in question has a high level of absence due to sickness in general or whether the absence is caused by a specific sickness, prognosis for return to work, prognosis for a relapse, whether the employer has accepted that that the employee has a reduction in working capacity, whether sickness or reduced working capacity was related to work, and finally length of employment.

A consequence of the assumption that the employer is within his or her right to expect that the employee delivers an agreed working performance, is that it is considered a rule of thumb, that a significantly higher frequency of absence due to sickness, as compared to the frequency of absence due to sickness of other employees will be considered reasonable grounds for dismissal. In a case from 1984, the Dismissals Tribunal stated that *"absence due to sickness, which significantly exceeds the normal level, will as a rule be considered a reasonable grounds for dismissal. Exception may be made where the employee has been with the company for a long period of time or where other special circumstances can be brought forward against a dismissal.'*[662] The assessment of whether the amount of

662 AN af 21.12.1984(151); Stenholm and Spiermann 2004, p. 89; AN af 16.7.1985 (171).

absence exceeds the *"normal level"* should be done by comparing with other employees in similar positions in similar companies.[663] This position illustrates clearly that employers may organise work on the assumption that employees do not have (significant) reductions in working capacity. The *"normal"* employee is an employee who delivers the agreed working performance.

The assumption that an employer should not be made to bear the burden of having employees who have 'abnormal' reductions in working capacity is codified in the so-called *"120-day-rule"*. According to Section 5(2) of the Act on White Collar Employees, an employer and an employee may agree that the employee can be dismissed with a shorter notice of one month, when he has been absent due to sickness *120 days within a period of 12 months*. The dismissal must take place in connection with the 120-day period and while the employee is still absent from work due to sickness. The 120 days must be calculated as calendar days and not as working days.[664] As illustrated by a judgment by the Supreme Court, the main rule is that a dismissal which takes place with reference to such an agreement is considered reasonable.[665] The case in question concerned the dismissal of a shop assistant who had been employed for 13 years and had developed back-problems. She was dismissed after 4 months of absence and the dismissal was found to be reasonable. The Supreme Court stated that dismissals with reference to the 120-day rule:

> *"will ordinarily be deemed reasonable so that compensation for a dismissal on unreasonable grounds will only be relevant under very special circumstances. Such very special circumstances are not in our opinion present in this case."*[666]

According to its wording, the 120-day rule applies when the 120-day absence is due to sickness. However until the implementation of the Framework Employment Directive, there was no doubt that also absence due to disability-related reduced working capacity would warrant a dismissal with shortened delay. Two cases lodged with the Danish Maritime and Commercial Court in 2009 raise this question and the Court decided to refer the following question for preliminary adjudication by the European Court of Justice regarding the 120-days rule and reasonable accommodation:[667]

---

663 AN 171.84, Stenholm and Spiermann 2004, p. 89.

664 Danish Maritime and Commercial Court judgment, UFR 1951.156 SH. Paulsen 1997, p. 598.

665 Danish Supreme Court judgment, UFR 2002.2626 H.

666 Danish Supreme Court judgment, UFR 2002.2626 H; One judge dissented and stated that 'very special circumstances' did not have to be present in order to find that a dismissal in accordance with the 120-day rule was unreasonable. In his opinion, a simple assessment of all the available facts could well lead to the conclusion that such a dismissal was unreasonable. Paulsen 1997, p. 333; Bruun 2003, p. 188.

667 Maritime and Commercial Court, Decision of 24 August 2009, F-13–06 and Decision of 24 August 2009, F-19–06. The decision to refer the above question to the ECJ was appealed to

> *"Is it in compliance with Council Directive 2000/78/EC of 27 November 2000 to dismiss an employee who has been absent from work due to a disability, as this concept is understood under the Directive, with a shortened delay which is applicable according to national legislation when a person has had 120 days of absence due to sickness within 12 consecutive months?"*

In my opinion, the CJEU cannot be expected to find that the 120-day rule, which applies under Danish law to white-collar employees, as such violates the prohibition of discrimination on the grounds of disability. However, it is likely that the CJEU will underline the duty of employers that the 120-day rule should be applied under consideration of the right of employees with disabilities to reasonable accommodation under the Employment Equality Directive. Thus, it should not be permitted to dismiss a person *with disabilities* who has had 120 days of leave unless he or she has been given the reasonable accommodation that he or she was entitled to.

As mentioned above, the expectations of the employer when the employee was hired are of central importance due to the dominance of contractual principles under Danish employment protection law. Consequently, an employee may be dismissed due to sickness which he has deceitfully failed to disclose when he or she took up a position.[668] This is confirmed indirectly by the Act on Health Information according to which an employee is obliged to inform the employer if he or she has a sickness or has symptoms of a sickness which will have significant importance for his or her working capacity.[669] If the employee has a significantly reduced working capacity due to a medical condition, which the employee had knowledge of when taking up a position without informing the employer, then the employer may dismiss him on these grounds.

Correspondingly, if an employer has hired an employee with full knowledge of his reduced working capacity and possibly even with a public wage subsidy to compensate for this reduction in working capacity, then the employer will be required to tolerate more inconvenience due to the sickness or reduction in working capacity. In a case from July 2006, Århus District Court found that a dismissal due to lower productivity was an unreasonable ground for dismissal of an employee with multiple sclerosis who had been hired with 66% salary subsidy.[670] The

---

the Supreme Court which has approved the referral, Supreme Court Decision of 7 May 2010, Case no. 284/2009, Dansk Almennyttigt Boligselskab v. HK som mandatar for B.

668 Act on White Collar Employees Section 5(1) according to which "absence due to illness is legal non-attendance unless he has become ill intentionally or as a result of gross negligence, or he has deceitfully failed to disclose when he took up a position".

669 Danish Act on Health Information, Act no. 286 of 24 April 1996, (Lov om Brug af Helbredsoplysninger m.v. på arbejdsmarkedet), Chapter III, Sections 6 and 7.

670 Århus District Court judgment of 13 July 2006, no. BS 5.2830/2005. The District Court had also decided that the complainant's impairments related to multiple sclerosis did not amount to

employee worked as a booker of sales meetings in a telemarketing company. The Court stated that the employer:

> *"had to be prepared for a greater amount of absence due to sickness than normal and a fall in the level of motivation due to an alteration in the calculation of the employee's remuneration after the employee went over to a new contract with salary subsidy. The defendant had not complained of the employee's performance before the dismissal. The employer had not offered the employee another relevant position. Under these circumstances the dismissal is not considered reasonable."*

When hiring an employee or after he or she has been hired, employers may enter into an agreement with local authorities that the local authorities will cover sickness benefits to be paid to an employee during the first two weeks of sick leave in accordance with Section 28 of the Act on Sickness Benefits. Without such an agreement, employers must cover these costs.[671] Such agreements are only possible where the employee has a high risk of absence due to sickness or reduction in working capacity. Where such an agreement has been made, the employer will be considered to have agreed to a higher level of absence due to sickness on the part of the employee. In a case from 1988, the Dismissals Tribunal acknowledged that a Section 28-agreement indicates that the employer has agreed to accept a higher frequency of absence due to sickness.[672] However the Tribunal underlined that such an agreement could not preclude the employer from dismissing an employee due to sickness. The case concerned an employee who had been employed eight years with the company and who during the last two years had been absent due to sickness 77% of the time. In its ruling, the Tribunal stated:

> *"When the employee and the employer have made a [Section 28] agreement, the employer must tolerate a greater amount of absence due to sickness before he can dismiss the employee due to sickness. However, if a [Section 28] agreement were to completely rule out the possibility of dismissing the employee due to sickness, employers would be reluctant to enter into [Section 28] agreements and the aim of the scheme would not be achieved."*

In view of the high amount of absence, the dismissal was considered reasonable.

Long period of employment with the same employer is a factor to be taken into consideration when performing an assessment of whether a dismissal is reasonable. Presumably, when an employee has been employed with the same employer for a

---

'disability' under the Act on Differential Treatment. This part of the judgment was upheld by the Danish Western High Court Judgment of 11 October 2007, published in UFR2008.306V (multiple schlerosis).

671 Danish Act on Sickness Benefits, LBK af 1047 af 28 October 2004 with latest amendment by act no. 596 of 9 June 2006, (lov om dagpenge ved sygdom eller fødsel), Section 28.

672 Danish Permanent Arbitration Tribunal on Dismissals, AN 23.88, Paulsen 1997, p. 330.

long period of time, the employee gains an expectation that he may stay in employment. In a case from 1984, the Dismissals Tribunal stated that *"absence due to sickness which significantly exceeds the norm will as a rule be reasonable grounds for a dismissal. Exception may have to be done where the employee has been employed with the company for a long period of time or where other special circumstances weigh against the dismissal."*[673] In a District Court judgment of 1989, the Court found it reasonable that an office employee was dismissed after 145 days of absence due to sickness even though she had 17 years of employment with the company. The Court underlined that she had informed the employer that she did not expect to be able to return to work within the near future.[674]

Also of importance in the case law is whether or not the cause of the reduction in working capacity is *work-related.* In a case from 2005, the Dismissals Tribunal reinstated a bus driver who was dismissed with reference to absence due to sickness caused by back pain as a result of a faulty driver's seat.[675] In a case from 2003, a worker in a ware-house became ill from working with a fork-lift truck. He had been employed with the company for 18 years.[676] The dismissal was found to be unreasonable with reference to his age, the length of employment and the fact that the sickness was work-related.[677] In a case from 1989, a District Court found that a dismissal was unreasonable in spite of the fact that it took place with reference to the 120-day rule.[678] The Court found that it was established that the absence was at least partially caused by work-related injury and sickness. The employee worked in an architect's practice with a photo-printing machine. It was undisputed that almost 50 days of absence due to sickness was caused by a respiratory ailment, which was work-related, and a finger injury, which was also work related. The remaining absence was caused by back problems. The Court could not reject that the back problems were also work-related and found that accommodation of the workplace was a prerequisite for the return of the employee. The Western High-Court came to a similar conclusion in a case from March 2009, where a laboratory technician in an industrial swine butchery was injured by an electrical shock while working.[679] During the first year after the injury, she worked part-time and was absent from work due to the injury for a period of approximately 2 months. One year after injury,

673 Danish Permanent Arbitration Tribunal on Dismissals, AN 151.84. Bruun 2003, p. 193.

674 Bruun 2003, p. 199.

675 Danish Permanent Arbitration Tribunal on Dismissals, AN 1322.05; Bruun 2003, p. 190–191. In AN 1984.151, the Dismissals Tribunal did not find that the back problems were caused by faulty accommodation of the work environment.

676 Danish Permanent Arbitration Tribunal on Dismissals, AN 1096.03.

677 See also a judgment from Ringsted District Court of 17 November 1989 mentioned below according to which a dismissal was unreasonable because the absence was caused by work-related illness and injury.

678 Ringsted District Court judgment of 17 November 1989, Bruun 2003, p. 154.

679 Danish Western High Court Judgment of 20 March 2009, 12. Afdeling, B-1160–08, HK Danmark som mandatar for A mod DI som mandatar for B.

she was dismissed. The Western High Court found that the dismissal was unjust in consideration of the fact that the injury was work-related, that she had worked with the same employer for ten years and that the long-term prognosis for a full recovery was good.[680] The decision by the Court was based on the prohibition of unfair dismissal contained in Section 2b of the Act on White Collar Employees. In addition, the Court underlined that an adjustment in the distribution of the work in the laboratory which would have enabled the employee to continue working would not have entailed a disproportionate burden on the employer.[681] The Act on Differential Treatment in Employment was not applicable in this case because the employee was not considered to have a disability as her impairment was not long-lasting or permanent.

In conclusion, no special employment protection applies in relation to disability-related reduced working capacity except where the person in question has been hired under special working conditions relating to long-lasting reduced working capacity such as Section 28 of the Act on Sickness Benefit or with wage subvention for employees with significantly reduced working capacity. For others, whose working capacity is not considered related to disability as it is defined under Danish discrimination law, but who may well have a disability as it is understood under the contemporary disability human rights approach, very few limitations apply. Only where the cause of the reduced working capacity was work-related and the employee has been employed with the same employer for many years, will the right of the employer to dismiss the employee be limited. In other cases, a proportionality assessment is performed, but the starting-point is that the employer should not have to tolerate that the employee's performance falls significantly. Thus, Danish employment legislation does not provide the required limitations in the right of employers to dismiss employees due to disability-related reduced working capacity and therefore does not comply with the contemporary disability human rights approach. In other words, Danish employment protection legislation does not contribute to the creation of general structures on the labour market which are inclusive to persons with disabilities and reduced working capacity.

3.1.2. Sweden

As mentioned above, the definition of disability under Swedish anti-discrimination law complies with the contemporary disability human rights approach. This means that Swedish anti-discrimination law provides protection against dismissals and an obligation to provide reasonable accommodation for the whole group of persons with disabilities as defined under the contemporary disability human rights

680 This case is discussed further in *Chapter IV Equality Law and Policy, Section 4 Definition of Disability.*

681 This case is discussed further in *Chapter IV Equality Law and Policy, Section 4 Definition of Disability.*

approach. The question still remains whether these obligations both towards persons with disabilities and persons with disability-related disabilities have been mainstreamed into Swedish employment protection legislation and health and safety legislation.

In Sweden, in contrast to Denmark, the *material protection* against unfair dismissals is relatively strong.[682] Thus the starting point is that reduced working capacity is not a fair ground for dismissal. A key passage from the Preparatory Works of the Employment Protection Act from 1974 makes this point:

> *"We must seek to prevent that we develop two employment markets, one for younger, well-qualified employees and one for older persons, persons with disabilities and undertrained employees. It follows that old age or sickness and the combination hereof should in principle not be accepted as reasonable grounds for a dismissal. The limitation on the employee's working capacity which age or sickness can result in should instead lead the employer to adopt special measures to support the employee, e.g. by providing special measures in his present position or by moving him to a less demanding position. Age or sickness can however result in a lasting reduction in working capacity which is so substantial that the employee can no longer perform work of any value. In such a case the reduction in working capacity may be grounds for a dismissal."*[683]

This perception of the role of employers in ensuring that the employment market be inclusive towards employees with reduced working capacity was translated into a relatively vague provision on unfair dismissals. According to Section 7 of the Employment Protection Act: *"dismissal by an employer must be objectively justified. A dismissal is not objectively justified if it is reasonable to require that the employer offers the employee a different position."* Both Preparatory Works to the Employment Protection Act and case law establish that sickness and reduced working capacity do not as a rule constitute a legitimate ground for dismissal. The problems resulting from sickness and reduced working capacity are expected to be solved through co-operation between employee and employer and not through dismissal. Thus, reduced working capacity can only warrant a dismissal where the reduced working capacity is *"long-lasting and prevents the employee from performing any work of importance to the employer"*.[684]

---

682 The present Section deals only with the situation for employees who are not on temporary contracts. According to the Employment Protection Act, employees on temporary contracts enjoy even stronger protection against dismissals on personal grounds than other employees.

683 Swedish preparatory works, Prop. 1973:129, p. 126.

684 Swedish preparatory works, Prop. 1973:129, p. 126, prop. 1981/82:71, p. 66; Inghammer 2007, p. 120; Lunning and Toijer 2006, p. 435; Källström and Malmberg 2006, p. 135 and 274. See e.g. Industrifacket Metall v. Teknikarbetsgivarna, AD 2006, no. 90, p. 16 and Fastighetsantälldas förbund v. Fastigo och HSB Filipstad Ekonomisk förening i Filipstad, AD 2001, no. 92, p. 8. Prop. 1973:129, p. 126.

It follows that a decision to dismiss an employee cannot be based merely on past reduced working capacity, but must be founded on an evaluation of the *future* working capacity of that employee.[685] As a rule, dismissal cannot take place as long as rehabilitation measures are still being taken and there is a possibility that the employee may return to work for the employer.[686] In practice, it is not uncommon that employees will have been on sick leave for periods of two to three years before they are dismissed.[687]

Both the Preparatory Works and case law have made an explicit link between the rules on a permanent sickness benefit or a disability pension under the General Insurance Act and the rules on fair dismissals under the Employment Protection Act.[688] According to the General Insurance Act, only a reduction in working capacity which is expected to last longer than one year will qualify for permanent sickness benefits. Thus case law has established that a dismissal on the grounds of sickness or reduced working capacity, which is not expected to last longer than one year, will only under very special circumstances qualify as an objective ground for dismissal.[689]

A case from 1996 illustrates that the Courts performs a relatively intense examination of whether the reduction in working capacity is such that it may warrant a dismissal. The case concerned a postal worker who had been working as a postman for almost 15 years. During the last 5 years she had been on sick leave part-time or full-time. During the last 9 months before her dismissal, she had been working part-time. The Court made reference to the Preparatory Works of the Employment Protection Act and stated that:

> *"The Permanent Secretary had [in the Preparatory Works]emphasised that age or sickness could result in a lasting reduction in working capacity which was so substantial that the employee in question could no longer perform work of any value. In such a case the reduction in working capacity could be grounds for a dismissal. As regards sickness, the employment relation should not be brought to an end before*

---

685 Swedish Labour Court judgment, AD 1996 no. 102. Lunning and Toijer 2006, p. 436, see also AD 1954 nr 35.

686 Swedish preparatory works, Prop. 1990/91, p. 52.

687 Swedish Labour Court judgment, AD 2007 no. 12, Facket för Service och Kommunikation (SEKO) mot Almega Tjänsteförbunden och Posten Aktiebolag i Stockholm; AD 2006 no. 11, Svenska Kommunalarbetareförbundet mot Hudiksval Kommun; Swedish Labour Court judgment, AD 2006 no. 57, SEKO Facket for Service och Kommunikation v. Almega Tjänsteförbunden och Posten Aktiebolag i Stockholm; AD 2006 no. 90, Industrifacket Metall v. Teknikarbetsgivarna och P.T. Rostfria o Mek Aktiebolag i Ramlösa. Swedish Labour Court judgment, AD 2006 no. 83, Svenska Kommunalarbetareförbundet v. Föreningen Vårdföretagarna och Falck Ambulans Aktiebolag i Lidingö.

688 Swedish preparatory works, Prop. 1973:129, p. 126.

689 Imghammar 2007, p. 122, Lunning and Toijer 2006, p. 437. See e.g. Swedish Labour Court judgment, AD 1997 no. 73, Vårdförbundet SHSTF v. Norrbottens läns landsting Luleå, p. 9.

the employee gained the right to a permanent sickness benefit or invalidity pension under the General Insurance Act. At least, the Permanent Secretary continued, dismissal should not become relevant as long as the employee received a sickness benefit on a temporary basis. (...) The mail company found that the employee could only manage to work half-time and that a full-time job would require a more light and varied job than that of postman."

The Court did not find that it had been established that the employee had a permanent reduction in her working capacity. On these grounds, the dismissal was not well-reasoned and the dismissal was declared null.[690]

Another case illustrates how the Labour Court requires that the person in question will as a rule be eligible for a permanent disability benefit in order for the dismissal to be legitimate. The case concerned a fireman who could no longer perform smoke-diving due to heart problems.[691] He was dismissed two years before his pension age. The Labour Court stressed that a working relationship should not be brought to an end before the employee had a right to receive permanent pension.[692]

Only in the exceptional situation where it is clear from the start that the employee has a reduction in working capacity, which must be expected to be long-lasting and where the employee cannot be expected to be rehabilitated to perform work of interest to this employer, will a dismissal be legal before one year has passed. For example in a case, which is referred to in more detail below, an electrician went on sick leave in November 2001 due to over-sensitivity of his hands caused by work with vibrating tools which meant that he could not work in temperatures colder than five degrees Celsius. The Labour Court found that his dismissal in January 2002 had been fair as it was already at the time of dismissal clear that he could not be expected to return to work in the company.[693]

In sum, the above examination shows the right of employers is strongly limited as regards dismissals due to disability-related reduced working capacity. Thus, the starting point under Swedish law is that dismissals due to reduced working capacity are considered unfair. The Swedish Labour Court operates with a requirement that the employee must have a substantial and lasting reduction in his working capacity before it can even be relevant to consider dismissing the employee. In addition, the Employment Protection Act prohibits dismissals where the employee can perform

690 Swedish Labour Court judgment, AD 1996 no. 115, Facket for Service och Kommunikation (SEKO) v. Alliansen och Posten Sverige Aktiebolag Stockholm,, p. 7 and 8.

691 Smoke-diving consists in entering zones where the fireman must breathe using bottled oxygen because of the high concentration of smoke in the air similarly to scuba-divers.

692 Swedish Labour Court judgment, AD 2002 no. 32, Svenska Kommunalarbetareförbundet v. Räddningstjänsten Östra Skaraborg i Skövde,, p. 9.

693 Swedish Labour Court judgment, AD 1993 no. 42, Svenska Elektrikerförbundet v. Elektriska Arbetsgivareföreningen och Svenska Elinstallationer Aktiebolag i Gävle, p. 17 and 18.

any work of value to the employer. In other words, the employer will have extensive duties to make adjustments for the needs of employees with disability-related reduced working capacity. The requirement that the employee must not be able to perform any work of value to the employer is an adequate mainstreaming of the duty to provide reasonable accommodation as long as essential work functions may be carried out. Thus, the protection under Swedish employment protection law complies with the requirements of the contemporary disability human rights approach and contributes to creating inclusive general structures on the labour market.

3.1.3. Conclusion

In conclusion, Denmark and Sweden differ significantly as regards the limitations which apply on the right of employers to dismiss employees on the grounds of disability-related reduced working capacity as defined under the contemporary disability human rights approach. In Denmark, disability is defined relatively narrowly under anti-discrimination law to cover just disability related to permanent and severe impairments. Consequently, minor long-term impairments which may lead to a disability under the contemporary disability human rights approach would not qualify for protection under Danish anti-discrimination law. Moreover, the starting point under Danish employment protection legislation is that an employer may dismiss an employee with a long-lasting reduced working capacity who may be considered disabled under the contemporary disability human rights approach. Limitations only apply when the reduced working capacity results from a work-related injury or sickness.

In Sweden, the concept of disability is defined broadly under anti-discrimination law in accordance with the contemporary disability human rights approach. This is reflected in Swedish employment protection legislation where dismissals due to reduced working capacity are only permitted if the employee is unable to carry out work of no value to the employer even after a re-organisation of work, training and adjustments of working conditions. In other words, the limitations imposed on employers under anti-discrimination law including the duty to provide reasonable accommodation have been mainstreamed into Swedish employment protection legislation in accordance with the contemporary disability human rights approach.

In the following *Sub-Section 3.2 Protection Against Unfair Dismissal*, I examine when employees enjoy protection from unfair dismissals in Denmark and Sweden. The material limitations under employment protection law are only relevant when a person is protected under employment law in the first place.

3.2. Protection against Unfair Dismissal

The present Sub-section analyses the coverage of protection against unfair dismissals in Denmark and in Sweden. As explained in *Section 2. Contemporary Disability Human Rights Approach* above, both UN and European human rights law impose a duty on States to provide protection against unfair dismissals. It is therefore necessary to examine whether all employees enjoy employment protection in Denmark and Sweden. The present Section falls into three Sub-Sections with the titles: Denmark, Sweden and Conclusion.

3.2.1. Denmark

In Denmark, employment protection is provided through collective agreements and three specific legal Acts: the Act on White Collar Employees, the Sailor's Act and the Act on Public Servants.[694] The first two of these legal Acts provide the only protection against unfair dismissals for employees in the private sector who are not covered by a collective agreement. The statutory protection was introduced in 1964 and 1973 respectively with inspiration from the Basic Agreement of 1960 between the main social partners, the Danish Confederation of Trade Unions and the Danish Confederation of Employers.[695] The Act on White Collar Employees applies to commercial and clerical staff, persons who do work of technical or clinical character which is not in craft or industry and persons whose main functions are to direct and allocate work.[696] Only employees who work at least 8 hours a week and who are subordinated to the employer are covered by the Act.[697] Importantly, the protection only applies after one year's continuous employment with the same employer.[698]

In the *public sector*, the Act on White Collar Employees is complemented by the Act on Public Servants. *"Public servants"* are public employees entitled to special job protection and pension. Employment as public servant is typically reserved for persons in managerial positions and for persons carrying out work of importance for the functioning of the State. For example prison guards and some postmen are employed as *"public servants"*. In return for the special job protection, public

694 Danish Act on White Collar Employees, Sailors' Act and Act on Public Servants.

695 The Danish Confederation of Trade Unions (LO) is the largest central organisation for workers on the Danish labour market. More than 1.3 million employees are in 2007 members of one of LO's affiliated unions, two thirds of all unionised employees in Denmark. LO covers both blue-collar workers and commercial and clerical staff in the public and the private sectors. The Confederation of Danish Employers (DA) is the main confederation for Danish employers representing the main employers' organisations with more than 29,000 private companies as members, covering the manufacturing, retail, transport, service and construction sectors.

696 Danish Act on White Collar Employees, Section 1(1).

697 Ibid., Section 1(2).

698 Ibid., Section 2(b).

servants may not go on strike.[699] The Act on Public Servants implicitly prohibits unfair dismissals by providing that both the public servant him or herself and his trade union shall be given the opportunity to comment on plans to dismiss him or her.[700] Public servants may be dismissed on the same grounds as other staff, but enjoy a right to pension when dismissal was not a consequence of a breach of duty or a criminal offence. Where dismissal takes place on the grounds of breach of duty or criminal offence, dismissal requires an official interrogation procedure or a court ruling. Dismissals on grounds relating to changes in the organisation of the administration additionally lead to an entitlement to salary for a period of three years. Finally, all publicly employed staff enjoy protection under general administrative law. It follows from administrative law principles that a decision to dismiss an employee must be founded on reasonable grounds. The principles of equality, proportionality, the ban against misuse of powers and the duty to perform an individual assessment ensure protection against unfair dismissals for all public employees.[701]

Persons working in sheltered employment in Denmark are publicly employed, but they are not considered to be employees under Danish Employment law.[702] Their work is considered to be a social measure rather than an employment. The only applicable standard to provide protection against losing sheltered employment would be administrative law according to which a decision to the detriment of an individual must be justified on sound grounds. However since the activation is not considered to be a job, it is likely that the interests of the individual to keep the employment will not be considered as strong as the interests of an employee to keep his employment.

As regards the protection against unfair dismissals under collective agreements in Denmark, the Basic Agreement of 1960 adopted by the main social partners provides a prohibition of unfair dismissals for members covered by the agreement. The protection under the Basic Agreement applies to members covered by the collective agreement, but only after nine months of employment with the same employer. Other collective agreements have since adopted corresponding protection.[703]

In sum, Danish employees in the public sector, with the exception of persons in sheltered employment, as well as white-collar employees and sailors in the private sector who have been employed for nine months or one year enjoy protection against

699 Danish Act on Public Servants, Chapter 10.

700 Danish Act on Public Servants, Chapter 4. Emborg and Schaumburg-Müller 1998, p. 297.

701 Andersen and others 2003, p. 176.

702 Persons employed in sheltered employment will not fall under the Act on White Collar Employees, the Sailor's Act, Act on Public Servants or collective agreements.

703 Nielsen and Roseberry 2008, p. 479.

unfair dismissals. Other employees on the private labour market only enjoy employment protection if they are covered by a collective agreement. Moreover, most collective agreements only convey employment protection after nine months of employment with the same employer. According to a survey by the Danish Confederation of Trade Unions, 71% of blue-collar workers in the private sector were in 2001 covered by a collective agreement.[704] This leaves approximately one-third of blue-collar workers in the private sector without protection against unfair dismissals as well as the significant number of employees who have not yet been employed for nine months or one year with the same employer.

The fact that such a significant part of the employees in Denmark are without protection against unfair dismissals under statutory law or collective agreement raises the question whether employers are completely free to dismiss the employees who are not covered by either employment protection under collective agreements or statutory law. *In Denmark*, it is undisputed that the managerial prerogative to dismiss at will was practically unrestricted until 1960 when the main social partners agreed to prohibit unfair dismissals.[705] Until 1964, when protection against unjust dismissals was introduced in the Act on White Collar Employees, the Supreme Court underlined that the *"assessment performed by the employer [in relation to a dismissal] could not be tried by the Courts"*.[706] Today, it is in Denmark disputed whether or not the prerogative of the employer to dismiss freely is still the fall-back position where protection against arbitrary dismissals under statutory law or collective agreement does not apply. A judgment from the Supreme Court from 2003 has unfortunately not resolved the issue. The case concerned a bartender on a ship who was dismissed by the privately owned shipping company after six months of employment. The protection against unfair dismissal contained in collective agreement and statutory law both require that a sailor has been in service at least nine months. The Supreme Court stated:

> *"The Supreme Court finds that the award of compensation on the grounds that a dismissal of a employee by a private entity is not justified by reasonable grounds relating to the employee or the entity can only take place if there is legal basis in statutory law, collective agreement or other agreement. This was the presumption when Section 2b of the Act on White Collar Employees and corresponding clauses in other legal acts and collective agreements were adopted and neither EU-law nor the ILO Convention on dismissals, which is not ratified by Denmark, can give grounds for a different result. (...) A's compensation claim on the grounds of an unfair dismissal unfounded on grounds relating to the employee is rejected already since there is no legal basis for such a compensation. It follows that there is no cause for an evaluation of whether the dismissal was fair. (...) There are no grounds to*

704 LO, Diskussionsoplæg om Fremtidens Arbejdsret, LO, March 2001, p. 214.

705 Ruling K 20 of 1910 by the Industrial Arbitration Tribunal (predecessor of the Danish Labour Court).

706 Danish Supreme Court judgment, UFR 1964.387H; Nielsen 2005, p. 422.

establish that the employer with the dismissal or what has been put forward in the case, has given rise to liability for a violation of A's freedom, peace, honour or person, cf. Liability for Damages Act Section 26. Also, there are no grounds for awarding A, who was dismissed under respect for the applicable prior notice, compensation according to the ordinary rules on compensation."[707]

This judgment was seen by some commentators as a rejection of a general requirement that dismissals be fair even when statutory or collective agreements do not provide this protection.[708] Others, including *Ruth Nielsen*, have argued that the Supreme Court acknowledged its capacity to try whether the employer is liable for loss according to general culpa-standard which will provide some protection against an unjust dismissal. *Ruth Nielsen* underlines that the culpa-standard should be interpreted in light of international soft-law obligations applicable in Denmark, including Article 30 of the EU Charter on the protection against unjustified which had not been made legally binding under EU law at the time of the judgment. In addition, the general duty to show loyalty to a contracting party should also be taken into account.[709] In my opinion, the judgment confirms the right of the employer to unilaterally dismiss his employees without justification unless the employee is covered by a specific employment protection clause under a legal act or a collective agreement. The Supreme Court recognises that the culpa-standard applies in relation to liability for economic loss and violation of a person's freedom, peace, honour or person. The question remains however what the material protection under this standard amounts to in practice. Where the agreed prior notice has been respected, it is difficult to see how an employer could become liable for compensation with reference to such a narrowly interpreted culpa-standard.

In conclusion, a substantial group of persons on the labour market are without protection against unfair dismissals due to a lack of legislative protection and lack of coverage of collective agreements in the private sector. Thus, Denmark does not comply with its obligations under the contemporary disability human rights approach and Denmark does not apply a rights-based approach in this regard.

3.2.2. Sweden

In contrast to Denmark, Sweden has adopted general statutory protection against unfair dismissals which applies to practically all employees on the labour market. This is a result of the fact that the Swedish Parliament has not had the same reluctance toward regulation of the labour market as the Danish Parliament. *Halvorsen and Hvindén* explain that the trade union movement has been stronger in Sweden than in Denmark and that the Social Democratic Party has been very strong

---

707 Danish Supreme Court judgment, UFR 2003.1570H.

708 Kristiansen 2005, p. 339.

709 Nielsen 2005, p. 422; Bruun 2003, p. 32.

in Sweden.[710] The Social Democratic Party was in government almost without interruption for four decades after World War II. It seems that in Sweden, the trade unions and the Social Democrats in Parliament have joined forces and have secured a relatively strong regulation by law of the rights of employees, whereas in Denmark, the employers' side has been stronger both in the industrial relations and in Parliament. This has resulted in a higher degree of autonomy for the social partners in Denmark which is not only reflected by a reluctance to pass national legislation in the area of the labour market, but also in a reluctance to undertake new human rights obligations which would affect the labour market.

In Sweden, the Employment Protection Act adopted first in 1974 provides protection against unfair dismissals and covers practically all employees.[711] The Employment Protection Act applies to all employees with the exception of employees in a managerial position, employees who are part of the employer's family, employees working in the household of the employer, and finally employees who are employed with special employment support or in protected employment.[712] It follows from the Preparatory Works of the Act that persons with disabilities employed on the open employment market with public support are covered by the Employment Protection Act.[713] The Swedish provisions prohibiting unfair dismissals cannot be set aside by agreements between an employer and an employee.[714]

The Swedish Labour Court has in relation to employees in managerial positions established that *"the free right to dismiss can never be used with an aim which violates law or good practice"*.[715] However, this does not entail an assessment of whether or not the dismissal was fair – as soon as the managing board has lost confidence in the administering director, there will be a right to dismiss him or her.[716] Instead, the Labour Court has limited its assessment to examining whether the employee has been given sufficient notice and sufficient severance pay and benefits.[717] Thus, although the Labour Court underlines that dismissals of managerial staff must be in accordance with good practice, this does not amount to a duty to ensure that dismissals are fair.[718] In addition, the general principles on

---

710 Halvorsen and Hvindén 2009b, p. 198.

711 Swedish Employment Protection Act (Lag om Anställningskydd), originally SFS 1974:12, which has been replaced by SFS 1982:80.

712 Swedish Employment Protection Act, Chapter 1, Section 1.

713 Swedish preparatory works on a renewed labour market policy on inclusion and growth, Prop. 1999/2000:98 (Fornyad arbetsmarknadspolitik för delaktighet och tillväxt), p. 78. Lunning and Toijer, p. 55.

714 Swedish Employment Protection Act, Sections 7 and 23.

715 Swedish Labour Court judgments, AD 1967 no. 26 and AD 1976 no. 33.

716 Swedish Labour Court judgment, AD 1997 no. 3.

717 Swedish Labour Court judgments AD 1988 no. 20, AD 1991 no. 86 and AD 2004 no. 90.

718 Lunning and Toijer 2006, p. 65.

compensation cannot warrant damages for a dismissal which violates good practice. Presumably, only compensation for economic loss can be awarded.[719]

In a case from 2005, the Labour Court has tried whether the dismissal of an employee in sheltered employment in the public concern *Samhall* was in accordance with general contractual principles. The Court confirmed that the Employment Protection Act did not apply and that the applicable collective agreement did not contain a requirement that dismissals be fair. Therefore, the Court contented itself with contractual principles: *"a dismissal must under all circumstances be possible where such fundamental breaches of contract have taken place which could, in accordance with general contractual principles, warrant the cancellation of a contract by a party to a reciprocally binding agreement"*[720] The employee had in this case stayed away from work for a period of almost a year and had refused to co-operate with the employer in finding tasks which were suitable for him. On these grounds, the Labour Court concluded that there was no doubt that the behaviour went beyond what the employer should be required to accept and that the dismissal was justified. Since the employee's lack of fulfilment of his working contract was so blatant in this case, it is difficult to use this case to assess the level of protection based on contractual principles. As with managerial staff, it seems likely that only compensation for economic loss could be awarded where a dismissal violated contractual principles. Compensation for non-economic damages and a reinstatement in a position would presumably require explicit legal authority.

In sum, the managerial prerogative to dismiss is the fall-back position under Swedish labour law. However, the Swedish Labour Court has established that a dismissal may not be in violation of good practice and must respect general contractual principles. Although this protection amounts to protection against the most unwarranted dismissals, it still leaves persons working in sheltered employment without full protection against unfair dismissals.

3.2.3. Conclusion

In conclusion, around one third of employees on the Danish labour market are without protection against unfair dismissals under either statutory law or collective agreements. This lack of protection is in violation of ICESCR Article 6 on the Right to Work.[721] In contrast, Sweden has adopted general legislation in accordance with the rights-based approach and practically all employees on the Swedish labour market are protected against unfair dismissals in line with Sweden's human rights

719 Swedish Labour Court judgments AD 1979 no. 146 and AD 1983 no. 46, Lunning and Toijer 2006, p. 68.

720 AD 2005 no. 43, P-A.W. i Bollstabruk v. Samhall Mitland AB, p. 4.

721 UN Committee on Economic, Social and Cultural Rights, General Comment No. 18 on the Right to Work adopted on 24 November 2005, E/C.12/GC/18, para. 4.

obligations. The consequences of the lack of protection in especially Denmark in relation to persons with disabilities are discussed immediately below in *Sub-Section 3.3. Conclusion.*

3.3. Conclusion

In conclusion, Denmark and Sweden differ significantly both as regards contents and coverage of the protection against unfair dismissal. In Denmark, the obligations to limit the right of employers to dismiss employees due to disability under the contemporary disability human rights approach are not reflected in Danish anti-discrimination law (which applies a too narrow definition of disability) or in employment protection law. Under employment protection law, the starting point is that an employer may dismiss an employee with a long-lasting reduced working capacity in line with the Danish flexicurity model.

In Sweden, the situation is completely different. The definition of disability under Swedish anti-discrimination law is in accordance with the contemporary disability human rights approach and the limitations on the right of employers to dismiss on the grounds of disability and disability-related reduced working capacity have been reflected in Swedish employment protection law.

In addition, a substantial group of persons on the private labour market in Denmark do not enjoy employment protection, which is in violation to the rights-based approach and the contemporary disability human rights approach. In Sweden, general employment protection legislation provides protection to practically all employees on the Swedish labour market with the exception of employees in sheltered employment.

As explained above, the contemporary disability human rights approach is founded on the substantive diversity equality model which requires that general structures are inclusive towards persons with disabilities. The above analysis of Danish and Swedish law shows that while Danish employment protection law does not create such inclusive general structures on the labour market, Swedish employment protection law does.

In the following Sub-Section, I examine how the different levels of protection against dismissal have corresponded with duties to make adjustments for the needs of employees with disabilities and disability-related reduced working capacities.

4. Adjustment for Reduced Working Capacity

As with *Section 3. Employment Protection*, the aim with the present Section is to ascertain whether general working conditions and working environments are inclusive towards persons with disabilities and disability-related reduced working capacity in line with the contemporary disability human rights approach. Whereas the previous Section examined the limitations imposed on the right of employers to dismiss employees due to reduced working capacity, the present Section examines the duties of employers to create generally accessible and inclusive work places and to make adjustments for employees with disabilities and disability-related reduced working capacity.

In Sub-Section 4.1, I examine duties under Danish law and policy and in Sub-Section 4.2, I examine the duties under Swedish law and policy. Sub-Section 4.3 contains a conclusion.

4.1. Denmark

As opposed to the area of employment protection, the work environment is closely regulated by the State, as opposed to the social partners in Denmark. A general Act on Work Environment was adopted in 1975 in Denmark with the aim of preventing work-related injuries and sicknesses.[722] The Work Environment Act is a framework act which sets out the general aims and requirements to the work environment.[723] Regulations and administrative guidelines are often adopted to supplement the Work Environment Act by the Danish Work environment Authority under the Ministry of Employment.[724] The Danish Work environment Authority oversees that employers comply with their obligations in relation to the work environment.[725] The Work Environment Act also recognises the right of the social partners to make agreements regarding the work environment. For example collective agreements may set aside the requirements in the Act on Work environment regarding the dialogue between employer and employees on security in the workplace.[726] A general Work Environment Council and several Sectoral Work Environment Councils with members appointed by the social partners ensure a formalised dialogue between the social partners and the State on issues relating to work

722 Nielsen and Roseberry 2008, p. 565. Danish Act on Work environment, No. 681 of 23 December 1975 (Lov om arbejdsmiljø).

723 Danish Act on Work environment, LBK no. 268 of 18 March 2005 with latest amendment by act no. 508 of 19 May 2010, (Lov om Arbejdsmiljø).

724 Danish Act on Work environment, Chapter 13, Section 73.

725 Danish Act on Work environment, Chapter 13.

726 Danish Act on Work environment, Section 8.

environment law.[727] Disabled persons organisations are not represented on Work Environment Councils.

The Danish Work Environment Act states that *"The employer has a duty to ensure that working conditions are completely adequate in relation to the health and safety of employees."*[728] The Work Environment Act does not establish an explicit duty to make adjustments for employees with a disability and disability-related reduced working capacity. Instead the principle of adjustment to the individual is mentioned in two daughter Regulations to the Working Environment Act. The Regulation on the Execution of Work provides that: "During the execution of work, consideration shall be given to the employee's age, knowledge, working capacity and other capacities."[729]

In addition the Regulation on Permanent Workplaces establishes that *"consideration shall when relevant be given to employees with disabilities when configuring workplaces. This especially applies to the aspects treated under [Sections on inter alia the individual work places, doors and toilets]"*.[730] The duty to adjust permanent workplaces to the needs of persons with disabilities is repeated in the Guidelines on the Design of Permanent Workplaces, but not in the Guidelines on the Performance of Work.[731] No specific guidelines have been prepared by the Work Environment Authority to detail the extent of the legally binding duty to adjust to the individual needs of persons with disabilities. The limitation of the duty to give consideration to employees with disabilities to relevant situations indicates that this is not a duty to create generally inclusive workplaces, but rather a duty to give consideration to specific needs of individual employees with disabilities.

In addition, the Work Environment Authority has created a *"work environment certificate"* which entities may obtain if they can document that they comply with the legally binding requirements under health and safety law and in addition can show that they work for integration of persons with disabilities labour market.[732] According to the *"Guidelines on Integration on the Labour Market"*, the main requirement is that the employers and employees must have a written agreement

727 Danish Act on Work environment, Chapters 12 and 3.

728 Danish Work Environment Act, Section 15.

729 Danish Regulation on the Execution of Work No. 599 o f 17 June 2004, Section 8(1), (Bekendtgørelse om Arbejdets Udførelse).

730 Danish Regulation on the design of permanent workplaces, BEK 96 of 13 February 2001 with latest amendment of BEK no. 1709 of 15 December 2010, (Bekendtgørelse om Faste Arbejdssteders Indretning), Section 18.

731 Danish Work Environment Authority Guidelines on the Design of Permanent Workplaces of March 2003, A.1.9; Danish Work Environment Authority Guidelines on workplace assessment of January 2005, AT-vejledning, Arbejdets Udførelse, D.1.1.

732 Danish Work Environment Authority Guidelines F.5.1. of April 2002, "Work Environment Certificate".

that they will work to prevent exclusion from the labour market, maintain employees at risk of exclusion from the labour market and recruit employees at risk of exclusion from the labour market.[733] As of December 2011, less than 3,000 entities have been awarded with the 'Certificate of Working Environment'.[734]

The few cases decided by courts or the Permanent Arbitration Tribunal on Dismissals concerning dismissals where violations of working environment law were at issue corroborate the impression that the duty to make adjustments to the needs of persons with disabilities under Danish Work Environment law does not enjoy much attention in practice.[735] All these cases, which raised issues of lack of compliance with the Work Environment Act, concerned general flaws in the work environment such as defective driving seats in a bus and a fork-lift which caused two drivers to develop backproblems.[736] I have found no case law in which employees with reduced working capacity have claimed that a failure to provide adjustments for their *individual* special needs under the Work Environment Act has resulted in the finding that a dismissal was unjust.

In sum, it seems that employers are merely obliged to fulfil general standards for a safe and healthy work environment. Although some daughter regulations to Working Environment Act impose a duty to give consideration to the working capacity and disabilities of employees, the exact extent of the duties is not specified and it would seem that these duties enjoy little focus in practice. Danish health and safety law does not impose a legally binding duty on employers to create generally accessible and inclusive work places, although employers may choose to adopt policies on integration of persons with disabilities and qualify for a work environment certificate. The relatively low level of obligations to make adjustments for employees with disabilities and disability-related reduced working capacity is in accordance with the findings under *Section 3 Dismissal Due to Disability-Related Reduced Working Capacity* according to which Danish employers may as a rule dismiss employees if their working capacity is reduced for a longer period of time.

---

733 Danish Work Environment Authority Guidelines F.5.3. of April 2002, "Integration on the Labour Market", (Det Rummelige Arbejdsmarket).

734 Frontpage of the homepage of the Danish Work Authority: www.at.dk, Entities with a green smiley with a crown have a work environment certificate.

735 The Permanent Arbitration Tribunal on Dismissals is established by the Basic Agreement between the Danish Confederation of Trade Unions and Employers' Union of 1973, Section 4(3) (Hovedaftalen mellem LO og DA).

736 Permanent Arbitration Tribunal on Dismissals Decisions AN 1322.05 and AN 1096.03, Bruun 2003, pp. 190–191. Ringsted District Court judgment of 17 November 1989, concerning an employee who developed breathing problems from working with a photoprinter. Dismissal was also found to be unreasonable, Bruun 2003, p. 154. Opposite result was reached in Permanent Arbitration Tribunal on Dismissals AN 926/00, concerning a dentist's assistant with arthritis who had to work reduced working hours. The Tribunal found that dismissal was unjustified because she had not been warned that her employers were dissatisfied with her performance, Bruun 2003, p. 202.

The findings indicate that duties to create inclusive labour market and make adjustments for individual needs of employees with disabilities and disability-related reduced working capacity have not been mainstreamed into health and safety law in accordance with the contemporary disability human rights approach.

4.2. Sweden

As in Denmark, the working environment is regulated primarily by law as opposed to collective agreements. The Swedish Work Environment Act was adopted in 1977 and is still in effect with numerous amendments. Like the Danish act, the Swedish Work environment Act is a framework act which aims at preventing work-related injuries and sicknesses and sets out general aims and requirements. The Swedish Work Environment Authority adopts more detailed regulations which must be fulfilled by employers.[737] Also as in Denmark, the Swedish Work Environment Authority is advised by the social partners when developing new standards and regulations for the work environment. The dialogue between the Swedish Work Environment Authority and the Swedish social partners is not formalised by the creation of a council, but the social partners and civil society will have the opportunity to express their opinions on planned legislation before it is adopted.[738]

However, in contrast to in Denmark, the duty of the employer to ensure that working tasks and conditions are adjusted to the needs of the employee is relatively far-reaching in Sweden. These duties follow firstly from the Work Environment Act, which applies from the moment the employee is hired, as well as the Social Insurance Act which applies once an employee experiences a reduced working capacity that leads to sick leave.[739] The general obligations of the employer to make adjustments for the disability and disability-related working capacity of the employees are described in *Sub-Section 4.2.1.* The rehabilitation obligations of the employer towards employees on sick leave are described in the following *Sub-Section 4.2.2.* And finally *Sub-Section 4.2.3.* contains an overview of the obligations of employers to transfer employees to a new position or reorganise work if the reduced working capacity or disability of the employee makes this necessary.

---

737 Swedish Act on Work environment, SFS 1977:1160 of 19 December 1977 with latest amendment by SFS 2009:870 of 25 June 2009, (Arbetsmiljölagen), Chapter 4.

738 See the homepage of the Swedish Work Environment Authority www.av.se/omoss/.

739 Swedish Work Environment Act, Chapters 2 and 3; Social Insurance Act, SFS 2010:110 of 4 March 2010 with latest amendment by SFS 2010:352 of 12 May 2010 (Socialförsäkringsbalk), Chapter 30. Breach of the Work Environment Act or the General Insurance Act will not in themselves result in a breach of the Employment Protection Act, but will indicate that the employer has not fulfilled his obligations to prevent dismissal, Swedish Labour Court judgment, AD 1999 no. 10. Källström and Malmberg 2006, p. 275.

4.2.1. General Duty to Adjust Working Tasks and Conditions

According to the Swedish Work Environment Act, employers are obliged to make adjustments for the needs of employees with disability or reduced working capacity. The Work Environment Act provides that working conditions *"shall be adjusted to the different physical and mental capabilities of persons"*.[740] The employer shall *"adjust working conditions or adopt other suitable measures to cater for the employee's specific capacity to carry out work"*.[741] In order to fulfil this obligation the employer shall *"ensure that there is an adequately organised rehabilitation and adjustment function in his entity"*.[742]

The Swedish Work Environment Authority, which is the administrative authority responsible for supervising the implementation of the Work Environment Act, has adopted a regulation on adjustment and rehabilitation.[743] This regulation provides that *"the employer shall make adjustments of the individual employee's working conditions in accordance with his or her capacities for the working tasks. Special consideration shall be taken where the employee has a disability or a reduction in working capacity."*[744] In the guidelines published by the Work Environment Authority, it is specified that adjustments may include technical aids and alterations of the physical work environment as well as changes in the organisation or distribution of work, working hours, working methods, and psychological and social conditions. Adjustments may also include dissemination of information, training or practical work trials.[745] The extent of the duties of the employer to reorganise work and transfer employees to other positions is examined in *Sub-Section 5.2.3.* below. The costs of accommodating measures undertaken by the employer will as a rule have to be borne by the employer, although contributions may be made by the authorities towards covering the costs of technical aids for employees who have been employed within the last 12 months.[746] The question of State support is examined in more detail in *Chapter VI State Measures.*

---

740 Swedish Work Environment Act, Chapter 2, Section 1.

741 Swedish Work Environment Act, Chapter 3, Section 3.

742 Swedish Work Environment Act, Chapter 3, Section 2a.

743 Swedish Work Environment Authority regulation on adjustment and rehabilitation, AFS 1994:1 of 26 january 1994, (Arbetarskyddsstyrelsens kungörelse med föreskrifter om arbetsanpassning och rehabilitering).

744 Ibid, Section 12.

745 Ibid, Kommentarer till enskilda paragrafer, Till § 12.

746 Swedish Act on Special Measures for persons with disabilities and reduced working capacity, SFS 2000:630 with latest amendment by SFS2010:394 of 20 May 2010, (Förordning om särskilda insatser för personer med funktionshinder som medför nedsatt arbetsförmåga), Sections 11–15.

4.2.2. Duty to Rehabilitate Employees on Sick Leave

Once an employee must take sick leave, the Social Insurance Act provides that employers have a duty to partake in the rehabilitation of the employee.[747] Whereas medical and social rehabilitation are the responsibility of public authorities, the employer has the primary responsibility for the employment rehabilitation of the employee insofar as he can be rehabilitated to a position with the employer.[748] According to the Labour Court employment rehabilitation may include both measures, which may be realised within the workplace of the employer as well as outside the work-place of the employer:

> *"... the employer is obliged to take measures for the employment rehabilitation, which may be realised within the workplace, e.g. employment training, education and reassignment. ... In addition, it can be required that the employer co-operates in finding e.g. relevant trial work, employment training or re-education outside of the workplace, and that the employer where necessary grants the employee leave to carry out such rehabilitation."*[749]

When an employee is on leave from work due to a sickness or injury, the General Insurance Authority supervises the rehabilitation process and facilitates the cooperation between the Work Environment Authority, the employer, the employee and his or her union in providing an effective rehabilitation effort.[750] The costs of employment rehabilitation activities will as a rule also have to be carried by the employer. However especially when education and training activities take place outside of the employer's entity, he may obtain a contribution towards covering their costs from the General Insurance Authority. The General Insurance Authority may also choose to contribute towards covering the costs of technical aids.[751]

It follows from both the Preparatory Works and case law that employers do not have a duty to rehabilitate an employee where the aim of the rehabilitation would be to enable the employee to carry out work for another employer. However, the limits of the employer's duty to provide employment rehabilitation of the employee are not clearly set out. In its case law, the Labour Court performs an individual assessment of whether the rehabilitation measures taken by the employer have been *sufficient and reasonable*. The Labour Court places great importance on whether or not the

---

747 Swedish Social Insurance Act, Chapter 30, Section 6.

748 Preparatory works to the Swedish General Insurance Act, Prop. 1990/91:141 p. 55–56. The Social Insurance Act is a new unified law which replaced 30 specialised legal acts including the General Insurance Act without introducing significant changes in relation to rehabilitation of employees.

749 Swedish Labour Court judgment, AD 1993 no. 42, Svenska Elektrikerförbundet v. Elektriska Arbetsgivareföreningen och Svenska Elinstallationer Aktiebolag i Gävle, p. 13 and 14.

750 Swedish Social Insurance Act, Chapter 30, Section 10.

751 Swedish Social Insurance Act, Chapter 30, Section 6; Regulation (1991:1046). Swedish Commission Report, SOU 2006:107, "Focus on compensation" (Fokus på Åtgärder), Chapter 13.

employer has demonstrated his willingness to undertake a serious rehabilitation effort. The employer must show that the management has understood and lives up to its far-reaching duty to rehabilitate the employee.[752] In a case concerning an employee who was dismissed after 22 years of employment with a regional authority, the Court stated the following:

> *"...according to the court it is not possible to disregard the impression that the management did not consider that there was a far-reaching duty for the employer to attempt to help [the employee] ER with organizing the work so that it fit her capacity better."*[753]

In this case, the employer had made three different assessments of the employee's psychological and physical working capacity, but it had not carried out an examination of whether rehabilitation measures or re-organisation of work could have helped. On these grounds, the Court found that the employer had not fulfilled its rehabilitation duties and that the dismissal was unjust.[754]

Another case illustrates the balance which has to be struck between the interests of the employer on the one hand and the interests of an employee on the other. An engineer who had become over-sensitive to electricity had had his office completely stripped of electrical impulses. As he still experienced difficulties due to electrical impulses from electrical appliances located outside of his office, he had asked that he be allowed to work from his home even though it would not be possible to install an electronic firewall to protect the data-security of the company. The Labour Court found that it was reasonable for the company to require protection of its data and that a re-organisation of work entailing that he worked 100% from home did not fall under the duty of the employer.[755]

From the case law of the Swedish Labour Court, it also transpires that the duty of the employer to rehabilitate depends on the cooperation of the employee. A case decided by the Swedish Labour Court illustrates this duty to cooperate: A home carer was dismissed from a city council after approximately 20 months of sick leave. The city council had during the two years preceding his dismissal taken a number of different rehabilitative measures including drawing up a rehabilitation plan, providing work-training as a receptionist and as an assistant teacher, participation in a rehabilitation course, offered a position as primary school kitchen

---

752 Lunning and Toijer 2006, p. 437; Inghammar 2007, p. 125.

753 Swedish Labour Court judgment, AD 1998 no. 57, Sveriges Kommunaltjänstemannaförbund v. Malmö Kommun, p. 14. See also Swedish Labour Court judgment, AD 2006 no. 90, Industrifacket Metall v. Teknikarbetsgivarna og P.T. Rostfria o Mek Aktiebolag i Ramlösa, p. 19 where the employer was again not found to have fulfilled his duty to rehabilitate the employee.

754 Ibid.

755 Swedish Labour Court judgment, AD 2001 no. 1, SIF v. Sveriges Verstadsförening och Erichsson Utvecklings Aktiebolag i Älvsjö, p. 7.

assistant and planning participation in a course to prepare him for work in a primary school. The employee decided to do a training to become an IT-assistant instead of attending the offered course. The Court stated the following:

> *"According to the Labour Court, TS has as described decided to interrupt the planned studies and thus he has not cooperated in his rehabilitation in such a manner as may be required of him. It cannot be required of the city council that it carries on its rehabilitation efforts. The conclusion is that the employer has fulfilled its duty to rehabilitate TS".*[756]

4.2.3. Reorganisation of Work and Transfer to Another Position

As mentioned above under Sub-Section 4.2.1, it follows directly from the wording of the Employment Protection Act Section 7 that an employer is under a *duty to transfer* employees to another vacant position where the alternative would be a dismissal on personal grounds, meaning a dismissal which is not based on work shortage: *"A dismissal is not objectively justified if it is reasonable to require that the employer offers the employee a different position"*[757] The Swedish Labour Court has established that employers have a duty to draw up a report on the possibilities for transfers to other positions in order to prove that they have examined this possibility thoroughly. Moreover, the Court has underlined that:

> *"doubts in relation to the question of transfers to another position will often lead to the conclusion that the transfer duty has not been fulfilled. A report on transferral to another position in a case such as the present requires a thorough examination of the wishes and qualifications of the employee and a systematic assessment of available positions if any."*[758]

The employer only has a duty to transfer employees to positions, which he or she is qualified to fulfil, and that it falls within the employer's prerogatives to define the required qualifications.[759] In several cases decided by the Swedish Labour Court,

---

756 Swedish Labour Court judgment, AD 2006 no. 11, Svenska Kommunalarbetareförbundet v. Hudiksvall Kommun, p. 12. See also Swedish Labour Court judgment, AD 1996 no. 26, Sveriges Civilingenjörsförbund v. Alliansen och Aktiebolaget IOF, p. 7, where the employee was a mentally ill researcher who had not co-operated sufficiently with the employer in the examination of this working capacity and need for rehabilitation. See also Swedish Labour Court judgment, AD 1997 no. 39 on lack of co-operation which relieves employer of duty to continue to rehabilitate the employee.

757 Inghammar 2007, p. 133–139; Lunning and Toijer 2006, p. 464–481.

758 See for example Swedish Labour Court judgment, AD 2002 no. 75 where the Court found that an employer's report on possibilities for transfers was insufficiently thorough.

759 Swedish Labour Court judgment, AD 1996 no. 54 Akademikerförbundet SSR v. Staten genom Arbetsgivarverket, p. 12 where the Court performs an in-depth evaluation of whether the dismissed employees could be said to have sufficient qualifications for a transfer to newly advertised positions. The positions were for specialists and the dismissed employees were

the reduction in working capacity has excluded the employee from being transferred to another position.[760] In a judgment of 2007, where a mail sorter was dismissed due to reduced working capacity related to pain in her shoulders and joints, the Swedish Labour Court first established that re-organisation of work could not be required and subsequently examined whether the employer had fulfilled its duty to transfer the employee to another position. The employer had made a thorough report on possible transfers and found that she was excluded from taking on the available positions due to her reduction in working capacity. The employer was found to have fulfilled its duties to attempt a transfer within the company.[761]

Although there may be a certain duty to re-organise work in the workplace and make accommodations for the capabilities of the employee, the rule is that an employer merely has a duty to transfer to existing, available positions. It is clear from case law that the employer does not have duty to expand the area of operation of the company in order to create a position for the employee.[762]

As was the case in relation to rehabilitation, the employee also has a duty to cooperate in relation to transfers. Thus, employees will, as a rule, have to accept to be transferred to positions that are lower-paid, reduced working time and even temporary positions where the alternative is a dismissal.[763] Case law has also established that the duty falls away when the reason for dismissal is gross misconduct on the part of the employee.[764]

It follows from the wording of the Employment Protection Act that the employer is also under an obligation to re-organise the distribution of work in order to avoid dismissal. The limits of the duty to re-organise work in the workplace also depend on an individual assessment. The question of re-organisation of work touches on an essential part of prerogative of the employer to manage his company. In acknowledgment hereof, the Labour Court has underlined that *"the employer even*

generalists. It had therefore been reasonable that the employer had not offered to transfer them. See also Inghammar 2007, p. 134–135.

760 Swedish Labour Court judgment, AD 2001 no. 59, Svenska Kommunalarbetareförbundet v. Uddevalla Kommun, p. 12. AD 1999 no. 124, Svenska Elektrikerförbundet v. Elektriska Installatörsorganisationen och Elmontage Eklind & Löfgren AB i Jönköping, p. 9.

761 Swedish Labour Court judgment, AD 2007 no. 7, Almega Tjänstförbunden v. Posten AB, p. 23 and 24.

762 Swedish Labour Court judgment, AD 1999 no. 10, Svenska Livsmedelsarbetareförbundet v. Livsmedelsbranschens arbetsgivareförbund och Scan Farmek Ekonomisk förening i Visby. See also Swedish Labour Court judgment, AD 1993 no. 42. Svenska Elektrikerförbundet v. Elektriska Arbetsgivareföreningen och Svenska Elinstallationer Aktiebolag i Gävle.

763 Swedish Labour Court judgment, AD 2006 no. 11, Svenska Kommunalarbetareförbundet v. Hudiksvalls Kommun, pp. 12 and 14.

764 In Swedish Labour Court judgment, AD 2004 no. 56, the Swedish Labour Court accepted that an employee who had been disloyal to his employer was not offered a transfer; Lunning and Toijer 2006, p. 468.

after the amendments in question must be considered to have a fundamental right to decide over his company".[765] Case law shows that the Labour Court balances the interest of the employee in the re-organisation of work on the one hand with disadvantages of the re-organisation of work, e.g. workload of other staff, security procedures and the prerogative of the employer to distribute work on the other hand.

In two cases concerning firemen with heart problems who could no longer participate in smoke-diving, the Labour Court found that it was reasonable to require that they be relieved of this work. Thus in both cases, it was considered reasonable to require that the firemen with heart problems be relieved of smoke-diving in spite of the need for increased planning which such a re-organisation of work entailed. The Court placed importance on the fact that fire departments in other regions of Sweden had succeeded in distributing the work so as to relieve older staff of smoke-diving and also that firemen could only retire with pension from the age of 58 years.[766]

In conclusion, the strong protection against dismissals on the grounds of disability-related reduced working capacity under Swedish employment protection law is complemented by strong obligations on the part of the employer to adjust working conditions and tasks to the needs of employee with reduced working capacity. Not only does the Work Environment Act impose explicit and detailed duties to make adjustments for disability and disability-related reduced working capacity of employees, but it also follows from the Social Insurance Act that employers must provide rehabilitation for employees who take sick leave. Finally, it follows from the Employment Protection Act that possibilities for transfers and re-organisation of work must be exhausted before dismissals due to reduced working capacity may be permitted.

---

765 Swedish Labour Court judgment, AD 1993 no. 42, Svenska Elektrikerförbundet v. Elektriska Arbetsgivareföreningen och Svenska Elinstallationer Aktiebolag i Gävle, p. 17.

766 Swedish Labour Court judgment, AD 2002 no. 32, Svenska Kommunalarbetareförbundet v. Räddningstjänsten Östra Skaraborg i Skövde, p. 10. See also Swedish Labour Court judgment, AD 2001 92, Fastighetsanställdas förbund v. FASTIGO och HSB Filipstad Ekonomisk förening i Filipstad, about a janitor who suffered from asthma and allergy which meant that he could not do cleaning work. The Court found that the employer should have re-organised the work so that his cleaning tasks which amounted to around 10% of his work load had been taken over by other staff. The dismissal was unreasonable. See also Swedish Labour Court judgment, AD 1993 no. 42, Svenska Elektrikerförbundet v. Elektriska Arbetsgivareföreningen och Svenska Elinstallationer Aktiebolag i Gävle, p. 17, as well as Swedish Labour Court judgment, AD 1991 no. 27.

4.3. Conclusion

In conclusion, whereas Danish employers have relatively few obligations to make adjustments for employees with disabilities and disability-related reduced working capacity, Swedish employers have extensive duties to do so. This finding is entirely in line with the significantly lower level of protection against dismissals in Denmark than in Sweden. In other words, while the duties to provide adjustments for the needs of employees with disabilities and disability-related reduced working capacity have not been mainstreamed into Danish health and safety legislation, this mainstreaming has taken place in Sweden. Thus, only Sweden complies with the contemporary disability human rights approach in this regard. The Swedish approach where employers are under clear and extensive obligations to make adjustments for employees with disabilities and disability-related reduced working capacity means that employers in Sweden are under an obligation to make extensive adjustments for individual employees with disability-related reduced working capacity. In addition, the extensive obligations towards individual employees, motivate employers to prepare for the situation when the working capacity of their employees falls. In other words, they are motivated to create generally inclusive policies and work places. Such generally inclusive policies and work places benefit not only employees who are presently employed. It is also likely that the creation of generally inclusive structures for ensuring that employees with reduced working capacity may carry out their work as efficiently as possible would also benefit future employees with disability-related reduced working capacity since the structures will already be in place.

5. Protection against Dismissals Due to Shortage of Work

In both Denmark and Sweden, dismissals, which are not founded on personal grounds, are considered founded on grounds relating to the employer's undertaking. Dismissals on grounds relating to the undertaking are as a starting point justified. The question to be examined under this Section is whether persons with disabilities and disability-related reduced working capacity enjoy special protection against being selected for dismissal in these situations. Thus, the present Section deals with positive action for the protection of persons with disabilities in contrast with the above Sections which dealt mainly with limitations in the right of employers to dismiss employees with disability-related reduced working capacity and related obligations to make adjustments under health and safety laws. As explained in *Section 2. Contemporary Disability Human Rights Approach* above, positive action for the promotion of equality is an essential characteristic of substantial diversity equality and the contemporary disability human rights approach. Moreover, the CRPD specifically requires the promotion of job retention programmes which would for example give employers economic incentives for retaining employees with disabilities. Thus, although special protection of persons with disabilities in situations of work shortage is in line with the contemporary disability human rights approach, it is not a requirement that States introduce such special protection. Below, I examine the state of law first in Denmark (Sub-Section 5.1) and then in Sweden (Sub-Section 5.2). A conclusion is provided in Sub-Section 5.3.

5.1. Denmark

In Denmark, the starting point is that a dismissal on the grounds of shortage of work or funding is justified. The Courts are reluctant to examine the economic or managerial soundness of such decisions. Even decisions which are objectively not in the best interest of the entity will not render dismissals unreasonable.[767]

There is however a requirement that the dismissal be a proportionate reaction to the actual shortage of work. Thus it is a requirement that the shortage can be expected to last for some time and that is not just a small fluctuation in the amount of work.[768] Where an employer hires new staff in the positions of employees who have been dismissed shortly after the dismissal, the dismissal cannot be seen as a result of shortage of work.[769] Also as a consequence of the proportionality requirement, the employer will be under a certain duty to transfer employees to vacant positions in other parts of the entity. This is not a general rule, but will apply where special circumstances are present such as when the employee has many years of service and has performed his or her job irreproachably. A demonstrated willingness to be transferred and to undergo training will weigh in favour of a duty to transfer the employee. It is clear that the employee must be qualified for the position that he wishes to be transferred to. However a need for a certain amount of training does not exclude a duty to transfer. The bigger the entity, the more reasonable it will be to require that the employee receive training in order to qualify for a transfer to a new position.[770]

Once it has been determined that there is a shortage of work which warrants the dismissal of employees then the employer enjoys a high degree of freedom in determining *which* employees to dismiss. In practice, the Courts and the Dismissals Tribunal are reluctant to find that the selection of one employee rather than another was unreasonable. It is up to the employee to show that unsuitable criteria has guided the employer.

---

767 Bruun 2003, p. 117.

768 Danish Permanent Arbitration Tribunal on Dismissals, AN 917.1999. Århus District Court, 14 December 1989, Jørgen Rønnov Bruun, p. 119.

769 Holsted District Court, 28 August 1992. Eastern High Court judgment of 17 December 1992; Bruun 2003, p. 121.

770 Danish Permanent Arbitration Tribunal on Dismissals, AN 255.1987, Bruun 2003, p. 136.

In the private sector it is legal for an employer to select which employees to dismiss on the basis of the last-in-first-out principle. Also in the private sector, a 25-years of service-rule has come to existence, according to which employers must show special grounds for dismissal of such employees.[771] This rule does not apply in the public sector. The Supreme Court has established that public employers must perform a concrete evaluation of each employee's aptitude to stay in order to determine who should be dismissed.[772] It is legal for the public authority to take years of service into account, but this may not be the only selection criterion. This follows from the administrative law principle according to which decisions must be based on a concrete evaluation of all available facts such as qualifications and years of service.[773]

In case law a few modifications to the rule that employers are free to choose whom they wish to dismiss have crystallised: Firstly, it is unreasonable to select a permanent member of staff rather than a *temporary* member of staff working in the same area.[774] Secondly, the employer will have to show special grounds for dismissing an employee with a *significantly longer length of service* than others in the same working area. See for example a ruling from 2005, where the Dismissals Tribunal rejected the dismissal of an employee with 20 years of service with the entity as it was undisputed that he was qualified as a storage worker and in view of the fact that the other two storage workers both had been employed for less than 8 years with the entity.[775] The importance of the duty to take length of service into consideration should not however be exaggerated. In a case, which was also mentioned above in *Chapter IV Equality Law and Policy,* the High Court did not object to the dismissal of an architect who had been with the same public employer for 29 years.[776] The architect in question had reduced-eye sight and had been singled out for redundancy because the management of the Danish Heritage Agency considered him to be less flexible than others due to his reduced eye-sight. Two out of the three High Court judges found that the use of the flexibility criteria was objectively justified. They argued that inspections of buildings constituted a significant part of the work of the employed architects, that it had been decided by management that the plaintiff could not conduct inspections on his own and that the decision that he could not conduct inspections on his own was justified on objective considerations for the efficient and correct handling of cases. On these grounds and based on an assessment that the accommodation in the form of a personal assistant would have resulted in an disproportionate burden on the Danish Heritage Agency,

---

771 Bruun 2003, p. 141.

772 Danish Supreme Court judgment, UFR 1995.177 H, Bruun 2003, p. 136. Andersen 1991, p. 272.

773 Ibid.

774 Danish Eastern High Court judgment of 11 April 1990, Bruun 2003, p. 127.

775 Danish Permanent Arbitration Tribunal on Dismissals, AN 9.2005, Bruun 2003, p. 127.

776 Danish Eastern High Court Judgment of 5 March 2008, 6. Section, No. B-413–07, Arkitektforbundet mod Kulturarvsstyrelsen.

two out of three judges found that discrimination on the grounds of disability had not taken place and that the dismissal was fair.

Thirdly, where an employee has a *work-related injury or sickness*, special consideration will have to be given to the interests of the employee and the employer will have to show that it would be unreasonable to require that the employee be transferred to another position. In a case from 2000, it was considered unreasonable to dismiss an employee who after 23 years of employment as a painter had contrived a reduced working capacity of 60% as a result of his work.[777] He was hired in a state subsidised position and the Dismissals Tribunal did not find that the employer had shown that it was necessary to dismiss him. The Dismissals Tribunal stated the following:

> *"...the company is under an obligation to provide very special and decisive reasons to warrant the dismissal of such an employee rather than an employee of lower age and length of employment."*

Another case from 1989 again underlines the need for special consideration where the employee has a work-related injury or sickness. The Dismissals Tribunal underlined that it was not proven that the dismissed employee could not have carried out the working tasks which new staff had been hired to perform:[778]

> *"The entity has referred to his lower level of flexibility as a ground for his dismissal. His reduced flexibility is however the result of an injury sustained during work for the entity. Under these circumstances the dismissal is considered unreasonable."*

In cases where the employee with a reduced working capacity due to work-related injury or sickness can no longer carry out his or her work or be transferred to another position, the Dismissals Tribunal has however found that dismissals were reasonable. For example, the Dismissals Tribunal found that the dismissal of an airplane cleaner was reasonable because she could not be transferred to another less demanding position.[779] The Tribunal attached importance to the fact that she had declined a position as security guard which would have been physically less demanding.

It has been argued by several authors that public employers are under a duty to take into consideration whether an employee will have special *difficulties in obtaining a*

[777] Danish Permanent Arbitration Tribunal on Dismissals, AN 969.00. Bruun 2003, p. 153.

[778] Danish Permanent Arbitration Tribunal on Dismissals, AN 365.89. Bruun 2003, p. 153.

[779] Danish Permanent Arbitration Tribunal on Dismissals, AN 1310.05. See also Danish Permanent Arbitration Tribunal on Dismissals, AN 1151.03 regarding the dismissal of an employee who could no longer fill out a position because of his reduced mobility. Bruun 2003, p. 153–154.

new job, e.g. due to a reduction in working capacity.[780] The obligation to take into consideration difficulties that the employee may have in finding a new job by no means constitutes a prohibition of dismissal of this group of employees. The public employer will simply have to show that this has been taken into consideration. Again the case mentioned above concerning the architect with reduced working capacity illustrates how reluctant the courts are to set aside the selection of which employees to dismiss.[781] In the private sector, the starting point will be that the employer will be under (even) less of an obligation to take into account such 'social' considerations. The starting point is that the private employer can base his decision on which employees to dismiss on mere operational considerations. A concrete evaluation of proportionality will have to be performed in each case.

In sum, the starting point under Danish law is that employees with disabilities and disability-related reduced working capacity enjoy no special protection where dismissals due to work shortage take place. Dismissals on the grounds of disability and disability-related reduced working capacity will only be prohibited when they are in violation of the prohibition of discrimination on the grounds of disability. In addition, some protection applies if the reduced working capacity results from a work-related sickness or injury. Since the definition of disability under the anti-discrimination legislation is narrower than the definition of disability under the contemporary disability human rights approach, the protection against dismissal in case of work shortage is inadequate in Denmark. The lack of special protection against dismissals of persons with disability and reduced working capacity does not itself violate the contemporary disability human rights approach which merely recommends the use of positive action measures for promoting substantive diversity equality on the labour market.

5.2. Sweden

Like in Denmark, dismissals due to shortage of work are as a rule justified in Sweden. Also, the Swedish Labour Court will as a rule be reluctant to assess whether a decision to dismiss employees on grounds relating to the undertaking are reasonable and whether they constitute an ideal decision from a business economic point of view.[782] However, as opposed to Denmark, Sweden has introduced both strict rules on which employees must be dismissed in situations of dismissals as well as special protection of persons with disabilities and reduced working capacity.

780 Illum, 1964, p. 191; Kristiansen 1997, p. 399. Bruun 2003, p. 141.

781 Eastern High Court Judgment of 5 March 2008, 6. Section, No. B-413–07, Arkitektforbundet mod Kulturarvsstyrelsen.

782 Inghammar 2007, p. 137, Lunning and Toijer 2006, p. 452. Calleman 2000, p. 103.

In Sub-Section 5.2.1., I describe the criteria provided by law for choosing which employee to dismiss in a situation of work shortage. In Sub-Section 5.2.2., I describe special protection of employees with reduced working capacity.

5.2.1. Criteria for Choosing Employees set by Law

As opposed to in Denmark, the starting point in Sweden is that employers are not free to choose which employee they want to dismiss. Instead, Section 22 of the Employment Protection Act provides that:

> *"a sequential list is made for each operative unit where the employer has several units. (...)The placement of an employee (...) is decided on the grounds of the sum of the duration of his employment with the employer. Employees with a longer duration of employment have priority before employees with a shorter duration of employment. When employees have the same duration of employment, higher age gives priority. If an employee can only continue to work for the employer after a transfer to another position, he will only be given priority if he has sufficient qualifications for continued employment."*[783]

Accordingly, employers are bound in the selection of employees to be dismissed to make a selection on the grounds of years of service and age. This rule ensures that employees with a reduced working capacity are not at a special risk of being disadvantaged in a selection process which could otherwise be based on more problematic criteria such as flexibility and productivity.

Section 22 of the Employment Protection Act is semi-dispositive in that other selection criteria may be agreed between employers and unions.[784] The criteria for the order of selection under such agreements must respect the ban against discrimination on the grounds of *inter alia* disability, but are not required to be founded on objective criteria such as duration of employment. They may be founded on more subjective criteria such as efficiency, flexibility etc which may place employees with reduced working capacity at a disadvantage compared to other staff.[785] The question of whether such criteria have an indirectly discriminatory effect on disabled employees has not been tried by the Labour Court.

In addition, an important exception has been made for smaller undertakings of less than 10 employees. These employers may, according to Section 22, *"exempt two*

---

783 It follows from the wording of Section 22 and the Swedish Preparatory Works that lists must be prepared for each 'operative unit' and for each group covered by different collective agreement. An operative unit typically consists of a unit which operates within the same premises, building or fenced-off area. Swedish Preparatory Works to the Act on Employment Protection, Prop. 1973:129, p. 260; Calleman 2000, p. 108.

784 Section 2 of the Employment Protection Act.

785 Inghammar 2007, p. 137.

employees who according to the employer's assessment are of special importance for the continued operation of the undertaking". In a case from 2005, the Labour Court found that a small employer had exempted two employees of special importance with the aim of selecting an employee with a disability for dismissal. The Court found that this amounted to discrimination on the grounds of disability.[786]

Finally, the Swedish Employment Protection Act also provides that persons who have been dismissed enjoy a priority for being employed again during nine months after the dismissal.[787]

In sum, although Section 22 of the Employment Protection Act does according to its wording offer strong protection against the use of selection criteria, which would most likely place employees with reduced working capacity at a disadvantage, the protection of persons with disabilities and disability-related reduced working capacity is reduced by two exceptions concerning collective agreements and small undertakings.

5.2.2. Special Protection of Persons with Disabilities

According to Section 23 of the Employment Protection Act, *"employees who have a reduced working capacity and as a result hereof have been employed under special conditions with the employer shall have priority to continued employment, if it can take place without serious inconvenience, be given priority for continued employment irrespective of the sequential order of dismissal."* Contrary to Section 22 above, Section 23 is not semi-dispositive and may not be exempted from by collective agreement.[788]

The reference in Section 23 to the sequential order of dismissal indicates that the provision only gives protection in a situation where there is a competition between employees for the working tasks which remain after a restructuring. This is illustrated by a case from 1983 in which a guard had been dismissed because his working tasks had been distributed to other staff. Since he was dismissed because his working tasks were no longer available and not because of his position in a sequential order list, the Court did not find that Section 23 was relevant.[789] It follows from the condition that continued employment must not cause a serious inconvenience on the employer. Thus, a re-organisation of work or a transfer of the

786 Swedish Labour Court judgment, AD 2005 no. 32, the case is described in more detail in *Chapter IV Equality Law and Policy.*

787 Swedish Employment Protection Act, Section 26.

788 Swedish Employment Protection Act, Section 2.

789 Swedish Labour Court judgment, AD 1983 no. 94, Calleman 2000, p. 324. See also Swedish Labour Court judgment, AD 1993 no. 139, p. 8.

person in question will only be required where the employee is qualified for the new tasks.[790] The provision does not grant special priority to persons with reduced working capacity in questions of re-employment.[791] Also, the provision is not relevant in cases of dismissals on personal grounds. The main aim of the provision is to ensure that persons with disabilities and reduced working capacity who are employed under special working conditions may continue to be employed.[792] The protection under Section 23 ceases to apply when a person reaches 67 years of age.[793]

According to the wording of Section 23, three conditions must be fulfilled in order to be protected under the provision: the employee must have a reduction in working capacity, he must be employed under special conditions and his continued employment must not result in a serious inconvenience to the employer.

As regards the first condition that the employee must have a *reduction in working capacity*, the Preparatory Works specified the following:

> *"the protection must be reserved for those who at a given time have difficulties in keeping and obtaining employment due to a reduced working capacity. The reason for the reduction in working capacity is irrelevant. It can be caused by a physical, intellectual or mental disability. The provision should even encompass employees who have a reduction in working capacity as a result of circumstances of a social nature.*[794] *[...] the provision does not grant special protection to older employees without special reductions in working capacity who may have received state-support for employment [...]."*[795]

Presumably, the reference to a reduction in working capacity of a social nature indicates that reductions in working capacity, which are a result of social problems, alcoholism or drug abuse, could be encompassed.[796] The fact that the Preparatory Works do not require a specific degree of reduction in working capacity and that they explicitly encompass also reductions in working capacity on social grounds, indicates that a broad definition of working capacities was intended. This seems to have been confirmed by the Labour Court in a case from 1977 where a man who was psychologically unstable and who had a history of alcohol and drug-abuse and had just been released from serving a long prison sentence was found to be

790 Calleman 2000, p. 327.
791 Swedish Labour Court judgment, AD 1986 no. 55.
792 Swedish Preparatory Works to Employment Protection Act, Prop. 1973:129, p. 215.
793 Swedish Employment Protection Act, Section 33, litra 3.
794 Swedish Preparatory Works to Employment Protection Act, Prop. 1973:129, p. 215.
795 Swedish Preparatory Works to Employment Protection Act, Prop. 1973:129, p. 262–263.
796 Calleman 2000, p. 325 agrees that the Preparatory Works have sought to define the concept of reduced working capacity broadly.

encompassed under Section 23.[797] In a case from 1993, a man with chronic sleeping disorder, which meant that he could not always sleep during the night and therefore at times would be tired during working hours, was also found to have a reduction in working capacity.[798] Additionally, in a case from 2003, an employee who had a third degree burn on her hand, who several years later suffered from pain in her hand and was awarded half-time sick-pension, was found to have a reduction in working capacity in the sense of Section 23.[799]

The opposite result was found in a case 1986 where man had been hired in a state-subsidised position because his age made it difficult for him to get a job. The Court stated that the provision only encompassed persons whose *"actual working capacity was reduced compared to what could normally be expected of them"* and that persons who were hired with wage-subsidies due to old age were not encompassed.[800]

In relation to the definition of disability under the contemporary disability human rights approach, the definition of persons with reduced working capacity under the Swedish Employment Protection Act is significantly narrower. Persons with disabilities may well have no reduced working capacity what so ever. This is not a problem in relation to the contemporary disability human rights approach since it is not a requirement that positive action be undertaken. Moreover, persons with disabilities as such do not have lower rates of employment than others. Only when disability is coupled with reduced working capacity does it lead to reduced employment rates. It is therefore in line with the contemporary disability human rights approach to target the special protection to persons with disabilities and reduced working capacity.

The second requirement is that the employee has been *employed under special conditions*. It is clear from the Preparatory Works that some form of special accommodation must have taken place, but whether it is always necessary with public wage subvention is unclear.[801] In a case from 2003 mentioned above, an employee had a third degree burn on her hand while working as a bookbinder. After months of sick leave, she was awarded half-time sick-pension. Due to her hand-injury she could not return to the same position as book binder. After job-training

[797] Swedish Labour Court judgment, AD 1977 no. 94.

[798] Swedish Labour Court judgment, AD 1993 no. 139, TCO-OF's sektor for affärsverk v. Staten gennem Televerket.

[799] Swedish Labour Court judgment, AD 2003 no. 83, Ledarna v. Grafiska Företagens Förbund och Parajett Aktiebolag i Landskrona.

[800] Swedish Labour Court judgment, AD 1986 no. 158. Inghammar sees this case as indicating a relatively narrow interpretation of the concept of reduced working capacity, Inghammar 2007, p. 141.

[801] Swedish Preparatory Works to Employment Protection Act, Prop. 1973:129 p. 262.

with her employer, she was given a half-time position assistant which she held for several years. The Labour Court acknowledged that she had a reduction in working capacity, but did not find that she was employed under special conditions. The Court stated that *"it is clear that every measure in form of a transfer to another position, re-organisation or re-distribution of working tasks which the employer is obliged to undertake within his duty to rehabilitate employees cannot entail that he has undertaken employment under special conditions in the sense of this provision".* Accordingly, the re-organisation of work which enabled the undertaking to keep the employee in a half-time position was not employment under special conditions.[802]

An example of a type of employment which qualified as being under special conditions was the employment of persons who had just been released after serving a long prison sentence. Even though his working tasks were no different from those of other staff, he had been hired in a position set up in order to re-integrate convicts in the ordinary employment market and the Court found that this was *"employment under special conditions".*[803]

In sum, the Labour Court does not require that the employee performs special tasks to be encompassed by the protection under Section 23. It is however necessary that the position be specially accommodated to meet the needs of the employee for example in a position with wage-subvention. The fact that an employee has been rehabilitated and works part-time is not sufficient.

Lastly, Section 23 is only applicable when it will not cause *serious inconvenience* to the employer to give employees with reduced working capacity special protection in situations of dismissals on grounds related to the undertaking. Thus, this protection is not absolute and allows for consideration to the interest of the employer. The Preparatory Works underline that *"the possibilities for upholding employment under special conditions must in this connection be taken into consideration. In this respect, exemption from the rule should be allowed under special circumstances."*[804] The Preparatory Works do not give more guidance as to when such special circumstances can be said to exist. Again very little case law exists about the interpretation of this requirement. In a case from 1993, dismissal was permitted since continued employment would cause too great an inconvenience on the employer who would have to carry out re-organisation of working tasks.[805]

802 Swedish Labour Court judgment, AD 2003 no. 83, Ledarna v. Grafiska Företagens Förbund och Parajett Aktiebolag i Landskrona, p. 6. Calleman 2000, p. 327, Inghammar 2007, p. 142.

803 Swedish Labour Court judgment, AD 1977 no. 94.

804 Swedish Preparatory Works to Employment Protection Act, Prop. 1973:129, p. 161.

805 Swedish Labour Court judgment, AD 1993 no. 94, TCO-OF's Sektor for Affärsverk v. Staten genom Televerket.

In conclusion, persons with disabilities and reduced working capacity are offered a relatively strong protection against dismissal on the grounds of shortage of work where they are employed with wage-subvention and continued employment does not amount to a disproportionate burden on the employer.

As described above the definition of persons with reduced working capacity seems quite broad whereas the requirement that they work under special conditions is more restrictive. In view of the fact that this provision gives special protection to a certain group of employees, it is necessary to define the group in question. On the one hand, whether or not conditions of employment qualify as 'special' may not always be objectively justified. An employee may well have refrained from applying for state-subsidies even though he or she would qualify. On the other hand, a too broad definition could be counter-productive by discouraging employers from taking special consideration to employees with reduced working capacity if such consideration could make the employee eligible for special protection against dismissal. Problems of delimitation are difficult to avoid and do not in my opinion undermine the protection granted under Section 23.

5.3. Conclusion

In conclusion, the starting points under Danish and Swedish law are opposites. Whereas Danish law hardly limits the right of employers to choose whom they wish to dismiss in a situation of work shortage, Swedish law dictates that the employees of the lowest age and length of service are dismissed first. Moreover, Swedish law grants special protection to employees with reduced working capacity who are employed under special conditions.

As argued under *Sub-Section 2 Contemporary Disability Human Rights Approach*, it is not a requirement under the contemporary disability human rights approach to introduce such special protection, but such protection is in line with the contemporary disability human rights approach. Thus, Denmark is not in violation due to lack of special protection for persons with disabilities in case of dismissals in situations of work shortage. In Denmark, dismissals on the grounds of disability and disability-related reduced working capacity will only be prohibited when they are in violation of the Danish prohibition of discrimination on the grounds of disability. Since the definition of disability under the anti-discrimination legislation is narrower than the definition of disability under the contemporary disability human rights approach, the protection against dismissal in case of work shortage is inadequate in Denmark. The Swedish protection of persons with disabilities in relation to dismissals due to work shortages is fully in accordance with the contemporary disability human rights approach. In Sweden, persons with disabilities are protected both by adequate protection against dismissals on grounds relating to disability and reduced working capacity and by special protective measures.

6. EU Law and Policy

In *Chapter III EU Law and Policy, Section 5 Employers' Obligations,* I concluded that EU law imposes relatively few obligations on employers to create working conditions which are inclusive towards persons with reduced working capacity. Thus, the EU has hardly harmonised employment protection and health and safety legislation imposes few duties to make adjustments for individuals with disabilities.

As regards EU policy in relation to employers' obligations, the EU recommends that labour market law and policy be based on the flexicurity model which entails relatively weak job protection legislation. Thus, present EU policy on employment protection does not explicitly take into account that protection against dismissals on the grounds of disability and disability-related reduced working capacity should be mainstreamed into general employment protection legislation and health and safety laws and policies in order for the general structures on the labour to become inclusive towards persons with disabilities and reduced working capacity.

However, the Employment Equality Directive may lead to significant change in national labour laws provided that the CJEU interprets the Directive in line with the contemporary disability human rights approach. As explained in *Chapter III EU Law and Policy*, the definition of disability under the Employment Equality Directive is still not clear and there are doubts as to whether the CJEU only finds that severe long-lasting impairments which in themselves lead to limitations on the labour market qualify as disability under the Employment Equality Directive. If the CJEU applies such a narrow definition of disability under the Employment Equality Directive, the Directive does not in itself obligate Member States to provide adequate protection to employees with disabilities and disability-related reduced working capacity under national anti-discrimination laws or general labour laws.

7. Conclusion

The present Chapter exposes significant differences in the obligations of employers towards persons with disabilities and disability-related reduced working capacity in Denmark and Sweden. Employers in Denmark are practically free to dismiss persons with reduced long-lasting working capacity related if they deem this to be in the interest of the entity.

Swedish employers however are obliged to make adjustments for all employees reduced working capacities who also enjoy special protection in situations of work shortage. This means that employers in Sweden have to organise the work place to cater for the needs of both persons with full working capacity and persons with reduced working capacity. In Denmark, employers have less of an incentive to create a work place which is inclusive towards persons with reduced working capacity.

In relation to the involvement of disabled persons organisations, neither Denmark nor Sweden have formalised their involvement. However, disabled persons organisations will often have the opportunity to comment on proposals for new legislation in the field of employment protection and health and safety.

Denmark does not live up to its duty under ICESCR to provide employment protection to all employees on the labour market since approximately one-third of all employees on the private labour market do not enjoy employment protection. In addition, the Danish employment protection and obligations on employers to employees with reduced working capacity does not live up to the contemporary disability human rights approach since the obligation to provide protection against dismissals on the grounds of disability and accommodation for reduced working capacity have not been mainstreamed into Danish employment protection legislation. In contrast, the Swedish employment protection complies with the contemporary disability human rights approach in that it has ensured adequate protection against dismissals on the grounds of disability and disability-related reduced working capacity and since persons with some disability-related reduced working capacity enjoy special protection against dismissals in case of work-shortage.

Finally, EU law is relatively weak in relation to employment protection and positive obligations on employers to make adjustments for employees with reduced working capacity. In addition, EU policy promotes flexicurity, which entails low employment protection for employees with disability-related reduced working capacity in line with the Danish model, rather than promoting a high level of protection for employees with disability-related reduced working capacity in line with the contemporary disability human rights approach.

Chapter VI
Employment Promotion

1. Introduction

The present Chapter examines how the State seeks to promote the employment of persons with disabilities with economic incentives, such as wage subvention. In *Chapter IV Equality Law and Policy*, I examined the extent to which private and public employers have a *duty* to give preferential treatment to persons with disabilities in employment situations. In *Chapter V Employers' Obligations,* I examined when employers have a *duty* to continue to employ an employee who develops a disability or disability-related reduced working capacity.

Public employment promotion consists of *general* measures which target all persons seeking employment, such as the provision of databases with information on job-seekers and available jobs, as well as *specific* measures targeting persons with disabilities seeking employment, such as subventions for assistive devices for employees with disabilities. Moreover, public employment promotional measures may encompass both measures which are aimed at immediate employment, such as for example wage subvention, and measures which seek to improve the employability of job-seekers, such as training and education. The present Chapter focuses on specific measures targeting job-seekers with disabilities. Moreover, this Chapter is also confined to examining employment promotional measures which are aimed specifically at obtaining employment immediately. Access to employment-oriented rehabilitation, which aims at improving a person's skills-level in order to make the person more employable, is examined in *Chapter VII Income-Replacement Benefits.*

Disability employment promotion measures aiming at employment fall into two main categories: *supported employment* on the one hand and *sheltered employment* on the other hand. Supported employment aims at encouraging employment on the open labour market and consists mainly in wage and cost subvention. Wage subvention is economic support which allows employers to employ persons with disabilities at a reduced cost. Cost subvention compensates employers for costs other than salary associated with employing persons with disability, such as for example technical aids. In contrast, sheltered employment entails a higher degree of specialised working conditions for persons with disabilities than supported employment. There will be significantly lower requirements to the employed person's work output than for a person employed in supported employment. Although there may be some work output to the benefit of the employer, sheltered employment will often have the character of therapy or work training for the benefit of the employee. Sheltered employment may take place both in segregated workplaces reserved for this type of employment or in special positions on the open labour market. There is no clear-cut line between supported and sheltered employment since sheltered employment may take place on the open labour market and may entail some work-output for the benefit of the employer. However, the higher the degree of specialised working conditions (segregation, reduced pay, reduced working hours), the more the employment should be characterised as sheltered employment.

Section 2 will examine what a disability employment promotion policy in line with the contemporary disability human rights approach entails. Section 3 gives an overview of the general employment promotion policies in Denmark and Sweden in order to put the disability employment promotion policies in context. Section 3 also sheds light on how social partners and disability organisations are involved in the development and implementation of public disability employment promotion. Sections 4 and 5 respectively compare Danish and Swedish law and policy on supported and sheltered employment in relation to the contemporary disability human rights approach. Section 6 analyses Danish and Swedish law and policy in relation to EU law and policy. Finally, Section 7 provides a conclusion.

2. Contemporary Disability Human Rights Approach

As described in *Chapter II Human Rights*, the contemporary disability human rights approach is based on four general principles or models:

- substantive diversity equality which entails that general structures must changed to reflect social diversity,
- the universality model of disability
- that the contemporary disability human rights approach is founded on a principle of participation of civil society in the conduct of relevant State functions, and
- that policies to redress inequality must be based on individual and enforceable rights.

In the following two Sub-Sections, I examine in more detail what a contemporary disability human rights approach entails in relation to the two main categories of disability employment promotion measures: sheltered employment is examined under Sub-Section 2.1. and supported employment is examined in Sub-Section 2.2. The reason that I start with the examination of sheltered employment is that the legal sources are clearer on this type of promotional measure than they are on supported employment.

2.1. Sheltered Employment

As mentioned above, sheltered employment entails a higher degree of specialised working conditions for persons with disabilities than supported employment. Thus, there will be significantly lower requirements to the work output of persons in sheltered employment than for a person employed in supported employment. Although there may be some work output to the benefit of the employer, sheltered employment will often have the character of therapy or work training for the benefit of the employee. Sheltered employment may take place both in segregated workplaces reserved for this type of employment or in special positions on the open labour market. As mentioned above, there is no clear dividing line between supported and sheltered employment since sheltered employment may take place on the open labour market and may entail some work-output for the benefit of the employer. However, the higher the degree of specialised working conditions, the more the employment should be characterised as sheltered employment.

In the Preparatory Works to the CRPD, the drafters take a clear stand on sheltered employment:

> *"The balance of views in the Committee on sheltered workshops was that such settings were undesirable because of the potential for segregation from the community and their conditions of employment."*

The negative opinion of the Committee on sheltered workshops resulted in 'sheltered employment' not being mentioned in Article 27(2) on means to achieve the realization of the right to work. Thus, Article 27 provides that States Parties must *"promote the employment of persons with disabilities in the private sector through appropriate policies and measures which may include affirmative action programmes, incentives and other measures."*[806] Presumably the drafters of the CRPD wished to underline the new approach to human rights of persons with disabilities that this convention represents compared to older human rights instruments, such as the UN Standard Rules on Equalization of Persons with Disabilities of 1993 which stated that

> *"For persons with disabilities whose needs cannot be met in open employment, small units of sheltered or supported employment may be an alternative. It is important that the quality of such programmes be assessed in terms of their relevance and sufficiency in providing opportunities for persons with disabilities to gain employment in the labour market."*[807]

---

806 CRPD Article 27(1) (h).

807 UN Standard Rules on Equalization of Opportunities for Persons with Disabilities, Rule No. 7.

Under the CRPD, the aim of creating an inclusive labour market takes the forefront. As such, while sheltered employment is not prohibited, it is envisaged to play a small role in promoting employment of persons with disabilities.

Also in the Council of Europe instruments, is it clear that there has been a shift in the perception of sheltered employment. In the European Social Charter of 1961, sheltered employment is mentioned as a preferred means of promoting employment of persons with disabilities. Thus, States Parties undertake:

> *"to take adequate measures for the placing of disabled persons in employment, such as specialised placing services, facilities for sheltered employment and measures to encourage employers to admit disabled persons to employment."*[808]

In contrast, the Revised European Social Charter underlines that employment *"in ordinary working environment"* is the primary goal and that sheltered employment shall be used only *"where [employment in the ordinary working environment] is not possible by reason of the disability."*[809]

In line herewith, the European Committee on Social Rights has laid down three requirements for sheltered employment under Article 15(2) and Article 1(2) on the right to work: Firstly, sheltered employment must be reserved for persons who due to their disability cannot be integrated into the open labour market. Secondly, the aim of sheltered employment should be to assist participants to enter the open labour market. Thirdly, persons working in sheltered employment facilities must enjoy the usual benefits of labour law and trade unions should be active in enforcing the labour rights of persons in sheltered employment. This last requirement regarding usual benefits of labour law applies at least when production is the main activity.[810]

The European Committee on Social Rights requires compliance with these principles also from States which have only committed themselves to Article 15 of the European Social Charter of 1961 and who have not ratified Article 15 of the Revised European Social Charter of 1996. The Committee requires that States provide information on sheltered employment and rates of progress from participation in sheltered employment into employment in the ordinary labour market.[811]

---

808 European Social Charter of 1961, Article 15(2).

809 Revised European Social Charter of 1996, Article 15(2).

810 See for example Council of Europe, European Committee of Social Rights, *European Social Charter (revised), Conclusions 2007, vol. 1, Estonia, 2005, p. 387.*

811 Council of Europe, European Committee of Social Rights, *Conclusions XVIII-2, vol. 2, Slovenia, 2007, p. 542.*

In conclusion, sheltered employment represents both a means of assisting persons with disabilities in obtaining employment and a differential treatment of persons with disabilities. However, since sheltered employment, which includes segregated employment, entails more differential treatment than supported employment, it follows that the use of sheltered employment should only be a last resort in order to comply with the human rights principles of inclusion and equality. Thus, sheltered employment used in accordance with the contemporary disability human rights approach should therefore be available to those who need it, but limited only to those without an alternative for employment on the ordinary labour market with or without support. Moreover, it should be given with the aim of promoting employment with less support and working conditions should be as similar as possible to those of persons employed on the ordinary labour market.

2.2. Supported Employment

As described above, supported employment consists mainly of economic incentives for employment of persons with disabilities on the open labour market, through for example wage and cost subvention. Wage subvention is economic support which compensates for reduced working capacity thus giving employers lower wage costs while ensuring that persons with disabilities and reduced working capacity maintain an acceptable income level. Cost subvention compensates employers for other costs than wages which are associated with employing persons with disability, such as for example technical aids required to carry out the job in question.

Supported employment can from a human rights perspective be perceived in three different manners which will be discussed below:

- as positive action necessary to overcome discrimination;
- as positive action necessary to compensate for a reduced working capacity related to biological differences, or
- as a differential treatment of persons with disabilities which limitations maintains discriminatory general structures on the labour market.

I would argue that all three perceptions of supported employment contain some relevance. Firstly, persons with disabilities do meet unfounded prejudice by employers and supported employment may help overcome such discriminatory practices because a prejudiced employer may become more inclined to employ persons with a disability and reduced working capacity after he or she has tried having employees with disabilities and reduced working capacity. Thus, supported employment may be seen as being in line with the social model of disability which explains a lack of participation in the labour market by referring *inter alia* to negative attitudes which colour the actions of employers.

Secondly, it should be acknowledged, as I do in *Chapter I, Section 4 Some Definitions*, that some severe impairments, such as excessive fatigue and pain may in themselves lead to serious limitations in possibilities for participation in the labour market. It is in my opinion unrealistic to envisage that private employers can be obliged to pay a sufficiently high wage to employees whose work-output is much lower than that of the average employee unless special circumstances, such as a work-related injury, warrant this. In relation to the social and medical models of disability, this perception of supported employment is founded on a mitigated social model of disability which takes into account that impairment may in itself lead to disability.

Thirdly, even though supported employment may as explained above have positive consequences for the participation of persons with disabilities on the labour market, it should be kept in mind that supported employment does entail differential treatment of persons with disabilities because employees in supported employment will often have a lower income than others even when they receive wage subvention because wage subvention often is relatively low. In addition, persons with disabilities in supported employment are continuously dependent on approval by public authorities for wage subvention. Moreover employment with wage subvention may be a hindrance for access to an ordinary position without support if the employer stands to gain from employment with wage subvention. This perception of supported employment, which problematises the use of supported employment, is also founded on a mitigated social model of disability since it identifies social structures in the form of too easy access to employment with wage subvention as a barrier to full participation on the labour market.

Below, I will first examine whether supported employment is recommended or required as a means of promoting and ensuring substantive equality on the labour market for persons with disabilities. Subsequently, I examine whether the possible negative effects for the inclusion of persons with disabilities on the labour market are also recognised under human rights law.

As explained also in *Chapter IV Equality Law and Policy, Sub-Section 2.3. Positive Action,* human rights instruments generally leave it up to States Parties to decide which types of positive action measures should be enacted in order to achieve substantive equality. However, both the CRPD and the Revised European Social Charter explicitly recommend the use of *"incentives"* and *"measures tending to encourage employers"* to promote employment of persons with disabilities on the labour market. Although *"incentives"* and *"measures tending to encourage employers"* may include many other measures, such as information campaigns and tax-incentives, I presume in the following that they also include economic incentives in the form of wage and cost subvention.

As mentioned above, CRPD Article 27 on Work and Employment provides that States Parties shall:

> *"Promote the employment of persons with disabilities in the private sector through appropriate policies and measures which may include affirmative action programmes, incentives and other measures."*[812]

According to the wording of Article 15(2) of the Revised European Social Charter of 1996, States Parties are required to undertake promotional measures:

> *"[...] the Parties undertake, in particular to promote their access to employment through all measures tending to encourage employers to hire and keep in employment persons with disabilities in the ordinary working environment and to adjust the working conditions to the needs of the disabled [...].*

Moreover, the European Committee on Social Rights also requires that Member States undertake employment promotional measures when it examines the performance of States Parties in relation to Article 15 of the Revised European Social Charter.[813] Thus, the European Committee on Social Rights operates with the heading: *"Measures to promote the employment of persons with disabilities"* when it examines States Parties under Article 15(2). Although the European Committee of Social Rights does not require the enactment of specific employment promotional measures, it does require that the employment promotional measures do lead to an increase in the employment rate for persons with disabilities and insufficient information will result in a finding of a violation of Article 15(2) of the Revised European Social Charter:

> *"The Committee reiterates that to assess the conformity of the situation under Article 15§2, it has to know how many disabled persons benefit from the measures in place to enable their integration into the ordinary labour market"*[814]

The Council of Europe Committee of Ministers Recommendation of 2006 also recommends the use of positive action measures for the promotion of employment of persons with disabilities without specifying which positive action measures should be used:

---

812 CRPD Article 27(1) (d) and (h).

813 See for example European Committee on Social Rights, Conclusions 2008 Revised European Social Charter, p.59 (Armenia) and p. 133 (Belgium).

814 European Committee on Social Rights, Conclusions 2008 Revised European Social Charter, p.59 (Armenia) and p. 133 (Belgium). Both Armenia and Belgium were found in violation of Article 15(2) due to lack of information on effectiveness of employment promotional measures.

> *"Equal access to employment should be enhanced by combining anti-discrimination and positive action measures and by mainstreaming issues related to the employment of people with disabilities in employment policies"*[815]

In sum, positive action measures, such as *"incentives"* and *"measures tending to encourage employers"*, are encouraged under human rights law. Moreover the wording of CRPD which provides that Member States shall promote employment and the fact that the European Committee requires that the positive effect of promotional measures is documented could indicate that States are obliged to undertake some form of promotional measures. Human rights law does not specify exactly which promotional measures should be undertaken, but they could include supported employment in the form of wage subvention and economic incentives for employment.

The next question is whether it is recognised under human rights law that supported employment may have negative effects on the inclusion of persons with disabilities on the labour market. I have not found indication that has been directly recognised under human rights law that supported employment may also have negative effects on the inclusion of persons with disabilities on the labour, such as segregated employment.

However, for the following reasons, it is my opinion that supported employment is potentially a problematic measure in line with sheltered employment under the contemporary disability human rights approach: Firstly, as explained above, it is difficult to draw a sharp line between supported and sheltered employment even though supported employment does not take place in a segregated workshop. Similarly to sheltered employment, supported employment does entail differential treatment of persons with disabilities because employees in supported employment will often have a lower income than others even when they receive wage subvention because wage subvention often is relatively low. In addition, persons with disabilities in supported employment are continuously dependent on approval by public authorities for wage subvention. Moreover even though supported employment does not take place in segregated workshops, employment with wage subvention may be a hindrance for access to an ordinary position without support if the employer stands to gain from employment with wage subvention. Finally, as I will also argue in *Section 3 Supported Employment*, the excessive use of a special measure for persons with disabilities, such as supported employment, to promote employment on the labour market may delay the creation of generally inclusive structures in the labour market.

---

815 Recommendation Rec(2006)5 of the Committee of Ministers to member states on the Council of Europe Action Plan to promote the rights and full participation of people with disabilities in society: improving the quality of life of people with disabilities in Europe 2006–2015, Action Line No. 5.

2.3. Conclusion

Both sheltered and supported employment are special employment measures for the promotion of employment of persons with disabilities. A clear line cannot be drawn between the two types of special measures and consequently they should be treated similarly in relation to the contemporary disability human rights approach. Firstly, supported and sheltered employment measures should be available to those who need it in order to obtain reasonable employment. However, sheltered and supported employment should only be used when employment under ordinary working conditions is not a reasonable option. Moreover, since sheltered employment entails a higher degree of special working conditions, sheltered employment should be reserved to those who cannot obtain reasonable employment with supported employment. Both supported and sheltered employment should be given with the aim of promoting employment with less support and working conditions should be as similar as possible to those of persons employed on the ordinary labour market. Finally, full compliance with the contemporary disability human rights approach requires that employment promotional measures are provided in the form of individual and enforceable rights.

3. Introduction to Danish and Swedish Labour Market Policy

The present Section gives a brief introduction to Danish and Swedish Labour Market policies in order to put the disability promotional measures in context. The Section falls into two Sub-Sections: Sub-Section 3.1., which gives a brief overview of the contents of Danish and Swedish general labour market policies, and Sub-Section 3.2 which introduces the implementation systems in the two countries with a special focus on the question of the involvement of social partners and civil society.

3.1. Danish and Swedish Employment Promotion Policies

Employment promotion policies are often classified as either focusing on creating incentives to encourage jobseekers to seek work or as focusing on building the jobseekers capacities so that he or she becomes more attractive to the labour market. Whereas a liberal type employment policy will *"take on a limited role, restricted to inciting individuals to seek work, providing quick information and simple matching services, as well as investing in short-term vocational training"*, the universalistic type *"caters for the provision of complex and extended services to all citizens, but simultaneously guarantees relatively high standards of living for the assisted"...*

"the 'negotiating' between the individual's and the society's interests appears much more balanced".[816]

Both Denmark and Sweden have appeared as classical proponents of the *"universalistic"* type of employment policy with high levels of employment promotional services and high standards of living for the assisted.[817] Both have traditionally had relatively generous benefits levels and provide a wide variety of relatively high-quality activation programmes.[818] In Denmark, the provision of strong employment services has been a cornerstone in the Danish flexicurity model.[819] According to Eurostat figures, Denmark and Sweden were in fact the only two countries of the EU-27 countries and Norway, which consistently spent more than 1% of their GDP on activation measures including training, rehabilitation and supported employment from 1998 to 2006.[820] In 2006, the average for expenditures on activation measures amounted to around 0.5% for EU-27. However, since the year 2000, the level of expenditures has dropped significantly in both Denmark and Sweden and it fell under 1% in Sweden in 2007 and in Denmark in 2008. In fact, the level of expenditures as a percentage of GDP had almost halved in Denmark and more than halved in Sweden from 2000 to 2008. In Denmark, it fell from 1.7% to 0.9% and in Sweden, it fell from 1.4% to 0.6%. Thus, in 2008, the level of expenditures on activation measures in Denmark and Sweden were significantly closer to the average level of EU-27 countries (0.5%) than they had been previously.[821]

As pointed out by *Johansson and Hvindén*, it is in fact misleading to view current Scandinavian activation policies as being proponents of a universalistic as opposed to a liberal approach.[822] Denmark has since the Labour Market Reform of 2002 undergone an explicit *"ideological repositioning"* of the status of the unemployed towards a liberal or a *"work-first"* approach.[823] Denmark has revised its previously very generous unemployment insurance system and has implemented stricter

816 Barbier and Ludwig-Meyerfoyer 2004, p. 427–8.

817 Dahl, Boesby and Ploug 2002, p. 4, which speaks of the group of 'Nordic welfare states' with strong emphasis on active efforts, generous income maintenance, low reliance on use of means-tested benefits, low level of unemployment, high level of labour market participation. Barbier and Ludwig-Meyerfoyer 2004, p. 429.

818 Bredgaard and Larsen 2005, p. 10.

819 Barbier, Colomb and Kongshøj Madsen 2009, p. 6.

820 Eurostat, Public Expenditure on labour market policies, by type of action,% of GDP, total LMP measures, categories 2–7, 1998–2008.

821 Eurostat, Public Expenditure on labour market policies, by type of action,% of GDP, total LMP measures, categories 2–7, 1998–2008.

822 Johansson and Hvindén 2007, p. 335.

823 Johansson and Hvindén 2007, p. 339. Preparatory works which speak of 'work-first' as a policy goal for the employment policy, 2002/1 LSF 193, p. 18.

eligibility rules and shorter duration of benefits.[824] The duty dimension of the employment policy system is increasing and jobseekers must fulfil a growing number statutory and contractual hurdles in order to be entitled to benefits.[825] In recent years, these requirements are also being applied in relation to a broader range of unemployed persons, including persons with disabilities. For example, unemployed persons are now required to apply for jobs more broadly than merely within the area of their previous occupation from the first day of unemployment.[826]

In Sweden, steps have also been taken to upgrade the incentives for obtaining employment. These changes have not however been defined as ideological or fundamental, but rather as incremental. The requirements for receiving unemployment benefits have become stricter and recipients' possibilities for renewing their entitlements through participation in different labour market programmes have been curtailed. Stronger demands for geographical and occupational mobility have been adopted.[827] As in Denmark, the activation policies are also being applied to persons with disabilities.[828]

However, as will be seen below in Sections 4 and 5, the increasing importance of active labour market policies on employment promotional policy has not lead to a reduction in the use of specific disability employment promotion measures. On the contrary, the use of especially wage subvention has risen significantly in both Denmark and Sweden since the year 2000, cf. *Sub-Section 4.1. Overview* below.

3.2. Implementation of Danish and Swedish Employment Promotion Policy

In Denmark, the responsibility for the implementation of employment promotion policies lies with the local councils (*kommunalbestyrelser*) under supervision by the State. On State level, the Minister of Employment and the national Employment Promotion Service (*Arbejdsmarkedsstyrelsen*) under the Ministry of Employment sets out national regulations on the implementation of Danish employment

---

824 See for example Act Amending the Act on Unemployment Insurance, Lov no. 703 of 25 June 2010, (Lov om ændring af lov om arbejdsløshedsforsikring), which changed the maximum period that a person may receive unemployment insurance benefit from 4 years within a 6-year period to 2 years within a 4-year period.

825 Johansson and Hvindén 2007, p. 339.

826 Danish Administrative Regulation on availability for the labour market, no. 179 of 19 February 2007, (Bekendtgørelse om Rådighed), Sections 8 and 9. The rules remain in place after the European Social Rights Committee, in 2006, found that Denmark was in breach of its obligations under ESC 1961 Article 12(3) because jobseekers are required to take any reasonable job from the first day of unemployment, including work outside the individual's unemployment field. Council of Europe, European Committee of Social Rights, *Conclusions XVIII-1, vol. 1, Denmark, 2006, p. 275.*

827 Johansson and Hvindén 2007, p. 340.

828 Johansson and Hvindén 2007, p. 340.

promotion policy. Moreover, the State has set up four regional employment bodies (*beskæftigelsesregioner*) to supervise the implementation regionally. One of the four regional employment bodies has been appointed as the *"special function on disability"* which provides information and counseling on employment promotion on persons with disabilities. Since 2007, the 'special function on disability' has published an annual report on the use of disability employment promotional measures in the different regions of Denmark.[829] On the local level, the local councils (*kommunalbestyrelser*) are responsible for the implementation of employment promotional policy. Each local council must create a job centre which makes decisions relating to supported employment. Decision to allow a person to take part in sheltered employment in workshops is taken by the social authorities and not by the job centres.[830]

At each of the three levels – local, regional and state – advisory Employment Councils (*beskæftigelsesråd*) have been set up by law with representation of both employers' and employees' organisations as well as disability organisations.[831] The Employment Councils give advice on political initiatives and plans.[832] The National and Regional Employment Councils prepare an employment policy report on an annual basis.[833] The Regional Employment Councils play an active part in the supervision of the local Job Centres and they supervise the State and Local Council employment efforts in the Job Centres in co-operation with the Regional Employment Bodies. Both Regional and Local Employment Councils have a special State budget to promote a fast and active effort in relation to mass dismissals and to undertake special business-oriented initiatives.[834] The national Employment Council may make recommendations to the Employment Minister on the use of the national budget.[835] It is established by law that the Regional Employment Councils must meet regularly and at least once a year with the Danish Disability umbrella-organisation and public employers to discuss the employment situation of persons with disabilities in the region.[836]

Furthermore, disability organisations are represented in the four Regional Employment Complaint Boards which hear complaints about decisions on disability employment measures taken by the Local Job Centres.[837] The Complaint Boards

---

829 The annual reports may be downloaded on the homepage of the 'special function on disability': www.bmhandicap.dk/.

830 Danish Act on Social Service, Chapter 19.

831 Danish Act on Management of the Active Employment Effort, Chapters 5, 6 and 7.

832 Ibid., Sections 35(1), 39(1) and 44.

833 Ibid., Sections 35(2) and 39(1).

834 Ibid. Section 43, 47(1) and 48.

835 Ibid. Section 36.

836 Danish Act on Compensation of Persons with Disabilities in Employment, Section 17.

837 Danish Act on Active Employment Effort, Section 128 and Act on Management of the Active Employment Effort, Chapter 8.

hears complaints about decisions taken both by the State or Local Council administration in the Job Centres regarding supported employment. They consist of a Chairman who is the Director of the Regional State Administration and six members who represent the Local Councils in the region, the Social Partners and the Disabled People's Organisation. Decisions by the Regional Employment Complaint Boards can be appealed to the National Social Appeals Board which will only hear the complaint if it considers that the case is of general importance.[838]

In Sweden, the responsibility for the implementation of employment promotion policy lies with the Swedish Employment Promotion Service (*Arbetsformedlingen)* under the Ministry of Employment. This State body has local units throughout the country which has been divided into ten employment areas and 69 employment sub-areas with in total more than 200 local units throughout the country. Complaints under the Swedish Act on Special Measures taken by the local units of the Employment Service are heard by the central complaint treatment authority of the Public Employment Service. These decisions are final and cannot be overturned by other administrative authorities.[839] In Sweden, disability organisations have not been given a formal advisory role in relation to the implementation of the employment policy by the Employment Service Authority. An advisory organ is established on national level, "*Partsrådet*" which comprises representatives of the social partners, but not disability organisations.[840]

As mentioned above in *Section 2 Contemporary Disability Human Rights Approach*, disability organisations and social partners should be involved in the development and implementation of State policies regarding the participation of persons with disabilities on the labour market. From this perspective, it is therefore positive that both Denmark and Sweden have created advisory bodies with the participation of social partners to advise the employment promotion authorities. Moreover, it is positive that Denmark has formalised the involvement of disability organisations in the implementation of employment promotion by creating advisory Employment Councils at national, regional and local levels. The fact that the responsibility for the implementation of employment promotion policy lies primarily with the local councils in Denmark and the State in Sweden entails that there may be greater differences in implementation in different parts of Denmark than between different parts of Sweden. However, the policy of local councils is supervised by the Danish

838 Danish Act on Management of the Active Employment Effort, Section 54.

839 Swedish Act on Special Measures, Sections 6, 43 and 43a. See also Swedish Act with instruction to the Employment Service, SFS 2007:1030 (Förordning med instruktion för Arbetsförmidlingen), and Swedish Preparatory Works to Act on Special Measures, prop. 2006/7:89, p. 78.

840 Swedish Act with instruction to the Employment Service, Section 21. See also however Swedish Act on Labour Market Politicy, SFS 2000:628, (Förordning om den arbetsmarkhadspolitiska verksamheten), Section 2, which provides that the employment policy shall be implemented in co-operation with other actors on the labour market such as the social partners, the councils and companies and organisations.

State and complaints are heard nationally which ensures a minimum of uniformity of practice in the different job centres also in Denmark.

3.3. Conclusion

Both in Denmark and Sweden, general employment promotion policies have undergone a significant development towards a more liberal work-first type of policy since the beginning of the new millennium. In the next Sections, the use of specific disability-related promotional measures will be analysed. As regards the implementation of employment promotional measures, Danish employment promotion policy is implemented by the local councils with State supervision, while Swedish employment promotion policy is implemented by a State body with local units throughout the country. Moreover, the involvement of both social partners and disability organisations has been formally ensured through the creation of employment councils in Denmark at local, regional and State level. The involvement of disability organisations is especially positive from the perspective of the contemporary disability human rights approach as it ensures the involvement of persons with disabilities in decisions which concern their participation in the labour market. In Sweden, a counselling body at national level ensures the involvement of social partners – but not disability organisations – in the implementation of employment promotion policy which is less favourable in relation to the contemporary disability human rights approach. In relation to the rights-based approach, it is problematic that complaints over decisions by the Swedish Public Employment Service cannot be treated by an independent administrative body. Moreover, the fact that local councils administer the rules on supported and sheltered employment in Denmark lead to significant differences in their administration which may also be problematic in relation to the rights-based approach.

4. Supported Employment in the Open Labour Market

4.1. Overview

As mentioned above in *Section 1. Introduction*, supported employment includes both support in the form of wage subvention and economic support to cover other costs related to employment, such as costs to cover assistive devices or personal assistants. It is however difficult to compare the support given, for example assistive devices and personal assistance in Denmark and Sweden meaningfully without comparing also support given for assistive devices and personal assistants by employers who do not receive public support, as well as support given under social laws. Thus, in 2008, public authorities in Denmark and Sweden spent 37 million euro and 26 million euro respectively on work-related personal assistants and assistive devices for persons with disabilities and reduced working capacity.[841] The higher level of work-related public support in Denmark could be the consequence of the lower level of obligations on employers (cf. *Chapter V Employers' Obligations*) and it could also be a consequence of lower level of general support to persons with disabilities under social legislation. In view of the significantly lower level of employment of persons with disabilities and reduced working capacity in Denmark compared to in Sweden, it seems unlikely that employees with disabilities in Sweden have access to less personal assistance and assistive devices on the labour market in practice.

The main focus of the present Chapter is wage subvention because it is the most widely used form of disability employment promotional measure in terms of the number of persons concerned and costs. Additional types of wage subvention exist for special groups, such as for example persons with disabilities who have completed higher education and who have not yet been employed, but I will concentrate on simple wage subvention because the other types of wage subvention are used so little compared to simple wage subvention.[842] In both countries, around 15% of persons with reduced working capacity received wage subvention for employment in a *"fleksjob"* in Denmark and wage subvention (*lönebidrag*) in Sweden during the year 2008 (see table below).[843] As mentioned above wage subvention is an economic compensation paid to the employer of a person with a disability who has been awarded wage subvention because of the employee's reduced working capacity.

841 Denmark: Act on Compensation of Persons with Disabilities in Employment, Chapter 3 on personal assistance, and Act on an Active Employment Effort, Sections 76–77 on assistive devices, Special Disability Function 2010, p. 22 and 29. In Denmark, 4,000 persons made use of personal assistants and no figures are available on number of persons using assistive devices. Sweden: Swedish Act on Special Measures, Sections 11–15 and 18–19. Arbetsförmedlingen 2009, p. 113 and 116. In Sweden, 5.500 persons made use of personal assistants and 4.500 made use of assistive devices.

842 In *Denmark*, an additional type of simple wage subvention for persons with disabilities who have completed an 18-month higher education course is also available (ice-breaker scheme), but this type of wage subvention will not be examined in more detail as it only used to a limited extent. No specific figures on the use of this scheme are available in the public on-line database of the Danish Employment Service www.jobindsats.dk or in Larsen and Høgelund 2008. In *Sweden*, wage subvention is also available to persons who qualify for 'development positions'. In addition to wage subvention, the employer may receive up to approximately 20 euro per day of employment to cover costs associated with accommodation for the employee's reduced working capacity. 'Development positions' are limited to a period of one year, but may under special circumstances be prolonged to two years. Persons in development positions are not covered by the Employment Protection Act, but other employment conditions must comply with general labour law, cf. Section 36 of the Swedish Act on Employment Promotional Measures for Persons with Disabilities and Reduced Working Capacity. In 2008, approximately 3,000 persons started in a 'development position', cf. Arbetsförmedlingen 2009, p. 128.

843 Dannmarks Statistik 2007.

In Denmark, wage subvention has been offered to *"persons with mental/physical handicaps"* since 1993 and to *"vulnerable groups"* since 1990.[844] The present *fleksjob* scheme was introduced in 1997 and the rules governing *fleksjobs* are contained in the Act on an Active Employment Effort.[845] According to Section 69 of the Act on an Active Employment Effort, *"the local council must ensure that a person under 65 years of age with a lasting reduction of his or her working capacity...has the opportunity for employment with public or private employers in a fleksjob."*[846]

In Sweden, wage subvention (*lönebidrag*) is part of a *"Labour Market Programme of the Swedish Public Employment Service for Persons with Reduced Working Capacity who have or are expected to experience difficulties with obtaining or keeping an ordinary job"*.[847] Swedish wage subvention (*lönebidrag*) was introduced for the first time in 1980 and the system was reformed in 1991 to target only employees with a disability.[848] Wage subvention (*lönebidrag*) is governed by the Act on Special Measures for Persons with Disabilities which Results in Reduced Working Capacity.[849]

As may be seen in Table 4 below, both in Denmark and in Sweden, the number of persons who receive wage subvention (*fleksjob/lönebidrag*) has risen significantly during the period from 2000 to 2008. In Denmark, the number of persons in a *fleksjob* has increased almost six times from a low figure of 10,000 persons in 2002 to close to 60,000 persons in 2008.[850] In Sweden, the rise in the number of persons receiving wage subvention was not as dramatic (from 50,000 to 70,000) over the same period of time. In 2008, the rise in the use of wage subvention in both countries meant that approximately 15% of persons with a disability and reduced working capacity of working age were awarded wage subvention in both Denmark and Sweden. However, since persons with reduced working capacity are approximately twice as likely to be in employment in Sweden compared to in Denmark, more than 60% of persons with a disability and reduced working capacity

844 Danish Act on an Active Employment Market Policy, Lov no. 434 of 30 June 1993 (Lov om en aktiv arbejdsmarkedspolitik), Section 37; Danish Act on a Municipal Employment Effort, lov no. 379 of 13 June 1990 (lov om kommunal beskæftigelsesindsats), Section 1.

845 Danish Act on an Active Employment Effort, Act no. 483 of 12 June 2009 with latest amendment of Act no. 639 of 14 June 2010, (Lov om en Aktiv Beskæftigelsesindsats).

846 Danish Act on an Active Employment Service which describes the target group, Section 2(7).

847 Danish Act on Special Measures, Section 1.

848 Swedish Preparatory Works, Prop. 1978/79:73 and Prop. 1990/91:100.

849 Swedish Act on Special Measures, SFS 2000:630 with latest amendment by SFS2010:394 of 20 May 2010, (Förordning om särskilda insatser för personer med funktionshinder som medför nedsatt arbetsförmåga).

850 Www.jobindsats.dk (fleksjob, hele landet, antal personer) and Miller, Høgelund and Geerdsen 2006, p. 35. No figures are available for the year 2000.

in employment were awarded wage subvention in Denmark while this is only true for 25% in Sweden.

Moreover, the sharp rise in the use of wage subvention in Denmark has not resulted in a rise in employment of persons of persons with reduced working capacity, but rather in a rise in the ratio of persons with disability and reduced working capacity *in employment* who are awarded wage subvention. Thus, the employment rate of persons with a disability and reduced working capacity has remained stable around 26% in Denmark, while it has fallen in Sweden from 56% to 50%. As may be seen also in *Table 4* below, the lack of rise in employment rates of persons with a disability and reduced working capacity cannot be explained either by a significant change in the percentage of persons with reduced working capacity or by a significant reduction in general employment in Denmark or Sweden.

Table 4. Wage subvention in Denmark and Sweden, 2000–2008

	Denmark		Sweden	
	2002	2008	2000[851]	2008[852]
Persons in *Fleksjob/lönebidrag*	10,000	60,000[853]	50,000	70,000
Percentage of persons with disability and reduced working capacity of population between 16 and 64 years of age	11%[854]	10%	10%	9%
Employment rate of persons with disability and reduced working capacity	26%	26%	56%	50%
Percentage of persons with disability and reduced working capacity who are employed with wage subvention	3%	16%	9%	13%
Percentage of persons with disability and reduced working capacity *in employment* who are employed with wage subvention	10%	62%	20%	25%
Employment rate of persons without disability	84%	83%	77%	77%

The following comparison of simple wage subvention schemes in Denmark and Sweden will be based on the requirements of the contemporary disability human rights approach: that simple wage subvention should only be given to persons who would otherwise be excluded from the labour market (Sub-Section 4.2.2.), that wage

851 Statistics Sweden 2009 and Statistics Sweden 2003.

852 Statistics Sweden 2009.

853 Www.jobindsats.dk (fleksjob, antal personer).

854 Miller, Høgelund and Geerdsen 2006, p. 49 (andel af personer med handicap * andel heraf, som har nedsat arbejdsevne).

subvention is available to those who need it (Sub-Section 4.2.3), that wage subvention aims at inclusion in the labour market without support (Sub-Section 4.3.4), that recipients limitations on an adequate standard of living (Sub-Section 4.3.5) and that working conditions are similar to those who do not receive wage subvention (Sub-Section 4.3.6).

4.2. Reserved to Persons Otherwise Excluded from the Labour Market

As pointed out above, the sharp rise in persons receiving wage subvention in especially Denmark, but also in Sweden has not amounted to a corresponding rise in employment rates of persons with disabilities and reduced working capacity. This indicates that both Denmark and Sweden may be having difficulties in ensuring that wage subvention is only granted to persons who would otherwise be excluded from the labour market or alternatively that more and more people become dependent on wage subvention in order to obtain employment. I will discuss this latter possibility in *Sub-Section 4.3. Available to Those Who Need It.* Both in Denmark and in Sweden, the legislation explicitly states that wage subvention can only be granted to persons who would otherwise be excluded from the labour market.[855] According to the Danish Act on an Active Employment Effort wage subvention may only be granted to persons:

> *"who cannot obtain or stay in employment on ordinary conditions on the labour market [...] Fleksjob may only be offered when all other relevant schemes under the present legal act and other measures, such as transfers to new positions have been attempted [...]."*[856]

The Swedish Act on Special Measures provides that *"wage subvention may only be granted if the authorities find that the person would otherwise not be able to keep or obtain employment due to his or her disability"*.[857] Moreover, the Administrative Guidelines underline that wage subvention should only be granted as a last resort where for example support in the form of technical aids or personal assistance is not sufficient.[858]

An important difference between the legislation in Denmark and Sweden consists in the fact that Danish legislation requires that the reduction in working capacity amounts to a minimum of 50% in relation to the job in question, whereas Swedish

855 Danish Act on Active Employment Effort, Section 70(1).

856 Danish Act on an Active Employment Effort, Section 70(1) and (2).

857 Danish Act on Special Measures, Section 26.

858 Swedish Public Employment Service General Guidelines on the administration of Act on Special Measures, AMSFS 2001:20 with latest amendment of AMSFS 2007:34, (Arbetsmarknadsstyrelsens allmänna råd om tillämpningen av förordningen om särskilda insatser), Section 10.

legislation does not require a minimum rate for the reduction in working capacity. No figures are available on the use of low rates of wage subvention as only the average wage subvention is provided for each sector in Sweden. Thus, in Sweden, the average wage subvention for employees of the State is given for 57% reduced working capacity and it is 70% reduced working capacity for employees of non-profit organisations which indicates that most persons do receive wage subvention around or above 50% in Sweden as well. In Denmark, the possibility for receiving wage subvention for a 33% reduced working capacity was removed in 2001 and since then only persons who qualified for 50% or 66% wage subvention could be found eligible. In connection with this amendment, the preparatory works underlined that the social partners have a responsibility towards persons with a small reduction in working capacity.[859] Interestingly however, the amount of persons hired under the social chapters of the collective agreements as described above under *Section 3 Overview of Employment Promotion Policy and Implementation* has fallen from 4,000 persons in 2005 to 3,000 persons in 2008.[860]

Moreover, the Danish National Social Appeals Board has conducted in-depth surveys of administrative practice regarding granting of wage subvention for employment in *fleksjobs* which show that a significant number of persons are granted wage subvention for employment in a *fleksjob* without meeting all requirements.[861] The main problem is that the administrative authorities do not make adequate tests of whether the person in question may be employed in another position on the labour market without support. In 2008, as many as 74% of the examined cases did not comply with the legal requirements for granting wage subvention for employment in a *fleksjob*.[862] In 2010, administrative practice had improved significantly, but the Danish National Appeals Board still found that requirements had not been met in 26% of the examined cases.[863]

Finally, in contrast to Denmark, which requires a certain rate of reduced working capacity, Sweden has imposed limitations regarding positions in which wage subvention (*lönebidrag*) may be granted. Thus, the Act on Special Measures establishes that wage subvention may only be granted when a person is hired, or when an employee returns to previous position after having received full sickness benefits. If an employee has received wage subvention within the past three years, he or she may also be granted wage subvention anew if his or her working capacity is reduced as compared to previously. Finally, wage subvention may also be given

---

859 Danish Preparatory Works, LF no. 136, 2000/01.

860 Larsen and Høgelund 2009, p. 50. Figures for the number of persons hired under the social chapters are not available for the years before 2005, cf. Mølgaard, Høgelund and Geerdsen 2006, p. 45.

861 Danish National Social Appeals Board 2010.

862 Danish National Social Appeals Board 2008.

863 Danish National Social Appeals Board 2010.

when a person who was previously in sheltered employment with a public employer is given a new position by the same employer.[864]

When assessing whether or not employment with wage subvention is necessary to avoid exclusion from the labour market, one is faced with the problem that the expectations of employers may change over time as wage subvention becomes more and more common. Employers may well become more and more reluctant to hire persons with a disability and reduced working capacity and the threshold for when the employers requires wage subvention before accepting to hire an employee with reduced working capacity may fall. This means that in each specific case the consequence of rejection of an application of wage subvention may well be exclusion from the labour market, while the rise in wage subvention at the same time leads to a less and less inclusive ordinary labour market.

In sum, although the legislation does provide that only persons who would otherwise be excluded from the labour market are eligible for wage subvention, statistics and surveys of administrative practice indicate that especially Denmark, but also Sweden, have not succeeded in reducing exclusion from the labour market in spite of sharp rises in the use of wage subvention. Instead it would seem that the threshold of employers for requiring wage subvention is falling in especially Denmark which means that the ordinary labour market is becoming *less* rather than *more* inclusive towards persons with disabilities.

4.3. Available to Those Who Need It

As mentioned above, 13% and 16% of persons with a disability and reduced working capacity of working age are employed with wage subvention in Denmark and Sweden respectively. This indicates that wage subvention is quite widely available in both countries. However, on the one hand, the relatively low overall employment rate of 26% in Denmark compared to 50% in Sweden of persons with disabilities and reduced working capacity indicates there could possibly be a higher need for wage subvention in Denmark.[865] On the other hand, as mentioned above, the low rate of employment of persons with a disability and reduced working capacity also means that a much higher percentage of disabled employed persons receive wage subvention in Denmark. In fact, the majority of persons with a disability and reduced working capacity who are in employment in Denmark receive wage subvention.

---

864 Danish Act on Special Measures Section 26. See also Sections 26a and 26b which permit granting wage subvention when a person is hired by a new employer and he or she left a position with wage subvention or left a position that he can no longer fulfil due to reduced working capacity.

865 Denmark: Larsen, Schademan and Høgelund 2008 and Extract by Social Research Institute 2009 for this thesis, kol 3, 4 and 6.

Moreover, it is difficult to see how the regulations on wage subvention in Denmark could be further relaxed without compromising the aim that wage subvention should only be given to those who would otherwise be excluded from the labour market.

In Sweden as opposed to in Denmark, a person cannot qualify for wage subvention in order to continue in his or her own position unless he or she has received a full sickness benefit.[866] This rule excludes persons with disabilities who have for example been able to continue to work part-time in spite of the reduction in working capacity that they have experienced from qualifying for wage subvention. However, this rule should be seen in conjunction with the strict duties imposed on employers not to dismiss employees who lose working capacity, but who can continue to perform work of value for the employer.[867] The fact that only persons who have received a full sickness benefit are eligible for wage subvention helps ensure that only persons, who would otherwise have been dismissed due to their reduced working capacity, will receive wage subvention.

As will be explained in more detail below in *Sub-Section 4.5. Usual Benefits of Labour Law*, in Sweden, the cap on eligible costs which may be subsidised through wage subvention is set at approximately half of an average salary. This means that wage subvention in Sweden typically will cover a significantly lower ratio of the employers' costs than in Denmark in spite of the fact that wage subvention cannot exceed 66% of total costs in Denmark. In other words, persons who would be entitled to a high salary can only receive a relatively low level of wage subvention in Sweden. Thus, one may question whether wage subvention is available to those who need it among persons who could qualify for a job with a high salary in especially Sweden.

Finally, as argued above under *Sub-Section 2 Contemporary Disability Human Rights Approach,* it should be kept in mind that wage subvention is a type of specialised treatment which should not take the place of generally inclusive structures. The aim of a wage subvention scheme should therefore not be to enable the employment of the *majority* of persons with disabilities and reduced working capacity. The problems of exclusion of persons with disabilities need to be solved through the creation of inclusive general structures and wage subvention should not become a prerequisite for employment of the majority of persons with disabilities.

In sum, it seems that wage subvention is widely available in both Denmark and Sweden. The question is whether partial wage subvention should be made more widely available in Denmark where approximately 75% of persons with disabilities and reduced working capacity are unemployed. However, the experience to date

866 Section 26 of Act on Special Measures.

867 See Chapter V Employers' Obligations.

with wage subvention in Denmark seems to counter-indicate the extensive use of wage subvention as it does not seem to have to contributed to raising the employment rate of persons with disabilities and reduced working capacity. Instead, it seems that employers in Denmark increasingly require wage subvention before hiring persons with disabilities and reduced working capacity. There is therefore a risk that the introduction of wage subvention for persons with less than 50% reduced working capacity in Denmark would further strengthen the vicious circle making it even more difficult for persons with disabilities and reduced working capacity to obtain ordinary employment with support.

4.4. Promote Transition to Open Labour Market

The second requirement in relation to the contemporary disability human rights approach is that wage subvention must be given with the aim of improving working capacity and enabling employment under ordinary working conditions, cf. *Section 2 Contemporary Disability Human Rights Approach*. In Denmark, the legislation on the *fleksjob*-scheme does not explicitly underline that the public authorities should use wage subvention with the aim of improving a person's working capacity and promoting inclusion on the ordinary labour market.[868] According to the Danish legislation, in order to have a *fleksjob* a person must have a 'longer-lasting reduction in his or her working capacity' and a *fleksjob* can only be granted

> *"When all other relevant schemes under this legal Act and other measures including for example transfer to a new position with the same employer, have been attempted in order to achieve or keep the person in question in ordinary employment".*[869]

In other words, wage subvention and employment in a Danish wage subvention *fleksjob* is seen as a last resort and primary focus is not on using *fleksjobs* for improving employability.

In contrast, Swedish legislation underlines that:

> *"the Employment Services shall work to promote that persons who receive wage subvention become employed without wage subvention. In order to support such a transition, an individual plan of action shall be prepared when a position with wage subvention is taken up."*[870]

868 Danish Act on an Active Employment Effort and Regulation on Fleksjob (Bekendtgørelse om Fleksjob), no 829 of 26 August 2009, Chapter 13.

869 Danish Act on an Active Employment Effort, Section 70(2).

870 Danish Act on Special Measures, Section 31.

Furthermore, Danish wage subvention for employment in a *fleksjob* is not time limited and may be given for an unlimited number of years.[871] However, the authorities are required to make a reassessment of whether the conditions for *fleksjob* are still present after six months the first time and thereafter on an annual basis.[872] In contrast, in Sweden wage subvention may only be granted for one year the first time and it is limited to a period of four years in total unless there are special reasons for a prolongation.[873] However, in spite of the difference in formulation of the legislation, both in Denmark and in Sweden, approximately 40% of persons receiving wage subvention had done so for three years or more in December 2008.[874]

Interestingly, the statistics on the percentage of persons who make the transition from employment with wage subvention to employment without wage subvention shows that the percentage is low in both countries, but that Sweden is more efficient in achieving this result than Denmark. In Denmark, 2.6% of persons employed with wage subvention made a transition to employment without wage subvention in 2008 while this was the case for 4.4% of persons employed with wage subvention in Sweden in 2008.[875] The better result in Sweden concurs with the fact that the employment rate for persons with a disability and reduced working capacity is twice as high in Sweden as in Denmark and that the majority of these persons are employed without wage subvention while this is only the case for 40% in Denmark.

In sum, Sweden more effectively lives up to the aim of using supported employment to promote employment on the ordinary labour market. As opposed to Denmark, this is an explicit goal with wage subvention in Sweden. Moreover, the rate of transition to ordinary employment without wage subvention is lower in Denmark than in Sweden.

---

871 Danish Act on an Active Employment Effort, Chapter 13.

872 Danish Act on Active Social Policy, Section 10(3). Ministry of Social Affairs, Administrative Guidelines no. 39 of 5 March 1998 on Act on Active Social Policy, para. 40.

873 Swedish Act on Special Measures, Section 30. Swedish Employment Service Administrative Regulation on the implementation of the Act on Special Measures, AMSFS 2000:6 with latest amendment by AMSFS 2006:7, (Arbetsmarknadsstyrelsens föreskrifter (AMSFS 2000:6) om tillämpningen av förordningen (2000:630) om särskilda insatser för personer med funktionshinder som medför nedsatt arbetsförmåga), Section 6.

874 Denmark: www.jobindsats.dk, fleksjob, 2006 (figur 1. antal forløb fordelt på varighed af ydelsen for hver af beskæftigelsesregionerne), Sweden: Swedish Employment Services 2009, p. 101.

875 Denmark: www.Jobindsats.dk (status 1 måneder efter afsluttet forløb, antal afsluttede forløb, antal personer i fleksjob); Sweden: Swedish Employment Services 2009, p. 100 and 102 (antal personer, antal övergånge till icke subventionerat arbete).

4.5. Usual Benefits of Labour Law

Finally the working conditions including pay of persons who receive wage subvention must, according to the contemporary disability human rights approach, be similar to those which apply to persons on the ordinary labour market.

In Denmark, persons employed with wage subvention are ensured working conditions in accordance with applicable collective agreements. The Act on an Active Employment Effort provides that:

> *"wages and other working conditions, including working time, are set according to applicable collective agreements and the social chapters contained herein. Where the position is not covered by a collective agreement, a collective agreement for comparable positions shall apply. Agreements on wages and other working conditions must take place in cooperation with the social partners."*[876]

Similarly, the Swedish Act on Special Measures provides that working conditions must be in accordance with the relevant collective agreements and that the work must be accommodated to the needs of the employee.[877]

Both in Sweden and in Denmark, ordinary protection against dismissal applies to persons employed with wage subvention.[878] However, as was explained in *Chapter V Employers' Obligations*, reduced working capacity which hinders an employee in performing his or her job over a substantial period of time is considered a legal ground for dismissal in Denmark.[879] Nevertheless, it has been established in the case law on dismissals of persons hired with wage subvention (*fleksjobs)* that the employee cannot be justly dismissed only on the grounds of reduced working capacity.[880] The reason is that the employer is considered to have accepted that the employee has a reduced working capacity when the employee was hired with wage subvention. Anti-discrimination legislation and working environment legislation also applies to persons employed with wage subvention in both Denmark and Sweden.[881]

---

876 Danish Act on an Active Employment Effort, Section 72.

877 Danish Act on Special Measures, Section 8.

878 Sweden: Section 2 of Act on Employment Protection. Denmark: *Section 4.2.1. Denmark of Chapter V Employers' Obligations.*

879 See Chapter V Employers' Obligations.

880 See for example Århus District Court, judgment of 13 July 2006, no. BS 5.2830/2005, (the rejection that the company had also committed discrimination on the grounds of disability has been appealed to the High Court.).

881 Denmark: Danish Act on Working Environment which does not exempt employment with wage subvention, Section 2; Danish Act on Differential Treatment on the Labour Market, Section 2. Sweden: Section 7 of Act on Labour Market Policy Programmes, SFS 2000:625 of 29 June 2000

The next question is whether the size of wage subvention is adequate in relation to ensuring that persons with disabilities on the labour market work under similar working conditions to others. Both in Denmark and in Sweden, wage subvention is paid to the employer who is obliged to pay a salary to the employee, which is in accordance with relevant collective agreements. This ensures that persons with disabilities and reduced working capacity will have an acceptable income. However, as explained below, the level of wage subvention is capped in both Denmark and Sweden, which will deter employers from giving employees in wage subvention-positions a higher salary than the required minimum under the applicable collective agreements.

In Denmark, the size of the subvention is calculated on the basis of the lowest salary set out in the applicable collective agreement for a person without experience or special qualifications plus obligatory employers' contributions up to DKK 445,000 or approximately 60,000 euro in 2010.[882] In practice the fact that only the minimum salary for a person without special qualifications or experience may be taken into account means that a significant number of persons in *fleksjobs* are only compensated partially for the income reduction associated with their working capacity. However, considering that the average annual salary was approximately 37,000 euro including most obligatory employers' contributions in 2008, then the wage-cap is relatively high in Denmark.

In Sweden, the amount of subvention is calculated on the basis of the actual gross wage; however any monthly wage above 20,400 euro per year before taxes and including all obligatory employers' contributions may not be taken into consideration.[883] The average annual salary before taxes was approximately 36,000 euro per year in 2008 in Sweden.[884] In other words, the cap on eligible costs is set at approximately half of an average salary in Sweden which means that wage subvention in Sweden typically will cover a significantly lower ratio of the employers' costs than in Denmark in spite of the fact that wage subvention cannot exceed 66% of total costs in Denmark.

In practice the lower wage subvention in Sweden means that employers will presumably be reluctant to pay wages above minimum wages to persons in wage subvention. In addition, the cap in wage subvention also limits the efficiency of the subvention system for employees entitled to a higher salary which is reflected in the low representation of persons with higher education under especially the Swedish

with latest amendment by SFS 2007:935 and Section 4 of Act on Work Environment; Section 1 of Chapter 2 of Swedish Discrimination Act.

882 Act on an Active Employment Effort, Section 75(2).

883 Act on Special Measures, Section 28. On calculation of gross wage see Section 16 of Public Employment Service General Guidelines on the administration of Act on Special Measures.

884 Sveriges Statistik, www.scb.se, (genomsnitlig månadslön, samtliga sektorer, samtliga yrken).

wage subvention scheme. In Sweden, only 12% of employees receiving wage subvention had a higher education, compared to 23% of persons with disabilities in general. In Denmark, the difference in representation of persons with a higher education was not as big as in Sweden. In Denmark, 18% of employees in *fleksjobs* had a higher education compared to 22% of persons with disabilities in general.[885]

In conclusion, both in Denmark and in Sweden, persons with disabilities and reduced working capacity receiving wage subsidies will experience limitations on an adequate standard of living since the level of salary that they receive must be in accordance with collective agreements. However, the possible level of compensation in Sweden is so low that it does not provide effective compensation for persons who would be entitled to relatively high wages if working without wage subvention. Thus, employers are unlikely to use it to employ people in higher wage jobs, even if the individuals' qualifications would make them potentially eligible for such positions.

Both in Denmark and in Sweden, the usual benefits of labour law apply to persons employed in supported employment. However, the low level of wage subvention available in Sweden means that wage subvention may not be sufficiently efficient in relation to promoting employment of persons who would be entitled to relatively high wages.

4.6. Conclusion

In conclusion, both Danish and Swedish supported employment schemes do in principle comply with the contemporary disability human rights approach since they both seek to provide necessary assistance to persons with disabilities and reduced working capacity, who would otherwise be excluded from the labour market. However, in Denmark, wage subvention has gone from being a support measure for a small minority of persons with disabilities and reduced working capacity to being provided to 60% of persons with a disability and reduced working capacity,who have obtained employment. Simple wage subvention is a form of individual compensation, which may be necessary in exceptional cases, but it should not take the place of generally inclusive labour market structures. Moreover, the strong growth in the ratio of persons receiving wage subvention has not been met with a corresponding reduction in persons excluded from the labour market. In other words, the practice of Danish simple wage subvention in particular, is not meeting the fundamental aim of moving persons from exclusion to inclusion in the labour market. Instead, especially Danish wage subvention may be maintaining general labour market structures, which are exclusive to persons with reduced

885 National Labour Market Board, Statistics Sweden, 2007, p. 24, Arbetsmarknadsstyrelsen, Årsrapport 2006, p. 160, Larsen, Schademan and Høgelund 2008, p. 103.

working capacity because it is becoming acceptable that the employer need not bear the costs of employing persons with reduced working capacity themselves.

Finally, in Sweden, the level of wage subvention is so low that the available wage subvention cannot ensure effective subvention to persons who would be entitled to relatively high levels of salaries.

5. Sheltered Employment

5.1. Overview

As explained above, sheltered employment entails a higher degree of specialised working conditions for persons with disabilities than supported employment. In addition to economic incentives provided under supported employment schemes, sheltered employment entails significantly lower requirements to the employed person's work output than for a person employed in supported employment. Although there may be some work output to the benefit of the employer, sheltered employment will often have the character of therapy or work training for the benefit of the employee. Sheltered employment may take place both in segregated workplaces reserved for this type of employment or in special positions on the open labour market.

As explained under *Section 2 Contemporary Disability Human Rights Approach*, sheltered employment represents both a means of assisting persons with disabilities in obtaining employment and a differential treatment of persons with disabilities. However, since sheltered employment (which includes segregated employment) entails more differential treatment than supported employment, it follows that the use of sheltered employment should be so much the more restricted to comply with the human rights principles of inclusion and equality. Thus, although sheltered employment used in accordance with the contemporary disability human rights approach should be available to those who need it, it must imperatively be limited to those without an alternative for employment on the ordinary labour market including with supported employment. Moreover, it should be given with the aim of promoting employment without support and working conditions should be similar to those of persons employed on the ordinary labour market.

As opposed to supported employment, which was used for an equally great share of persons of working age with disabilities and reduced working capacity in Denmark and in Sweden, a significantly greater share of persons of working age with disabilities and reduced working capacity are in sheltered employment in Sweden than in Denmark. Thus, as may be seen from *Table 5. Sheltered Employment* below, approximately 3.5% of all persons with disabilities and reduced working capacity are employed in sheltered employment in Denmark while this is the case for 5.7% in Sweden. This difference is especially significant when one takes into account that approximately 50% of persons of working age with reduced working capacity are in employment in Sweden while this only holds true for 26% in Denmark.

In Denmark, sheltered employment is available only to persons who receive a disability pension (*førtidspension*) which, as explained in *Chapter VII Income-Replacement Benefits*, is a permanent income-replacement benefit for persons less than 65 years of age who are unable earn an income on the labour market due to reduced working capacity related to a disability.[886] In Denmark, two different types of sheltered employment exist: *"employment with sheltered workshops"*, which are specialised workshops established by city councils under the Act on Social Service, and *"sheltered employment with ordinary employers"* which entails that the employer receives wage subvention under the Act on an Active Employment Effort.[887]

As may be seen in *Table 5. Sheltered Employment* below, approximately 8,000 persons were in employed in sheltered workshops in Denmark in 2008.[888] There are approximately 200 sheltered workshops in Denmark and they are typically located in the vicinity of other activities funded under the Act on Social Services ranging from production work to activation and stimulation of the senses of the users.[889] Some localities with sheltered workshops also have living quarters and approximately 750 persons employed in sheltered workshop work and live in the same locality.[890] In 2008, approximately 5,000 persons were in "sheltered employment with ordinary employers".

In Sweden, three types of sheltered employment exist: employment with *"Samhall"*, *"public protected employment"* (*offentlig skyddat arbete*) and *"positions with high employment protection"* (*trygghetsanställning*) with both public and private employers. Samhall is a public limited company established in 1980 with the aim of realising the goals of employment also for persons with reduced working capacity. Samhall replaced the former decentralised workshops and other more loosely organised types of segregated employment.[891] In 2008, Samhall had almost 19,500

---

886 Act on Social Pension, LBK nr 1005 af 19 August 2010 without amendments (Bekendtgørelse af lov om social pension), Chapter 3.

887 Danish Act on Social Services, LBK no. 1117 of 26 September 2007 with latest amendment of Lov no. 549 of 26 September 2008 (Lov om Social Service), Section 103. Danish Act on an Active Employment Effort, Section 2(6), Chapters 12 and 14 of.

888 Center for Ligebehandling af Handicappede 2008, p. 34.

889 Ministry of Social Affairs, Administrative Guidelines on Housing Offers, no. 95 of 10 December 2007, (Vejledning til botilbud mv), para. 226. Bengtsson and Mateu 2009, p. 14.

890 Bengtsson and Mateu 2009, p. 15.

891 Inghammar 2007, p. 69.

employees with a disability out of a total of almost 22,000.[892] According to the articles of association of the company, *"The assignment is to produce goods and services that are in demand in order to provide meaningful and developing employment for persons with disabilities, where there is a need. The company shall be adapted to the capacities of these persons and shall be run in accordance with business principles on market conditions."*[893] The business areas fall into three categories which roughly employ one third of the staff each: production, services including cleaning and services for older persons and manning solutions for other companies.[894] Manning solutions entails that a group of staff from Samhall carry out work for another company in that company's workplace under supervision by Samhall.[895]

"Public protected employment" was established in 1986 and, as indicated by the name, this scheme is limited to employment with public employers. The employers of the participants in this scheme are entitled to wage subvention under the same provisions as the ordinary Swedish wage subvention scheme (*lönebidrag*). The scheme aims specifically at creating employment opportunities with especially social councils which are under an obligation to assist persons with disabilities with obtaining employment and aims specifically at creating employment opportunities for persons with socio-medical conditions, such as long-lasting addictions of alcohol.[896]

As may be seen in *Table 5. Sheltered Employment* below, approximately 6.300 persons were in *"public protected employment"* in 2008. In accordance with the Act on Special Measures, 57% of participants in this scheme had a socio-medical condition and their background was in most cases a long-lasting addiction to alcohol and/or drugs, 23% had a mental or an intellectual disability.[897]

Lastly, the *"positions with high employment security"*-scheme was established in 2006 in order to allow for a sheltered employment alternative with private employers. Employers of participants in this scheme are entitled to wage subventions under the ordinary wage subvention scheme as well as up to approximately 20 euro per day of employment to cover costs associated with accommodation for the

---

892 Samhall 2009, p. 4.

893 Samhall Articles of Association, Samhalls Bolagsordning, Section 3.

894 Samhall, Annual Report 2007, p. 15.

895 Samhall, Annual Report 2007, p. 16.

896 Swedish Act on Special Measures, Section 35. Swedish Commission Report "Labour Force", SOU 2003:95, (ArbetsKraft), p. 82. Act on Social Services, SFS 2001:453 with latest amendment SFS 2010:741, (Socialtjänstlag), Section 7. Swedish Act on Support and Service to certain Persons with Disabilities, (Lag om stöd och service till vissa funktionshindrade), SFS 1993:387 with latest amendment by SFS 2010:480, Section 15(4).

897 Arbetsmarknadspolitiska program, Årsrapport 2006, p. 168.

employee's reduced working capacity.[898] Employment in a 'position with high employment security' is not intended to be short term and is without a time limitation. As may be seen in *Table 5. Sheltered Employment* below, approximately 5,000 persons were employed in a position with high employment security in 2008.

Table 5. Sheltered Employment (2008)

Schemes	Number of participants	As % of persons of working age with disability and reduced working capacity	% of participants with mental and intellectual disabilities	Annual rate of transfer to other employment (both supported and non-supported)
Sheltered workshops (DK)[899]	8,000	2.1%	82%	0.5%
Sheltered employment with ordinary employers (DK)[900]	5,200	1.4%	Information not available	Information not available
Samhall (SE)	19,500	3.6%	Information not available	4.9%
Public protected employment (SE)[901]	6,300	1.2%	22% (sociomedical: 57%)	2% (to non-supported employment)
Positions with high employment protection (SE)[902]	5,000	0.9%	42% (sociomedical: 7%)	12% (to non-supported employment)

In the Sub-Sections below, the differences between the Danish and Swedish schemes are analysed from a human rights' perspective. As described under *Section 2 Contemporary Disability Human Rights Approach* above, law and policy in accordance with the contemporary disability human rights approach must ensure that sheltered employment is (1) reserved to those to persons excluded from the open labour market, (2) available to those who need it, (3) promotes transition to open labour market and (4) that usual benefits of labour law are available.

898 Act on Special Measures on 'positions with high employment security' (trygghetsanställning), Sections 37 and 37a. Wage subvention under this scheme may not be combined with support for personal assistance.

899 Bengtsson and Mateu 2009.

900 Statistics Denmark, Statistikbanken, Arbejdsmarkedet, Tabel AUH01 Personer Uden Ordinær Beskæftigelse.

901 Arbetsförmedlingen 2009.

902 Arbetsförmedlingen 2009.

5.2. Reserved to Persons Excluded from the Open Labour Market

According to the contemporary disability human rights approach, sheltered employment must be limited to persons who are excluded from employment on the open labour market, including supported employment.

In Denmark, sheltered employment is reserved to persons who receive a disability pension and disability pension can only be awarded to a person whose working capacity is reduced to such an extent that the applicant cannot become self-supporting through work on the ordinary labour market, including supported employment.[903] However, as explained in *Chapter VII Income-Replacement Benefits*, a disability pension may well have been awarded on the basis of a relatively superficial assessment especially when it was awarded before 2003 or when it was awarded with reference to an intellectual disability from birth.[904] Moreover, the working capacity of disability pensioners is not reassessed regularly by the authorities.[905] This means that additional assessments of a person's working capacity could be necessary before approval is given for sheltered employment.

According to the Act on an Active Employment Effort, it is an explicit requirement that "sheltered employment with ordinary employers" only be granted to persons who are not capable of keeping or obtaining employment with reduced working hours on ordinary conditions on the labour market. Also, according to the Act on Social Service, it is an explicit requirement that sheltered employment in workshops only be granted to persons *"who are not capable of keeping or obtaining employment with reduced working hours on ordinary conditions on the labour market, or who are unable to make use of schemes under other laws."* However the decision to allow a person to take part in sheltered employment in workshops is taken by the social authorities and not by the job centres.[906] Moreover it is not a requirement that a new formalised assessment of the applicant's work capacity in the form of a 'job plan' be performed in relation with an application to take part in any form of sheltered employment.[907]

In Sweden, as opposed to in Denmark, the decision to enrol a person in sheltered employment with Samhall or *"positions with high employment security"* or *"public*

---

903 Danish Act on Social Pension, Section 16(2).

904 Danish Administrative Guidelines on early retirement no. 105 of 23 october 2002, pkt. 12 according to which it is not necessary to perform an assessment of a person's working capacity after the 'working capacity method' when he or she has a mental disability from birth, e.g. has Down's syndrome.

905 See Chapter VII Income Replacement Benefits, Section 3 on Disability Pension.

906 Danish Act on Social Service Chapter 19.

907 Danish Act on an Active Employment Effort Chapter 9, Ministry of Social Affairs, Administrative Guidelines no. 95 of 5 December 2005, (Vejledning om botilbud m.v. til voksne), para. 224–226.

sheltered employment" is taken by the Employment Service and not by the social authorities.

As regards employment with Samhall, it is an explicit requirement under law that the applicant's *"working capacity is so reduced that he or she cannot obtain other work and whose needs cannot be met through other measures."*[908] Moreover, since 2006, employment with Samhall should be preceded by employment in a *"development position"* in order to determine whether the person in question could work in the ordinary field of employment, i.e. a job trial. Finally the job-seeker, the Employment Service and Samhall must make an agreement which includes personal goals, need for support and development and a time table for a possible transition to work outside of Samhall prior to employment.[909]

As regards employment in *"public sheltered employment"* and *"positions with high employment security"* in Sweden, it is also explicitly required under law that the applicant's working capacity must be so reduced that he or she cannot obtain other employment.[910] However, it is not a requirement that applicants for *"public sheltered employment"* or *"positions with high employment security"* that a job-trial take place. Instead, an examination of the applicant's disability and working capacity will have to be made which will not necessarily include a job-trial.[911]

In sum, it is in accordance with the contemporary disability human rights approach that both the Danish and the Swedish legislation underline that sheltered employment may only be used when employment under ordinary conditions or with support would not be possible. However, it seems that practical safeguards are not always in place to ensure that this rule is complied with. Thus, it is only prior to employment with Samhall in Sweden that a job-trial must take place. In Denmark, a job-trial may or may not have taken place when the applicant was granted a disability pension and in Sweden, job-trials are not required to take place when an examination of a person's disability and working capacity is prepared by the Swedish Employment Service. The lack of a requirement that job-trials take place may result in the placement in sheltered employment of persons who could have been capable of working in supported employment instead.

---

908 Swedish Act on Special Measures, Section 32.

909 Swedish Public Employment Service General Guidelines on the administration of Act on Special Measures, AMSFS 2001:20 Sections 25 and 26.

910 Swedish Act on Special Measures, Section 32 and 37.

911 Swedish Employment Service Administrative Regulation on the Implementation of the Act on Special Measures, Sections 3, 14 and 9 which mentions a medical examination, but not a job-trial.

5.3. Available to Those Who Need It

The question treated in this Sub-Section is whether sheltered employment is available to those who need it in order to facilitate their inclusion in the labour market. As mentioned above, approximately 3.5% of all persons with disabilities and reduced working capacity are employed in sheltered employment in Denmark while this is the case for 5.7% in Sweden. As mentioned above, the fact that the percentage of persons with disabilities and reduced working capacity in sheltered employment is 50% higher in Sweden compared to Denmark is surprising in view of the fact that in Denmark persons with disabilities and reduced working capacity of working age are half as likely to be employed as in Sweden. The lower level of employment in Denmark could indicate that there is a greater need for sheltered employment to help persons make the transition from exclusion to inclusion on the labour market in Denmark than in Sweden.

As will be discussed in the following Sub-Section, Danish sheltered employment does not effectively promote the transition of participants/employees to the open labour market. If however, the Danish sheltered employment were to become more effective in promoting transition to the open labour, then it could be recommendable to employ more persons in sheltered employment in Denmark.

5.4. Promote Transition to Open Labour Market

As explained in *Section 2 Contemporary Disability Human Rights Approach* above, it is imperative under the contemporary disability human rights approach that sheltered employment promotes the transition to the open labour market for the participants who can be made capable hereof.

In Denmark, the aim of promoting a transition to open employment only follows *indirectly* from the Act on Social Services, which states that sheltered employment is reserved for those persons who cannot make use of measures under other legal acts, and the Administrative Guidelines which recommend that participation in sheltered employment is made temporary so that the possibility of employment on the open labour market is the subject of a renewed assessment on a regular basis.[912] The lack of a clear statement that one of the main goals of segregated employment should be to assist in the transition to open employment means that it is left up to the local councils to decide whether or not to prioritise this goal. In fact, according to a recent study on sheltered employment in workshops in Denmark, only one sixth of all the local councils have established promotion of employment on the open

912 Swedish Act on Social Services, Ministry of Social Affairs, Administrative Guidelines no. 95 of 5 December 2005, para. 224, Section 103.

labour market as explicit goals for their sheltered employment schemes.[913] The surveys shows that most Danish local councils see sheltered employment in workshops as an activation measure for the benefit of the participant and do not make a link between sheltered employment and employment promotion.[914]

As regards the Danish *"sheltered employment with ordinary employers"*, the Act on Special Measures applies in contrast to the social legislation which governs employment in sheltered workshops. According to the Act on Special Measures, the goal of *"sheltered employment with ordinary employers"* is *"obtaining or retaining employment"*.[915] This goal is not forward-looking and does not include improving the person's possibilities for being employed with less support. In line herewith, the local jobcentres, which grant sheltered employment with ordinary employers, are not required to prepare a plan for promoting the individual's possibilities for employment with less support.[916] Finally, this type of wage subvention may be given for an unlimited period of time which also signals that improved employment possibilities are not an expected outcome of this type of special measure.[917] Rates of transition from sheltered employment to other types of employment are not collected systematically by the Danish authorities.

In Sweden, it follows directly from the Act on Special Measures that both employment in Samhall, *"public sheltered employment"* and *"positions with high employment security"* must aim at *"strengthening the possibilities that [persons with disabilities] may obtain or keep employment"* as all other measures listed in the Act on Special Measures.[918] Moreover it is specifically underlined that *"the Employment Service shall promote the transition from segregated employment to employment in the ordinary labour market"* when persons are employed with Samhall, in public sheltered employment' or in "positions with high employment security".[919] In line with the fact that it is clearly established that sheltered employment should aim at promoting employment without support, the authorities systematically measure the rate of participants who make the transition from sheltered employment to employment on ordinary conditions or with less support. As may be seen from *Table 5. Sheltered Employment* above, the rate of transfer from sheltered to less supported employment is significantly higher in Sweden than in Denmark. In Sweden, the rate of transfer was almost 5% for persons employed in Samhall, 2% for persons in 'public sheltered employment' and 12% for persons in

913 Bengtsson and Mateu 2009, p. 95.
914 Bengtsson and Mateu 2009, p. 95.
915 Danish Act on an Active Employment Effort, Section 52.
916 Danish Act on an Active Employment Effort, Section 27. A plan for employment under ordinary working conditions is for example required before granting wage subvention (fleksjob).
917 Danish Act on an Active Employment Effort, Section 53(2).
918 Danish Act on Special Measures, Section 4.
919 Danish Act on Special Measures, Sections 32 and 37a.

"positions with high employment security" in 2008. In Denmark, the transition rate is not measured systematically, but a recent survey of sheltered employment in workshops showed that the transition rate was approximately 0.5% in 2008.[920]

In sum, Danish sheltered employment is not line with the contemporary disability human rights approach in that it has not been established that it should aim at enabling participants/employees to become employed with less support. In contrast, Swedish law clearly provides that sheltered employment must aim at employment with less support. The actual transition rates also show a marked difference between Danish and Swedish policy in this regard. Thus, transitions in Denmark seem to be practically non-existent while they are substantial in Sweden.

5.5. Usual Benefits of Labour Law

According to the third requirement relating to sheltered employment of the European Committee on Social Rights, persons working in sheltered employment facilities must enjoy the usual benefits of labour law, such as protection against dismissal and anti-discrimination, wages in accordance with collective agreements etc, at least when production is the main activity, cf. *Section 2 Contemporary Disability Human Rights Approach* above. Moreover, trade unions should be active in enforcing the labour rights of persons in sheltered employment. Initially, I will examine the two forms of sheltered employment in Denmark (sheltered workshops and sheltered employment with ordinary employers) and subsequently, the three Swedish forms of sheltered employment will be studied.

In Denmark, persons who take part in activities in sheltered workshops are not considered to be employees under Danish Employment law. Their placement in a sheltered workshop is considered to be a social measure rather than an employment. Persons in sheltered employment are therefore not covered by protection against unjust dismissals,[921] they do not have a right to a certificate of employment,[922] to

920 Bengtsson and Mateu 2009.

921 Danish Act on White Collar Employees, LBK no. 81 of 3 February 2009 without amendments (Lov om retsforholdet mellem arbejdsgivere og funktionærer); Danish Sailors' Act, LBK no. 766 of 19 September 1995 with latest amendment by Lov no. 493 of 12 May 2010 (Sømandsloven); Danish Act on Public Servants, LBK 488 of 6 May 2010 without amendments (Tjenestemandsloven), cf. Chapter V on Employers' Obligations.

922 Danish Eastern High Court Judgment UFR 2005.1429/2Ø and Danish Western High Court Judgment of 23 September 2009, 7. Section, No: B-0796–08 quoted in *Chapter IV Equality Law and Policy* which concludes that persons in sheltered workshops are not encompassed by legislation on sickness benefits, employment contracts and the Act on Differential Treatment on the Labour Market.

sickness benefits,[923] to pay during vacations.[924] In addition, persons in sheltered workshops are not covered by the Danish Act on Differential Treatment on the labour market.[925] However, legislation on safety and health does apply at least to some extent.[926]

The perception of sheltered workshops as a social measure was also the reason why the Danish Eastern High Court rejected that persons in sheltered workshops could be covered by the legislation on employment certificates.[927] The case concerned a workshop which produced machines for the dispensing of draught beer. The Court stated that:

> *"The offered employment was not oriented towards support for future employment possibilities, but had the character of a socio-pedagogical offer. The salary which is paid aside from social benefits has the size of pocket money. The authority normally vested in an employer is not present as 'A' cannot be dismissed if he does not show up in the morning. The production which is made is purchased by a regular buyer, but there is no agreement on the amount to be produced. The production results in an economic deficit which supports the view that the employment has another aim than being business oriented. In addition, the Court has been informed that the employment is not encompassed by the Act on Vacation Pay. On these grounds, and in spite of the fact that income tax is paid on the 'work reward', the High Court finds that there is no employment relationship. The institution therefore was not obliged to issue a certificate of employment."*[928]

Also in relation to pay, the participants in sheltered workshops do not enjoy the usual benefits of labour law as they merely receive a symbolic 'work reward' in addition to their disability pension instead of receiving pay in accordance with the

923 Danish Western High Court Judgment of 23 September 2009, 7. Section, No: B-0796–08. Also, the Employment Service has informed the Equal Opportunities Centre for Disabled People that it does not consider persons in sheltered employment to be encompassed by the legislation on sickness benefits since they do not consider them to be in an ordinary employment relationship under employment law, cf. Center for Ligebehandling af Handicappede 2008, p. 26.

924 The Danish Labour Market Appeals Board upheld a decision by the Employment Service that participants in sheltered employment were not encompassed by the Act on Vacation pay "since the work does not constitute regular salaried work with employment with ordinary conditions of pay", cf. Center for Ligebehandling af Handicappede 2008, p. 25.

925 Danish Western High Court Judgment of 23 September 2009, 7. Section, No: B-0796–08 quoted in *Chapter IV Equality Law and Policy.*

926 Danish Act on Health and Safety, LBK no. 268 of 18 March 2005 with latest amendment by Lov no. 559 of 17 June 2008, (Lov om Arbejdsmiljø), Section 2, and Administrative Guidelines of the Health and Safety Authority on Safety organisation for employees on special conditions of March 2006 (AT-vejledning om sikkerhedsorganisation for ansatte på særlige vilkår i beskyttede værksteder mm, øvrige områder F.2.2.).

927 Danish Eastern High Court Judgment UFR 2005.1429/2Ø.

928 Ibid. and Danish Western High Court Judgment of 23 September 2009, 7. Section, No: B-0796–08.

level of pay on the ordinary labour market. According to an executive order issued by the Ministry of Welfare:

> *"persons who are in employment shall to widest extent possible be paid in accordance with their effort... Where a person has a severe disability which means that he or she can only make a working contribution which gives a very limited income, a work reward amounting to a minimum of 5% of the lowest pay according to the collective agreement on the area shall be paid"*.[929]

As illustrated by the Eastern High Court judgment referred to above, the payment has the size of pocket money and the lack of substantial pay is one of the reasons that sheltered employees are not considered to be 'employees' under general labour law.[930]

In relation to the second type of sheltered employment in Denmark, namely *"sheltered employment with ordinary employers"*, the situation is different although they also only receive symbolic pay because they keep their disability pension. The main reasons for the differentiation between persons in sheltered workshops and persons in *"sheltered employment with ordinary employers"* are firstly that persons in *"sheltered employment with ordinary employers"* are not segregated in separate workshops for persons with reduced working capacity, but work in ordinary workplaces. Secondly, *"sheltered employment with ordinary employers"* is considered an employment promotional measure rather than a social measure. Lastly, *"sheltered employment with ordinary employers"* is governed by the Act on an Active Employment Effort under the Ministry of Employment whereas *"sheltered workshops"* are governed by the Act on Social Service under the Ministry of Welfare.

Consequently, Persons in "*sheltered employment with ordinary employers"* are not exempted from Danish legislation on employment protection,[931] they do have a right to a certificate of employment,[932] to sickness benefits, to pay during vacations.[933] In addition, persons in *"sheltered employment with ordinary employers"* are covered by the Danish Act on Differential Treatment on the labour market as well as the Act on Work Environment.[934] The salary and other working

---

929 Danish Ministry of Welfare, Executive Order no. 628 of 15 June 2006, Section 1(1) and (2)(3).

930 Danish Eastern High Court Judgment UFR 2005.1429/2Ø.

931 Danish Act on White Collar Employees; Danish Sailors' Act; Danish Act on Public Servants, cf. Chapter V on Employers' Obligations.

932 Danish Act on the employer's duty to inform the employee about the conditions applicable to the employment, LBK no. 240 of 17 March 2010 without amendments, (Lov om ansættelsesbeviser).

933 Danish Ministry of Employment, Administrative Regulation on an active employment effort, BEK no. 865 of 1 July 2010, (bekendtgørelse om en aktiv beskæftigelsesindsats), Section 58.

934 Danish Western High Court Judgment of 23 September 2009, 7. Section, No: B-0796–08 quoted in *Chapter IV Equality Law and Policy.* Section 2 of Act on Work Environment, LBK no. 268 of

conditions must be agreed between the employer and the employee in cooperation with the social partners.[935] However, as mentioned above, since persons in *"sheltered employment with ordinary employers"* receive a disability pension, the level of pay will be significantly lower than for persons in supported employment who receive wage subvention (*fleksjob*).[936] As will be seen below, the Swedish law and policy entails that persons in sheltered employment receive pay in accordance with applicable collective agreements possibly combined with a partial disability pension if they do not work full-time. Salary constitutes an important benefit associated with working and the fact that a person only receives a symbolic salary signals that the work only has symbolic value as opposed to the work of others whose work is highly valued. In sum, based on the contemporary disability approach, Denmark should enable persons in sheltered employment to receive salaries at a level in accordance with the level agreed in collective agreements at least for persons in *"sheltered employment with ordinary employers"*.

In Sweden, both employees of Samhall and persons in Swedish *"public sheltered employment"* are exempted from ordinary protection against dismissal in the Act on Employment Protection similarly to persons working in sheltered workshops in Denmark.[937] However, as opposed to Denmark, the Swedish Labour Court has established that similar principles as those contained in the Employment Act do apply to persons employed in Samhall.[938] In addition, many persons employed in Samhall and *"public sheltered employment"* are covered by collective agreements. Employees in Samhall and *"public sheltered employment"* are encompassed by legislation on sickness benefits and health and safety as well as the Swedish Discrimination Act. As opposed to persons working in Danish sheltered workshops, employees of Samhall do not receive a disability pension, but salary for their work in Samhall.

Both in Denmark and in Sweden, the allocation of support to the workshops/ Samhall is not given as individual wage subvention, but rather as a lump sum covering all participants/employees at once.[939] This constitutes a differentiation between persons employed in sheltered employment and in supported employment which may make the transition to supported employment more difficult. The Report by a Government Commission on Samhall of 2003 pointed out that a person who has been awarded an individual wage subsidy may find it easier to obtain a new job

---

18 March 2005 with latest amendment by Lov no. 559 of 17 June 2008, (Lov om Arbejdsmiljø).

935 Danish Act on an Active Employment Effort, Section 58.

936 Danish Act on an Active Employment Effort, Section 64.

937 Swedish Act on Special Measures Section 32.

938 Swedish Labour Court judgment, AD 2005 no. 43, P-A. W. i Bollstabruk v. Samhall Midland AB, p. 22. The Court *inter alia* applied Section 7(4) of the Employment Protection Act which requires that a dismissal may not be based on occurrences dating further back than two months.

939 Samhall, Annual Report 2007, p. 8.

knowing that he or she is entitled to a wage subsidy. Also it would underline that the Employment Service was responsible for promoting integration into the field of ordinary field of employment of these persons also.[940] Moreover, it would also unify the system of promotion of employment in the ordinary field of employment.

Lastly, as regards persons employed in the two other types of sheltered employment in Sweden, namely *"positions with high employment security"* and *"sheltered public employment"*, the situation is similar to that of employees in Samhall except that persons employed in *"positions with high employment security"* are covered by the Swedish Act on Employment Protection. Another difference consists in the fact that persons employed in *"positions with high employment security"* and *"sheltered public employment"* are awarded wage subvention by the Employment Service on an individual basis which should make it easier for them to move on to supported employment.

In sum, it is problematic in relation to the contemporary disability human rights approach that especially persons in Danish sheltered workshops do not enjoy usual benefits of labour law since they are not considered to be employees under Danish law. Moreover, both persons in sheltered workshops and in *"sheltered employment with ordinary employers"* in Denmark do not enjoy the usual benefits since they do not receive a salary in accordance with usual benefits of labour law because they receive a disability pension. In Sweden, persons in sheltered employment do enjoy usual benefits of labour law. Although persons employed with Samhall and in *"public sheltered employment"* in Sweden are not covered by the Employment Protection Act, they are ensured protection against unfair dismissal under general contractual principles.

5.6. Conclusion

In sum, the situation for persons in sheltered workshops in Denmark is not in accordance with the contemporary disability human rights approach. Employment in sheltered workshops is considered a social measure rather than an employment promotional measure. Consequently it is not a clear aim to promote transition to the open labour market and employment legislation, with the exception of health and safety regulations, does not apply. In Sweden, however, sheltered employment with Samhall has a clear goal to promote transition to the open labour market and ordinary employment protection applies either directly or based on analogical interpretation in case law.

940 Swedish Commission Report "Not Just Samhall", SOU 2003:56 (Inta Bara Samhall), pp.78 and 111.

Finally, as regards both Danish *"sheltered workshops"* and *"sheltered employment with ordinary employers"*, the participants receive a disability pension and only a symbolic salary for their work. As illustrated with the Swedish system where all employees receive pay according collective agreements instead of a full disability pension, this differentiation between persons in sheltered employment and others on the labour market is unnecessary and should be abolished.

6. EU Law and Policy

As explained in *Chapter III EU Law and Policy, Section 6 Employment Promotion*, although the EU places great importance on the creation of jobs, no primary or secondary legislation has been adopted with a view to harmonising national employment promotion services. However, EU law and policy seeks to promote active labour market policies, 'making work pay' (meaning that there must be economic incentives for starting to work) and contracting out employment services (meaning that employment services should be contracted out to private service providers) which may be of relevance for national employment promotional laws and policies.[941] In addition, EU law on State aid sets limitations on subventions to companies which entail limitations on the use of wage subvention for employees with reduced working capacity which will be discussed further below.

In relation to the active labour market policies, both Denmark and Sweden have taken steps in the direction of more active labour market policies, 'making work pay' as well as privatisation of employment promotional services, cf. *Section 3 Introduction to Danish and Swedish Employment Promotion* above. There is a risk that persons with disabilities who are more likely to be dependent on social benefits and may have more difficulties in obtaining employment may be disadvantaged disproportionately by these policies. However, as mentioned above, it goes beyond the scope of the present research to study whether or not these developments in the general promotional services are an advantage or a disadvantage to unemployed persons with disabilities in Denmark and Sweden.

Secondly, in relation to State aid, Article 107 TFEU sets limitations to the amount of subsidies, such as wage subvention, which may be paid to individual undertakings. However, the Commission's General Block Exemption Regulation describes certain types of State aid, which may be granted without prior notification to the Commission.[942] The General Block Exemption Regulation for example provides in

941 Freedland, Craig, Jacqueson and Koutouris 2007, p. 360.

942 Commission Regulation (EC) No. 800/2008 of 6 August 2008 declaring certain categories of aid compatible with the common market in application of Article 87 and 88 of the Treaty, OJ [2008] L 214/3. See also European Commission Vadecuum on Community Law on State Aid of 30 September 2008, Factsheet No. 7 Employment Aid.

Article 41 that 'aid for the employment of disabled workers in the form of wage subsidies' shall be permitted provided that *"the aid intensity shall not exceed 75% of the eligible costs"* understood as *"wage costs over any given period during which the disabled worker is employed"*.[943] Aid for compensating the additional costs of employing disabled workers shall not exceed 100% of the eligible costs.[944] In relation to sheltered employment, the additional costs include for example, *"the costs of constructing, installing or expanding the establishment concerned, and any costs of administration and transport which result directly from the employment of disabled workers."*[945] Sheltered employment is defined in the Regulation as *"employment in an undertaking where at least 50% of workers are disabled."*[946]

In relation to supported employment, it seems that both Denmark and Sweden do not exceed the limit of 75% of wage costs. In Denmark, a subvention can cover a maximum of 66% of the wages an individual receives in supported employment (*fleksjob*) while Sweden has no percentual limitation, but has a cap of approximately 20,000 euro per year on eligible wage costs which may be subsidised. The average salary in Sweden is approximately 40,000 euro per year, so it is highly unlikely that an employer will receive a wage subvention amounting to more than 75% of actual costs unless the person in question receives a low salary.

The situation is a little different in relation to sheltered employment. In Denmark, the main income of persons in sheltered employment is a disability pension, which could be seen as a form of subvention to the employer. And especially as regards sheltered workshops where the activities of the workshop are not income-generating then practically all costs will have to be covered through public subventions. According to a recent study on employment in sheltered workshops, approximately 45% of workshops stated that income-generation through for example production had no or little importance with respect to their economic foundations. Also in Sweden, the annual report of Samhall showed that public wage subventions amounted to 76% of its costs related to personnel amounted in both 2008 and 2009. This ratio will be even higher if only costs related to personnel in sheltered employment with Samhall is taken into account as opposed to all personnel including the management. In sum, it seems that the levels of wage subvention in sheltered employment in both Denmark and Sweden may be too high to comply with the European rules on State aid.

Whether it is recommendable to allow higher levels of subvention from the perspective of the contemporary disability human rights approach is debatable. The present Block Exemption Directive adopted in August 2008 did in fact raise the

943 Ibid. Article 2(20) and (21).
944 Ibid. Article 42.
945 Ibid. Article 42(3)(d).
946 Ibid. Article 2(21).

permitted levels of subvention compared to the previous Block Exemption, which only permitted wage subvention to amount to 60% of total wages, but provided no explicit limit for subventions to cover other costs.[947]

On the one hand high levels of wage subvention would allow employers to hire employees with little capacity for value-generation through their work which would promote inclusion of the weakest into the labour market. On the other hand, too high levels of wage subvention may deter employers from effectively promoting the transition of employees from sheltered employment into employment on the ordinary labour market.

Thus, as long as the aim of transition to supported employment is strongly enforced, then it would seem to be an advantage under the contemporary disability human rights approach to allow wage subvention-personnel cost ratios to be higher than 75%.

In conclusion, no EU laws have been adopted with a view to harmonising State employment promotion of persons with disabilities. Nevertheless, EU policy clearly promotes active labour market policies which have also been a trend in Danish and Swedish policies. As indicated at the outset of this Chapter, it goes beyond the scope of the present thesis to examine whether this development in general employment promotion has had problematic consequences for persons with disabilities. The EU has adopted limitations on the use of State Aid which are also of relevance to national employment promotion. Interestingly, both Denmark and Sweden seem to be in violation of EU law as the levels of subvention for persons in sheltered employment seem to exceed the EU limit of 75% of eligible costs. It is recommended that the EU Block Exemption Regulation be altered once again as high ratios of wage subvention may be necessary to ensure that persons with very low working capacity may take part in sheltered employment.

7. Conclusion

In conclusion, the contemporary disability human rights approach requires that supported and sheltered employment are (1) available, (2) reserved to those who need support, (3) promote employment on the ordinary labour market and (4) take place under working conditions which are similar to those on the ordinary labour market. Both Danish and Swedish supported and sheltered employment schemes are to a large extent in accordance with the contemporary disability approach. The

947 Articles 5 and 6 of Commission Regulation No. 2204/2002 of 12 December 2002 on the application of Articles 87 and 88 of the EC Treaty to State aid for employment, OJ [2002] L 337 which was replaced by Commission Regulation (EC) No. 800/2008 of 6 August 2008 mentioned above.

exceptions will be mentioned below. Most interestingly, the present Chapter shows that even generous and widely available supported employment schemes cannot replace the creation of general structures on the labour market which are inclusive to persons with disabilities. Strong focus on employment promotion for the unemployed is a cornerstone of the Danish flexicurity model and the flexicurity model promoted by the EU. Although it is important to provide employment promotion, these measures cannot in themselves ensure the realisation of substantive diversity equality for persons with disabilities on the labour market.

In relation to *supported employment*, the present chapter shows that a significantly greater share of employed persons with disabilities and reduced working capacity are in supported employment in Denmark than in Sweden. Thus, while only a minority of employed persons with disabilities and reduced working capacity are in supported employment in Sweden, this is true for a majority of 60% of persons with disabilities and reduced working capacity in Denmark.

Moreover, in spite of a sharp rise in the use of supported employment in Denmark, the rate of employment of persons with disabilities and reduced working capacity has not improved from 2002 to 2008. This indicates that a vicious circle may be reinforcing the use of supported employment without leading to higher employment of persons with disabilities. Higher use of supported employment may lead employers to require wage subvention for more and more employees with less and less reduced working capacity which once again leads employers to require wage subvention for more and more employees etc. It seems that Swedish authorities have better succeeded in avoiding such a negative spiral *inter alia* by prohibiting the use of wage subvention for existing employees unless special circumstances are present.

Danish supported employment schemes need to be reformed, but this can only be done as part of a greater reform of the duties of employers towards employees with disabilities. A mere reduction of the supported employment schemes could lead to further exclusion of persons with disabilities from the labour market without changing the attitudes of employers towards employees with disabilities.

In relation to sheltered employment, the main differences between Denmark and Sweden are firstly that sheltered employment is less used in Denmark where approximately 3.5% of persons with a disability and reduced working capacity are in sheltered employment compared to 5.6% in Sweden. Secondly, sheltered employment is in Denmark largely seen as a social therapeutic measure for persons without aiming at inclusion in the labour market whereas Swedish sheltered employment aims at improving the employability of participants/employees. This perception of sheltered employment is reflected in significantly lower rates of transition to ordinary employment in Denmark and lack of enjoyment of the usual benefits of labour law.

In other words, a reform of the Danish sheltered employment scheme is also needed for full compliance with the contemporary disability human rights approach. However, once again, a reform cannot stand alone and would have to be coupled with a reform of disability pension schemes to ease the transition from disability pension to employment.

In relation to the rights-based approach, it is problematic that complaints over decisions by the Swedish Public Employment Service cannot be treated by an independent administrative body. Moreover, the fact that local councils administer the rules on supported and sheltered employment in Denmark lead to significant differences in their administration which is also problematic in relation to the rights-based approach.

On a more positive note, social partners are included by both Danish and Swedish authorities and disability organisations have also been awarded a formal consultative role in Denmark in Employment Councils. This inclusion of persons with disabilities in the development of policies and implementation of employment promotional measures in especially Denmark is positive from the perspective of the contemporary disability human rights approach.

Chapter VII Income-Replacement Benefits will examine the related question of social benefits for persons with disabilities outside the labour market, which may or may not influence the participation of persons with disabilities on the labour market.

Chapter VII
Income Replacement Benefits

1. Introduction

The focus of this Chapter is on income-replacement benefits which are paid to persons unable to support themselves due to reduced working capacity. The Chapter focuses on four different types of income-replacement benefits: firstly, disability pension, which is a long-term benefit for persons who have a long-term reduced working capacity, secondly, sickness benefits, which are short-term benefits for persons with reduced working capacity, thirdly, rehabilitation benefits, which are benefit paid to persons who undergo employment-oriented rehabilitation and fourthly, benefits for persons who have incurred a reduced working capacity due to a work injury.

The present Chapter aims at examining how income-replacement benefits linked to reduced working capacity should be shaped to be in accordance with the contemporary disability human rights approach and to determine whether law and policy in Denmark and Sweden are in accordance herewith. Moreover, Danish and Swedish law and policy are examined in relation to EU policy and legislation.

The policies and laws governing these benefits are of great importance to the analysis of disability policies in the field of employment. These benefits are given to persons who are outside the labour market due to a reduced working capacity and the benefits may determine whether or not they return to the labour market. As will be discussed in detail below, from the perspective of the contemporary disability human rights approach, income-replacement benefits must strike a balance between providing support for returning to the labour market on the one hand and ensuring an adequate standard of living to all persons who cannot support themselves on the other hand.

It should be noted that the present Chapter will not examine the prerequisite conditions for qualifying for income-replacement benefits in Denmark and Sweden, such as years of residence and annual income of a certain size in the two countries in question. Only the disability-specific conditions for entitlement to the different benefits are examined.

The remainder of this Chapter falls into 8 Sections: Section 2 seeks to define income-replacement benefits in accordance with the contemporary disability human rights approach, Sections 3 to 6 deal with the specific benefits and Section 7 analyses the benefits in relation to EU law and policy. A conclusion is provided in Section 8.

2. Contemporary Disability Human Rights Approach

The purpose of the present section is to define how income-replacement benefits linked to reduced working capacity should be shaped to be in accordance with the contemporary disability human rights approach. Initially, I will discuss how the shift from the medical model of disability and formal equality model to the social model of disability and the substantive equality model have influenced how income-replacement benefits should be designed. Subsequently, I will analyse in more detail the provisions on income-replacement benefits to persons with disabilities in human rights instruments.

As discussed previously in *Chapter II Human Rights*, it is relatively recent that the universality model of disability, which is a social model of disability, and the substantive diversity equality model were recognised as the foundation for the human rights approach to disability. Previously, the medical model of disability and formal equality laid the foundation for the human rights approach to disability. According to the medical model of disability, the impairment itself led to disability and exclusion from the labour market and social life. Consequently, human rights instruments based on the medical model of disability provide that Member States shall seek to cure impairments through rehabilitation and that persons with disabilities unable to take part in the labour market should have access to income-replacement benefits to ensure an adequate standard of living.[948] In other words, the main focus of these older human rights instruments is to ensure that persons with disabilities can sustain an adequate standard of living either with the support of income-replacement benefits or by becoming less disabled.

As will be seen from the provisions in newer human rights instruments below, the shift from the medical model of disability and formal equality to the social model of disability and substantive equality mean that income-replacement benefits play a less central role in contemporary disability human rights approach, but their role is nevertheless an important one. Whereas the provision of income-replacement benefits was a goal in itself under the medical model of disability, the goal under the contemporary disability human rights approach is to create a society with inclusive structures where the need of persons with disabilities for income-replacement benefits will be as small as possible. Thus, under the contemporary disability human

[948] European Social Charter of 1961 Article 15 on the right of physically or mentally disabled persons to vocational training, rehabilitation and social resettlement compared to the Revised European Social Charter of 1996 on the right of persons with disabilities to independence, social integration and participation in life of the community.

rights approach, the income-replacement benefit schemes must support inclusion which is the central goal.

In *Chapter II Human Rights*, it was concluded that the contemporary disability human rights approach is based not only on the universality model of disability and the substantive diversity equality model, but also on the principles of participation of civil society in the conduct of State functions and the rights-based approach. This means firstly that disabled persons' organisations may be involved for example in the preparation of legislation governing income-replacement benefits as well as being represented in bodies which consider complaints about administrative decisions regarding applications for income-replacement benefits. Secondly, access to income-replacement benefits should be provided through individual and enforceable rights. I will discuss compliance with these last two principles in the Sections of this Chapter on specific types of income-replacement benefits.

In the following two Sub-Sections, the main provisions on income-replacement benefits for persons with disabilities in human rights instruments are analysed. In Sub-Section 2.1 the provisions in disability-specific instruments and provisions such as the CRPD and the Revised European Social Charter Article 15 are examined. In Sub-Section 2.2, general provisions on income-replacement benefits are analysed. In Sub-Section 2.3, the right to persons with disabilities to work injury compensation under the contemporary disability human rights approach is examined. A conclusion is provided in Sub-Section 2.4.

2.1. Disability-Specific Provisions

The main disability-specific instruments and provisions are the CRPD, ILO Convention No. 159 on Rehabilitation and Employment and the Revised European Social Charter of 1996 Article 15. In the present Sub-Section, it will be examined how income-replacement benefits for persons with disabilities should be designed according to these instruments and the contemporary disability human rights approach.

According to Article 3 of the CRPD, the CRPD is based *inter alia* on the principle of full and effective inclusion and participation in society and all the provisions of the convention must be read in the light of this principle. Thus, in spite of the fact that Article 28 on *"Adequate Standard of Living and Social Protection"* does not mention inclusion specifically, it follows that measures enacted to ensure that persons with disabilities have an adequate standard of living and access to social protection must promote full and effective inclusion and participation for persons with disabilities. Article 28(1) and (2) have the following wording:

"States Parties recognize the right of persons with disabilities to an adequate standard of living for themselves and their families, including adequate food, clothing and housing, and to the continuous improvement of living conditions, and shall take appropriate steps to safeguard and promote the realization of this right without discrimination on the basis of disability.
States Parties recognize the right of persons with disabilities to social protection and to the enjoyment of that right without discrimination on the basis of disability, and shall take appropriate steps to safeguard and promote the realization of this right, including measures."

The Preparatory Works of this Article show that it was suggested that the Article be split into two articles on *"social security"* and *"an adequate standard living"* respectively because an adequate standard of living should be seen as one aspect of inclusion in society which should not necessarily be achieved through the provision of social security, but rather through the removal of barriers to active participation on the labour market. Canada thus stated the following:

"we believe that by including them as 2 paragraphs in the same article, we may perpetuate a negative assumption about persons with disabilities. [...] We believe that our suggestion is consistent with the approach of seeking to create conditions of equal participation and full inclusion by persons with disabilities in all aspects of life through barrier removal and prevention."[949]

In other words, the Canadian representatives wished to underline that inclusion and participation would not mainly be achieved through the provision of social security benefits. However, in spite of the fact that the Article was not split up, it is clear from the context of Article 28 in the CRPD, which aims at the creation of an inclusive society, that an adequate standard of living and social protection should be provided with this goal in mind. Thus, persons with disabilities who receive income-replacement benefits should also receive support for becoming self-supporting for example through continued access to rehabilitation.[950] Article 26 on Habilitation and Rehabilitation is closely related with Article 28 on Social Protection and reads:

"States Parties shall take effective and appropriate measures [...] to enable persons with disabilities to attain and maintain maximum independence, full physical, mental, social and vocational ability, and full inclusion and participation in all aspects of life. To that end, States Parties shall organize, strengthen and extend comprehensive habilitation and rehabilitation services and programmes [...] in such

949 Canadian electronic submission on Draft Article 28 on Social Security and an Adequate Standard of Living made during Sixth Session of Ad-Hoc Committee on a Comprehensive and Integral International Convention on Protection and Promotion of the Rights and Dignity of Persons with Disabilities, August 2005.

950 CRPD Articles 26 on Habilitation and Rehabilitation.

a way that these services and programmes [...] Support participation and inclusion in the community and all aspects of society[...]."

Moreover, the provision in Article 28(2)(b) of the CRPD underlines the right of persons with disabilities to equal access to social protection. Thus, States Parties must ensure that the conditions for entitlement of income-replacement benefits do not place persons with disabilities at a disadvantage in comparison to other applicants and that necessary adjustments are made for the needs of persons with disabilities for example when recipients are activated in job-training.

In sum, the CRPD provides firstly that inclusion and participation are the overall aims of the convention, which must be achieved through the creation of inclusive general structures. Secondly, social protection, rehabilitation services and income-replacement benefits must be provided in such a way that they promote inclusion in society. And thirdly, persons with disabilities have a right to an adequate standard of living and equal access to social protection.

Similarly to the CRPD, the Revised European Social Charter of 1996 Article 15, is based on a social model of disability and substantive equality as opposed to being based on a medical model of disability. Thus, the European Committee on Social Rights has underlined that Article 15 on persons with disabilities, *"considers that this provision reflects and advances the change in disability policy that has occurred over the last decade or more away from welfare and segregation and towards inclusion and choice."*[951] Since the provision of welfare benefits to persons with disabilities is no longer seen as a goal in itself, Article 15 of the Revised European Social Charter does not deal with the right of persons with disabilities to social security. Instead, this issue is dealt with in Article 12 of the Revised European Social Charter which is a not a disability-specific provision. I therefore examine the contents of this provision in the next Sub-Section.

ILO Convention No. 159 on Vocational Rehabilitation and Employment (Disabled Persons) of 1983 provides that persons with disabilities shall have access to vocational rehabilitation in order *"to enable a disabled person to secure, retain and advance in suitable employment"*.[952] Thus, the gist of this instrument is that States Parties should compensate the individual for his or her disability rather than altering general structures to make them more inclusive towards persons with disabilities. In other words, this instrument is based on the medical model of disability and therefore not relevant for the definition of the contemporary disability human rights approach.

---

951 European Committee on Social Rights, Conclusions 2003, Statement of Interpretation on Article 15 p. 10.

952 Article 1(2) of ILO Convention No. 159.

In the following Sub-Section, provisions on income-replacement benefits in human rights instruments, which are not disability-specific, are examined.

2.2. Non-Disability-Specific provisions

Several general human rights instruments, which are not disability-specific, provide the right to an adequate standard of living and to social security. Thus, the UN Covenant on Economic, Social and Cultural Rights of 1966, recognises *"the right of everyone to social security, including social insurance"* as well as *"the right to an adequate standard of living"*.[953] In its General Comment on Persons with Disabilities, the ICESCR Committee does not state directly that income-replacement benefits should aim at inclusion in social life, but it does state that an adequate standard of living is necessary to assist persons with disabilities *"to increase their level of independence in their daily living and to exercise their rights"*.[954]

Similarly, the Revised European Social Charter provides in Articles 12 and 13 that all workers and their dependents have the right to social security and that anyone without adequate resources has the right to social and medical assistance. Read in conjunction with Article 1 on the right to work and Article 15 on the right of persons with disabilities to independence, integration and participation in life of the community, it may be concluded that States Parties should ensure that persons with disabilities receive income-replacement benefits when they are unable to support themselves for reasons linked with their disability and that the State shall continue to promote their inclusion on the labour market while they receive income-replacement benefits.

The Revised European Social Charter Article 12 on the right of workers to social security provides that the States Parties undertake *"to maintain the social security system at a satisfactory level at least equal to that necessary for the ratification of the European Code of Social Security"*[955] In the European Social Charter of 1961, reference was made instead to ILO Convention No. 102 on Social Security (Minimum Standards) of 1952. Both the European Code of Social Security of 1964 and ILO Convention No. 102 on Social Security represent a codification of minimum standards for social security. A protocol to the European Code of Social Security adopted also in 1964 represented the *"the desirable standard"*.[956] Both Denmark and Sweden have ratified the European Code of Social Security of 1964

953 CESCR Articles 9 and 11.

954 UN Committee on Economic, Social and Cultural Rights, General Comment No. 5 on "Persons with Disabilities, paras. 28 and 33.

955 Revised European Social Charter Article 12(2).

956 Explanatory Report to the Revised European Code of Social Security of 1990, p. 10.

which entered into force in 1968 and ILO Convention No. 102 on Social Security.[957] The Protocol on *"the desirable standard"* for social security has been ratified by Sweden and only signed by Denmark.

Since 1964, both the minimum and desirable standards for social security have developed significantly. The European Council has adopted a Revised European Code of Social Security in 1990 in order to reflect developments in the field of social security in Europe. The main aims of the revision were to extend the personal scope of the Code, to improve the nature and level of benefits, to ensure greater flexibility in conditions governing entitlements and to ensure elimination of discrimination on the grounds of gender.[958] No States have yet ratified the Revised European Code of Social Security of 1990 which has therefore not entered into force.

According to the European Code of Social Security of 1964, the contingencies covered by disability pensions (invalidity benefit) shall include: *"inability to engage in any gainful activity, to an extent prescribed, which inability is likely to be permanent or persist after the exhaustion of sickness benefit."*[959] In the Revised European Code (which no States have ratified), the contingency covered was broadened to include incapacity to engage in usual activities for persons who are not economically active.[960]

Both Codes also set standards for sickness benefits and work injury benefits, but they only describe the general framework and do not describe how for example a balance shall be struck between providing income security to persons with reduced working capacity on the one hand and supporting their active participation in the labour market on the other hand. For example, the Codes do not touch upon the central question of rehabilitation of persons with disabilities.

Within the ILO and apart from ILO Convention No. 159 on Vocational Rehabilitation and Employment (Disabled Persons) of 1983 and ILO Convention No. 102 on Social Security (Minimum Standards) mentioned above, the following three conventions provide relatively detailed standards on the issues income-replacement benefits linked to disability: ILO Convention No. 121 on Employment Injury Benefits of 1964, Convention No. 128 on Invalidity, Old-Age and Survivors Benefits of 1964, Convention No. 130 on Medical Care and Sickness benefits Convention of 1969. With the exception of Conventions No. 121 and 128, which have not been ratified by Denmark, these Conventions have all been ratified by both Denmark and Sweden.

957 Sweden is bound by the Code in full, including Parts III-VII and IX as modified by the Protocol. Denmark is bound by all parts except Part X on Survivor's benefit.

958 Explanatory Report to the Revised European Code of Social Security of 1990, p. 9.

959 European Code of Social Security, 1964, European Treaties Series No. 48.

960 Article 58 of Revised European Code of Social Security, 1990, European Treaties Series No. 139.

ILO Convention 128 on Invalidity, old-age, survivors benefits of 1964 underlines that Member States shall *"provide rehabilitation services which are designed to prepare a disabled person wherever possible for the resumption of his previous activity, or, if this is not possible, the most suitable alternative gainful activity, having regard to his aptitudes and capacity; and (b) take measures to further the placement of disabled persons in suitable employment."*[961] Neither ILO Convention No. 121 on Employment Injury Benefits and ILO Convention No. 130 on sickness benefit provide a duty for the State to provide support for returning to the labour market.[962]

In sum, the non-disability specific human rights instruments provide rights to income-replacement benefits which apply both to persons with and without disabilities. These provisions deal mainly with the obligation of ensuring access to the income-replacement benefits and ensuring an adequate income. For example, the European Committee on Social Rights requires that income-replacement benefits ensure an income of a minimum of 50% of average equivalised income.

2.3. Work Injury Benefit from a Human Rights' Perspective

The following Sub-Section deals with the right of persons with disabilities to work injury benefit under the contemporary disability human rights approach. Persons with disabilities may have a certain predisposition to work injuries due to their impairment. The question is whether persons with disabilities who may have a predisposition to injury should be entitled to the same work injury compensation as a person without a predisposition to injury. The reason that a person with a predisposition to injury should not be entitled to the work injury compensation would be that the injury was not entirely work-related since it would not have occurred if the person in question was not predisposed for injury.

The CRPD does not take up the question of equal treatment of persons with disabilities in relation to work injuries. However, based on the principles of full and effective inclusion and non-discrimination, it follows that predisposition to injury should not prevent persons with disabilities from obtaining work injury compensation.[963]

The European Social Charter establishes a duty to ensure *"the effective exercise to safe and healthy working conditions"*, but it does not mention the right to

961 Article 13 of ILO Convention No. 128. Sweden has accepted all parts of Convention no. 128. Other relevant ILO Conventions include ILO Convention no. 117, Social Policy, Basic Aims and Standards of 1962 which has not been ratified by Scandinavian countries.

962 Article 12 of ILO Convention No. 121.

963 Article 3 of the CRPD on General Principles.

compensation for work injuries in this connection.[964] However, the European Code of Social Security has a separate Part on 'Employment Injury Benefit', which provides that the contingencies covered shall include inter alia loss of working capacity *"due to accident or prescribed disease resulting from employment".*[965] The requirement that the accident or disease must result from employment could mean that there must be a causal-link between the injury and the employment. However, the opposite is the case under the non-binding ILO Employment Injury Benefits Recommendation No. 121 which provides that *"Each Member should, under prescribed conditions, treat the following as industrial accidents: (a) accidents, regardless of their cause, sustained during working hours at or near the place of work or at any place where the worker would not have been except for his employment;"* This provision underlines that all accidents (but not injuries) regardless of their cause must be considered as industrial accidents which give a right to compensation as long as they were sustained at any place where the worker would not have been except for his employment. Thus, under the definition in this non-binding ILO Recommendation, persons with disabilities would have a right to compensation even if the accident is linked with a predisposition to injury.

In conclusion, the human rights standards which deal specifically with work injuries do not touch upon the question of predisposition to injury although ILO Recommendation underlines that no causal link is needed for accidents which take place while a person is carrying out work or transporting him or herself to work. However, it follows from the principles of inclusion and equal treatment underlying the CRPD, that employees with disabilities must be guaranteed same level of protection against the negative consequences of work injuries as other employees without disabilities.

2.4. Conclusion

The above analysis shows that persons with disabilities have a right to social protection in the form of income-replacement benefits and an adequate standard of living. This means both that persons with disabilities should have equal access to income-replacement benefits when they are unable to support themselves and that the level of the benefits should ensure an adequate standard of living.

Moreover the right to social security and an adequate standard of living should be administered in such a way that they promote the fundamental goal of inclusion in social life. In other words, persons with disabilities who receive income-replacement benefits should receive continuous support in the form of for example access to

964 Article 3(1) of the European Social Charter.

965 Article 32 of the European Code of Social Security of 1961 and Article 32 of ILO Convention No. 102 of 1952.

rehabilitation services in order to promote that they become self-supporting. All promotion of inclusion may not compromise the dignity of the recipients of income-replacement benefits.

Moreover, as found in *Chapter II Human Rights*, the contemporary disability human rights approach is based on the principles of participation of civil society in the conduct of State functions. Disabled persons' organisations may be involved for example in the preparation of legislation governing income-replacement benefits as well as being represented in bodies which consider complaints about administrative decisions regarding applications for income-replacement benefits.

Lastly the contemporary disability human rights approach is rights-based which means that access to income-replacement benefits should be provided in individual and enforceable rights, that information should be available on the state of law and that administrative complaints procedures should be available.

3. Disability Pension

As stated in *Chapter I Introduction*, in Denmark approximately 75% persons with disabilities and reduced working capacity of working age are outside the labour market while 50% are outside of the labour market in Sweden. This leads to the expectation that more persons receive a disability pension in Denmark as compared to Sweden. However, in 2008, 240,649 persons or 6.4% of the working age population in Denmark received a disability pension whereas 531.500 persons or around 8.6% of the working age population did so in Sweden.[966] In Denmark, partial disability pensions could only be awarded until the year 2003 and the present statistics do not specify the rate of persons who continue to receive a partial disability pension in Denmark.[967] In Sweden, approximately 25% of all disability pensions were partial pensions for persons with ¼, ½ or ¾ reduced working capacity.[968]

As explained above under *Section 2. Contemporary Disability Human Rights Approach*, disability pension schemes should firstly provide sufficient income to persons who are unable to be self-supporting due to their disability and secondly, persons with disabilities who receive a disability pension should be encouraged and supported to enter or return to the labour market where possible. Thirdly, disabled persons' organisations should be involved in the design and implementation of the disability pension system.

966 Nordic Social Statistical Committee (NOSOSKO) 2009, p. 158.

967 Ibid.

968 Statistik Försäkringskassan, sjuckersättning/aktivitetsersättning i December 2008.

In Sub-Section 3.1, I examine whether disability pensions are available to those who need them and whether the level of benefit is sufficient to uphold an adequate standard of living, in Sub-Section 3.2. I examine whether persons who receive a disability pension are supported and encouraged to enter or return to the labour market. Finally, in Sub-Section 3.3, I examine the inclusion of disabled persons' organisations in the design and administration of disability pensions.

3.1. Available to Those Who Need it and Ensures an Adequate Standard of Living

In Denmark, a disability pension is considered a permanent pension, on a par with old-age pension and accordingly, the Act on Social Pension covers both disability pensions and old-age pensions.[969] The Danish name for disability pension is *"førtidspension"* or literally *before-time-pension.* In Sweden, however, the disability pension system was separated from the old-age pension systems with a reform in 2003. In Sweden, the concept of 'pension' is no longer used. Instead, a person with reduced working capacity under 30 years of age may qualify for *"activity compensation"* (*aktivitesersättning*) and a person between 30 and 64 years of age may qualify for *"sickness compensation"* (*sjuckersättning*).[970]

3.1.1. Long-Lasting Reduced Working Capacity

In Denmark, a disability pension can only be awarded on a permanent basis and only when the working capacity is considered to be long-lasting.[971] In Sweden, it is also a requirement that the working capacity be long-lasting, i.e. the loss is assumed to last for the foreseeable future.[972] This requirement was introduced in the Swedish legislation in 2008, before which it was possible to award a time limited disability pension for persons over 30 years of age (*sickness compensation*). However, as regards the disability pension for persons under the age of 30 years (*activity compensation*) which is not a permanent benefit, it is not a requirement that the reduction in working capacity be permanent. Instead, it is sufficient that the reduction in working capacity be expected to last one year.[973]

969 Danish Act on Social Pension.

970 Chapter 33of Swedish Act on Social Insurance.

971 Section 16 (2) of Danish Act on Social Pension.

972 Section 6 of Chapter 33 of Swedish Social Insurance Act. Swedish Social Insurance Agency: Guidelines 2004:9 Version 9, 18 November 2008, p. 43.

973 Section 7 of Chapter 33 of Swedish Social Insurance Act. Swedish Social Insurance Agency: Guidelines 2004:9 Version 9, 18 November 2008, p. 43.

3.1.2. Partially Reduced Working Capacity

Since 2003, it has not been possible to qualify for a partial disability pension in Denmark. Thus, the Danish Act on Social Pension provides that *"the working capacity must be reduced to such an extent that the person in question will not be able to be self-supporting in spite of the possibilities for support under social or other legislation, including supported employment in a flexjob"*.[974] According to the Act on Active Employment Effort, wage subvention for employment in a so-called *'flexjob'* may be awarded to persons with 50% or 66% reduced working capacity.[975] In other words, a person whose working capacity is more reduced than 66% may qualify for a full disability pension in Denmark. The reference to supported employment rather than to sheltered employment in the legal text means that persons who are able to work in sheltered employment will not be disqualified from obtaining a disability pension.[976]

In Sweden, however, it is possible to be awarded four different levels of disability pensions or *"illness and activity compensations"* depending on the the applicant's remaining working capacity. *"Illness and activity compensations"* may thus be awarded for 25%, 50%, 75% and 100% reduced working capacity.[977]

In Sweden, the applicant's working capacity must be reduced in relation to the whole labour market, including employment with wage subvention. However, in Sweden as opposed to Denmark, sheltered employment is considered to be employment and thus a person who can perform sheltered employment will not qualify for full illness and activity compensations (*disability pension*).[978] This is the result of a recent amendment of the legislation which took effect on 1 July 2008. Before that date, a person's working capacity was measured in relation to 'normal work on the labour market' which did not include sheltered employment.

3.1.3. Documentation of Reduced Working Capacity

In Denmark, it must be documented through work-trials or completely evident that a person's working capacity cannot be improved through employment promotion, employment-oriented or medical rehabilitation or other measures in order to receive

---

974 Section 16(2) of Danish Act on Social Pension.

975 Section 71(2) of Danish Act on an Active Employment Effort, Act no. 483 of 12 June 2009 with latest amendment of Act no. 639 of 14 June 2010, (lov om aktiv beskæftigelsesindsats). See *Chapter VI State Measures, Section 4. Supported Employment.*

976 Section 16(2) of Danish Act on Social Pension.

977 Section 9 of Chapter 33 of Swedish Social Insurance Act. Swedish Social Insurance Agency: Guidelines 2004:9 Version 9, 18 November 2008, p. 43.

978 Swedish Social Insurance Agency: Guidelines 2004:9 Version 9, 18 November 2008, p. 43.

a disability pension.[979] An example of a case where the National Social Appeals Board has considered that it is 'completely evident' that a person has no residual working capacity and no additional exploration of a person's working capacity is necessary is a case where the applicant has Down's syndrome and constant motor unrest which lead to a need for constant assistance.[980]

In 2006 and in 2007, the National Social Appeals Board examined the administration of the disability pension legislation by analysing a total of approximately 200 sample cases from Local Councils from all regions of Denmark.[981] In 23% and 33% of the cases respectively, the National Social Appeals Board found that the Local Councils did not have sufficient grounds for awarding a disability pension. The main problem in the deficient cases was that the Local Councils had not performed relevant work-trials and did not have a sufficient focus on the possibilities for developing the working capacity of the applicant. The high rate of cases where a residual working capacity was not explored indicates that there is a discrepancy between the aim of the system, which is to only grant disability pensions to persons who have no significant working capacity and who have had this fully tested and documented, and the administration of the rules in practice.

An example of such a case where the work-trial was not sufficiently accommodated to a person's individual capacity concerned a 25-year old woman with a language learning disability due to a blood clot in the brain in early childhood. She had been enrolled in an agricultural college and a technical college, but had dropped out. She had also had five different jobs as a shop assistant, but in all five cases she had been dismissed due to suspicions of having stolen from the cash register. She said that she loved cars and would like to work in a garage and that she would also like to work in a garden centre. The Appeals Board criticised the Local Council, which had awarded her a disability pension, because the Local Council had not given her a work-trial in a garage and a garden centre where the woman could have been given manual tasks without direct responsibility for the cash register.[982]

In Sweden, there is no explicit requirement that work-trials must be carried out with a view to assessing a person's working capacity prior to awarding a disability pension. However, as regards sickness compensation (disability pension for persons over 30 years of age), the possibilities for regaining working capacity through medical or employment-oriented rehabilitation must be considered to be

979 Sections 18 and 19 of Danish Act on Social Pension.
980 National Social Appeals Board 2006 p. 28 case no. 010.
981 National Social Appeals Board 2006 and 2007.
982 National Social Appeals Board, Ankestyrelsens praksisundersøgelse, Førtidspension efter arbejdsevnemetoden, juli 2006, p. 26, case no. 003.

exhausted.[983] In order to qualify for activity compensation (disability pension for persons under the age of 30), it is sufficient that possible rehabilitation steps have either been taken or are planned to last more than one year during which the person in question may receive activity compensation.[984]

3.1.4. Level of Benefit

In addition to examining whether or not a disability pension is available to those who need it, it is also necessary to examine whether the level of the benefit is sufficient to enable persons who receive it to uphold an adequate standard of living. The following assessment only deals with public disability pensions and does not take into account that persons who receive a disability pension may also be awarded other benefits to cover for example expenses related to medical treatment. However a housing benefit, which is integrated with the Swedish disability pension, is taken into account.[985]

A comparison of the levels of benefit for a person who receives a full disability pension according to present benefit levels shows that Danish disability pensions are independent of prior income and amounts to 1,150 euro in all cases.[986] In comparison, Swedish "*illness and activity compensation*" (disability pension for persons over and under 30 years of age) consist of an income-related benefit, meaning that the benefit level is related to the individual's prior income, and a guarantee benefit which is a minimum level of benefit for those who only qualify for a small or no income-related benefit. The minimum guaranteed benefit is 950 euro per month and the maximum income-related monthly benefit is 1,450 euro.[987] Approximately 40% of persons who receive a full disability pension in Sweden receive the maximum income-related disability pension and only approximately 20% receive only the minimum guaranteed benefit.[988]

The European Committee on Social Rights has examined the level of benefits in both Denmark and Sweden in 2009. The European Committee on Social Rights concluded that the level of disability benefits in both Denmark and Sweden comply with Article 12(1) of the European Social Charter of 1961 as regards Denmark and

---

983 Section 6 of Chapter 33 of Swedish Social Insurance Act. Swedish Social Insurance Agency: Guidelines 2004:9 Version 9, 18 November 2008, p. 43.

984 Section 7 of Chapter 33 of Swedish Social Insurance Act. Social Insurance Agency: Guidelines 2004:9 Version 9, 18 November 2008, p. 43 and 44.

985 Nordic Social Statistical Committee (NOSOSKO) 2009, p. 157.

986 Nordic Social Statistical Committee (NOSOSKO) 2009, p. 156, table 6.3.1. Euros adjusted for purchasing power parity.

987 Ibid.

988 Swedish Social Insurance Agency 2008, (Försäkringskassan: Sjukersättning/aktivitetsersättning i december 2008 med fördelning efter beloppstyp).

Article 12 of the Revised European Social Charter of 1996 as regards Sweden.[989] Both under Article 12(1) of the European Social Charter of 1961 and the Revised European Social Charter of 1996, the European Committee on Social Rights require that income-replacement benefits exceed 50% of the median equivalised income which amounted to approximately 1,000 euro in Denmark and 850 euro in Sweden in 2008.[990]

As mentioned above, the EU has adopted a non-binding at-risk-of-poverty threshold set at 60% of the median equivalised income for a household and not for an individual person. Although this threshold is not a legally binding human rights standard, it is interesting to note that neither the Danish nor the Swedish minimum levels of full disability pension amount to 60% of the median equalivalised income in Denmark and Sweden respectively if the recipient of a disability pension is the only person with an income in the household in question. Only the maximum level of income-related disability pension in Sweden significantly exceeds the EU at-risk-of-poverty threshold.[991]

In sum, the minimum level of full disability pensions in Denmark and Sweden are set at similar levels just above 50% of the median equivalised income. This means that they only just comply with minimum requirements under the European Social Charter. While the Danish benefit is a flat-rate for all irrespective of prior income, the Swedish disability pension is partially income-related and as a result, only 20% of persons who receive full disability pension in Sweden must content themselves with the minimum guaranteed benefit. In conclusion, the level of disability pensions in Sweden is more in accordance with the contemporary disability human rights approach than the Danish disability pension which only just comply with minimum levels.

3.1.5. Conclusion

In conclusion, there are both significant similarities and differences between the law and policy on entitlement to disability pensions. In Denmark as well as in Sweden, approximately 7% of the working age population receive a full disability pension and the minimum disability pension in both countries amounts to just over 50% of the median equivalised income.

---

989 European Social Charter Conclusions on Denmark, 2009, p. 20, and on Sweden, 2009, p. 19.

990 Eurostat, At-risk-of-poverty thresholds (50% of median equivalised income), 2008.

991 European Council 17 June 2010 Conclusions, Annex 1, where it is agreed that at-risk-of-poverty set at The population is defined as the number of persons who are at risk-of-poverty and exclusion according to three indicators of social inclusion (at-risk-of poverty; material deprivation; jobless household).

However, the differences are also considerable. Firstly only full disability pensions are awarded in Denmark, while persons who are down to 25% reduced working capacity may qualify for a disability pension in Sweden. Secondly, disability pensions for persons under 30 years of age are time limited in Sweden and thirdly, the size of a disability pension is related to prior income in Sweden while a relatively low flat-rate is awarded in Denmark irrespective of prior income.

Persons with a reduced working capacity of 50% or 66% in Denmark cannot qualify for a disability pension in Denmark because they may obtain employment with wage subvention. If they obtain employment with wage subvention they receive a salary which is in accordance with applicable collective agreements and they may thus uphold an adequate standard of living. If however they are approved for employment with wage subvention and do not find employment then they will receive a special reduced unemployment benefit (*flexydelse*) which is approximately 5% lower than ordinary unemployment benefits and disability pensions.[992]

3.2. Dignified Support for Entry into Labour Market

As stated above, in Denmark, disability pension can only be awarded on a permanent basis and only when all possibilities for improving an individual's working capacity have been explored. There is no requirement that the review of the right to entitlement to the pension be done regularly. However, persons who receive a disability pension are obliged to inform the Local Council of any changes, which may affect the right to entitlement to the pension and the Local Council should keep itself informed about the working capacity of persons who receive a disability pension.[993] The legislation and the administrative guidelines do not specify how the Local Council should keep itself informed about the working capacity of persons on a disability pension.[994] A person of over 60 years of age may not be disqualified from receiving a disability pension due to an increase in his or her working capacity.[995]

Although the starting point in Denmark is that a disability pension is a permanent benefit, Danish law permits the granting of a disability pension with a set date for a

992 Special unemployment benefit for persons approved for employment with wage subvention amountsed to approximately 95% of disability pension. Ministry of Employment, Administrative Guideline No. 10239 of 14 November 2007 (vejledning om satser m.v. i 2008). See also Chapter VI on wage subvention (flexjob) and unemployment benefit for persons who are approved for wage subvention (flexydelse).

993 Section 41 of Danish Act on Social Pension.

994 Section 90 of Administrative Guidelines no. 105 of 23 October 2002 about early retirement from 1 January 2003 with amendments contained in Administrative Guidelines no. 55 of 31 August 2007adopted by the Ministry of Social Affairs.

995 Section 44(3) of Danish Act on Social Pension.

renewed evaluation with regard to entitlement in narrowly-defined situations.[996] Thus, only where the reduction in working capacity is caused by a condition which has an unpredictable course of development will it be permitted to set a date for a renewed evaluation. In two cases decided by the National Social Appeals Board, chronic pain syndrome and personality disorder were not considered to be illnesses with unpredictable courses of development. Therefore, the National Social Appeals Board decided that the persons in question should have been awarded a disability pension without a set date for a renewed evaluation.[997] The administrative guidelines stress that young age may count towards allowing a set-date for a renewed evaluation.[998]

In Sweden, the starting point is the opposite, namely that an entitlement to a disability pension must be re-assessed regularly. Thus, Swedish *"sickness compensation"* (disability pension for persons between 30 and 65 years of age) is awarded with a set date for a renewed evaluation with regard to entitlement. A renewed evaluation with regard to entitlement is required at least every three years.[999] Only where the disability pension was granted before 1 January 2005 or where the person in question is over 60 years old, should an evaluation not be performed.[1000] The Swedish Social Insurance Agency must assess whether the working capacity is still reduced to the same degree as when the benefit was granted and whether there are new possibilities for rehabilitation.[1001] If there are possibilities for improving the recipient's working capacity through rehabilitation, a plan for return to work must be prepared in close co-operation with the person in question.

Moreover, *"activity compensation"* (disability pension for persons under 30 years of age) is a time limited benefit which is granted for a maximum period of three years at a time. The Swedish Social Insurance Agency shall continuously examine whether activities could be undertaken to improve the working capacity of the person in question.[1002]

---

996 Section 20 of Danish Act on Social Pension.

997 National Social Appeals Board, Decision no. P-35–04 of 1 September 2004 (chronic pain syndrome) and Decision no. P-10–08 of 16 April 2008 (personality disorder).

998 Section 20(1) of Danish Act on Social Pension and Sections 11 and 32 of Administrative Guidelines no. 105 of 23 October 2002 about disability pension from 1 January 2003 with amendments contained in Administrative Guidelines no. 55 of 31 August 2007adopted by the Ministry of Social Affairs. National Social Appeals Board, Decision P-35–04 of 13 October 2004.

999 Section 17 of Chapter 33 of the Swedish Social Insurance Act.

1000 Section 17 of Chapter 33 of the Swedish Social Insurance Act.

1001 Swedish Social Insurance Agency: Guidelines 2007:1 Version 3, 18 June 2008, p. 30.

1002 Swedish Social Insurance Act, Section 17 of Chapter 33.

3.2.1. Suspension of Disability Pension

In Denmark, a person who receives a disability pension may apply to have his or her disability pension suspended in order to attempt to work without jeopardising his or her right to a disability pension. The right to a disability pension may be suspended for an unlimited period of time, but the Local Council may also decide to set a time limit for the duration of the suspension.[1003] In cases where a person who receives a disability pension applies to be approved for a job with wage subvention, the pension payment may only be suspended from the moment the person in question has received a specific job offer with wage-subvention.[1004]

Similarly in Sweden, the right to both *"sickness and activity compensation"* (disability pension) may be suspended either partly or fully while the person in question explores his or her capacity to work or study.[1005] The suspension may last a maximum of two years and may only take place after a minimum of one year after a disability pension was awarded.[1006] In addition, a person may apply to be granted a three-month trial-period every twelve months during which he or she continues to receive *"sickness or activity compensation"* while he or she attempts to work or study.[1007]

In sum the above comparison of disability pensions in Denmark and Sweden shows that the nature of disability pensions differs in the two countries. While a disability pension is a permanent pension in Denmark, in Sweden it is a benefit which at least for persons under the age of 30 years is time limited and aims at enabling an entry or a return to the labour market. While the starting point in Denmark is that an entitlement for a disability pension is not re-assessed, disability pensions for persons under 30 years of age in Sweden are time limited and entitlements for disability pensions for persons over 30 years of age must be re-assessed at least every three years. Thus also in this regard, the Swedish disability pensions are more in accordance with the contemporary disability human rights approach because it is based on the assumption that a person may become able to take part in the labour market again with the proper support.

3.3. Design and Administration of Disability Pension

In Denmark, the general rules on the disability pension scheme are adopted by law, which are complemented by administrative regulations adopted by the Ministry of

---

1003 Danish Act on Social Pension, Section 43a.
1004 Danish National Social Appeals Board, Decision P-18–04 of 3 March 2004.
1005 Swedish Social Insurance Act, Section 10 and 12 of Chapter 36.
1006 Swedish Social Insurance Act, Section 14 of Chapter 36.
1007 Swedish Social Insurance Agency: Guidelines 2007:1 Version 3, 18 June 2008, p. 71.

Employment.[1008] As explained in *Chapter VI Employment Promotion*, advisory Employment Councils (*beskæftigelsesråd*) have been set up under law with representation of both employers and employees' organisations as well as disabled persons' organisations at both local, regional and State levels.[1009] The Employment Councils advise the Ministry of Employment and Local Councils on political initiatives and supervise the administration of legislation in the employment political field.[1010]

The consideration of applications for a disability pension is done under the management of the Local Councils (*kommunalbestyrelser*).[1011] Complaints about decisions regarding disability pensions by the Local Councils may be made to one of the five regional Employment Complaints Boards.[1012] The Employment Complaints Boards have eight members appointed by the Minister of Employment after recommendation by *inter alia* the social partners and the Disabled Peoples' Organisation Denmark which is an umbrella organisation for Danish disabled persons' organisations.[1013] The decisions of the Employment Complaints Boards are final, but the National Social Appeals Board may hear complaints about the decisions of the Employment Complaints Boards when it considers that a case raises questions of general importance.[1014] The members of the National Social Appeals Board are appointed by the Minister of Welfare after recommendation once again from *inter alia* the social partners and the Disabled Peoples' Organisation Denmark.[1015]

In Sweden, the general rules on the disability pension scheme are adopted by law which are complemented by administrative regulations adopted by the Swedish Social Insurance Agency (*Försäkringskassan*).[1016] The dialogue between the Swedish Social Insurance Agency and the Swedish disabled persons' organisations has not been formalised through the creation of for example an advisory board, but the Swedish disabled persons' organisations are consulted during the ordinary

---

1008 Danish Act on Social Pension, LBK nr 1005 of 19 August 2010 without amendments (Bekendtgørelse af lov om social pension). Administrative Regulation No. 1438 of 13 December 2006 on Social Pension with latest amendment by Administrative Regulation No. 825 of 28 June 2010 (Bekendtgørelse om social pension).

1009 Danish Act on Management of the Active Employment Effort, Chapters 5, 6 and 7.

1010 Danish Act on Management of the Active Employment Effort, Sections 35(1), 39(1) and 44.

1011 Danish Act on Social Pensions, Section 17.

1012 Danish Act on Social Pensions, Section 49(2).

1013 Danish Act on Management of the Active Employment Effort, LBK No. 731 of 15 June 2010 (Bekendtgørelse af lov om ansvaret for styringen af den aktive beskæftigelsesindsats), Chapter 8.

1014 Danish Act on justice and administration in the social field, LBK 1054 of 7 September 2010 with without amendments, (Lov om retssikkerhed og administration på det sociale område), Chapter 9.

1015 Danish Act on justice and administration in the social field, Section 52.

1016 Swedish Act on Social Insurance, Chapter 33.

legislative process which includes asking relevant non-governmental organisations about their opinion before new legislation is proposed to Parliament.

The Swedish disability pension legislation is also administered by the Swedish Social Insurance Agency (*Försäkringskassan*) which has local branches covering all of Sweden.[1017] Complaints about decisions by the Social Insurance Agency cannot be heard by any other administrative body, but may be heard by the Swedish Administrative Court.[1018]

In sum, Danish disabled persons' organisations have strong representation in advisory bodies to the authorities, which prepare legislation for adoption by the Danish Parliament as well as in complaints bodies. In Sweden, the involvement of disabled persons' organisations in the design and administration of legislation on disability pensions is minimal. Thus, the Danish system is more in accordance with the contemporary disability human rights approach with regard to the involvement of disabled persons' organisations in the design and implementation of disability pension law and policy.

3.4. Conclusion

In conclusion, neither Danish nor Swedish disability pensions fully ensure an adequate standard of living for all persons who need it. Firstly, in order to achieve this level, the Danish flat-rate disability pension and the Swedish minimum level disability pension should be increased to ensure that all persons who receive a full disability pension have an income which amounts to 60% of the median equivalised income for households. Secondly the Danish disability pension scheme only covers persons whose working capacity is reduced by more than 66% which leaves especially unemployed persons who have been approved for jobs with wage subvention (*flexjobs*) with a relatively low income. Thirdly, Danish law and policy on disability should continuously ensure support for returning to the labour market to persons who receive a disability pension. This support should be provided in a dignified manner. In sum, especially the Danish disability pension law and policy needs to be reformed in order to ensure compliance with the contemporary disability human rights approach.

4. Sickness Benefit

The present Section examines laws and policies on sickness benefits in Denmark and Sweden from the perspective of the contemporary disability human rights

[1017] Swedish Act on Social Insurance, Section 5 of Chapter 23.
[1018] Swedish Act on Social Insurance, Section 10 of Chapter 113.

approach. Persons who receive a sickness benefit have a temporarily reduced working capacity and thus they are not necessarily disabled which would require that they have a longer-lasting impairment. However, many persons who become disabled while they are on the labour market will at least in the beginning qualify for a sickness benefit and the treatment and support that they get while receiving a sickness benefit may determine whether they return to the labour market or are excluded from the labour market. Thus, 40% of new recipients of a disability pension in the first quarter of 2008 in Denmark had received a sickness benefit in the period prior to receiving a disability pension.[1019]

In Sub-Section 4.1, I examine whether a sickness benefit is available to those who need it and whether the level of benefit is sufficient to uphold an adequate standard of living, in Sub-Section 4.2. I examine whether persons who receive sickness benefits are supported and encouraged to enter or return to the labour market. Finally, in Sub-Section 4.3, I examine the inclusion of disabled persons' organisations in the design and administration of sickness benefits.

4.1. Available to Those Who Need It and Ensures an Adequate Standard of Living

The rate of absence from work due to sickness is slightly higher in Sweden than in Denmark as is the public expenditure relating to sickness benefits. In Denmark, approximately 1,9% of the workforce had more than one week of absence due to sickness in 2008. In Sweden, 2.4% of the workforce had more than one week of absence due to sickness in 2008.[1020]

In Denmark and Sweden, the employer pays a sickness benefit to the person in question with or without public reimbursement during an initial period. In Denmark, the first 14 days of sick leave are paid by the employer without public reimbursement.[1021] In Sweden, the employer will only receive public reimbursement if the period of sick leave lasts more than 14 days.[1022] As a starting point, public reimbursement is not given for the first day of sick leave in Sweden unless the previous period of sick leave had ended within 5 days of the new period of sick leave or the period of sick leave was taken in order to undergo preventive or rehabilitative treatment.[1023] If an employee is at special risk of numerous periods of sick leave, the employer may make an agreement with the public authorities in both

1019 Den Sociale Ankestyrelse, *Tema: Sygedagpenge og førtidspension,* 2008.

1020 Nordic Social Committee (NOSOSKO) 2009, p. 100.

1021 Danish Act on Sickness Benefit, Act No. 536 of 9 June 2006 with latest amendment by Act no. 701 of 25 June 2010 (Lov om Sygedagpenge), Section 6. Swedish Act on Sick pay, SFS 1991:1047 (Lag om Sjuklön), Section 6, and Swedish Social Insurance Act, Section 9 of Chapter 27.

1022 Swedish Social Insurance Act, Section 26(2) of Chapter 27.

1023 Swedish Social Insurance Act, Section 27–29 of Chapter 27.

Denmark and Sweden that the authorities reimburse the first two weeks of sick leave.[1024]

4.1.1. Measurement of Working Capacity

According to the Danish Act on Sickness benefit, *"It is a prerequisite for the right to a sickness benefit that the person in question is incapable of working due to his or her own illness."*[1025] The Swedish Social Insurance provides that: *"Sickness benefit is given out when a sickness reduces the working capacity of the insured person by at least one fourth."*[1026] In Denmark, the reduction in working capacity must amount to at least 4 hours of absence from work per week for any worker irrespective of working hours.[1027]

In Denmark, already from the first day of illness, the authorities may measure the person's working capacity against not only his or her current position, but also against other relevant positions with the same employer. After three months, the assessment is made in relation to a broader employment area, which takes account of the person's prior experience and education. This assessment in relation to a broader employment area must take place regardless of whether the person in question is still employed unless it seems that a recovery of the capacity to perform relevant work for the present employer is imminent.[1028] The working capacity of job-seekers always takes place in relation to the broader employment area which takes account of prior experience and education.[1029]

Since a reform of sickness benefit scheme in Sweden entered into force in July 2008, the legislation in both Denmark and Sweden requires that the working capacity of an employee who receives a sickness benefit must be measured in relation to other jobs than the current job after a certain period of time on sick leave. If the working capacity of the person in question is not reduced in relation to other jobs than the current job, then he or she will no longer be entitled to a sickness benefit. If the person in question was not dismissed from his or her current employment, he or she would still have to leave that employment to seek a new employment. During the period of time when he or she sought new employment, he or she could apply for unemployment benefit or needs-based social security.

1024 Danish Act on Sickness benefit, Section 56. Swedish Social Insurance Act, Sections 39 and 40 of Chapter 27.

1025 Danish Act on Sickness benefit, Section 7.

1026 Swedish Social Insurance Act, Section 27.

1027 Danish Act on Sickness benefit, Section 7.

1028 Danish Act on Sickness benefit, Section 7(3), and Danish Labour Market Agency, Guidelines on sickness benefit no. 9300 of 25 June 2008, p. 26.

1029 Danish Act on Sickness benefit, Section 7(4), and Danish Labour Market Agency, Guidelines on sickness benefit no. 9300 of 25 June 2008, p. 51.

In Sweden, a newly adopted 'rehabilitation chain' provides that the working capacity of a person on sick leave shall be measured against the person's current job during the first 90 days.[1030] After 90 days of sick leave, the possibilities for transfer into another position with the same employer shall be explored.[1031] And after 180 days of sick leave, the person's working capacity shall be assessed in relation to employment on the "regular labour market and other suitable work".[1032] After 365 days of sick leave, a person's working capacity must always be submitted to the same evaluation as after 180 days.[1033]

In relation to the contemporary disability human rights approach, one may question whether the assessment of a person's working capacity in relation to other positions than the current position is accordance with the principle that all persons in need of a sickness benefit should receive it. In Denmark, a person on sick leave is only required to apply for employment with an employer other than the current one after just three months, unless a recovery is imminent. In Sweden, an employee is only obliged to apply for employment with another employer after sick leave lasting six months. This delay ensures that persons who receive a sickness benefit have a reasonable initial period during which they are not required to seek new employment with other employers even if their working capacity is only reduced in relation to jobs with their current employer. However, in view of the fact that employees whose recovery is imminent are exempted, it cannot be considered in violation of the contemporary disability human rights approach that employees on sick leave are required to apply for employment with other employers after three months in Denmark.

The fact that in Denmark the working capacity of a person on sick leave is measured in relation to all relevant positions with the *current* employer from the first day of sick leave does not seem problematic in view of the fact that a return to his or her original position with the same employer would presumably be possible after a full recovery.

In sum, it seems that sickness benefits are generally available to those who need it in both Denmark and Sweden in accordance with the contemporary disability human rights approach. In Sub-Section 4.2. below, it is discussed whether the limitations on the period of time during which a person may receive a sickness benefit in Denmark and Sweden are also in accordance with the contemporary disability human rights approach.

1030 Swedish Social Insurance Act, Section 46 of Chapter 27.
1031 Ibid., Section 47 of Chapter 27.
1032 Ibid., Section 48 of Chapter 27.
1033 Swedish Social Insurance Act, Section 49 of Chapter 27.

4.1.2. Level of Sickness Benefits

As mentioned above, employees in both Denmark and Sweden are entitled to full pay during the first two weeks of sick leave.[1034] Moreover, in both countries, collective agreements provide that public employees receive full pay (90% of full pay in Sweden) during the whole period of sickness and that many white-collar employees in the private sector receive full pay (90% of full pay in Sweden) during the first two months of a period of sick leave.[1035] An employer who pays the employee a salary during a period of sick leave will be entitled to receive the sickness benefit that the employee would otherwise have been entitled to.[1036]

As mentioned above under *Section 2 Contemporary Disability Human Rights Approach*, both under Article 12(1) of the European Social Charter of 1961 and the Revised European Social Charter of 1996, the European Committee on Social Rights requires that income-replacement benefits exceed 50% of the median equivalised income.[1037] In Denmark, the maximum sickness benefit amounts to approximately 1,000 euro after taxes have been paid which is the equivalent of 50% of the equivalised median income.[1038] In Sweden however, the maximum sickness benefit amounts to approximately 1,200 euro after taxes have been paid, which is more than 50% of the median equivalised income in Sweden which was 850 euro in 2008.[1039] In addition, the EU has adopted a non-binding at-risk-of-poverty threshold set at 60% of the median equivalised income and only the Swedish sickness benefit exceeds this limit.[1040]

In conclusion, Denmark only just complies with the requirement that sickness benefits must amount to 50% of the median equivalised income under the contemporary disability human rights approach whereas Sweden complies with a larger margin.

1034 Danish Act on Sickness Benefit, Section 6; Swedish Act on Sick pay, Section 6.

1035 Nordic Social Statistics Committee (NOSOSKO) 2009, pp. 94–95.

1036 Danish Act on Sickness Benefit, Section 54; Swedish Social Insurance Act, Section 56 of Chapter 27.

1037 Eurostat, At-risk-of-poverty thresholds (50% of median equivalised income), 2008.

1038 Nordic Social Statistics Committee (NOSOSKO) 2009, pp. 99 (euros adjusted for purchasing power parity).

1039 Ibid.

1040 The at-risk-of-poverty threshold is calculated as available income for a household so only where the recipient of sickness benefit is the only person with an income in the household will he or she be under the at-risk-of-poverty threshold.

4.2. Dignified Support for Entry into the Labour Market

In Denmark, it is an explicit aim of the Act on Sickness Benefit that the "working capacity of the person on sick leave is improved and that he or she returns to the labour market as fast as possible".[1041] In order to promote a rapid return to the labour market, a time limit has been imposed on the period of time, which a person may be entitled to a sickness benefit. Thus, a sickness benefit may not be claimed for a period that is longer than 12 months spread over an 18-month period.[1042] This means that a person can only claim sickness benefits during for example the months of January to June, for two consecutive years. If the person in question is still sick in July of the second year, he or she will not be entitled to claim a sickness benefit.

Based on the Danish Act on Sickness Benefits, The conditions for extending entitlement to claim sickness benefits for a longer period of time than 12 months are:

- That it is highly likely that employment rehabilitation may enable the person in question to return to the ordinary labour market (employment without wage subvention).[1043]
- That it is necessary to place the person in question in a trial-job in order to assess his or her working capacity.[1044]
- That the person in question is undergoing medical treatment which is expected to enable the person in question to return to the ordinary labour market within one year from the time that the working capacity became reduced.[1045] Only when the person in question was already employed in a position with wage subvention may the period on sickness benefits be prolonged with reference to the likelihood that he or she will return to work in a position with wage subvention.[1046]
- That the person in question has a life-threatening illness and that all possibilities for treatment have been exhausted.[1047]
- That an application for compensation for work-related injury or illness has been placed.[1048]
- That an application for a disability pension is being considered.[1049]

1041 Danish Act on Sickness Benefit, Section 2(1).
1042 Ibid., Section 24.
1043 Ibid., Section 27(1)(1).
1044 Ibid., Section 27(1)(2).
1045 Ibid., Section 27(1)(3).
1046 Labour Market Agency, Guidelines on sickness benefit no. 9300 of 25 June 2008, p. 85.
1047 Danish Act on Sickness Benefit, Section 27(1)(4).
1048 Ibid., Section 27(1)(5).
1049 Ibid., Section 27(1)(6).

The Administrative guidelines provide that if a person's reduced working capacity becomes permanent, will be eligible for a sickness benefit during the time necessary to assess whether the person should be rehabilitated, be approved for a job with wage-subvention or be approved for a disability pension.[1050] The Local Council shall in all cases assess whether the person in question has a right to be approved for a job with wage-subvention, rehabilitation benefit or a disability pension before ending the period with a sickness benefit.[1051]

In practice, the strictly enforced time limits on periods with a sickness benefit in Denmark mean that certain groups are unable to return to the labour market when their entitlement to a sickness benefit ends. The only possibility that they will have to access a social benefit when the entitlement to a sickness benefit ends, will be needs-based social security. For example, consider the situation of a person who is still receiving medical treatment, but who is unlikely to be able to obtain employment without wage subvention in the future. If that person does have some remaining working capacity, he or she will not qualify for a disability pension. This problem is evidenced by research carried out by a trade union representing secretarial staff employed in the State which has collected 22 examples among their members who have in 2008 lost their job and their right to a sickness benefit without qualifying for a disability pension. Three of the examples concerned women who had had blood clotts in the brain, but who had some remaining working capacity and therefore did not qualify for a disability pension.[1052]

In comparison to the time limits in Denmark, the Swedish time limits regarding entitlements to claim a sickness benefit are significantly more lenient. In fact, as a time limit was only introduced in July 2008 the concept of a time limit is relatively recent in Sweden. Sweden was the last Nordic country to introduce a time limit on the period of time that a person may claim a sickness benefit. In the preparatory works, the need for a time limit was explained in the following manner:

> *"Sweden's extremely long periods of sick leave are unique and it is a fact that a limitation on how long a sickness benefit can be provided is missed. The Commission report found that there is nothing which indicates that long periods of sick leave have positive effects. On the contrary, there are indications that the long periods in themselves have a negative effect on the possibilities for returning to the labour market".*[1053]

[1050] Ibid., Section 7(5) and Danish Labour Market Agency, Guidelines on sickness benefit no. 9300 of 25 June 2008, p. 29.

[1051] Danish Labour Market Agency, Guidelines on sickness benefit no. 9300 of 25 June 2008, p. 79.

[1052] HK Stat, *HK Statbladet*, "22 eksempler", May 2008.

[1053] Swedish Preparatory Works, Prop. 2007/08:136, p. 76. Swedish Commission Report SOU:86 of 9 November 2006, "More Insurance and More Work", (Mera försäkring och mera arbete).

In contrast to Denmark, which has strict a one-year time limit, the Swedish sickness benefit is only reduced after one year and the actual time limit only applies after 30 months. In Sweden, persons with reduced working capacity may claim a full sickness benefit for a period of 12 months within a 15-month period. In Sweden, a full sickness benefit amounts to 80% of a person's income, cf. *Sub-Section 4.1 Available to Those Who Need It and Adequate Standard of Living* above. After the first 12-month period with a sickness benefit has elapsed, a person with reduced working capacity may claim a reduced sickness benefit amounting to 75% of his or her income for an additional period of 18 months.[1054] However, a person may continue to receive a full sickness benefit for more than 12 months if the person in question is seriously ill.[1055] Examples of such situations would be a person who is waiting to have a transplant of a vital organ or a person who is receiving treatment for a serious illness such as cancer. There is no time limit on how long a person can receive a full sickness benefit if these conditions are fulfilled.[1056]

A person may be entitled to claim a reduced sickness benefit for a period of more than 18 months if the cause of the reduced working capacity was work-related, if the person is receiving substantial medical treatment, if the person in question has lost his or her perception of reality due to his or her illness, or if a return to the labour market would entail a risk of deteriorating the person's condition.[1057]

In sum, there are several differences between the Danish and Swedish limitations on the period of time during which a person may be entitled to a sickness benefit. Most importantly, the starting point in Denmark is that a sickness benefit may only be awarded for a period of 12 months while the maximum period of time with a sickness benefit is 30 months in Sweden (with a reduced benefit after 12 months). In addition, a person may continue to receive a sickness benefit in Sweden beyond 30 months for example when a return to the labour market would entail a risk of deterioration of the person's condition. In Denmark, the only reasons for an extension of the 12 month period are significantly more limited.

In relation to the contemporary disability human rights approach, it is not problematic in itself that there should be a time limit on the period of time during which a person may receive a sickness benefit since the nature of sickness is that it is time limited as opposed to an impairment which is long-lasting. The main concern seems to be that Danish legislation differentiates between persons who are expected to recover only a partial working capacity and persons who are expected to recover full working capacity. Only persons who are expected to recover full

1054 Swedish Social Insurance Act, Section 24 of Chapter 27.

1055 Ibid., Section 23 of Chapter 27.

1056 Swedish Social Insurance Agency, Guidelines on sickness benefit and co-ordinated rehabilitation, 2004:2 Version 11 of 16 December 2008, p. 52.

1057 Swedish Social Insurance Act, Section 25 of Chapter 27.

working capacity can continue to receive a sickness benefit for more than 12 months. Presumably, the reason for this provision is that a sickness benefit is not meant to be a long-term benefit and that it aims at promoting a quick return to full working capacity.

However, the differential treatment of persons who cannot be expected to regain full working capacity in comparison with persons who can be expected to regain full working capacity leads to a undignified treatment of persons with reduced working capacity. If the working capacity of a recipient of a sickness benefit is still improving and he or she can be expected to regain sufficient working capacity to enable him or her to become employed with wage subvention within one year, then he or she should be treated in the same way as persons who are expected to recover to full working capacity and be permitted to continue to receive a sickness benefit. Thus, the current Danish sickness benefit scheme is not in accordance with the contemporary disability human rights approach, as it does not provide to persons with disabilities and reduced working capacity, dignified support to return to work.

In contrast, the relatively lenient Swedish rules on sickness benefits promote a return to the labour market in a dignified manner for persons with disabilities and reduced working capacity.

4.3. Design and Administration of Sickness Benefits

Similarly to the disability pension schemes described above in *Section 3 Disability Pension*, the sickness benefit schemes in Denmark are governed by laws which are complemented by administrative regulations adopted by the Ministry of Employment.[1058] As explained above, advisory Employment Councils (*beskæftigelsesråd*) have been set up under law with representation of both employers and employees' organisations as well as disabled persons' organisations at both local, regional and State levels.[1059] The consideration of applications for a sickness benefit is done under the management of the Local Councils (*kommunalbestyrelser*).[1060] Complaints about decisions regarding sickness benefits by the Local Councils may be made to one of the five regional Employment Complaints Boards and the National Social Appeals Board.[1061] The Disabled

1058 Danish Act on Social Pension, LBK nr 1005 of 19 August 2010 without amendments (Bekendtgørelse af lov om social pension). Administrative Regulation No. 1438 of 13 December 2006 on Social Pension with latest amendment by Administrative Regulation No. 825 of 28 June 2010 (Bekendtgørelse om social pension).

1059 Danish Act on Management of the Active Employment Effort, Chapters 5, 6 and 7.

1060 Danish Act on Social Pensions, Section 17.

1061 Danish Act on Social Pensions, Section 49(2). Danish Act on justice and administration in the social field, LBK 1054 of 7 September 2010 with without amendments, (Lov om retssikkerhed og administration på det sociale område), Chapter 9.

People's Organisation recommends persons for membership of both the Employment Complaints Boards and the National Social Appeals Board.[1062]

In Sweden, the general rules on the sickness benefit scheme are adopted by law, which are complemented by administrative regulations adopted by the Swedish Social Insurance Agency (*Försäkringskassan*).[1063] As explained above, the dialogue between the Swedish Social Insurance Agency and the Swedish disabled persons' organisations has not been formalised. As mentioned above, the decisions of the Swedish Social Insurance Agency (*Försäkringskassan*) cannot be heard by any other administrative body, but may be heard by the Swedish Administrative Court.[1064]

In sum, Danish disabled persons' organisations have strong representation in advisory bodies to the authorities, which prepare legislation for adoption by the Danish Parliament as well as in complaints bodies. In Sweden, the involvement of disabled persons' organisations in the design and administration of legislation on sickness benefits is minimal. Thus, the Danish system is more in accordance with the contemporary disability human rights approach with regard to the involvement of disabled persons' organisations in the design and implementation of sickness benefit law and policy.

4.4. Conclusion

In conclusion, both the Danish and the Swedish sickness benefit scheme are in accordance with the contemporary disability human rights approach in that persons who receive a sickness benefit are only expected to apply for new jobs with a new employer after 3 and 6 months respectively unless a recovery is imminent. Furthermore, although the sickness benefits in both countries are in accordance with the minimum level set by the European Social Charter of set at 60% of the median equivalised income. Finally, while the Swedish limitation on the period of time that a person may be entitled to a sickness benefit is in accordance with the contemporary disability human rights approach, the Danish sickness benefit scheme does not promote a return to the labour market in a dignified manner for persons who are not expected to recover full working capacity. In sum, the Swedish sickness benefit scheme is in greater accordance with the contemporary disability human rights approach while the Danish counterpart should be modified to ensure full compliance.

1062 Danish Act on justice and administration in the social field, Section 52.

1063 Swedish Act on Social Insurance, Chapter 33.

1064 Swedish Act on Social Insurance, Section 10 of Chapter 113.

5. Rehabilitation

The subject of this Section is employment-related rehabilitation, which is aimed at enabling a person to regain working capacity through mainly in-work training, general training or education. A rehabilitation benefit is awarded to the person in question in order to replace his or her income while he or she takes part in rehabilitation activities. In addition, rehabilitation benefits may also consist in covering the costs associated with rehabilitation such as the cost of a training course and training material.

Whereas the duties of the employer to rehabilitate their employees was examined in *Chapter V Employers' Obligations*, the present Section deals with the employment-related rehabilitation measures and benefits provided by the State.

Rehabilitation benefits under the contemporary disability human rights approach are discussed above in *Section 2. Contemporary Disability Human Rights Approach*. Firstly, disabled persons' organisations must be included in the design and administration of rehabilitation services and benefits for national policy to be in accordance with the contemporary disability human rights approach. Secondly, employment-related rehabilitation benefits should, in accordance with the contemporary disability human rights approach, be provided to persons with disabilities who need them in order to achieve inclusion on the labour market. Thirdly, employment-related rehabilitation services must be provided in a dignified manner which takes into account the wishes and capabilities of the persons under rehabilitation.

5.1. Available to Those Who Need It and Ensures an Adequate Standard of Living

Approximately the same share of persons of working age received a rehabilitation benefit during the year of 2008 in both countries, namely approximately 0.6% of working age population in Denmark and 0.5% of working age population. However, the average time period on the rehabilitation benefit was set as approximately eight months in Denmark and just three months in Sweden.[1065] In both countries approximately 40% of persons who had received a rehabilitation benefit were in employment six months after the end of the period in rehabilitation.[1066]

1065 Denmark: www.Sweden: Swedish Employment Service (Arbetsformedlingen) 2010, p. 20. Both the figures for Denmark and Sweden cover only public costs related to rehabilitation benefit and not public costs related to covering for example training courses and materials.

1066 Danmark: www.jobindsats.dk, Revalidering. Status 1, 3, 6 og 12 mdr. efter afsluttet forløb; Sweden: Swedish Employment Service (Arbetsformedlingen) 2010, p. 22.

Both in Denmark and in Sweden, employment-oriented rehabilitation measures are reserved for persons with reduced working capacity who need retraining or education so that the person in question may return to the labour market and become self-supporting. According to the Danish Act on an Active Social Policy:

> *"Rehabilitation concerns employment-oriented activities and economic assistance which help to enable a person with reduced working capacity to stay or enter the labour market so that his or her possibilities for supporting him or herself and his or her family are improved. [...] The Local Council provides rehabilitation when the employment-oriented activities under the present Act and other legislation, including the Act on an Active Employment Effort, are not sufficient to enable the person in question to become self-supporting."*[1067] *According to the Swedish Social Insurance Act, "Rehabilitation according to this Chapter shall aim at reinstating a person who has become ill with working capacity and qualifications which will enable him or her to become self-supporting through work."*[1068]

In Denmark, it is not specified how much a person's working capacity should be reduced before he or she may be entitled to undergo rehabilitation as long as it is necessary to promote re-entry into the labour market. Although rehabilitation in Denmark is considered a full-time activity, it does not follow that a person's working capacity must be fully reduced to take part in rehabilitation activities. In Sweden, a person receives a rehabilitation benefit according to how much his or her working capacity is reduced. Thus, a person with 25% reduced working capacity, will receive 25% of the full rehabilitation benefit while undergoing rehabilitation.[1069] He or she will naturally continue to be entitled to salary if he or she is still employed or unemployment benefit if he or she is unemployed while undergoing rehabilitation. Both in Denmark and in Sweden, the expenses incurred while undergoing rehabilitation, such as expenses to buy necessary training materials and for technical aids, may be reimbursed by the authorities.[1070]

In both Denmark and in Sweden, rehabilitation benefits amount to the same as full unemployment or sickness benefits Thus, the level of rehabilitation benefits in both countries are in accordance with the minimum level set by the European Social Charter of 50% of the median equivalised income. However, while the Danish level of rehabilitation benefits ensures an income, which is only just above the minimum requirement, especially the Swedish level of rehabilitation benefits is significantly higher than the minimum required level and is in better accordance with the contemporary disability human rights approach in this regard.

1067 Danish Act on an Active Social Policy, Section 46.

1068 Swedish Social Insurance Act, Section 2 of Chapter 29.

1069 Swedish Social Insurance Act, Sections 3 and 8 of Chapter 31.

1070 Danish Act on an Active Social Policy, Section 63, and Swedish Social Insurance Act, Section 14 of Chapter 31.

In sum, access to rehabilitation benefits seems to be relatively similar in both Denmark and Sweden. The above comparison indicates that persons whose working capacity has been reduced have access to employment-rehabilitation in line with the contemporary disability human rights approach, although Danish rehabilitation benefit should in some cases be increased in order to fully meet the requirements of this approach. In fact, the main difference between the rehabilitation schemes in Denmark and Sweden concern the length of the rehabilitation periods which will be discussed in *Sub-Section 5.3 Design and Administration of Rehabilitation Benefit*, below.

5.2. Promotes Re-entry into Labour Market in a Dignified Manner

As explained above in *Section 2 Contemporary Disability Human Rights Approach*, rehabilitation should promote the return to the ordinary labour market, but persons who will not be able to obtain employment without support should also have access to rehabilitation. Moreover, the fact that the promotion should take place in a dignified manner means that the wishes and capabilities of the person in question should be taken into account as opposed to choosing the shortest possible rehabilitation which could enable the person in question to return to the labour market.

Both the Danish and Swedish legislations specify that the rehabilitation must be planned in cooperation with the person in question and must take account of the capabilities and wishes of that person.[1071] In addition, it is also specified in both Danish and Swedish legislation that the employer, if there is one, should be included in the planning process.[1072]

In Denmark, it is underlined that rehabilitation should aim at enabling a person to achieve employment in a field where employment possibilities are either *"good or very good"*.[1073] Moreover, *"rehabilitation should last as short a period of time as possible while meeting the needs of the person in question. The Local Council may plan that a person receives rehabilitation benefit for a maximum period of five years."*[1074] Rehabilitation may however be planned to last a longer time than five years where the person in question *"has significantly reduced working capacity and his or her capabilities and personal interests speak strongly for rehabilitation through higher education."*[1075]

[1071] Danish Act on an Active Social Policy, Section 47, and Swedish Social Insurance Act, Section 3 of Chapter 30.

[1072] Danish Act on an Active Social Policy, Section 47, and Swedish Social Insurance Act, Section 10 of Chapter 30.

[1073] Act on an Active Social Policy, Section 47.

[1074] Act on an Active Social Policy, Section 49.

[1075] Act on Active Social Policy, Section 49.

In Sweden, the preparatory works and administrative guidelines provide that rehabilitation may only last a maximum of one year when it does not aim at enabling return to the same employer. If rehabilitation is given with the aim of returning to the same employer as before the illness, the rehabilitation must be shorter. The preparatory works state that education of up to three years may be possible in limited cases when it is necessary to allow for longer time due for example to a person's disability.[1076]

In sum, rehabilitation may be planned to last five years under Danish law and only three years under Swedish law. This difference in the legislation is also reflected in the different practices in the two countries: In Denmark, the average rehabilitation lasts eight months while it lasts only three months in Sweden. This difference may be caused by the fact that more persons who undergo rehabilitation with the aim of returning to their current employer in Sweden than in Denmark, where rehabilitation typically targets the unemployed. The presumption that the person undergoing rehabilitation does not have a current employer is reflected in the Danish legislation which only mentions the involvement of employers who have agreed to provide job-training or employment with wage subvention and not employers in general.[1077]

5.3. Design and Administration of Rehabilitation Benefits

In Denmark, rehabilitation is governed by the Act on an Active Social Policy. The Local Councils are responsible for work-related rehabilitation both for persons who are employed and for persons who are unemployed.[1078]

In Sweden, rehabilitation is governed by the Swedish Social Insurance Act while the National Social Insurance Agency is responsible for co-ordinating rehabilitation. Rehabilitation which is aimed at enabling a return to work with the existing employer is the responsibility of the employer. General labour market rehabilitation for persons who cannot return to work with their existing employer and for the unemployed is the responsibility of the Employment Service.[1079]

1076 Swedish Social Insurance Agency, Guidelines on sickness benefit and co-ordinated rehabilitation, 2004:2 Version 11 of 16 December 2008, p. 293. Report on the treatment of proposal for amendment of Act on General Insurance, 1990/91:SfU16, s. 33–34 (Socialförsäkringsutskottets betänkande Rehabilitation och rehabiliteringsersättning).

1077 Danish Act on an Active Social Policy, Section 47.

1078 Danish Act on an Active Social Policy, LBK no. 946 of 1 October 2010 with latest amendment by Act no. 573 of 31 May 2010, Chapter 6. See also Danish Act on an Active Employment Effort, Chapters 10 and 11, which allow for in-work training of unemployed persons and persons who need rehabilitation.

1079 Swedish Social Insurance Agency, Guidelines on sickness benefit and co-ordinated rehabilitation, 2004:2 Version 11 of 16 December 2008, p. 259 and 278.

As explained above in *Sub-Section 3.1. Design and Administration of Disability Pension*, Danish disabled persons' organisations have strong representation in advisory bodies to the employment-related authorities at both local, regional and State level, as well as in complaints bodies. In Sweden, the involvement of disabled persons' organisations in the design and administration of legislation on disability pensions is minimal. Thus, the Danish system is more in accordance with the contemporary disability human rights approach with regard to the involvement of disabled persons' organisations in the design and implementation of rehabilitation law and policy.

5.4. Conclusion

In conclusion, it seems that both the Danish and the Swedish rehabilitation schemes provide rehabilitation which aims at enabling a return to the ordinary labour market in a dignified manner. The difference in the length of time during which rehabilitation may be provided reflects a difference in the situation of employees whose working capacity becomes reduced. Whereas employees in Denmark cannot expect to stay with their current employer, the contrary is the case in Sweden. In Denmark, rehabilitation will therefore not aim at a specific job and may therefore be more broad and longer-lasting, whereas in Sweden, it will be more specific and last a shorter period of time. Thus, the differences in the two schemes reflect differences in the general organisation of the labour market. Both the Danish and the Swedish rehabilitation schemes are in line with the contemporary disability human rights approach.

6. Work Injury Compensation

Compensation for a work injury is a benefit which an employee receives in order to compensate him or her for negative consequences of an injury resulting from work. Similarly to a sickness benefit, temporarily reduced working capacity is a condition for qualifying for this benefit. As a result it is not reserved for persons with disabilities. However, work injury compensation is especially relevant to persons with disabilities who are likely to be over-represented in the group of applicants both because the work injury may potentially lead to a disability and because an existing impairment in itself may heighten the risk of being victim of a work injury where sufficient accommodations have not been made for the impairment. For example, a person with an existing back-injury may be more at risk of getting serious back-problems if accommodations in working equipment and working routines have not been made for his existing back injury than a person who has a healthy back.

In this Section, I will first compare law and policy on work accident compensation and secondly carry out an analysis in relation to the contemporary disability human rights approach. It should be noted that the compensation provided under collective agreements is substantial in both countries but especially in Sweden. However, this will not be discussed in the following Sections.

6.1. Design and Administration of Work Injury Compensation

The design and administration of work injury compensation differ quite significantly in Denmark and Sweden. In Denmark, all employees are guaranteed a certain level of compensation for work injuries under law and all employers are required by law to take out insurance against work injuries, which finances the system of work injury compensation.[1080] In addition, certain collective agreements may also provide rights to additional compensation. In Sweden, the system of work injury compensation is split between a system of public compensation administered and financed by the State, and a system based on collective agreements financed by employers' insurances.[1081] In Sweden, the State compensation provides only a minimum compensation for severe loss of working capacity and leaves it to the system, based on collective agreements, to provide additional compensation. For example, the Swedish State compensation only provides compensation for loss of a minimum of 1/15 of working capacity, when it lasts for a minimum of one year, but Swedish State compensation does not compensate for an impairment in itself or pain and suffering.[1082] In contrast, the Danish State compensation covers both loss of working capacity above 15% as well as longer-lasting impairments (*varige mén*).[1083] The Danish State compensation also does not cover pain and suffering.[1084]

A comparison of statistics on the number of persons who are granted public compensation illustrates that the Swedish public compensation only provides minimal protection. In 2007, there were approximately 30,000 work-accidents resulting in sick-days in Sweden and 50,000 in Denmark. In Sweden, only approximately 3,000 persons were granted State compensation whereas 10,000 persons were granted State compensation in Denmark.[1085] Thus, in Sweden approximately 10% of persons who were victims of a work-related accident were

1080 Danish Act on Employment Injury Protection, LBK 154 af 07/09/2009 with latest amendment by Act no. 718 of 25 June 2010, Section 48.

1081 AFA Försäkring provides private insurance for work injuries in Sweden. www.afaforsakring.se.

1082 Swedish Social Insurance Act, Section 2 of Chapter 41 of Chapter 42.

1083 Danish Act on Employment Injury Protection, Sections 17 and 18.

1084 Danish Act on Employment Injury Protection, Section 11.

1085 Denmark: Arbejdstilsynet, Anmeldte Arbejdsulykker 2002–2007, Årsopgørelse for 2007, juni 2008, p. 8, Sweden: Lindquist and Wadensjö, 2008, pp. 68 and 73.

granted State compensation whereas 20% were granted State compensation in Denmark.

The consequence of both the Danish and the Swedish systems of work injury compensation is that an individual employee is ensured compensation regardless of whether or not his or her employer is solvent and willing to pay compensation.[1086] However, as the employer is not held directly responsible for work injuries, the employers may not be as motivated to prevent work injuries as they would otherwise be. The fact that the Swedish system of compensation is split into a system of minimum compensation from the State and additional compensation based on collective agreements means that approximately 8% of all employees on the labour market in Sweden are only entitled to minimal compensation for work injuries because they are not covered by a collective agreement.[1087] Moreover, individual victims of work injuries must make applications for compensation under collective agreements themselves. Although it is free of charge to place a claim for compensation under the collective agreements, it seems that a significant number of victims do not place their claims due to lack of information and resources.[1088] In sum, the Swedish system of work injury compensation is organised in such a way that persons who are not covered by collective agreements and who do not have sufficient resources do not enjoy an equal access to compensation for work injury as others. Although this is not in direct violation with Sweden's human rights obligations, which do not require more than minimal compensation or prohibit differentiation of persons who are covered by collective agreements, it would be more in line with the contemporary disability human rights approach to ensure an equal access for all employees on the labour market to compensation for work injuries.

The system of compensation for work-related injuries is closely linked to the promotion of a safe working environment, which was discussed in *Chapter V Empoyers' Obligations* on the duties of employers towards employees with disabilities. In *Chapter V Employers' Obligations*, it was shown that protection against unfair dismissal is based to a large extent on collective agreements in Denmark and based on law in Sweden. In this light, it seems surprising that the systems of work injury compensation are based to a larger extent on collective agreements in Sweden and on law in Denmark.

1086 Swedish General Insurance Agency, Administrative Guidelines 2003:4, version 4 of 3 December 2007, p. 19.

1087 Lindquist and Wadensjö 2008, p. 110.

1088 Lindquist and Wadensjö 2008, p. 111.

6.2. Equal Right of Persons with Disabilities to Public Work Injury Compensation

In the present Sub-Section, it is examined whether persons with disabilities who may be predisposed to work injury due to their impairment enjoy an equal right to compensation for work injuries as persons who are not predisposed to work injury.

The wording in both Danish and Swedish legislation on when an injury is work-related is quite brief. The Danish legislation provides that:

> *"By work injury is understood an accident or a sickness which is a consequence of work or the conditions under which it takes place. [...] By accident in this Act is understood an injury on a person caused by an incident or an impact which happens suddenly or within five days. Injury may also be caused by sickness which according to medical documentation results from certain impacts and which certain groups of persons are more likely than others to have experienced through their work or the conditions that the work takes place under."*[1089]

In Swedish law, *"Work injury shall according to this Act be understood as injury which is caused by an accident or another damaging cause related to work. An injury shall be seen as related to work when prevailing grounds favour this result."*[1090] As opposed to Denmark, Swedish law does not require that an injury can qualify as either a *work-accident* or a *work-related illness. Work injury* is a general concept which covers both.

Guidance as to how these relatively broadly formulated provisions shall be implemented is found *inter alia* in the preparatory works which show that there is a significant difference between Denmark and Sweden when it comes to the treatment of people who have a predisposition to injury. The Danish preparatory works state that *"an occurrence can only be seen to be the cause of an injury where it was biologically natural and logical that the injury incurred as a result of that occurrence at work [...]"*. An assessment will have to be made to determine whether *"such an occurrence would normally provide a biologically natural and logical explanation for the injury [...]"*.[1091]

Thus, the assumption is that a predisposition to injury should not be taken into account and that an assessment shall be made on the basis of what a *"normal"* person should be expected to withstand. This is also reflected in the case law on

---

1089 Danish Act on Employment Injury Protection Sections 5, 6(1) and 7(1).

1090 Swedish Social Insurance Act, Section 3 of Chapter 38.

1091 Danish Preparatory Works on Act on Employment Injury Protection, LF216 of 9 April 2003 (Forslag til Lov om Arbejdsskadesikring), "Bemærkninger til lovforslagets enkelte bestemmelser", Til § 6.

Danish work injury compensation. For example a decision by the National Appeals Board involved a waitress who had to lift boxes of soft drinks, which weighed approximately 13.5 kilograms from the stockroom to the shop. When she lifted her second box that day, she experienced a sharp pain in her back. She was given an emergency MR-scanning which showed that she had a slipped disk. The application for compensation for work injury was rejected because her work could not be expected to result in such an injury unless a person has a special disposition for such an injury.[1092] In another case, a day-care mother lifted a child weighing 15 kilograms and had a bone injury because of severe osteoporosis. This occurrence was not suited to create such an injury in a person without predisposition to such injuries and the application for compensation was rejected.[1093] In a third case, the captain of a ship with undiagnosed severe arteriosclerosis, died of shock after his ship ran aground. Even though the authorities recognised that death would not have occurred without this incident, it was not considered that it would normally lead to death in a person without arteriosclerosis.[1094] Again, the occurrence was not suited to create such an injury in a 'normal' person and the application for compensation was rejected.

In contrast, in Sweden, it was made clear in the preparatory works to the amendment of the Act on Employment Injury Insurance that the protection applies to persons *"in the state that they are in" (befintligt skick).* This means that *"it should be taken into account that different persons have different levels of tolerance [...] The evaluation of the impact of work on a person should be done in relation to the individual person and not in relation to a 'normal person'. [...] There is however a limit to the importance which may be given to the individual's physical or mental vulnerability. Factors related to the work in question which are generally not harmful should not be found to be the cause of an injury to an extremely sensitive person."*[1095] The preparatory works underline that the exact delimitation of the protection under this Act will have to be made on a case-by-case basis.[1096]

The Swedish approach, which provides that the assessment of whether or not an injury is work-related shall be done in relation to the individual person in question and not a 'normal' person, results in a higher level of protection for persons with disabilities than under Danish law which may be illustrated with the following examples from case law. A case decided by the Swedish Social Insurance Agency

1092 National Social Appeals Board, Decision No. 28–09 of 3 December 2008.

1093 Danish Work Injury Agency, Administrative Guidelines, "Vejledning om anerkendelse af ulykker – skader sket 1. januar eller senere", 4. udgave, 21 December 2006, example no. 5b, p. 8.

1094 Danish Work Injury Agency, Administrative Guidelines, "Vejledning om anerkendelse af ulykker – skader sket 1. januar eller senere", 4. udgave, 21 December 2006, example no. 5a, p. 8. (Find sagsnummer på Ankestyrelsens afgørelse i sagen).

1095 Swedish Preparatory Works, Prop. 2001/02:81, p. 103 and 104.

1096 Ibid.

concerned a kitchen chef who had developed pain in her neck and shoulders. In her work she lifted heavy loads without support and her working place had not been accommodated to her low height of 158 cm. When assessing whether the lifting and her working position could lead to a work injury, the assessment was not made in relation to a 'normal' person, but to a woman of her height and build.[1097] Another case decided by the Swedish Social Insurance Agency concerned a man who worked in the food sector. Before he took up this position, he had degenerative disc disorder in his lower back. The work required that he lift heavy objects and caused strain to his back. This led to a deterioration of his degenerative disc disorder and the deterioration became permanent. The Swedish Social Insurance Agency took into account that he was especially vulnerable and awarded him compensation for the deterioration of the condition of his back.[1098]

The above shows that the assessment of whether a person is entitled to work injury compensation is performed on a case-by-case basis in both countries. However, the comparison between the two countries also shows that there is a significant difference in the starting points under the Danish and the Swedish legislation. Under Danish law, the starting point is that the incident or impact must be suited to create the injury in question to a 'normal' person. In Sweden, the starting point is the opposite, namely that the incident or impact must be suited to cause the injury to the individual person in question. In other words, the starting point under Swedish legislation, is that both persons who fall within and outside of the definition of "*normal*" persons, are ensured protection against the consequences of work accidents.

This finding concurs with the findings in *Chapter VI Employers' Obligations,* which showed that employers in Sweden are under a significantly stronger obligation to make accommodations for employees with disabilities than employers in Denmark. In other words, in Sweden as opposed to in Denmark, employers are obliged to take into account that employers may have a reduced working capacity and the same is the case in relation to work injuries. Thus, there is a parallelism between the duty to make accommodation for employees with disabilities and the protection of employees with disabilities against the consequences of working in an environment which has not taken account of their special vulnerability.

1097 Swedish Social Insurance Agency, Guidelines on Compensation under the Act on Employment Injury, 2003:4, Version 8, p. 70.

1098 Swedish Social Insurance Agency, Guidelines on Compensation under the Act on Employment Injury, 2003:4, Version 8, p. 70.

6.3. Conclusion

Firstly, the Danish and Swedish systems of administration of work injury compensation are different in that the Danish system consists of one unified system while the Swedish system is split into two systems. The Swedish State employment-injury scheme provides minimal protection for longer-lasting severely reduced working capacity and the system based on collective agreements provides other types of compensation. In order to ensure compliance with the contemporary disability human rights approach, the Swedish system should be reformed to ensure that in practice all persons receive full work injury compensation irrespective of coverage by a collective agreement and their own capacity to make an application for compensation.

Secondly, while Sweden ensures that the assessment of whether or not an injury is work-related is done in relation to the individual person in question including his or her sensitivities, the opposite is the case in Denmark. In Denmark, the assessment of whether or not an injury is work-related is done in relation to a "*normal*", non-disabled person which means that persons with disabilities do not enjoy an equal right to work injury compensation in Denmark. In sum, Denmark should reform its work injury compensation scheme in order to ensure full compliance with the contemporary disability human rights approach.

7. EU Law and Policy

As explained in *Chapter III EU Law and Policy,* EU legislation and policy on income-replacement benefit remain relatively general in nature. Thus, while the European Charter of Fundamental Rights states that *"The Union recognises and respects the entitlement to income-replacement benefits",* it also only recognises that the entitlements must be *"in accordance with the rules laid down by Community law and national laws and practices."* Similarly, (for example) Article 48 TFEU provides that *"The European Parliament and the Council shall [...] adopt such measures in the field of social security as are necessary to provide freedom of movement for workers"* while at the same time allowing Member States to declare that a legal act will not have legal effect in their State if it would *"affect important aspects of its social security system"* or require unanimity in the Council.[1099] Thus, instead of adopting harmonising secondary legislation on income-replacement benefits, some legislation has been adopted which provides for fundamental principles of freedom of movement and prohibition of discrimination on the grounds of nationality, gender and race apply in relation to income-replacement benefits. The Employment Equality Directive does not cover social security, but the new proposal for an equality directive may require that Member States impose a

1099 Article 48 TFEU and Article 153(2) TFEU.

prohibition of discrimination on the grounds of disability in the field of social security.[1100]

In contrast to EU legislation, EU *policy* does seek to influence general laws and policies on income-replacement benefits in the Member States on social security. Thus, the Council Employment Guidelines and the Commission's Proposal for a Joint Report on Social Protection and Social Inclusion of 2010 promote income-replacement benefits as an integrated part of active labour market policy.[1101] In other words, the policies relating to income-replacement benefits must be aimed at employment while ensuring adequate support for those who cannot work. On the one hand, there is a risk that a too-strong focus on incentives for re-employment, may result in benefits, which are not sufficient to ensure an adequate standard of living and the dignity of persons who receive the benefit may also be disregarded in the effort to stimulate their return to work. On the other hand, an increased focus on return to the labour market may also be positive in relation to persons with disabilities, who, have in some cases have been 'parked' outside of the labour market on life-long income-replacement benefits with little incentives or support for returning to the labour market.

The analysis in the present Chapter shows that both Danish and Swedish income-replacement benefit policies are in fact both increasingly becoming a part of / or affected by an active (EU) labour market policy and thus increasingly focused on creating incentives for a rapid return to the labour market. As described above, it seems that this has negative as well as positive consequences for persons with disabilities. On the one hand, the level of income-replacement benefits in especially Denmark does not ensure an adequate standard of living for persons who are forced to live on income-replacement benefits. On the other hand, it is positive if an increased focus on promoting participation in the labour market in Denmark will ensure that disability pensioners receive incentives and support to return to the labour market where this is possible.

In sum, EU law and policy in the field of income-replacement leaves it up to Member States to define national laws and policies as long as they comply with general principles of freedom of movement and non-discrimination. However, EU policy does point in the direction of active labour market policies which also plays

---

1100 European Commission Proposal for a COM (2008) 426 of 2 July 2008 on implementing the principle of equal treatment between persons irrespective of religion or belief, disability, age or sexual orientation. Draft Joint Report on Social Protection and Social Inclusion submitted to the European Council (EPSCO) on 15 February 2010, 6500/10, Communication from the Commission COM (2010) 25 final, Proposal for the Joint Report on Social Protection and Social Inclusion.

1101 Council Decision 707/2010 of 21 October 2010 on Guidelines for the Employment Policies of the Member States, [2010] OJ L308/46, Guideline No. 7.

an important part in Danish and Swedish policy in the field of income-replacement benefits. Altogether, it seems that Danish and Swedish laws and policies are in line with the rather vague EU law and policy on income-replacement benefits.

8. Conclusion

The present Chapter shows that income-replacement benefits based on the contemporary disability human rights approach should aim at inclusion in the labour market. In addition, persons with disabilities should have equal access to income-replacement benefits and the levels of the benefits should ensure an adequate standard of living. Moreover, it follows from the contemporary disability human rights approach that the adoption and implementation of laws and policies on income-replacement benefits should involve disabled persons' organisations. Finally, access to income-replacement benefits should be based on individual and enforceable rights.

The above analysis of law and policy regarding income-replacement benefits for persons with disabilities demonstrates that Danish law and policy on income-replacement is to some extent not based on the contemporary disability human rights approach. Thus the rules and policies on neither disability pensions, sickness benefits and work injury compensation in Denmark can be said to promote full inclusion on the labour market of persons with disabilities. For example, disability pensions are awarded as a benefit for life with little support for returning to the labour market and sickness benefits are only available for more than twelve months if the person in question is expected to regain *full* working capacity. Moreover, work injury is awarded only where the injury would have occurred if the person was 'normal' which means that any vulnerabilities associated with disability are not taken into account.

Swedish law and policy on income-replacement benefits is more in line with the contemporary disability human rights approach as the law and policy is to a higher degree founded on the right to inclusion of persons with disabilities.

Moreover, the levels of income-replacement benefits in especially Denmark, but also as regards minimum benefits in Sweden, should be increased in order to ensure that all persons living on income replacement-benefits enjoy an adequate standard of living in accordance with the contemporary disability human rights approach.

In relation to the inclusion of disabled persons' organisations in the adoption and implementation of laws and policies on income-replacement benefits, Denmark has included representatives of disabled persons' organisations in the administrative complaints board, whereas Sweden has not formally included disabled persons' organisations.

Finally, in relation to the rights-based approach, the main problem concerns the fact that only minimum work injury benefits are based on individual and enforceable rights in the law of Sweden. A substantial part of work injury benefits are based on collective agreements. This means that almost 10% of employees on the Swedish labour market are only entitled to minimum work injury benefits, as they are not covered by a collective agreement.

In conclusion, neither Denmark nor Sweden has income-replacement policies and laws, which fully live up to the contemporary disability human rights approach.

PART IV

CONCLUSION

Chapter VIII
Conclusion

1. Main Findings

This thesis defines a contemporary disability human rights approach and applies it to Danish, Swedish and EU law and policy. The thesis shows that Sweden complies with the contemporary disability human rights approach to a greater extent than Denmark. The main difference between Danish and Swedish disability employment law and policy is that employers in Sweden have significantly more far-reaching obligations towards employees with disability-related reduced working capacity. This thesis argues that such difference in law and policy is the main reason that the Swedish labour market is significantly more inclusive towards persons with disabilities and reduced working capacity than the Danish labour market. EU law and policy on disability employment also complies with the contemporary disability human rights approach to a high degree. However the EU promotes the flexicurity model for the labour market which entails low levels of obligations for employers, and which is not conducive to inclusion of persons with disabilities and reduced working capacity on the labour market.

Below, I describe firstly the four main principles or models on which the contemporary disability human rights approach is founded. Thereafter, I describe how these principles should be understood in relation to employment policy and law.

Firstly, the contemporary disability human rights approach is founded on an obligation to promote substantive diversity equality rather than substantive difference equality or formal equality. In relation to persons with disabilities, this paradigm-shift towards the substantive diversity equality model entails that general structures of society must be made inclusive in order to reflect the equal right of persons with disabilities to take part in social life. Thus, according to the substantive diversity equality model, it is not sufficient merely to provide disability-specific measures, which promote employment of persons with disabilities.

Secondly, the contemporary disability human rights approach is founded on a new concept of disability. A shift has taken place in relation to the perception of disability and the causes of disability from medical models of disability to the social minority model of disability, and finally to the social universality model of disability. Common to the two social models of disability is that disability is understood as resulting from the interaction between impairment and barriers in society rather than resulting merely from medical conditions inherent to the individual. As in the social minority model of disability, disability is not seen as the common characteristic of a specific group in society under the social universality model of disability. Instead, disability is perceived as a general human condition and all persons are seen as more or less disabled at different times in their lives, and in different situations. Similarly to the substantive diversity equality model, it follows from the social universality model of disability that the range of what is considered "normal" in society must be broadened and general social structures must be amended accordingly.

Thirdly, the contemporary disability human rights approach is founded on the principle of participation of civil society in the conduct of State affairs. In order to ensure that society becomes inclusive and in order to compensate for the fact that persons with disabilities are under-represented in positions of power, the contemporary disability human rights approach requires that civil society organisations representing persons with disabilities, be included in the conduct of the legislative and executive powers of the State.

Fourthly and finally, the contemporary disability human rights approach is rights-based, meaning that persons with disabilities must to the widest extent possible be provided with legally binding and enforceable individual rights to inclusion.

When applied specifically to disability *employment* law and policy, my research on the contemporary disability human rights approach translates into the following main points:

(1) General law and policy governing the labour market such as legislation on employment protection and health and safety laws must limit the right of employers to dismiss on the grounds of disability-related reduced working capacity and must impose duties on employers to make adjustments for the needs of employees with disability-related reduced working capacity. Only in this way will the general structures of the labour market become inclusive towards persons with disabilities and reduced working capacity.

(2) Persons with disabilities must enjoy effective protection against discrimination on the grounds of disability including an effective right to reasonable accommodation in the work place. However, the prohibition of discrimination is secondary to the creation of inclusive general structures on the labour market. In fact, a prohibition of discrimination on the grounds of disability in itself is unlikely to be effective if the general structures on the labour market are not inclusive.

(3) Persons with disabilities must have access to effective employment promotion services as well as supported employment measures such as wage subvention for persons with disabilities and reduced working capacity and economic support for covering the costs of technical aids in the work places. However,

once again, employment support measures will not be effective in promoting employment of persons with disabilities and reduced working capacity without the creation of inclusive general structures on the labour market. In fact, employment support measures may lead to more exclusion of persons with disabilities from the ordinary labour market if the general structures of the labour market have not been made inclusive.

(4) Persons with disabilities must be ensured an adequate standard of living as well as continued support for returning to the labour market in a dignified manner both when they are temporarily unemployed and when they are outside of the labour market for longer periods of time. However, once again, support for returning to the labour market will not be effective as long as general structures on the labour market have not been made inclusive towards persons with disabilities.

(5) Organisations of persons with disabilities must be included in the formulation and implementation of employment law and policy.

(6) The promotion of inclusion of persons with disabilities on the labour market must to the largest extent possible be secured with individually enforceable rights. In order to ensure an effective implementation of individual rights, it is also important to adhere to the fundamental human rights principles of predictability and transparency regarding the state of law as well as the possibility to have easy access to a complaints procedure, which allows for independent judicial bodies to review decisions taken by the authorities.

(7) The comparison between the actual policies and their effects on the employment situation of persons with disabilities and reduced working capacity in Denmark and Sweden seems to confirm that an employment policy in line with the contemporary disability human rights approach is necessary in order to ensure effective disability employment policies.

One of the triggers of my research was the significant difference in the rates of employment of persons with disabilities and reduced working capacity in Denmark and Sweden. Only 26% of persons with disabilities and reduced working capacity of working age are in employment in Denmark, while persons with disabilities and reduced working capacity are twice as likely to be in employment in Sweden where the employment rate is 50%. Interestingly, persons with disabilities, but without reduced working capacity, have higher or identical rates of employment to persons without disabilities in Denmark and Sweden (around 80% in both countries). This means that the research into more effective disability employment policy should concentrate on how policies affect persons with disabilities *and* reduced working capacity specifically rather than persons with disabilities in general.

The main difference between Danish and Swedish disability employment policies, lies in the strong protection against dismissals enjoyed by persons with disabilities and reduced working capacity in Sweden, as opposed to Denmark. Employers in

Sweden are prohibited from dismissing employees due to reduced working capacity as long as the employees can perform work of value to the employer, and the employer must provide training and adjustments to enable the employee to carry out his or her work. In addition, employees with reduced working capacity who are hired under special conditions are also protected from dismissals in cases of shortage of work. These far-reaching constitute a mainstreaming of the obligations to provide protection against discrimination and promote substantial equality persons with disabilities into general employment protection laws and health and safety laws. As opposed to anti-discrimination laws, employment protection and health and safety laws are not limited to persons with disabilities and they impose relatively clear and detailed obligations on employers to take responsibility for employees whose working capacity reduces. It seems that the strong protection of persons with reduced working capacity under general labour laws in Sweden is the main reason for the more inclusive labour market in Sweden, which leads to a significantly higher rate of employment for persons with disabilities and reduced working capacity than in Denmark.

The necessity of creating generally inclusive structures in the labour market rather than relying on specific support to persons with disabilities is underlined by the fact that the policies and laws in Denmark and Sweden are relatively similar as regards other aspects of the labour market such as employment promotion and support and income-replacement benefits for persons with disabilities. However, in spite of these similarities, the employment rate of persons with disabilities and reduced working capacity remains half as high in Denmark compared to Sweden.

In relation to EU law and policy, the main findings are that the EU's disability policy is based on the contemporary disability human rights approach. However, the EU's disability policy has not been fully mainstreamed into general policies such as the European Employment Strategy. For example, the EU promotes the flexicurity model which is the model on which the Danish labour market is based. This model of regulation of the labour market is characterised by a high degree of flexibility for employers combined with a high degree of security and support for the unemployed. However, as explained above, even assuming that a high degree of security and support is provided for unemployed persons with disabilities and reduced working capacity, then this will not in itself lead to high rates of employment of persons with disabilities. Only by limiting the right of employers to dismiss employees due to reduced working capacity, will the general structures of the labour market become inclusive towards persons with disabilities. A modified flexicurity model, which takes account of the needs of persons with disabilities and reduced working capacity, therefore needs to be promoted by the EU to ensure better compliance with the contemporary disability human rights approach.

* * *

In Sections 2 to 7 below, I make more detailed concluding remarks regarding the different main requirements under the contemporary disability human rights approach as listed above: Employers' obligations, equality law and policy, employment promotion, income-replacement benefits, participation of disability organisations and legally enforceable rights. In Section 6, I also take up the question of the role of social partners in influencing employment law and policy. In Section 8, I discuss EU law and policy in the light of the contemporary disability human rights approach. Finally, in Section 9, I sum up the main recommendations for changes in Danish, Swedish and EU policy with a view to achieving the most effective disability employment policies in line with the contemporary disability human rights approach.

2. Employers' Obligations

From all areas compared in this thesis, the area of employers' obligations under general labour law is where Danish and Swedish employment law and policy differs the most. In Sweden, employers are prohibited from dismissing employees due to reduced working capacity as long as the employees can perform work of value to the employer. Moreover, employers are obliged to provide training and make adjustments to enable the employee to carry out his or her work. In Denmark, employers are as a starting point, permitted to dismiss employees due to significantly reduced working capacity, after a certain period of time.

Based on the fact that all other Danish and Swedish disability employment laws and policies were relatively similar, I conclude that the mainstreaming of limitations in the right of employers to dismiss employees with disability-related reduced working capacity into general labour laws is necessary in order to create a inclusive labour market in line with the requirements under the contemporary disability human rights approach.

3. Equality Law and Policy

An effective protection against discrimination on the grounds of disability is central to the contemporary disability human rights approach founded on the principle of equality and individual rights. The prohibition of discrimination and the duty to provide reasonable accommodation are the embodiment of the rights-based approach and are based on the fundamental principle of equality. An effective protection against discrimination ensures *inter alia* that individuals are not subjected to direct or indirect discrimination on the grounds of disability and that they enjoy an individual right to reasonable accommodation.

However, this thesis also shows that an effective prohibition of discrimination in the field of employment, especially as regards the duty to provide reasonable accommodation, will to a large extent depend on whether *general* legislation governing the labour market is inclusive towards persons with disabilities. Anti-discrimination legislation provides only minimum protection and the courts are influenced by for example duties to provide adjustments for disability and protection against dismissals on the grounds of reduced working capacity when they interpret anti-discrimination laws.

As shown in *Chapter III Equality Law and Policy*, the prohibition of discrimination on the grounds of disability has been implemented in significantly different legal contexts and consequently the levels of protection are different in Denmark and Sweden. As explained above, the general legislation governing the labour market in Denmark is not inclusive towards persons with reduced working capacity. In this legal context, Danish protection against discrimination on the grounds of disability is relatively weak and unclear. Thus, the definition of disability is not clear as different courts at different times have required either long-lasting or permanent impairments as well as more or less far-reaching needs for compensation. Similarly, the duty to provide reasonable accommodation has also been interpreted more or less narrowly by different courts. The lack of clarity has led the Danish Maritime and Commercial Court to refer questions on both the definition of disability and the duty to provide reasonable accommodation to the CJEU for preliminary rulings.

In Sweden, the legal context was different to the Danish legal context, in that general legislation governing the labour market in Sweden limits the right of employers to dismiss employees due to reduced working capacity and imposes far-reaching duties to make adjustments for disability and reduced working capacity. This means that the prohibition of discrimination on the grounds of disability and especially the duty to make reasonable accommodation for needs associated with disability, fit well with existing employers' obligations. Consequently, the protection against discrimination on the grounds of disability and the duty to make reasonable accommodation are relatively strong in Sweden. The definition of disability is broad and encompasses for example minor disabilities as well as past and future disabilities and employers have relatively far-reaching duties to make accommodations for employees with disabilities. In sum, the Swedish but not the Danish protection against discrimination, complies with the contemporary disability human rights approach.

Duties to enact positive action are practically not used in either Denmark or Sweden. Denmark has imposed legal obligations on public employers to give preferential treatment to jobseekers with disabilities, but this possibility is only rarely used in practice. Neither in Denmark nor in Sweden are private employers under an obligation to give preferential treatment to persons with disabilities. Sweden has however adopted legislation, according to which the Public Employment Service may impose duties on private employers to give preferential treatment to jobseekers with reduced working capacity, but this possibility is also rarely used in practice. According to the contemporary disability human rights approach based on substantive diversity equality, the State should not only permit some forms of positive action, it should also establish legally binding duties to promote equality of opportunities through positive action. Consequently, neither Denmark nor Sweden comply with the contemporary disability human rights approach in this regard.

4. Employment Promotion

As mentioned above, employment promotion of persons with disabilities, mainly in the form of economic incentives for employers of persons with disabilities, is an important component of the contemporary disability human rights approach in the field of employment. Thus, it is recognised that persons with disabilities face barriers to employment both due to reduced working capacity and negative attitudes of employers, which may be reduced by economic incentives to employers of persons with disabilities. However, although employment promotional measures may be necessary, they cannot alone ensure high employment rates of persons with disabilities, which can only be achieved through inclusive general structures. There is in fact even a risk that too easy access to employment promotional measures may amount to a barrier in itself to employment in the ordinary employment sector which does not provide special support. The disadvantage of employment with support is that the employee's salary will often be lower than that of his or her colleagues and that he or she will be dependent on continuously qualifying for State support.

The comparison of employment promotion policies in Denmark and Sweden do in fact illustrate quite well that although these policies may help reduce barriers to employment, there is also a risk that they become a barrier to full inclusion on the labour market. In both Denmark and Sweden, approximately 15% of persons with disabilities and reduced working capacity between the ages of 15 and 64 years are in supported employment. However, since the employment rate of persons with disabilities and reduced working capacity is much lower in Denmark, this means that a significantly greater share of *employed* persons with disabilities and reduced working capacity are in supported employment in Denmark. Thus, while only a minority of *employed* persons with disabilities and reduced working capacity are in supported employment in Sweden, this is true for a majority of 60% of persons with disabilities and reduced working capacity *in employment* in Denmark. In other words, the difference in the general structures on the labour market in Denmark and Sweden most likely mean that supported employment measures come to play a different role in the two countries. Whereas supported employment may increasingly be perceived as a prerequisite for employment for a majority of persons with disabilities and reduced working capacity in Denmark, employment with ordinary working conditions without support is still the norm for employed persons with disabilities and reduced working capacity in Sweden. In other words, employment support schemes may create a separate labour market for persons with disabilities with little mobility to the ordinary labour market if the general structures on the labour market are not inclusive towards persons with disabilities and reduced working capacity.

In relation to employment promotion, the contemporary disability human rights approach also entails a new approach to sheltered employment which must aim at inclusion on the ordinary labour market and must take place under working conditions which are as similar as possible to ordinary employment.

5. Income-Replacement Benefits

According to the contemporary disability human rights approach, persons with disabilities must have access to adequate income-replacement benefits when they are unable to obtain suitable employment. In addition support and encouragement for returning to the labour market must continuously be provided in a dignified manner.

Denmark and Sweden are among the countries in Europe that spend the highest percentages of GDP on income-replacement benefits for persons with disabilities and reduced working capacity. However, the level of income-replacement benefits only just reaches 50% of the median equivalised income in especially Denmark which is the required level under the contemporary disability human rights approach. In both countries, the rate of persons receiving a disability pension in Denmark and Sweden is approximately 7% of the population of working age. The main difference in relation to income-replacement policies and laws in Denmark and Sweden is the increasing adherence to active labour market policy in Denmark. Thus, conditions governing entitlements to income-replacement benefits such as disability pensions and sickness benefits have become increasingly tightened in Denmark since around the turn of the new millennium. In addition, the first steps are being taken to reform the disability pension scheme in Denmark to provide continued support for disability pensioners for returning to the labour market. In Sweden, law and policy on income-replacement benefit has also been influenced by active labour market policies, but the changes have been more minor.

Active labour market policies are in accordance with the contemporary disability human rights approach as long as they do not entail a violation of the right to an adequate standard of living. It is also in accordance with the contemporary disability human rights approach to promote continued support for returning to the labour market. However, laws and policies must not compromise the dignity of the recipients and should reflect that reduced access to social benefits will not in itself remove barriers to inclusion on the labour market for persons with disabilities and reduced working capacity.

6. Disability Organisations and Social Partners

As mentioned above, it follows from the contemporary disability human rights approach that disability organisations should be included in the conduct of State affairs in order to compensate for the lack of representation of persons with disabilities in State bodies.

In Denmark, the dialogue between State and disability organisation is highly formalised as opposed to in Sweden. The formalisation of the dialogue with disability organisations regarding employment policy takes the form of representatives of disability organisations in advisory boards on employment policy at local, regional and state levels as well as representatives of disability organisations in key administrative judicial bodies which handle complaints regarding disability employment promotion measures, disability pension and discrimination on the grounds of disability. In Sweden, the dialogue between State bodies and disability organisations has not been formalised to the same degree as in Denmark. As is the case in Denmark, disability organisation will for example be asked for their opinion regarding planned legislation. However, no advisory boards on employment policy or administrative judicial bodies have been set up in Sweden and consequently disability organisations are not represented in such bodies.

However, in spite of a more formalised dialogue between authorities and disability organisations in Denmark, the Danish labour market remains less inclusive towards persons with disabilities than the Swedish labour market. This indicates that a dialogue does not in itself guarantee that opinions and interests are taken into account. In fact, it is possible that the establishment of the formalised dialogue between authorities and disability organisations is a side-effect of a strong political consensus in Denmark that the State should play a withdrawn role in the regulation of the labour market which should to the highest extent possible be left to the social partners. Formalised dialogues between authorities and social partners have therefore been set up in order to ensure that the social partners are involved in the formulation of all public policies and laws on the labour markets. Disability organisations have then been invited to take part in these formalised dialogues. However, where the interests of social partners and disability organisations differ, it would seem that the opinions and interests of the social partners prevail. In Sweden, the social partners also play a strong part in the regulation of the labour market, but they do not enjoy the same degree of autonomy as in Denmark.

In Sweden, a majority of employees are also members of employees' organisation and the social partners also enjoy a great deal of freedom in agreeing on salary and other working conditions. However, the Swedish State has not had the same degree of hands-off policy towards the regulation of the labour market as in Denmark. Most importantly, general employment protection legislation has been adopted limiting the right of employers to dismiss employees due to reduced working capacity. Working environment legislation also imposes strong obligations on employers to make adjustments for the needs of employees with reduced working capacity. In other words, in spite of a less formalised dialogue between authorities and disability organisations in Sweden, the general structures on the labour market are more inclusive towards persons with disabilities.

7. Rights-Based Approach

According to the contemporary disability human rights approach, the promotion of inclusion of persons with disabilities on the labour market must to the largest extent possible be secured with individually enforceable rights. In order to ensure an effective implementation of individual rights, it is also important to adhere to the fundamental human rights principles of predictability and transparency regarding the state of law as well as the possibility to have easy access to a complaints procedure which allows for independent judicial bodies to review decisions taken by the authorities.

In both Denmark and Sweden, the prohibition of discrimination is ensured by law and administrative complaints procedures have been set up to promote effective implementation of this right. In relation to protection against dismissals on the grounds of reduced working capacity and employers' obligations to make adjustments, Sweden has provided legally binding rights to employees. In contrast, employment protection is not ensured to all employees in Denmark and duties to make adjustments for employees with disabilities and reduced working capacity are hardly enforced in Denmark. In relation to employment promotion and income-replacement benefits, decisions are to some extent taken at the discretion of the relevant public authorities which means that the rights-based approach is not fully implemented in these important areas of law and policy. Additionally, in Sweden, an independent administrative complaints procedure against decisions regarding employment promotion and income-replacement benefits does not exist.

8. EU Law and Policy

The EU's disability-specific law and policy is to a large extent in accordance with the contemporary disability human rights approach. Not only has the EU adopted the Employment Equality Directive from the year 2000 which is a key piece of legislation as regards equal treatment of persons with disabilities in the EU. The EU has also concluded the UN Disability Convention which has become the first human rights convention concluded by the EU. Finally, the EU's newly adopted disability strategy also promotes the contemporary disability human rights approach.

However, as mentioned above, the EU's general employment policy does not promote changes of general structures on the labour market to include persons with disabilities and reduced working capacity. Existing EU legislation on health and safety is relatively weak as regards the imposition of obligations on employers to make adjustments for employees with disabilities. Moreover, as part of the non-binding European Employment Strategy, the EU promotes the flexicurity model for labour markets, which is characterised by a high degree of flexibility for employers to organise the work and dismiss employees, and which disencourages employers from creating inclusive structures for employees with reduced working capacity.

The flexicurity model promoted by the EU also promotes adequate social security and support for obtaining employment to unemployed persons, which is in line with the contemporary disability human rights approach. Moreover, the EU also promotes active labour market policies according to which social benefits should be linked with support and incentives for return to the labour market. It is in accordance with the contemporary disability human rights approach to promote continued support for returning to the labour market as long as this is done with respect for the dignity of the persons in question.

The EU has a policy of active participation of disability organisations in the development of its disability policy, which is in line with the contemporary disability human rights approach. There is however room for improvement as regards the participation of disability organisations in the formulation of general employment policy.

Lastly, the EU promotes a rights-based approach to disability, which is also in line with the contemporary disability human rights approach. However, once again, there is room for improvement as regards the mainstreaming of disability in the general legislation adopted by the EU.

9. Main Recommendations

Firstly, protection against dismissals on the grounds of disability-related reduced working capacity should be strengthened in Denmark. A general employment protection act should be adopted in Denmark, which would ensure that all employees and not just employees covered by collective agreements and or legislation on white-collar employees enjoy employment protection. Moreover, the starting point under Danish law should be changed so that the right of employers to dismiss employees due to disability-related reduced working capacity becomes more limited. Employers should share the responsibility with public authorities to ensure a rapid return to the workplace of the employee and only when rehabilitation, training and adjustments cannot enable the employee to carry out work of value to the employer should it be permitted to dismiss him or her. Positive obligations of employers towards employees with disabilities and reduced working capacity should also be set out in work environment legislation as well as legislation on sickness benefits.

Secondly, the prohibition on discrimination on the grounds of disability in the field of employment in Denmark should be made more effective. Clear and broad definitions of the central concepts of disability and reasonable accommodation should be ensured.

Thirdly, supported employment schemes in Denmark should be maintained and sheltered employment should take place under working conditions which are more similar to those on the ordinary labour market and with the aim of promoting inclusion on the ordinary labour market.

Fourthly, persons who receive a disability pension in Denmark should be offered rehabilitation measures and support for returning to the labour market. Moreover, both rehabilitation measures and sickness benefits should be made more widely available in Denmark also to persons who are not expected to regain full working capacity.

Fifthly, both in Denmark and in Sweden, the inclusion of disabled persons' organisations in the conduct of State functions should be strengthened. In Denmark, the opinions and interests of disability organisations should be taken more into account. In Sweden, formal structures for dialogue between public authorities and disabled persons' organisations should be strengthened.

Sixthly, both in Denmark and Sweden, the rights-based approach should be adhered to more stringently to ensure compliance with the contemporary disability human rights approach. In Denmark, as mentioned above, an individual right to employment protection should be provided in a general law rather than being spread out in several laws and based on collective agreements which do not cover all employees on the labour market. In Sweden, an independent administrative board should handle complaints about decisions made by the Social Insurance Agency.

Finally, it is also recommended that the European Union promotes a modified flexicurity-model for labour markets which includes a limited right to dismiss employees due to disability-related reduced working capacity. The concept of 'disability' should be understood broadly in line with the contemporary disability human rights approach.

Summary in English

This thesis examines the evolving principles of disability human rights law in the field of employment and applies them to Danish, Swedish and EU law and policy. The thesis questions firstly what constitutes a contemporary disability human rights approach in the field of employment. Based on an analysis of the newly-adopted UN Convention on the Rights of Persons with Disabilities and present-day interpretations of international and European human rights instruments, four key requirements are identified. Secondly, the book compares Danish and Swedish employment law and policy and their compliance with the contemporary disability human rights approach. In addition, EU law and policy in the field of disability employment law and policy is examined and it is asked, inter alia, whether the 'flexicurity' model promoted by the EU is consistent with the contemporary disability human rights approach. The comparison of Danish and Swedish law and policy is done on the basis of legal sources and statistical information on the use and effects of different laws and policies. The comparison concentrates on four different areas of employment law and policy: disability equality, employers' obligations towards employees with disabilities and reduced working capacity, employment promotion for unemployed persons with disabilities and income-replacement for persons with disabilities outside the labour market. The comparison shows that the main difference between Danish and Swedish disability employment law lies in the level of employers' obligations towards employees with disabilities and reduced working capacity under employment protection law and health and safety law. It is argued that a high level of employers' obligations leads to more inclusive general structures in the labour market in Sweden and constitutes the main explanation for the extreme difference in employment rates for persons with disabilities and reduced working capacity in Denmark and Sweden.

* * *

The research in this thesis has been triggered by three factors: firstly, a transformation of international disability human rights law over the last two decades which should also be reflected in domestic law and policy; secondly, a surprisingly low rate of employment of persons with disabilities in Denmark compared to Sweden; and thirdly, a growth in EU disability policy and law which is exerting an increasingly strong influence on the disability laws and policies of the EU Member States.

Human rights law, which addresses disability has been transformed since the 1990s due to a change in the underlying perception of disability. Whereas limitations in participation in social life were in the past seen as inevitable consequences of impairment, limitations are now perceived as resulting from the inter-action between man-made barriers and impairment. Previously, disability-related human rights were limited to rights to rehabilitation and social security whilst today, it is recognised that persons with disabilities may encounter discrimination in the enjoyment of all human rights. One by one, human rights bodies are embracing this new perception of the human rights of persons with disabilities. By far the strongest evidence of this new approach to disability under human rights law is the United Nations Convention on the Rights of Persons with Disabilities (CRPD) adopted in 2006. The CRPD has already been ratified by almost one hundred States and signed by almost one hundred and fifty States.

The second trigger of my research was the significant difference in the rates of employment of persons with disabilities and reduced working capacity in Denmark and Sweden. Only 26% of persons with disabilities and reduced working capacity of working age are in employment in Denmark, while persons with disabilities and reduced working capacity of working age are twice as likely to be in employment in Sweden, where the employment rate is 50%. Interestingly, persons with disabilities, but without reduced working capacity, have higher or identical rates of employment to persons without disabilities in Denmark and Sweden (around 80% in both countries). Consequently, my research on a more effective disability employment policy concentrates on how policies affect persons with disabilities and reduced working capacity specifically rather than just persons with disabilities.

The third trigger was the growing influence of EU law and policy on disability laws and policies in Member States. A directive on equal treatment in employment was adopted in the year 2000 and in 2010, the CRPD became the first international human rights treaty formally concluded by the European Union. EU law and policy in the field of employment has also developed quite significantly since the 1990s and exerts an increasingly strong influence on the employment policies and laws of the Member States. Interestingly, the EU promotes the so-called flexicurity-model on the labour market which is the labour market model adhered to in Denmark. According to the European Employment Guidelines adopted by the European Council, flexicurity entails a combination of flexible contractual agreements between employers and employees, and adequate social security as well support for obtaining employment.

Definition of the Contemporary Disability Human Rights Approach

In this thesis, I define a contemporary approach to human rights of persons with disabilities based on an analysis of the obligations under the CRPD and present-day interpretations of other human rights instruments in relation to persons with disabilities. I find firstly and most importantly that the contemporary disability human rights approach is based on a substantive diversity equality model according to which general structures of society must be made inclusive in order to reflect the equal right of persons with disabilities to take part in social life. According to the substantive diversity equality model, it is not sufficient merely to provide disability-specific measures to promote employment of persons with disabilities.

Secondly, the contemporary disability human rights approach is founded on a universality social model of disability. This is a social model of disability, which understands disability as resulting from the inter-action between impairment and barriers in society, rather than resulting merely from medical conditions inherent to the individual. In addition, disability is perceived as universal, or as a general human condition. Accordingly, it is recognised that all persons may be more or less disabled at different times in their lives and in different situations. It follows from the universality social model of disability that the range of what is considered "normal" in society must be broadened and that general social structures must be amended accordingly.

Thirdly, the contemporary disability human rights approach is founded on the principle of participation of civil society in the conduct of State functions. In order to ensure that society becomes inclusive and in order to compensate for the fact that persons with disabilities are under-represented in positions of power, the contemporary disability human rights approach requires that civil society organisations representing persons with disabilities be included in the conduct of the legislative and executive powers of the State.

Fourthly and lastly, the contemporary disability human rights approach is rights-based meaning that persons with disabilities must to the widest extent possible be provided with legally binding and enforceable individual rights to inclusion in the labour market.

Below, I summarise the main findings when Danish and Swedish disability employment law and policy are compared and examined in relation to compliance with the contemporary disability human rights approach.

Employers' Obligations

Among the compared areas in this thesis, the area of employers' obligations under general labour law is where Danish and Swedish employment law and policy differs the most. In Sweden, employers are prohibited from dismissing employees due to reduced working capacity as long as the employees can perform work of value to the employer. Moreover, employers are obliged to provide training and make adjustments to enable the employee to carry out his or her work. In Denmark, employers are as a starting point permitted to dismiss employees due to significantly reduced working capacity after a certain period of time. Based on the fact that all other Danish and Swedish disability employment laws and policies were relatively similar, I conclude that the mainstreaming of limitations in the right of employers to dismiss employees with disability-related reduced working capacity into general labour laws is necessary in order to create a inclusive labour market in line with the requirements under the contemporary disability human rights approach.

The EU's general employment policy does not promote changes of general structures on the labour market to include persons with disabilities and reduced working capacity. Existing EU legislation on health and safety is relatively weak as regards the imposition of obligations on employers to make adjustments for employees with disabilities. Moreover, as part of the non-binding European Employment Strategy, the EU promotes the flexicurity model for labour markets, which is characterised by a high degree of flexibility for employers to organise the work and dismiss employees, and which disencourages employers from create inclusive structures for employees with reduced working capacity.

Equality Law and Policy

In spite of the overall similarity in Danish and Swedish law regarding the prohibition of discrimination on the grounds of disability, the levels of protection are different in Denmark and Sweden. Danish protection against discrimination on the grounds of disability is relatively weak and does not fully comply with the requirements of the contemporary disability human rights approach. Thus, both the definition of 'disability' and the duty to provide reasonable accommodation have been interpreted narrowly and remain unclear. In contrast, in Sweden, the prohibition of discrimination and the duty to make reasonable accommodation are relatively strong. The definition of disability is broad and encompasses for example minor disabilities as well as past and future disabilities. In addition, employers have relatively far-reaching duties to make accommodations for employees with disabilities. In addition, lack of provision of reasonable accommodation amounts to direct discrimination under Swedish law.

Duties to enact positive action are practically not imposed in either Denmark or Sweden and, where they exist, they are hardly used in practice. According to the contemporary disability human rights approach based on substantive diversity equality, the State should not only permit some forms of positive action, it should also establish legally binding duties to promote equality of opportunities through positive action. Consequently, neither Denmark nor Sweden comply with the contemporary disability human rights approach in this regard.

EU equality law and policy to a large extent complies with the contemporary disability human rights approach. However, in relation to positive action, EU law also does not comply with the contemporary disability human rights approach since the use of positive action is not mandatory under EU law either.

Employment Promotion

Both Denmark and Sweden have relatively generous wage subvention schemes for the promotion of employment of persons with disabilities, which is in accordance with the contemporary disability human rights approach. However, the comparison of employment promotion policies in Denmark and Sweden shows that although wage subvention policies may help reduce barriers to employment, there is also a risk that they become a prerequisite for employment and thus become a barrier to full inclusion on the labour market. In both Denmark and Sweden, approximately 15% of persons with disabilities and reduced working capacity between the ages of 15 and 64 years are in supported employment. However, since the employment rate of persons with disabilities and reduced working capacity is much lower in Denmark, a significantly greater share of employed persons with disabilities and reduced working capacity are in supported employment in Denmark. Thus, while only a minority of employed persons with disabilities and reduced working capacity are in supported employment in Sweden, this is true for a majority of 60% of persons with disabilities and reduced working capacity in employment in Denmark.

The EU promotes the use of supported employment and is in compliance with the contemporary disability human rights approach in this regard.

Income-Replacement Benefits

Denmark and Sweden are among the countries in Europe that spend the highest percentages of GDP on income-replacement benefits for persons with disabilities and reduced working capacity. However, the level of income-replacement benefits only just reaches 50% of the median equivalised income in especially Denmark which is the required level under the contemporary disability human rights approach. In both countries, the rate of persons who receive a disability pension in

Denmark and Sweden is approximately 7% of the population of working age. The main difference in relation to income-replacement policies and laws in Denmark and Sweden is the increasing adherence to active labour market policy in Denmark. Conditions governing entitlements to income-replacement benefits, such as disability pensions and sickness benefits, have become increasingly tightened in Denmark since around the turn of the new millennium. The EU also promotes active labour market policies, according to which social benefits should be linked with support and incentives for return to the labour market.

Active labour market policies are in accordance with the contemporary disability human rights approach as long as the right to an adequate standard of living is respected. It is also in accordance with the contemporary disability human rights approach to promote continued support for returning to the labour market. However, laws and policies must not compromise the dignity of the recipients and should reflect that reduced access to social benefits will not in itself remove barriers to inclusion on the labour market for persons with disabilities and reduced working capacity.

Disabled persons' organisations and Social Partners

In Denmark, the dialogue between State and disabled persons' organisations is highly formalised as opposed to in Sweden. However, in spite of a more formalised dialogue between authorities and disabled persons' organisations in Denmark, the Danish labour market remains less inclusive towards persons with disabilities than the Swedish labour market. This indicates that a formalised dialogue does not in itself guarantee that all relevant opinions and interests are taken into account. In Denmark, it would seem that where the interests of social partners and disabled persons' organisations have differed, the opinions and interests of the social partners have prevailed.

The EU has a policy of active participation of disabled persons' organisations in the development of its disability policy, which is in line with the contemporary disability human rights approach. There is however room for improvement as regards the participation of disabled persons' organisations in the shaping of general employment policy.

Rights-Based Approach

Denmark and Sweden have adopted the rights-based approach in some areas of employment disability policy, but not in all areas. The prohibition of discrimination is an example of the implementation of the rights-based approach. However, in the area of employment protection, Denmark still relies mainly on regulation by collective agreements, which leave a considerable part of employees on the labour market without employment protection. In relation to employment promotion and income-replacement benefits, the relevant public authorities in both countries operate with a significant element of discretion, which means that the rights-based approach is not fully implemented in these important areas of law and policy. Additionally, in Sweden, an independent administrative complaints procedure for decisions regarding employment promotion and income-replacement benefits does not exist.

The EU promotes a rights-based approach to disability which is also in line with the contemporary disability human rights approach. However, once again, there is room for improvement as regards the mainstreaming of disability in the general legislation adopted by the EU.

Summary in Dutch (Samenvatting)

In dit proefschrift wordt onderzoek gedaan naar de zich steeds meer ontwikkelende mensenrechtelijke beginselen met betrekking tot mensen met een handicap op het gebied van werkgelegenheid en worden deze beginselen toegepast op beleid en wetgeving in Denemarken, Zweden en de Europese Unie. De eerste vraag die wordt gesteld, is wat de huidige mensenrechtelijke aanpak van 'handicap' in relatie tot werkgelegenheid inhoudt. Aan de hand van een analyse van het onlangs aangenomen VN Verdrag inzake de rechten van personen met een handicap en de hedendaagse uitleg van internationale and Europese mensenrechteninstrumenten worden vier elementaire vereisten geïdentificeerd. Ten tweede wordt in het boek een vergelijking getrokken tussen de werkgelegenheidswetgeving en het werkgelegenheidsbeleid in Denemarken en Zweden en de mate waarin deze beantwoorden aan de huidige mensenrechtelijke aanpak van 'handicap'. Daarnaast wordt onderzoek gedaan naar de werkgelegenheidswetgeving en het werkgelegenheidsbeleid van de Europese Unie ten aanzien van mensen met een handicap en wordt onder andere de vraag gesteld of het door de EU gestimuleerde 'flexicurity' model zich verdraagt met de huidige mensenrechtelijke aanpak van 'handicap'. De vergelijking tussen wetgeving en beleid in Denemarken en Zweden wordt getrokken aan de hand van rechtsbronnen en statistische gegevens over het gebruik en de werking van diverse wetten en vormen van beleid. De vergelijking concentreert zich op vier verschillende gebieden van werkgelegenheidswetgeving en -beleid: gelijke behandeling van mensen met een handicap; verplichtingen van de werkgever ten opzichte van werknemers met een handicap en/of een verminderd arbeidsvermogen; het stimuleren van werkgelegenheid voor werklozen met een handicap; en inkomensvervanging voor personen met een handicap buiten de arbeidsmarkt. De vergelijking laat zien dat het voornaamste verschil tussen de Deense en Zweedse werkgelegenheidswetgeving ten aanzien van mensen met een handicap is gelegen in de zwaarte van de werkgeversverplichtingen ten opzichte van werknemers met een handicap en/of een verminderd arbeidsvermogen op grond van beschermende arbeidsvoorschriften en wetgeving ten aanzien van gezondheid en veiligheid op de werkplek. Ik betoog dat in Zweden een hoog niveau aan werkgeversverplichtingen tot meer inclusieve algemene structuren op de arbeidsmarkt leidt en de belangrijkste verklaring is voor de extreme verschillen tussen Denemarken en Zweden in arbeidsparticipatie van personen met een handicap en een verminderd arbeidsvermogen.

* *
*

Aanleiding voor het in dit proefschrift neergelegde onderzoek zijn de volgende drie factoren: ten eerste, een transformatie gedurende de laatste twee decennia van het internationale mensenrechtenrecht met betrekking tot personen met een handicap, die ook terug te vinden zou moeten zijn in het nationale recht; ten tweede, een verrassend lage arbeidsparticipatie van mensen met een handicap in Denemarken in vergelijking tot Zweden; en ten derde, de toename van EU wetgeving en beleid ten aanzien van mensen met een handicap, die een steeds sterkere invloed uitoefenen op de wetgeving en het beleid van de Lidstaten ten aanzien van mensen met een handicap.

Vanaf de negentiger jaren heeft, als gevolg van de veranderde achterliggende opvatting van 'handicap', mensenrechtenrecht dat zich richt op 'handicap' een transformatie ondergaan. Waar belemmering van deelname aan het maatschappelijke leven in het verleden werd gezien als een onontkoombaar gevolg van het hebben van een functiebeperking, worden zulke beletsels tegenwoordig gezien als een gevolg van de interactie tussen de door mensen opgetrokken hindernissen en het hebben van een functiebeperking. Waar vroeger mensenrechten gericht op 'handicap' beperkt waren tot revalidatie en sociale zekerheid, wordt tegenwoordig erkend dat personen met een handicap, bij het genieten van welk mensenrecht dan ook, kunnen worden geconfronteerd met discriminatie. Een voor een omarmen mensenrechtenorganen deze nieuwe opvatting van mensenrechten van mensen met een handicap. Verreweg het beste bewijs van deze nieuwe aanpak van 'handicap' binnen het mensenrechtenrecht is het in 2006 aangenomen VN Verdrag inzake de rechten van personen met een handicap. Het Verdrag is reeds door honderd Staten goedgekeurd en door bijna honderdvijftig Staten ondertekend.

De tweede aanleiding voor het onderzoek was het significante verschil in arbeidsparticipatie van mensen met een handicap en een verminderd arbeidsvermogen tussen Denemarken en Zweden. In Denemarken neemt slechts 26% van de personen met een handicap en een verminderd arbeidsvermogen die deel uitmaken van de beroepsbevolking, deel aan het arbeidsproces, terwijl het in Zweden, met 50% arbeidsparticipatie, tweemaal zo waarschijnlijk is dat mensen met een handicap en een verminderd arbeidsvermogen die deel uit maken van de beroepsbevolking, werkzaam zijn. Interessant is dat in Denemarken en Zweden mensen die wel een handicap, maar geen verminderd arbeidsvermogen hebben, een hogere of eenzelfde arbeidsparticipatie kennen als mensen zonder handicap, namelijk ongeveer 80% in beide landen. Om die reden richt het onderzoek naar een meer doeltreffend werkgelegenheidsbeleid voor mensen met een handicap zich op de manier waarop beleid eerder specifiek van invloed is op personen met *zowel* een handicap *als* een verminderd arbeidsvermogen dan op personen met alleen een handicap.

De derde aanleiding was de toenemende invloed van EU wetgeving en beleid op de wetgeving en het beleid ten aanzien van personen met een handicap in de Lidstaten. In 2000 werd een richtlijn inzake gelijke behandeling in arbeid en beroep aangenomen en in 2010 was het VN Verdrag inzake de rechten van personen met een handicap het eerste internationale mensenrechtenverdrag waarbij de Europese Unie zelf partij werd. Vanaf de negentiger jaren hebben de werkgelegenheidswetgeving en het werkgelegenheidsbeleid van de Europese Unie eveneens een belangrijke ontwikkeling doorgemaakt. Er gaat een grote invloed van uit op het werkgelegenheidsbeleid en de werkgelegenheidswetgeving van de Lidstaten. Het is interessant te zien dat de Europese Unie het zogenoemde "flexicurity model" voor de arbeidsmarkt stimuleert, aangezien dit het arbeidsmarktmodel is dat in Denemarken wordt gehanteerd. Volgens de door de Europese Raad aangenomen Europese Werkgelegenheidsrichtsnoeren houdt flexicurity een combinatie in van flexibele contractuele afspraken tussen werkgevers en werknemers en passende sociale zekerheid alsook ondersteuning bij het verkrijgen van werk.

De hedendaagse mensenrechtenrechtelijke aanpak van 'handicap'

In dit proefschrift wordt de huidige opvatting van mensenrechten van personen met een handicap omschreven aan de hand een analyse van de onder het VN Verdrag inzake de rechten van personen met een handicap opgelegde verplichtingen en de tegenwoordige uitleg van andere mensenrechteninstrumenten met betrekking tot personen met een handicap. Ik heb in de allereerste plaats gevonden dat de huidige mensenrechtelijke aanpak stoelt op een materiële-gelijkheid-in-verscheidenheid model ("substantive diversity equality model"), op grond waarvan de algemene structuren van de maatschappij inclusief dienen te worden gemaakt, zodat zij het gelijke recht van mensen met een handicap aan het maatschappelijk leven deel te nemen, weerspiegelen. Volgens het materiële-gelijkheid-in-verscheidenheid model volstaat het niet specifiek op handicaps gerichte maatregelen ter stimulering van de arbeidsparticipatie van mensen met een handicap te nemen.

Op de tweede plaats stoelt de huidige mensenrechtelijke aanpak van 'handicap' op een universeel sociaal handicap model. Dit sociale handicap model ziet 'handicap' eerder als een gevolg van de interactie tussen functiebeperking en hindernissen in de maatschappij dan louter als een gevolg van medische condities eigen aan het individu. Daar komt bij dat 'handicap' wordt gezien als universeel of als een algemene menselijke conditie. Op grond hiervan wordt erkend dat alle mensen op verschillende momenten in hun leven en onder verschillende omstandigheden in mindere of meerdere mate gehandicapt kunnen zijn. Uit het sociale handicap model dat uitgaat van universaliteit volgt dat de reikwijdte van wat als "normaal" wordt gezien, moet worden verbreed en dat algemene sociale structuren overeenkomstig dienen te worden aangepast.

Op de derde plaats stoelt de huidige mensenrechtelijke aanpak van 'handicap' op het beginsel van participatie van de burgermaatschappij in het uitvoeren van staatsambten. Om er voor te zorgen dat de maatschappij inclusief wordt, en ter compensatie van het feit dat mensen met een handicap zijn ondervertegenwoordigd in machtsposities, vereist de huidige mensenrechtelijke aanpak van 'handicap' dat organisaties binnen de burgermaatschappij die personen met een handicap vertegenwoordigen, participeren in de uitvoering van de wetgevende en uitvoerende macht van de Staat.

En op de vierde en laatste plaats stoelt de huidige mensenrechtelijke aanpak van 'handicap' op het toekennen van rechten, dat wil zeggen dat aan mensen met een handicap zo veel mogelijk juridisch bindende en afdwingbare individuele rechten op integratie in de arbeidsmarkt moeten worden verleend.

Hieronder wordt een samenvatting gegeven van de belangrijkste uitkomsten van de vergelijking tussen de werkgelegenheidswetgeving en het werkgelegenheidsbeleid ten aanzien van mensen met een handicap in Denemarken en Zweden en het onderzoek naar de mate waarop die beantwoorden aan de huidige mensenrechtelijke aanpak van 'handicap'.

Werkgeversverplichtingen

Onder de gebieden die in dit proefschrift worden onderzocht, verschillen werkgelegenheidswetgeving en -beleid in Denemarken en Zweden het meest op het gebied van de in de algemene arbeidswetgeving neergelegde werkgeversverplichtingen. In Zweden is het werkgevers verboden werknemers te ontslaan als gevolg van een verminderd arbeidsvermogen zolang de werknemer in staat is werk uit te voeren dat van waarde is voor de werkgever. Bovendien zijn werkgevers verplicht scholing aan te bieden en aanpassingen aan te brengen zodat de werknemer zijn of haar werk kan uitvoeren. In Denemarken is het werkgevers, na zeker verloop van tijd, in ieder geval toegestaan werknemers te ontslaan als gevolg van een aanzienlijke vermindering van hun arbeidsvermogen. Gezien het feit dat de overige werkgelegenheidswetgeving en het overige werkgelegenheidsbeleid in Denemarken en Zweden ten aanzien van mensen met een handicap in betrekkelijk mate overeenkomen, kom ik tot de conclusie dat de beperking van het recht van werkgevers werknemers met een verminderd vermogen tot het verrichten van arbeid als gevolg van een handicap te ontslaan, opgenomen dient te worden in de algemene arbeidswetgeving om zo een inclusieve arbeidsmarkt te creëren die voldoet aan de eisen die onder de huidige mensenrechtelijke aanpak van 'handicap' worden gesteld.

Het algemene werkgelegenheidsbeleid van de Europese Unie stimuleert geen veranderingen in de algemene structuren op de arbeidsmarkt die het mogelijk zou maken mensen met een handicap en een verminderd arbeidsvermogen daarin op te nemen. De geldende EU wetgeving op het gebied van gezondheid en veiligheid op de werkplek is nogal zwak waar het gaat om het opleggen van verlichtingen aan werkgevers aanpassingen aan te brengen ten behoeve van werknemers met een handicap. Bovendien stimuleert de EU, als onderdeel van de niet-bindende Europese Werkgelegenheidsstrategie, het "flexicurity" model voor arbeidsmarkten, dat wordt gekenmerkt door een hoge mate van flexibiliteit voor werkgevers met betrekking tot het organiseren van werk en het ontslaan van werknemers, en het ontmoedigt werkgevers om inclusieve structuren te creëren voor werknemers met een verminderd arbeidsvermogen.

Wetgeving en beleid op het gebied van gelijke behandeling

Ondanks de globale overeenkomsten tussen de Deense en Zweedse wetgeving met betrekking tot het verbod van het maken van onderscheid op grond van een handicap, verschillen de beschermingsniveaus in beide landen. De in Denemarken geboden bescherming tegen discriminatie op grond van een handicap is betrekkelijk gering en zij beantwoordt niet volledig aan de eisen die worden gesteld in de tegenwoordige mensenrechtelijke aanpak van 'handicap'. Zowel het begrip 'handicap' als de plicht redelijke aanpassingen aan te brengen worden beperkt uitgelegd en zijn nog steeds vaag. In Zweden daarentegen zijn het verbod van discriminatie en de plicht redelijke aanpassingen aan te brengen betrekkelijk sterke begrippen. 'Handicap' wordt ruim omschreven en omvat bij voorbeeld zowel minder ernstige handicaps als in het verleden ervaren handicaps en toekomstige handicaps. Daar komt bij dat werkgevers een betrekkelijk vergaande plicht hebben aanpassingen aan te brengen ten behoeve van werknemers met een handicap. Bovendien levert het niet voorzien in redelijke aanpassingen naar Zweeds recht directe discriminatie op.

Er bestaat in zowel Denemarken als Zweden bijna geen verplichting tot positieve actie over te gaan en waar die er wel is, wordt er in de praktijk nauwelijks gebruik van gemaakt. Onder de huidige mensenrechtelijke aanpak van 'handicap' die is gebaseerd op materiële gelijkheid in verscheidenheid, zou de Staat niet alleen sommige vormen van positieve actie moeten toestaan, maar zou hij tevens juridisch bindende plichten moeten creëren om gelijke kansen middels positieve actie te stimuleren. Dit betekent dat Denemarken noch Zweden in dit opzicht beantwoordt aan de huidige mensenrechtelijk aanpak van 'handicap'.

Wetgeving en beleid van de Europese Unie met betrekking tot gelijke kansen beantwoordt voor een groot deel aan de huidige mensenrechtelijke aanpak van 'handicap'. Wat betreft positieve actie beantwoordt EU recht echter evenmin aan de huidige mensenrechtelijke aanpak van 'handicap', aangezien onder EU recht het ondernemen van positieve actie niet is verplicht.

Stimuleren van werkgelegenheid

Zowel Denemarken als Zweden kennen betrekkelijk ruime loonsubsidiestelsels ter stimulering van de werkgelegenheid van mensen met een handicap. Dit beantwoordt aan de huidige mensenrechtelijke aanpak van 'handicap'. Een vergelijking van het stimuleringsbeleid op het gebied van werkgelegenheid tussen Denemarken en Zweden leert dat, hoewel loonsubsidiestelsels hindernissen bij het vinden van arbeid kunnen helpen verminderen, er ook een gevaar is dat zij een eerste voorwaarde voor arbeidsparticipatie worden en zo een barrière vormen voor volledige arbeidsintegratie. In zowel Denemarken als Zweden doet ongeveer 15% van de mensen met een handicap en een verminderd arbeidsvermogen van tussen de 15 en 64 jaar begeleid werk, maar aangezien de arbeidsparticipatie van personen met een handicap en een verminderd arbeidsvermogen in Denemarken veel lager is, doet een significant groter deel van de *werkende* personen met een handicap en een verminderd arbeidsvermogen daar begeleid werk. Dat is dus zo voor een meerderheid van 60% van de *werkende* personen handicap en verminderd arbeidsvermogen in Denemarken, terwijl in Zweden slechts een minderheid van de *werkende* personen met een handicap en een verminderd arbeidsvermogen begeleid werk doet.

De Europese Unie stimuleert begeleid werk en beantwoordt in dit opzicht aan de huidige mensenrechtelijke aanpak van 'handicap'.

Inkomensvervangende uitkeringen

Denemarken en Zweden zijn twee landen in Europa die het hoogste percentage van hun bruto binnenlands product aan inkomensvervangende uitkeringen voor mensen met een handicap en een verminderd arbeidsvermogen uitgeven. Het niveau van een inkomensvervangende uitkering haalt, in het bijzonder in Denemarken, maar net 50% van het mediaan equivalent inkomen. Dit is het vereiste niveau onder de huidige mensenrechtelijke aanpak van 'handicap'. In beide landen is het percentage mensen dat een arbeidsongeschiktheidspensioen geniet ongeveer 7% van de beroepsbevolking. Het grote verschil tussen Denemarken en Zweden in inkomensvervangend beleid en -wetgeving is dat in Denemarken steeds meer wordt overgegaan tot een actief arbeidsmarktbeleid. Vanaf de eeuwwisseling zijn in Denemarken de voorwaarden voor het recht op inkomensvervangende uitkeringen, zoals arbeidsongeschiktheidspensioenen en ziekte-uitkeringen, steeds meer verscherpt. De Europese Unie stimuleert eveneens actieve vormen van arbeidsmarktbeleid, waarbij sociale uitkeringen dienen te worden gekoppeld aan begeleid werk en prikkels om terug te keren op de arbeidsmarkt.

Actief arbeidsmarktbeleid beantwoordt aan de huidige mensenrechtelijke aanpak van 'handicap', zolang het recht op een passende levensstandaard wordt gerespecteerd. Het strookt eveneens met huidige mensenrechtelijke aanpak van 'handicap' die voortdurende begeleiding bij terugkeer op de arbeidsmarkt stimuleert. Wetgeving en beleid mogen echter de waardigheid van de uitkeringsgerechtigden niet aantasten en dienen te weerspiegelen dat minder toegankelijke sociale uitkeringen de hindernissen om te komen tot arbeidsintegratie van personen met een handicap en een verminderd arbeidsvermogen op zich niet wegnemen.

Organisaties van personen met een handicap en sociale partners

In tegenstelling tot Zweden is in Denemarken de dialoog tussen de Staat en organisaties waarin mensen met een handicap zich hebben georganiseerd zeer geformaliseerd. Ondanks een meer geformaliseerde dialoog in Denemarken tussen de autoriteiten en dergelijke organisaties blijft de Deense arbeidsmarkt echter minder toegankelijk voor mensen met een handicap dan de Zweedse arbeidsmarkt. Dit wijst er op dat een geformaliseerde dialoog op zich geen garantie is dat met alle in het spel zijnde opvattingen en belangen rekening wordt gehouden. Het lijkt erop dat in Denemarken de meningen en belangen van de sociale partners waar die niet overeenkomen met de belangen van de organisaties waarin mensen met een handicap zich hebben georganiseerd, voorop staan.

De Europese Unie stimuleert actieve deelname van organisaties van personen met een handicap bij het ontwikkelen van beleid ten behoeve van personen met een handicap, hetgeen strookt met de huidige mensenrechtelijke aanpak van 'handicap'. Er is echter ruimte voor verbetering van de deelname van organisaties van personen met een handicap aan het vormen van een algemeen werkgelegenheidsbeleid.

Een op rechten stoelende aanpak

Denemarken en Zweden hebben op een aantal terreinen van werkgelegenheidsbeleid voor personen met een handicap, maar niet op alle, gekozen voor een aanpak die bestaat uit het toekennen van rechten aan deze groep. Het verbod van discriminatie is zo'n voorbeeld van uitvoering van een dergelijke aanpak. Op het gebied van werkgelegenheidsbescherming gaat Denemarken nog steeds uit van regelgeving per collectieve arbeidsovereenkomst, waardoor een aanzienlijk deel van de werknemers op de arbeidsmarkt geen werkgelegenheidsbescherming geniet. Ten aanzien van het stimuleren van werkgelegenheid en inkomensvervangende uitkeringen hebben de betreffende openbare autoriteiten in beide landen een grote beleidsvrijheid, hetgeen betekent dat een aanpak die stoelt op het toekennen van rechten op deze belangrijke rechtsgebieden en beleidsterreinen niet wordt nagevolgd. Daar komt bij dat in Zweden geen onafhankelijke klachtenprocedure bestaat voor bestuursbesluiten aangaande het stimuleren van werkgelegenheid en inkomensvervangende uitkeringen.

De Europese Unie stimuleert een op rechten stoelende aanpak van 'handicap', die eveneens beantwoordt aan de huidige mensenrechtelijke opvatting. Waar het gaat om opname van 'handicap' in de door de Europese Unie aangenomen algemene wetgeving kan in dit opzicht echter ook nog het een en ander verbeteren.

List of Literature

Andersen, A., R. Nielsen and K. Precht. (2008). *Ligestillingslovene, Bind 1.* Copenhagen, DJØF.

Andersen, A., R. Nielsen and K. Precht. (2010). *Ligestillingslovene Bind 2.* Copenhagen, DJØF.

Andersen, J. (1991). “”SIFU-princippet i offentligretlig belysning.”.” *Ugeskrift for Retsvæsen* 272.

Andersen, J., M. Engberg, et al. (2003). *Forvaltningsret.* Copenhagen, DJØF.

Andersen, L. S. (2004). *Funktionærret.* Copenhagen, DJØF.

Arbetsförmedlingen (2009). “Arbetsmarknadspolitiska Program – Årsrapport 2008.” **Ure 2009:1**.

Arbetsmarknadsstyrelsen (2006). Personer med Funktionshinder och Nedsat Arbetsförmåga. Stockholm. **Ura 2006:3**.

Arnardóttir, O. M. (2003). *Equality and Non-Discrimination under the European Convention of Human Rights.* The Hague, Martinus Nijhoff Publishers.

Arnardóttir, O. M. (2009). A Future of Multidimensional Disadvantage Equality? *The UN Convention on the Rights of Persons with Disabilities – European and Scandinavian Perspectives.* O. M. Arnardóttir and G. Quinn. Leiden, Martinus Nijhoff Publishers.

Bamforth, N. (2004). “Conceptions of Anti-Discrimination Law.” *Oxford Journal of Legal Studies* **24**(4): 693–716.

Barbier, J.-C., F. Colomb, et al. (2009). Flexicurity – an open method of coordination, at the national level. *Documents de travail du Centre d’Economie de la Sorbonne* Université Panthéon-Sorbonne (Paris 1), Centre d’Economie de la Sorbonne. **09046**.

Barbier, J.-C. and W. Ludwig-Meyerfoyer (2004). “Introduction: The Many Worlds of Activation.” *European Societies* **6**(6): 423–436.

Bardenfleth, L. and M. S. Madsen (2005). *Arbejdspladsens Kommenterede Love: Forskelsbehandlingsloven.* Copenhagen, Dansk Arbejdsgiverforening.

Barlett, P., O. Lewis, et al. (2007). *Mental Disability and the European Convention on Human Rights.* Leiden, Martinus Nijhoff Publishers.

Barnard, C. (2006). *EC Employment Law, Third Edition.* Oxford, Oxford University Press.

Barnard, C. and B. Hepple (2000). “Substantive Equality.” *Cambridge Law Journal* **59**: 562–585.

Bell, M. (2002). *Anti-Discrimination Law and the European Union.* Oxford, Oxford University Press.

Bell, M. (2007). Direct Discrimination. *Non-Discrimination Law.* D. Schiek, L. Waddington and M. Bell. Oxford, Hart Publishing.

Bell, M. and L. Waddington (2003). “Reflecting on Inequalities in European Equality Law.” *European Law Review* **28**: 349–369.

Bengtsson, S. (1997). *Handicap og funktionshæmning i halvfemserne.* Copenhagen, The Danish National Institute of Social Research.

Bengtsson, S. and N. C. Mateu (2009). Beskyttet Beskæftigelse – En Kortlægning. Copenhagen, SFI Det Nationale Forskningscenter for Velfærd. **09:09**.

Bickenbach, J. E. (1999a). Minority Rights or Universal Participation: The Politics of Disablement. *Disability, Divers-ability and Change*. M. Jones and L. A. Basser. The Hague, Martinus Nijhoff Publishers.

Bickenbach, J. E., S. Chatterji, et al. (1999b). "Models of Disablement, Universalism and the International Classifications of Impairments, Disablements and Handicaps." *Social Science and Medicine* **48**: 1173–1187.

Björgvinsson, D. T. (2009). The Protection of the Rights of Persons with Disabilities in the Case Law of the European Court of Human Rights. *The UN Convention on the Rights of Persons with Disabilities – European and Scandinavian Perspectives*. O. M. Arnardóttir and G. Quinn. Leiden, Martinus Nijhoff Publishers.

Bloch, F. S. and R. Prins (2001). *Who Returns to Work and Why?*

A Six-Country Study on Work Incapacity & Reintegration. New Brunswick and London, Transaction Publishers.

Board, D. N. S. A. (2010). Flexjob og Flexydelse. Copenhagen. **June 2010**.

Board, N. S. A. (2006). Førtidspension efter arbejdsevnemetoden. Copenhagen, Ankestyrelsen.

Board, N. S. A. (2007). Førtidspension til personer med psykisk lidelse. *Ankestyrelsens Praksisundersøgelser*. Copenhagen.

Bogdan, M. (2004). On the value and method of rule-comparison in compartive law. *Festschrift für Erik Jayme*. T. Frantzen. München, Sellier.

Bredgaard, T. and F. Larsen (2005). Introduction. *Employment Policy from Different Angles*. T. Bredgaard and F. Larsen. Copenhagen, DJØF.

Bredgaard, T., F. Larsen, et al. (2007). "Flexicurity – Afklaring af et begreb i bevægelse." *Tidsskrift for Arbejdsliv* **9**(4): 8–24.

Bruun, J. R. (2003). *Usaglig Afskedigelse*. Copenhagen, Thomson GadJura.

Bruun, N. and J. Malmberg (2005). Arbetsrätten i Sverige och Finland efter EU-inträdet. *Tio år med EU – effekter på arbetsrätt, partsrelationer, arbetsmarknad och social trygghet*. K. Ahlberg, Arbetslivsinstitutet. **2005:5**.

Calleman, C. (2000). *Turordning vid Uppsägning*. Stockholm, Norstedts Juridik AB.

Christoffersen, J. (2000). "Højesteret og den Europæiske Menneskerettighedskonvention." *Ugeskrift for Retsvæsen*: 593–600

Christoffersen, J. (2001). "Folkerettens virkning i dansk ret,." *Ugeskrift for Retsvæsen*: 143–148.

Christoffersen, J. (2009). *Fair Balance: Proportionality, Subsidiarity and Primarity in the European Convention of Human Rights*. The Hague, Martinus Nijhoff Publishers.

Clements, L. and J. Read (2005). The Dog That Didn't Bark: The Issue of Access to Rights under the European Convention of Human Rights by Disabled People. *Disability Rights in Europe, from theory to practice*. A. Lawson and C. Gooding. Oxford, Hart Publishing.

Dahl, K., D. Boesby, et al. (2002). Welfare Systems and the Management of the Economic Risk of Unemployment: Denmark. *Working Paper nr. 8*. Copenhagen, The Danish National Institute of Social Research.

De Burca, G., ed. (2005). *EU Law and the Welfare State*. Oxford, Oxford University Press.

De Burca, G. and B. De Witte (2005). *Social Rights in Europe*. Oxford, Oxford University Press.

De Schutter, O. (2005). Reasonable Accommodation and Positive Obligations in the European Convention on Human Rights. *Disability Rights in Europe – From Theory to Practice*. A. Lawson and C. Gooding. Oxford, Hart Publishing.

De Schutter, O. (2007). Chapter Seven Positive Action. *Non-Discrimination Law*. D. Schiek, L. Waddington and M. Bell. Oxford, Hart Publishing.

De Schutter, O. and S. Deakin (2005). *Social Rights and Markets Forces: Is the Open Coordination of Employment and Social Policies the Future of Social Europe?*. Brussels, Bruylant.

Denmark, S. (2007). Arbejdskraftundersøgelsen 2006. *Statistiske Efterretninger*. **2007:5**.

Driessen-Reilly, M. and B. Driessen "Don't Shoot the Messenger: A Look at Community Law Relating to Harassment in the Workplace " *European Law Review* **28**(4): 493–507.

Editor, C. M. L. R. (2006). "Horizontal direct effect – A law of diminishing coherence?" *Common Market Law Review* **43**(1): 1–8.

Editorial, C. M. L. R. (2006). "Editorial Comments: Horizontal direct effect – A law of diminishing coherence?" *Common Market Law Review* **43** (1): 1–8.

Edwards, P. (2003). *Industrial Relations: Theory and Practice*. Oxford, Blackwell Publishing.

Ellis, E. (2005). *EU Anti-Discrimination Law* Oxford, Oxford University Press.

Emborg, O. and P. Schaumburg-Müller (1998). *Offentlig Arbejdsret*. Copenhagen, GadJura.

Finke, B. (2007). "Civil Society Participation in EU Governance." *Living Reviews in European Governance (www.europeangovernance.livingreviews.org)* **2**(2).

Frederiksen, Y. and M. Krarup (2008). *Lov om Forbud mod Forskelsbehandling på Arbejdsmarkedet med Kommentarer*. Copenhagen, Thomson.

Fredman, S. (2002). *Discrimination Law*. Oxford, Oxford University Press.

Fredman, S. (2005a). Disability Equality, A Challenge to the Existing Anti-Discrimination Paradigm? *Disability Rights in Europe*. C. Gooding and A. Lawson. Oxford Portland, Hart Publishing.

Fredman, S. (2005b). "Changing the Norm: Positive Duties in Equal Treatment Legislation." *Maastricht Journal of European and Comparative Law* **12**(4): 369–398.

Freedland, Craig, et al. (2007). *Public Employment Services and European Law*. Oxford, Oxford University Press.

Friedrich, D. (2007). "Old Wine in New Bottles: The Actual and Potential Contribution of Civil Society to Democratic Governance in Europe." *RECON Online Working Papers (www.reconproject.eu)*(07/2007).

Function, S. D. (2010). Beretning 2009 – Status på job og handicap, Arbejdsmarkedsstyrelsen, Beskæftigelsesregionerne i Danmark.

Gerards, J. H. (2004). "Intensity of Review in Equal Treatment Cases." *Netherlands International Law Review*: 135–183.

Gijzen, M. (2006). *Selected Issues in Equal Treatment Law: A multi-layered comparison of European, English and Dutch Law.* Antwerp, Intersentia.

Gordley, J. (1998). "Is comparative law a discipline." *The American Journal of Comparative Law* **46**: 607–615.

Gundersen, T. (2008). Kvoteordninger i Europeiske Land for Personer med Nedsatt Funksjonsevne. Oslo, Norsk Institut for Forskning om Oppvekst, Velferd og Aldring. **8/08**.

Hahn, H. (1993). "The Potential Impact of Disability Studies on Political Science (as well as vice-versa)." *Policy Studies Journal* **1**(4): 740–751

Halvorsen, R. and B. Hvinden (2009a). Nordisk politikk for funksjonshemmede møter internasjonal likebehandlingspolitikk. *Funksjonshemming – politikk, hverdagsliv og arbeidsliv.* J. Tøssebro. Oslo, Universitetsforlaget.

Halvorsen, R. and B. Hvindén (2009b). Nordic Disability Protection meeting Supranational Equal Treatment Policy – A boost for the Human Rights of People with Disabilities? *Human Rights, Dignity and Autonomy in Health Care and Social Services.* H. S. Aasen, A. B. d. Silva and R. Halvorsen. Brussels, Intersentia Publisher.

Helgadóttir, R. (2009). The UN Convention in Nordic Domestic Law – Lessons Learned from Other Treaties. *The UN Convention on the Rights of Persons with Disabilities – European and Scandinavian Perspectives.* O. M. Arnardóttir and G. Quinn. Leiden, Martinus Nijhoff Publishers.

Hendricks, A. (2002). Different Definition – Same Problem – One Way Out? *Disability Rights Law and Policy – International and National Perspectives.* M. L. Breslin and S. Yee. Ardsley Transnational Publishers.

Hendricks, A. (2005). Promoting Disability Equality after the Treaty of Amsterdam: New Legal Directions and Practical Expansion Strategies. *Disability Rights in Europe – From Theory to Practice.* A. Lawson and C. Gooding. Oxford, Hart Publishing.

Hendricks, A. and M. V. Liisberg (2009). Entry on 'Disability'. *Encyclopedia of Human Rights.* D. P. Forsythe. Oxford, Oxford University Press.

Hendriks, L. W. a. A. (2002). "The Expanding Concept of Employment Discrimination in Europe: From Direct and Indirect Discrimination to Reasonable Accommodation Discrimination." *The International Journal of Comparative Labour Law and Industrial Relations* **18**(3): 403–427.

Hoecke, M. v. and M. Warrington (1998). "Towards a New Model of Comparative Law." *International and Comparative Law Quaterly* **47**: 495–536.

Hoskins, D. L. (2006). "Great Expectations: Protection From Discrimination Because of Disability in Community Law." *European Law Review* **31**(5): 667–689.

Hoskins, D. L. (2007). "European Developments, A High Bar for EU Disability Rights." *Industrial Law Journal* **36**(2): 228–237.

Hvindén, B. (2008). Cultures of Activation: the shifting relationship between income maintenance and employment promotion in the Nordic context. *Culture and Welfare State – Values and Social Policy in Comparative Pespective.* W. v. Oorschot, M.

Opielka and B. Pfau-Effinger. Cheltenham, Edward Elgar Publishing Limited: 205–224.

Høgelund, J. (2003). *In Search of Effective Disability Policy*
Comparing the Developments and Outcomes of Dutch and Danish Disability Policies. Amsterdam, Amsterdam University Press.

Illum, K. (1964). *Kollektiv Arbejdsret, 3. udgave.* Copenhagen, Nyt Nordisk Forlag Arnold Busk.

Inghammar, A. (2007). *Funktionshindrad – med rätt till arbete?*
En komparativ studie av arbetsrättliga regleringar kring arbete och funktionshinder. Lund, Juristförlaget.

Institute, D. T. (2009). Success med Flexicutiry. *Analyse og Erhvervsfremme.* Copenhagen. **July 2009**.

Jacobsen, B.D. (2005). "Mere om Føtex-sagen", *Ugeskrift for Retsvæsen* **2005,** p. B 301.

Jans, J. H. (2007). "The Effect in national Legal Systems of the Prohibition of Discrimination on Grounds of Age as a General Principle of Community Law." *Legal Issues of Economic Integration* **34**(1): 53–66.

Johansson, H. and B. Hvindén (2007). "Re-activating the Nordic Welfare States: do we find a distinct universalistic model?" *International Journal of Sociology and Social Policy* **27**(7/8): 334–346.

Justesen, P. (2008). "Handicap og Arbejdsmarked." *Ugeskrift for Retsvæsen* **2008**, p. B 295.

Kahn-Freund, O. (1974). "On Uses and Misuses of Comparative Law." *Modern Law Review* **37**: 1–27.

Kallehauge, H. (2009). General Themes Relevant to the Implementation of the UN Disability Convention into Domestic Law: Who is Responsible for the Implementation and How Should it be Performed? *The UN Convention on the Rights of Persons with Disabilities – European and Scandinavian Perspectives.* O. M. Arnardóttir and G. Quinn. Leiden, Martinus Nijhoff Publishers.

Kayess, R. and P. French (2008). "Out of Darkness and Into Light." *Human Rights Law Review* **8**(1): 1–34.

Ketscher, K. (2008). *Socialret – Principper, Rettigheder, Værdier.* Copenhagen, Thomson.

Kimber, C. J. M. (1996). Equality or Self-Determination. *Understanding Human Rights.* C. Gearty and A. Tomkins. London, Mansell Publishing.

Koch, I. E. (2009). From Invisibility to Indivisibility: The International Convention on the Rights of Persons with Disabilities. *The UN Convention on the Rights of Persons with Disabilities – European and Scandinavian Perspectives.* O. M. Arnardóttir and G. Quinn. Leiden, Martinus Nijhoff Publishers.

Koch, I. E., K. Røberg, et al. (2004). *Menneskerettigheder og Magtfordeling.* Århus, Århus Universitetsforlag.

Kohler-Koch, B. and B. Finke (2007). "The Institutional Shaping of EU-Society Relations: A Contribution to Democracy via Participation " *Journal of Civil Society* **3**(3): 205–221.

Kristiansen, J. (1997). *Lønmodtager Beskyttelse i Dansk Arbejdsret.* Copenhagen, DJØF.

Kristiansen, J. (2005). *Grundlæggende Arbejdsret.* Copenhagen, DJØF.

Kristiansen, J. (2008). "Laval, Viking og den danske model." *Juristen*(3).

Källström, K. and J. Malmberg (2006). *Anställningsförhållandet: Inledning till den individuella arbetsrätten*. Uppsala, Iustus Förlag.

Larsen, B. and J. Høgelund (2009). Handicap og Beskæftigelse – Udviklingen mellem 2002 og 2008. Copenhagen, SFI – Det Nationale Forskningscenter for Velfærd. **09:05**.

Larsen, B., K. H. Schademan, et al. (2008). Handicap og beskæftigelse i 2006. Copenhagen, Danish National Centre for Social Research, SFI. **08:10**.

Lawson, A. (2007). "The United Nations Convention on the Rights of Persons with Disabilities: New Era or False Dawn." *Syracuse Journal of International Law and Commerce* **34**: 563–614.

Lawson, A. (2009). The UN Convention on the Rights of Persons with Disabilities and European Disability Law: A Catalyst for Cohesion? *The UN Convention on the Rights of Persons with Disabilities – European and Scandinavian Perspectives*. O. M. Arnardóttir and G. Quinn. Leiden, Martinus Nijhoff Publishers.

Liisberg, M. V. (2009). Deltagelse i Samfundslivet for Handicappede – Rettighed eller Privilegium? *Den Europæiske Menneskerettighedsdomstol – 50 års samspil med dansk ret og politik*. J. Christoffersen and M. R. Madsen. Copenhagen, Dansk Jurist og Økonom Forbund.

Lindquist, G. S. and E. Wadensjö (2008). *Dags för en ny arbetsskadeförsäkring*. Stockholm, SNS förlag.

LO, D. C. o. T. U. (2001). Diskussionsoplæg om Fremtidens Arbejdsret. Copenhagen, LO.

Loucaides, L. G. (2007). *The European Convention on Human Rights. Collected Essays*. Leiden, Martinus Nijhoff Publishers.

Lunning, L. and G. Toijer (2006). *Anställningsskydd – Kommentarer til Anställningsskyddslagen*. Stockholm, Norstedts juridik AB.

Madsen, P. K. (2007). Distribution of Responsibility for Social Security. *Amsterdam Institute for Advanced Labour Studies*. Amsterdam, University of Amsterdam. **Working Papers Number 07/51**.

McCrudden, C. and H. Kountouros (2007). Human Rights and European Equality Law. *Equality Law in an Enlarged European Union – Understanding the Article 13 Directives*

H. Meenan. Cambridge, Cambridge University Press.

Miller, M. M., J. Høgelund, et al. (2006). Handicap & beskæftigelse. Udviklingen mellem 2002 og 2005. Copenhagen, Danish Institute for Social Research, SFI. **06:24**.

Mølgaard, M. M., J. Høgelund, et al. (2006). Handicap og Beskæftigelse – Udviklingen mellem 2002 og 2005. Copenhagen, SFI. **06:24**.

Nergelius, J. (1996). *Konstitutionellt Rättighetsskydd: Svänsk Rätt i Komparativt Perspektiv*. Stockholm, Fritzes.

Nergelius, J. (2008). Between Collectivism and Constitutionalism. *Constitutionalism: New Challenges – European Law from a Nordic Perspective*. J. Nergelius. Leiden, Martinus Nijhoff Publishers.

Nielsen, H. K. (2004). *Funktionærlov med Kommentarer*. Copenhagen, Thomson.

Nielsen, R. (1996). *Employers' Prerogatives*. Copenhagen DJØF.

Nielsen, R. (1999). *Retskilderne, 6. reviderede udgave*. Copenhagen, Jurist og Økonomforbundets Forlag.

Nielsen, R. (2005). *Lærebog i Arbejdsret*. Copenhagen, DJØF.

Nielsen, R. and L. Roseberry (2008). *Dansk Arbejdsret*. Copenhagen, DJØF.

Norström, T. (2010). *Nya sociallagarna*. Stockholm, Norstedts Juridik.

NOSOSKO, N. S. k. (2009). Social Tryghed i de nordiske lande 2007/08

Omfang, udgifter og financiering. J. Nielsen. Copenhagen.

Nowak, M. (2005). *U.N. Covenant on Civil and Political Rights – CCPR Commentary, 2nd Revised Edition*. Kehl, Norbert Paul Engel Verlag.

Numhauser-Henning, A. (2001). *Legal Perspectives on Equal Treatment and Non-Discrimination*. The Hague, Kluwer Law International.

Numhauser-Henning, A. (2007). Funktionshindrades rätt till arbete – ett område under snabb förändring *Inkluderande arbetsliv*. A. Kunskapsrådet. Stockholm, Fritze. **SOU 2009:93**.

Numhauser-Henning, A. (2009). En samlad diskrimineringslagstiftning. *Arbeid og Rett, Festkrift til Henning Jahellns 70-årsdag*. H. Aune, O. K. Fauchald, K. Lilleholt and D. Michalsen. Oslo, Cappelen Damm.

O'Cinneide, C. (2005). A New Generation of Equality Legislation? Positive Duties and Disability Rights. *Disability Rights in Europe – From Theory to Practice*. A. Lawson and C. Gooding. Oxford, Hart Publishing.

O'Cinneide, C. (2006). "Positive Action and the Limits of Existing Law." *Maastricht Journal of European and Comparative Law* **13**(3): 351–364.

O'Cinneide, C. (2009). Extracting Protection for the Rights of Persons with Disabilities from Human Rights Frameworks: Establishing Limits and New Possibilities. *The UN Convention on the Rights of Persons with Disabilities – European and Scandinavian Perspectives*. O. M. Arnardóttir and G. Quinn. Leiden, Martinus Nijhoff Publishers.

Ovey, C. and R. C. A. White (2006). *Jacobs and White, The European Convention of Human Rights*. Oxford, Oxford University Press.

Paulsen, J. (1997). *Afskedigelse*. Copenhagen, GadJura.

Priestley, M. (2007). "In Search of European Disability Policy: Between National and Global." *Alter, Revue Europeenne de recherche sur le handicap* **1**: 61–74.

Quinn, G. (2005). The European Social Charter and EU Anti-Discrimination Law in the Field of Disability: Two Gravitational Fields With One Common Purpose. *Social Rights in Europe*. G. d. Búrca and B. d. Witte. Oxford, Oxford University Press.

Quinn, G. (2007). Disability Discrimination Law in the EU. *Equality Law in an Enlarged European Union*. H. Meenan. Cambridge, Cambridge University Press.

Quinn, G. (2007). People with Disabilities: Active Players in the internal Market *European Day of Persons with Disabilities*. Brussels: (summary of presentation).

Quinn, G. (2009). Resisting the 'Temptation of Elegance': Can the Convention on the Rights of Persons with Disabilities Socialise States to Right Behaviour? *The UN Convention on the Rights of Persons with Disabilities – European and Scandinavian Perspectives*. O. M. Arnardóttir and G. Quinn. Leiden, Martinus Nijhoff Publishers.

Quinn, G. and T. Degener (2002). *The Current Use and Future Potential of the United Nations Human Rights Instruments in the Context of Disability.* Geneva, United Nations High Commissioner for Human Rights.

Read, L. C. a. J. (2005). The Dog that Didn't Bark: The Issue of Access to Rights under the European Convention on Human Rights by Disabled People. *Disability Rights in Europe – From Theory to Practice.* A. Lawson and C. Gooding. Oxford, Hart Publishing.

Roseberry, L. (2004) "Tørklædediskrimination på arbejdsmarkedet", *Ugeskrift for Retsvæsen*, p. B 189.

Samhall (2009). Års- och hållbarhetsredovisning 2008. Stockholm, Samhall.

Scheinin, M. (2008). Constitutionalism and Approaches to Rights. *Constitutionalism: New Challenges – European Law from a Nordic Perspective.* J. Nergelius. Leiden, Martinus Nijhoff Publishers.

Schiek, D. (2002). "A New Framework on Equal Treatment of Persons in EC Law?" *European Law Journal* **8**(2): 290–314.

Schiek, D. (2009). From European Union non-discrimination law towards multidimensional equality law for Europe. *European Union Non-Discrimination Law – Comparative perspectives on multidimensional equality law.* D. Schiek and V. Chege. London, Routledge Cavendish.

Schiek, D., L. Waddington, et al., Eds. (2007). *Non-Discrimination Law.* Oxford, Hart Publishing.

Schiek, D., L. Waddington, et al. (2007a). *Non-Discrimination Law – Cases, Materials and Texts on National, Supranational and International Non-Discrimination Law.* oxford, Hart Publishing.

Schiek, D., L. Waddington, et al. (2007b). A Comparative Perspective on Non-Discrimination Law. *Non-Discrimination Law.* D. Schiek, L. Waddington and M. Bell. Oxford, Hart Publishing.

Schultze, M. (2010). A Handbook on the Human Rights of Persons with Disabilities – Understanding the UN Convention on the Rights of Persons with Disabilities. New York, Handicap International.

Shakespeare, T. (2006). *Disability Rights and Wrongs.* Oxon, Routledge.

Shaw, M. N. (1991). *International Law, 3rd Edition.* Cambridge, Cambridge University Press.

Spiermann, O. (2002). "Om tilbageholdenhed i anvendelsen af internationale menneskerettighedskonventioner." *Ugeskrift for Retsvæsen*: 412–421.

Spiermann, O. (2006). *Moderne Folkeret.* København, DJØF.

Statistics-Denmark (2009). Statistical Yearbook. Copenhagen, Statistics Denmark

Statistics-Sweden (2003). Labour Market Situation for Disabled Persons – 4th quarter 2002 Stockholm, Statistics-Sweden. **2003:3**.

Statistics-Sweden (2007). Labour Market Situation for Disabled Persons – 4th quarter 2006 *Information on Education and the Labour Market.* Stockholm, Statistics Sweden. **2007:2**.

Statistics-Sweden (2009). Labour Market Situation for Disabled Persons – 4th quarter 2008 *Information on Education and the Labour Market* Stockholm, Statistics Sweden. **2009:3**.

Stein, M. A. (2007). "Disability Human Rights." *california Law Review* **95**: 75–122.

Stein, M. A. and J. E. Lord (2009). Future Prospects for the United Nations Convention on the Rights of Persons with Disabilities. *The UN Convention on the Rights of Persons with Disabilities – European and Scandinavian Perspectives*. O. M. Arnardóttir and G. Quinn. Leiden, Martinus Nijhoff Publishers.

Stenholm, P. S. and K. B. Spiermann (2004). *Afskedigelsesnævnet*. Copenhagen, Danish Confederation of Employers (DA).

Tobler, C. (2007). "Putting *Mangold* in perspective: in response to *Editorial comments*, Horizontal direct effect – A law of diminishing coherence." *Common Market Law Review* **44**(4): 1177–1183.

Tobler, C. and K. Waaldijk (2009). "Case C-267/06, *Tadao Maruko v. Versorgungsanstalt der deutschen Bühnen*, Judgment of the Grand Chamber of the Court of Justice of 1 April 2008, not yet reported." *Common Market Law Review* **46**(2): 723–746.

Traustadóttir, R. (2009). Disability Studies, the Social Model and Legal Developments. *The UN Convention on the Rights of Persons with Disabilities – European and Scandinavian Perspectives*. O. M. Arnardóttir and G. Quinn. Leiden, Martinus Nijhoff Publishers.

Tömmel, I. (2010). Civil society in the EU: a strong player or a fig-leaf for the democratic deficit? *Canada-Europe Transatlantic Dialogue: Seeking Transnational Solutions to 21st Century Problems* www.carleton.ca/europecluster.

Waddington, L. (1995). *Disability, Employment and the European Community*. Antwerpen, Maklu.

Waddington, L. (2004). Implementing and Interpreting the Reasonable Accommodation Provision of the European Equality Directive: Learning from Experience and Achieving Best Practice, European Commission.

Waddington, L. (2006a). *From Rome to Nice in a Wheelchair – The development of European Disability Policy*, Europea Law Publishing.

Waddington, L. (2006b). "Recent Developments and the Non-Discrimination Directives: Mangold and More." *Maastricht Journal of European and Comparative Law* **13**(3): 365.

Waddington, L. (2007a). Reasonable Accommodation. *Non-Discrimination Law*. D. Schiek, L. B. Waddington and M. Bell. Oxford, Hart Publishing.

Waddington, L. (2007b). "Case C-13/05, *Chacon Navas v. Eurest Colectividades SA*, judgment of the Grand Chamber of 11 July 2006." *Common Market Law Review* **44**: 487–499.

Waddington, L. (2008a). "When it is Reasonable for Europeans to be Confused: Understanding when a Disability Accommodation is Reasonable from a Comparative Perspective." *Comparative Labour Law and Policy Journal* **11**(1).

Waddington, L. (2008b). "Case C-411/05: Félix Palacios de la Villa v. Cortefi el Servicios SA, Judgment of the Court (Grand Chamber) of 16 October 2007" *Common Market Law Review* **45**(3): 895.

Waddington, L. (2009a). "Case C-303/06, S. Coleman v. Attridge Law and Steve Law, Judgment of the Grand Chamber of the Court of Justice of 17 July 2008, not yet reported." *Common Market Law Review* **46**: 665–681.

Waddington, L. (2009b). Breaking New Ground: The Implications of Ratification of the UN Convention on the Rights of Persons with Disabilities for the European Community. *The UN Convention on the Rights of Persons with Disabilities – European and Scandinavian Perspectives*. O. M. Arnardóttir and G. Quinn. Leiden, Martinus Nijhoff Publishers.

Waddington, L. (2009c). "Case C-267/06, *Tadao Maruko v. Versorgungsanstalt der deutschen Bühnen*, Judgment of the Grand Chamber of the Court of Justice of 1 April 2008, not yet reported." *Common Market Law Review* **46**: 723–746.

Waddington, L. and M. Bell (2006). "Equality and Diversity: Challenges for EU Anti-Discrimination Law." *Maastricht Journal of European and Comparative Law* **12**(3): 227–228.

Waddington, L. and M. Diller (2002). Tensions and Coherence in Disability Policy: The Uneasy Relationship between Social Welfare and Civil Rights Models of Disability in American, European and International Employment Law. *Disability Rigths Law and Policy*. M. L. Breslin and S. Yee. Ardsley, Transnational Publishers.

Waddington, L. and A. Hendricks (2002). "The Expanding Concept of Employment Discrimination in Europe: From Direct and Indirect Discrimination to Reasonable Accommodation Discrimination." *The International Journal of Comparative Labour Law and Industrial Relations*(Winter): 403–427.

Wells, K. (2003). "The Impact of the European Equality Directive on UK Disability Discrimination Law." *Industrial Law Journal* **32**(4): 253–273.

Whittle, R. (2002). "The Framework Directive for Equal Treatment in Employment and Occupation: An Analysis from a Disability Rights Perspective." *European Law Review* **27**(3): 303–326.

Williams, A. (2004). *EU Human Rights Policies*. Oxford, Oxford University Press.

Åhman, K. (2004). Rättighetsskyddet i Pratiken – Skydd på papperet eller verkligt gennomslag? *Konstitutionell Demokrati*. E. Smith and O. Pettersson. Stockholm, SNS.

Aasen, H. S. (2009). Dignity and Human Rights in the Modern Welfare State. H. S. Aasen, R. Halvorsen and A. B. d. Silva. Antwerp, Intersentia.

School of Human Rights Research Series

The School of Human Rights Research is a joint effort by human rights researchers in the Netherlands. Its central research theme is the nature and meaning of international standards in the field of human rights, their application and promotion in the national legal order, their interplay with national standards, and the international supervision of such application. The School of Human Rights Research Series only includes English titles that contribute to a better understanding of the different aspects of human rights.

Published titles within the Series:

1 Brigit C.A. Toebes, *The Right to Health as a Human Right in International Law*
ISBN 90–5095–057–4

2 Ineke Boerefijn, *The Reporting Procedure under the Covenant on Civil and Political Rights. Practice and Procedures of the Human Rights Committee*
ISBN 90–5095–074–4

3 Kitty Arambulo, *Strengthening the Supervision of the International Covenant on Economic, Social and Cultural Rights. Theoretical and Procedural Aspects*
ISBN 90–5095–058–2

4 Marlies Glasius, *Foreign Policy on Human Rights. Its Influence on Indonesia under Soeharto*
ISBN 90–5095–089–2

5 Cornelis D. de Jong, *The Freedom of Thought, Conscience and Religion or Belief in the United Nations (1946–1992)*
ISBN 90–5095–137–6

6 Heleen Bosma, *Freedom of Expression in England and under the ECHR: in Search of a Common Ground. A Foundation for the Application of the Human Rights Act 1998 in English Law*
ISBN 90–5095–136–8

7 Mielle Bulterman, *Human Rights in the External Relations of the European Union*
ISBN 90–5095–164–3

8 Esther M. van den Berg, *The Influence of Domestic NGOs on Dutch Human Rights Policy. Case Studies on South Africa,Namibia, Indonesia and East Timor*
ISBN 90–5095–159–7

9 Ian Seiderman, *Hierarchy in International Law: the Human Rights Dimension*
ISBN 90–5095–165–1

10 Anna Meijknecht, *Towards International Personality: the Position of Minorities and Indigenous Peoples in International Law*
ISBN 90–5095–166-X

11 Mohamed Eltayeb, *A Human Rights Approach to Combating Religious Persecution. Cases from Pakistan, Saudi Arabia and Sudan*
ISBN 90–5095–170–8

12 Machteld Boot, *Genocide, Crimes Against Humanity, War Crimes: Nullum Crimen Sine Lege and the Subject Matter Jurisdiction of the International Criminal Court*
ISBN 90–5095–216-X

13 Corinne Packer, *Using Human Rights to Change Tradition. Traditional Practices Harmful to Women's Reproductive Health in sub-Saharan Africa*
ISBN 90–5095–226–7

14 Theo R.G. van Banning, *The Human Right to Property*
ISBN 90–5095–203–8

15 Yvonne M. Donders, *Towards a Right to Cultural Identity?*
ISBN 90–5095–238–0

16 Göran K. Sluiter, *International Criminal Adjudication and the Collection of Evidence: Obligations of States*
ISBN 90–5095–227–5

17 Nicola Jägers, *Corporate Human Rights Obligations: in Search of Accountability*
ISBN 90–5095–240–2

18 Magdalena Sepúlveda, *The Nature of the Obligations under the International Covenant on Economic, Social and Cultural Rights*
ISBN 90–5095–260–7

19 Mitsue Inazumi, *Universal Jurisdiction in Modern International Law: Expansion of National Jurisdiction for Prosecuting Serious Crimes under International Law*
ISBN 90–5095–366–2

20 Anne-Marie L.M. de Brouwer, *Supranational Criminal Prosecution of Sexual Violence: The ICC and the Practice of the ICTY and the ICTR*
ISBN 90–5095–533–9

21 Jeroen Gutter, *Thematic Procedures of the United Nations Commission on Human Rights and International Law: in Search of a Sense of Community*
ISBN 90–5095–557–6

22 Hilde Reiding, *The Netherlands and the Development of International Human Rights Instruments*
ISBN 978–90–5095–654–3

23 Ingrid Westendorp, *Women and Housing: Gender Makes a Difference*
ISBN 978–90–5095–669–7

24 Quirine A.M. Eijkman, *We Are Here to Serve You! Public Security, Police Reform and Human Rights Implementation in Costa Rica*
ISBN 978–90–5095–704–5

25 Antoine Ch. Buyse, *Post-conflict Housing Restitution. The European Human Rights Perspective with a case study on Bosnia and Herzegovina*
ISBN 978–90–5095–770–0

26 Gentian Zyberi, *The Humanitarian Face of the International Court of Justice. Its Contribution to Interpreting and Developing International Human Rights and Humanitarian Law Rules and Principles*
ISBN 978–90–5095–792–2

27 Dragoş Cucereanu, *Aspects of Regulating Freedom of Expression on the Internet*
ISBN 978–90–5095–842–4

28 Ton Liefaard, *Deprivation of Liberty of Children in Light of International Human Rights Law and Standards*
ISBN 978–90–5095–838–7

29 Laura van Waas, *Nationality Matters. Statelessness under International Law*
ISBN 978–90–5095–854–7

30 Jeroen Denkers, *The World Trade Organization and Import Bans in Response to Violations of Fundamental Labour Rights*
ISBN 978–90–5095–855–4

31 Irene Hadiprayitno, *Hazard or Right? The Dialectics of Development Practice and the Internationally Declared Right to Development, with Special Reference to Indonesia*
ISBN 978–90–5095–932–2

School of Human Rights Research Series

32 Michał Gondek, *The Reach of Human Rights in a Globalising World: Extraterritorial Application of Human Rights Treaties*
ISBN 978–90–5095–817–2

33 Jeff Handmaker, *Advocating for Accountability: Civic-State Interactions to Protect Refugees in South Africa*
ISBN 978–90–5095–910–0

34 Anna Oehmichen, *Terrorism and Anti-Terror Legislation: The Terrorised Legislator? A Comparison of Counter-Terror Legislation and Its Implications on Human Rights in the Legal Systems of the United Kingdom, Spain, Germany and France*
ISBN 978–90–5095–956–8

35 Simon Walker, *The Future of Human Rights Impact Assessments of Trade Agreements*
ISBN 978–90–5095–986–5

36 Fleur van Leeuwen, *Women's Rights Are Human Rights: The Practice of the United Nations Human Rights Committee and the Committee on Economic, Social and Cultural Rights*
ISBN 978–90–5095–980–3

37 Eva Rieter, *Preventing Irreparable Harm. Provisional Measures in International Human Rights Adjudication*
ISBN 978–90–5095–931–5

38 Desislava Stoitchkova, *Towards Corporate Liability in International Criminal Law*
ISBN 978–94–000–0024–7

39 Paulien Muller, *Scattered Families. Transnational Family Life of Afghan Refugees in the Netherlands in the Light of the Human Rights-Based Protection of the Family*
ISBN 978–94–000–0021–6

40 Bibi van Ginkel, *The Practice of the United Nations in Combating Terrorism from 1946 to 2008. Questions of Legality and Legitimacy*
ISBN 978–94–000–0076–6

Christophe Paulussen, *Male captus bene detentus? Surrendering suspects to the International Criminal Court*
SBN 978–94–000–0100–8

nne McGonigle Leyh, *Procedural Justice? Victim Participation in International inal Proceedings*
978-1-78068-020-0

entegodt Liisberg, *Disability and Employment. A Contemporary Disability ghts Approach Applied to Danish, Swedish and EU Law and Policy*
-78068-028-6